WAFFEN-SS

WAFFEN-SS

Hitler's Army at War

———

ADRIAN GILBERT

DA CAPO PRESS

Da Capo Press
Hachette Book Group
1290 Avenue of the Americas, New York, NY 10104
dacapopress.com
@DaCapoPress, @DaCapoPR

Printed in the United States of America

First Edition: June 2019

Published by Da Capo Press, an imprint of Perseus Books, LLC, a subsidiary of Hachette Book Group, Inc. The Da Capo Press name and logo is a trademark of the Hachette Book Group.

The Hachette Speakers Bureau provides a wide range of authors for speaking events. To find out more, go to www.hachettespeakersbureau.com or call (866) 376-6591.

The publisher is not responsible for websites (or their content) that are not owned by the publisher.

Print book interior design by Trish Wilkinson.

Library of Congress Cataloging-in-Publication Data
Names: Gilbert, Adrian, author.
Title: Waffen-SS : Hitler's Army at War / Adrian Gilbert.
Description: First edition. | New York, NY : Da Capo Press, Hachette Book Group, Inc., 2019. | Includes bibliographical references and index.
Identifiers: LCCN 2019014507| ISBN 9780306824654 (hardcover : alk. paper) | ISBN 9780306824661 (ebook : alk. paper)
Subjects: LCSH: Waffen-SS—History. | World War, 1939–1945—Germany. | World War, 1939–1945—Campaigns—Europe. | Germany—History, Military—20th century.
Classification: LCC D757.85 .G55 2019 | DDC 940.54/1343—dc23
LC record available at https://lccn.loc.gov/2019014507

ISBNs: 978-0-306-82465-4 (hardcover), 978-0-306-82466-1 (ebook)

LSC-C

10 9 8 7 6 5 4 3 2 1

CONTENTS

MAPS

TABLE OF COMPARATIVE RANKS

Waffen-SS	German Army	U.S. Army
Commissioned Officers		
—	Generalfeldmarschall	General of the Army*
Oberstgruppenführer	Generaloberst	General
Obergruppenführer	General der Infanterie etc	Lieutenant General
Gruppenführer	Generalleutnant	Major General
Brigadeführer	Generalmajor	Brigadier General
Oberführer	—	—
Standartenführer	Oberst	Colonel
Obersturmbannführer	Oberstleutnant	Lieutenant Colonel
Sturmbannführer	Major	Major
Hauptsturmführer	Hauptmann	Captain
Obersturmführer	Oberleutnant	First Lieutenant
Untersturmführer	Leutnant	Second Lieutenant
Noncommissioned Officers		
Sturmscharführer	Stabsfeldwebel	—
Stabsscharführer	Hauptfeldwebel	Master Sergeant
Hauptscharführer	Oberfeldwebel	First Sergeant
Oberscharführer	Feldwebel	Technical Sergeant
Oberjunker	Fähnrich	—
Scharführer	Unterfeldwebel	Staff Sergeant
Unterscharführer	Unteroffizier	Sergeant
Rottenführer	Obergefreiter	Corporal
Other Ranks		
Sturmmann	Gefreiter	Private 1st Class
Mann/Schütze	Soldat/Schütze	Private

*Officer ranks between the Waffen-SS and U.S. Army (1942–1948) correspond closely, unlike noncom ranks, which are only broadly approximate (U.S. technician grades have not been included).

The German Reich at Its Height, November 1942

FINLAND

Lake Onega

Helsinki

Lake Ladoga

Leningrad

Rybinsk Reservoir

Demyansk

Riga

SOVIET UNION

Moscow

Smolensk

Minsk

Kursk   Voronezh

R. Don

Kiev   Kharkov   Stalingrad

R. Dnieper   *R. Volga*

Lemburg   Caspian Sea

ROMANIA

Rostov

Odessa

Grozny

Sevastapol

Ploiesti

Bucharest

Black Sea

BULGARIA

Sofia

Skopje

Istanbul   **IRAN**

Klidi

toria

GREECE   **TURKEY**

Gulf of Corinth

Patras   Athens   **IRAQ**

SYRIA

Crete

	Greater Germany
	Countries & territories allied with Germany or under German control
	International boundaries, November 1, 1942
	Front Line, November 1, 1942

| 0 | 100 | 200 | 300 | 400 | 500 | | 1000 |

MILES

INTRODUCTION

THE SS HAS come to personify the evil at the heart of Nazi Germany, its sinister influence seemingly undiminished by the passage of time. Originally intended as Adolf Hitler's bodyguard, the Schutzstaffel (protection squad) grew into a Hydra-like monster under the leadership of Heinrich Himmler, administering the concentration-camp system; controlling the Reich's police, security, and intelligence agencies; as well as overseeing a sprawl of economic interests throughout Germany and its occupied territories. But, most significantly, it developed its own military force—the Waffen-SS—with more than 900,000 men passing through its ranks. The Waffen-SS fought in all the major European campaigns of World War II, earning a deserved reputation for aggression in attack and steadfastness in defense. It also became infamous for its cooperation with other perpetrators of the Holocaust and for the battlefield atrocities it committed against civilians and prisoners.

The Waffen-SS was always an organization in flux. Before the advent of war in 1939, the armed units of the SS were drawn from German volunteers, selected for their physical aptitude and appropriate Aryan background. As the war developed, so the Waffen-SS grew massively in size, an expansion that compromised its overall military quality and, through the recruitment of non-Germans, its racial integrity. By the end of the war it had been transformed into a partially conscripted multinational army.

The scale and nature of these changes seemed to fly in the face of Nazi racial doctrine, as well as running counter to Hitler's original demand for an elite, ultraloyal German bodyguard. Himmler, however, saw things differently. Obsessed by racial matters, he looked beyond nationality to the concept of a Pan-Germanic Europe, where the countries of northern and western Europe, with their Germanic peoples, would eventually be incorporated into a Greater Germany, which in turn would rule over a new empire in central and eastern Europe.[1]

Once the war was won, Himmler reasoned, he would use his Germanic formations as a template for a new army,[2] while the other units of lesser racial quality would prove useful in controlling the slave populations of the empire in the East and protecting it from external threat. Himmler also saw the advantage of possessing a powerful military force during the inevitable postwar struggles with other Nazi leaders. For these reasons Himmler accepted the myriad difficulties and contradictions that came with raising this multinational army, substantial parts of which were of poor quality and doubtful motivation. Hitler, while not sharing these Pan-Germanic racial enthusiasms, allowed Himmler a relatively free rein, thanks mainly to the exceptional battlefield performance of the German-recruited Waffen-SS panzer divisions.

Germany, of course, did not win the war, and post-1945 the Allies insisted on finding and punishing those they believed responsible for the destruction and killings carried out by Hitler's regime. The Wehrmacht (army, navy, air force) was swift to transfer blame onto other Nazi organizations, insisting it had played no part in the Nazis' genocidal policies. As a consequence of the friendly cooperation between senior German commanders and the Western Allies, the concept of the "clean" Wehrmacht began to emerge. This idea was supported in memoirs and other accounts from German officers, among them the influential voices of Heinz Guderian, Erwin Rommel, and Erich von Manstein. Their publications were critically and commercially successful and set the parameters for the understanding of the war among Western readers.[3] The Wehrmacht had in fact perpetrated numerous atrocities, especially on the Eastern Front, and was fully aware of Nazi intentions toward its subject peoples. This knowledge was successfully hidden for several decades, until more recent investigations revealed the true extent of Wehrmacht complicity.[4]

The success of the "clean" Wehrmacht story left the Waffen-SS in a difficult position, especially when critics condemned the SS as a single monolithic entity. Waffen-SS veterans fought back, insisting that their force was an apolitical military elite—the "fourth branch of the Wehrmacht"—quite separate from other parts of the SS, who, with other Nazi agencies, were the ones responsible for the killings. They maintained that the Waffen-SS knew nothing of these events and, instead, was a corps of soldiers motivated by comradeship, patriotism, and a desire to protect Western civilization from the threat of communism. That this defense—or apologia—was fundamentally flawed did not stop the veterans from hammering home their argument. They were sufficiently successful to enlist a new generation of writers from North America and Europe, who adopted and further promoted the idea of the "honorable" Waffen-SS.[5]

In reality, thousands of Waffen-SS soldiers took part in the systematic killing of Jews, Slavs, and other civilians on the Eastern Front and in the Balkans, while smaller numbers of troops moved between the concentration camps and Waffen-SS field units and vice versa. Likewise, Waffen-SS troops engaged in the battlefield massacres of civilians and captured soldiers throughout Europe, on a scale sufficiently large that entire books have been written describing these atrocities.[6] A few of the better-known incidents have been included in this work, if only to counter the fraudulently disingenuous nature of so many Waffen-SS apologias.

In defense of the Waffen-SS, they were far from alone in committing battlefield atrocities. All armies throughout history have behaved badly on campaign: raping and looting, murdering civilians and prisoners. While the Western Allies were swift to take the moral high ground during the war, crimes of this nature were committed by British, American, and French troops in Italy and northwest Europe. In one, albeit exceptional, instance, seventy-three Axis prisoners were shot by U.S. troops at Biscari in Sicily in July 1943, and although the American commanding officers (COs) were subsequently court-martialed, their punishment was minimal. To the Waffen-SS veteran, this was a typical example of the hypocrisy of "victor's justice."

There were, however, important distinctions between the battlefield crimes of the Waffen-SS and the Western Allies. The Waffen-SS certainly committed more atrocities and on a larger scale than their Western opponents. And in contrast to the Allied political leadership, Hitler and Himmler repeatedly demanded that their troops ill-treat and kill civilians and prisoners on the Eastern Front. These attitudes were passed down the chain of command, providing a sense of legitimacy to the men carrying out the actions.

A history of the Waffen-SS needs to go beyond just a listing of atrocities. It was one of the more intriguing organizations to come out of the Nazi system. For some of its officers it was a unique experiment in how to wage a new type of war, while to its political masters it was a means to ensure the ascendancy of the National Socialist revolution over the German establishment. And, of course, there was Himmler's intention to use the Waffen-SS as military backing for his SS-controlled Europe.

Germany's defeat in 1945 prevented the Nazis from achieving their goal of European domination, but the association of the Waffen-SS with some of the most terrible deeds of the war has inspired revulsion and fascination ever since. It has gained cult status, a popular subject for modelers, war gamers, and historical reenactment societies, as well as the general military reader. Much of this interest derives from its aura of toughness as an elite fighting force, the charismatic nature of its officers, and from more technical aspects, such as the early adoption of camouflage uniforms and, from 1942 onward, the use of some of the best weapons produced in the war. It was also fortunate in being able to call upon first-rate war photographers to provide a detailed visual record of its activities, which has subsequently filled many illustrated volumes of its soldiers at war.

The Waffen-SS has also become a subject of interest to academic historians, considering such factors as its ideology, structural development, social background, criminality, and transnational character. This book charts a middle course. Set within a narrative framework of the campaigns and battles fought by the Waffen-SS, it also examines its transformation as a military organization, from Hitler's palace guard to Himmler's mass army.

———

WHILE AWARE OF the dual military-political character of the Waffen-SS, the emphasis in this book has been placed on its military nature. Greater attention had been devoted to the units and formations that did the most fighting over the longest periods. As a consequence, divisions such as

Leibstandarte and Das Reich are considered in some depth, while the ragbag of formations created toward the end of the war—of no military and little political significance—plays only a very minor role. Some basic information on all the divisions can be found in Appendix A.

Anyone writing on this or other German military subjects faces the dilemma of how much "German" to use in the narrative text. Some authors—presumably keen to identify with their subject—copiously use German words and terms. For the sake of clarity, I have tended to rely on English expressions, even though I have arguably broken this rule by using the distinctive SS rank system (see the Table of Comparative Ranks). Many place-names, especially in Eastern Europe, have changed in the years since 1945; I have used the versions most familiar to English-speaking readers, but with local names included where necessary. The (fairly) standard system of describing military units and formations is employed here: armies written out, corps in roman numerals, and the rest in arabic numerals (an exception is made for the German tradition of using roman numerals to describe battalions within a regiment).

Part One

HIMMLER'S ARMY

I know there are many people who fall ill when they see black uniforms; we understand that and don't expect that we will be loved by many people.

—HEINRICH HIMMLER

Chapter 1

FOUNDATION STONES

O N 16 January 1929, Adolf Hitler appointed Heinrich Himmler as his Reichsführer-SS. Although few at the time could have realized its significance, the promotion of the twenty-eight-year-old Nazi functionary to head the Schutzstaffel would transform a disparate group of bodyguards into the most powerful and malevolent organization within the entire Nazi empire.

The origins of the SS dated back to March 1923, when Hitler formed a small headquarters guard to protect himself from attack by rival political factions. In 1925, after his release from prison following the failed Munich Beer Hall Putsch, he called upon his chauffeur Julius Schreck to organize another bodyguard, which on this occasion adopted the title Schutzstaffel.

When Himmler took command of the SS, it comprised no more than 300 men. The SS had been conceived as a small elite force whose allegiance was not to the Nazi Party but exclusively to Adolf Hitler. Himmler was determined to maintain this special status while at the same time expanding the scope and size of the SS. When Hitler became German chancellor in January 1933, its membership had grown to 52,000.

Born on 7 October 1900, Heinrich Himmler was a product of a solid Bavarian middle-class family. He experienced a normal upbringing by the standards of his day and maintained close ties with his parents after he had left home. Himmler's various biographers have been unable to find anything seriously untoward in his childhood to suggest the nature and course of his subsequent career.[1] He enthusiastically volunteered for the army in 1917, but before he could complete officer training the armistice of November 1918 had come into effect. That he had never experienced frontline action would weigh heavily upon him throughout his life.

Himmler drifted in the postwar world, studying agriculture at a university in Munich at the behest of his parents while still hoping to develop a military career. Unable to find a place in the Reichswehr—a force limited to 100,000 men by the Versailles Treaty—Himmler signed up with various paramilitary groups. In January 1922 he met Ernst Röhm, a decorated soldier from the trenches and an early convert to the Nazi cause. Influenced by Röhm, Himmler joined the Nazi Party in 1923 and was accepted into the SS two years later. As a Nazi official, Himmler developed a fixation on the idea of German racial superiority and the notion that the SS should act as a standard-bearer in matters of race. By 1927 he had worked himself up to the position of SS deputy leader.

Himmler's physical characteristics—slight frame, sloping chin, poor vision—alongside a fussy, often pedantic manner, made him an unlikely candidate for control of the SS. Yet at the time, the position of Reichsführer-SS was not considered to be of much importance, the SS being very much a subordinate part of the Sturmabteilung (Storm Section), or SA.

Founded in 1921, the brown-shirted SA was the Nazi Party's paramilitary force, its prime function to intimidate political opponents and provide vocal and physical support for National Socialism. Under Röhm's leadership, the SA expanded into a vast, unruly organization of more than 300,000 followers by early 1933. With Hitler in power it would grow larger still and become a semi-independent body within the Nazi system.

During most of the 1920s Himmler was a minor figure in the Nazi world, easy to underestimate. In 1930 he briefly came under the direction of Joseph Goebbels, the future head of German propaganda. In a suitably patronizing tone, Goebbels described Himmler in his diary: "He's not particularly clever, but hard-working and well meaning." Goebbels concluded that he got "too bogged down in details."[2] But Goebbels had misread the man. Himmler was a shrewd and intelligent political operator, and it was his mastery of detail that would prove so useful in his ascent to power.

Himmler has been considered as the archetypal bureaucrat, and while he was undoubtedly a highly capable administrator he was also far more than that. He possessed a capacity for hard work and a focused vision rare among other leading Nazis, transforming the SS from almost nothing to make it the vehicle to realize his ambitions for a Germanic Europe. His command of Hitler's bodyguard was only a first step on this road to power, and through his determination and political skills he extended the role of the SS to encompass control of the police, security, and intelligence services as well as the creation of the military force that would become the Waffen-SS.

In retrospect, it might seem that the SS—given its ubiquity and success—was an inevitable consequence of Nazism itself, but without Himmler it would have remained a minor organization at best. Himmler's importance in the creation of the Waffen-SS also needs to be underlined in light of postwar attempts by former Waffen-SS generals to downplay his role. A recent biographer, Peter Longerich, has written, "Himmler was the complete opposite of a faceless functionary interchangeable with any other. The position he built up over the years can instead be described as an extreme example of the almost total personalization of political power."[3]

THE TONE AND style of the SS owed much to the Freikorps movement that flourished at the end of World War I. In the immediate aftermath of the conflict, Germany seemed poised on the brink of civil war, with the newly established republican government threatened by communists and other Far Left political groups. The response of the political Right in Germany was to form ad hoc military units, or Freikorps, to suppress these leftist uprisings by force, its members recruited from the many disgruntled former soldiers who seemed unable to return to civilian life. By early 1919 the putative communist revolution in Germany had been snuffed out, the Freikorps earning a reputation for enthusiastic brutality. Apart from its battles with the German Left, the Freikorps fought in various border disputes, notably against Polish insurgents for control of Upper Silesia in 1921.

Varying in size and capability, Freikorps units were typically based around a charismatic individual with frontline experience in the trenches, embodying a ferocious fighting attitude with a casual approach to formal discipline. They took as their model the freebooting Landsknecht mercenaries of sixteenth-century Germany.

Manfred von Killinger, a Freikorps leader and subsequent Nazi politician, wrote that his soldiers "didn't care why or for whom they fought. The main thing for them was that they were fighting. War had become their career. They had no desire to look for another. War made them happy—what more can you ask?"[4] Another Freikorps member, Ernst von Salomon, praised his comrades for their "ruthless action against armed or unarmed enemy masses, their limitless contempt for the so-called sanctity of life and their marked disinclination to take prisoners under any circumstances."[5] Although the Freikorps withered away in the early 1920s, their nihilistic attitude influenced the conduct of the SS from the outset. Many senior Waffen-SS officers served in Freikorps units.

The Freikorps also made their mark on the cumbersome unit and rank designations adopted by the SA and then SS. The old system of the regular army was rejected in favor of more Germanic styles derived from the trenches, so that, for example, a battalion was retitled a "storm unit" (Sturmbann), commanded not by a major but by a Sturmbannführer.

Senior and far larger than the SS, the SA dominated the Nazi movement during the 1920s. Himmler, however, chafed under his subordination to the SA, and at the end of 1930 he persuaded Hitler to grant the SS a substantial degree of autonomy. The SS swiftly repaid Hitler's favor during the Stennes revolts of 1930–1931, when the SS supported the party against attacks on its offices led by Berlin's maverick SA leader, Walther Stennes. After the revolt's suppression, Hitler publicly praised the SS: "SS Mann, deine Ehre heisst Treue" (SS man, your honor is loyalty). This was amended to the SS motto—"My honor is loyalty"—subsequently inscribed on the belt buckles of all SS men. Encouraged by this new degree of independence, Himmler issued instructions for the production of a new uniform and insignia to underline the separateness of the SS from its parent organization.

The SA had adopted the brown uniforms that provided its nickname as a result of a chance acquisition of large stocks of khaki-brown military shirts originally destined for Germany's tropical colonies. During the 1920s the SS also wore the brown SA uniform, but with black breeches and a black kepi that included the Totenkopf (Death's Head) insignia. On Himmler's orders a new SS uniform was introduced in 1932.

Designed by two SS officers, Professor Karl Diebitsch and Walter Heck, the black uniform issued to all ranks was modeled on that of a German Army officer, far superior to the clumsy attempts at a paramilitary outfit made by the SA. The choice of black reflected its popularity among fascist movements and was also a nod to the black uniforms worn by the Prussian lifeguard hussars. And the sinister nature of the uniform was not lost on Himmler, who took a keen interest in all aspects of SS regalia. The uniforms were manufactured in the factories of Hugo Boss, a dedicated Nazi supporter whose tailoring business had been rescued from bankruptcy by SS contracts.

For use in the field, from 1935 onward, the militarized or armed SS dispensed with black uniforms for a more practical version made from earth-gray or earth-brown material. This experiment did not last long, however, when in 1937 both uniform types were replaced by a field-gray version similar to that worn by the army. From then onward, field units of the armed SS could be distinguished from their army counterparts only by their special insignia.

Since the late nineteenth century, German interest in Nordic runes had been encouraged by various right-wing Volkish (nationalist folk) groups. The most famous of these rune symbols was, of course, the Hakenkreuz (hooked cross), or swastika, which came to visually define the Nazi regime. Among other related signs was the lightning flash of the Siegrune, the symbol of victory. Walter Heck—a graphic designer by training—placed two Siegrunes side by side to create the iconic insignia worn by SS men.[6] Karl Diebitsch, one of Himmler's favorite artists, helped design the ceremonial sword and the talismanic dagger. He was also a director of the Bavarian Allach porcelain works, which produced objets d'art using slave labor from the nearby Dachau concentration camp.

The Totenkopf and crossbones had a long history in the German armed forces, dating back to the time of Prussia's Frederick the Great. During World War I it had become a popular symbol among storm troopers and fighter pilots, and its use continued among the many Freikorps bands. Thus, it was hardly surprising that the Totenkopf was adopted by the SS from its inception, worn as a cap badge by all members. It was through the use of such iconic uniforms and insignia that Himmler was able to present the SS as an organization glamorous and sinister at the same time.

————————

THERE WOULD BE little difficulty in attracting men for service in the SS. Indeed, such was the rush of volunteers after Hitler had come to power that Himmler temporarily halted recruitment to prevent its elite status from being fatally dissipated. Yet the expansion of the SS to more than 50,000 members had already caused its own problem: it was just too big and unwieldy to give Hitler the close protection he required as German chancellor.

Prior to January 1933 Hitler had been able to rely on a circle of a dozen or so chauffeurs and bodyguards, tough street fighters armed with blackjacks and concealed pistols. Now that he was Germany's political leader, Hitler faced wider and larger threats, not least from sections of the army who despised and feared the Nazis and even from some of his old but now disgruntled supporters.

On 17 March 1933, Hitler personally resolved the problem by ordering Sepp Dietrich, one of his old bodyguards, to form an SS-Stabswache (staff or headquarters guard) to protect the Reich Chancellery in Berlin. Just 117 men strong, this unit was the first manifestation of what became the armed SS. Dietrich, a Bavarian of humble background, was the sort of man invaluable to Hitler and the Nazi cause. Loyal to his master, he reveled in the cut and thrust of street politics; his cool head under fire and rough and easy manner made him a natural leader. Having served in Bavarian storm-troop units during World War I, he fought as a Freikorps soldier in Upper Silesia before gravitating toward the fledgling Nazi Party. Although his fighting credentials were established in the Beer Hall Putsch of 1923, he dropped out of the movement until 1928, when he formally joined the party and the SS.

Under the patronage of both Himmler and Hitler, Dietrich rose swiftly through the ranks and by 1930 was an Oberführer. A postwar

Allied interrogation described him as having "a flair for the dramatic in gesture and speech, and a crude sense of humor, coupled with a forceful energy that could be hard and ruthless" and noted that this "undoubtedly enabled him to achieve his meteoric success in the SS."[7]

Dietrich's guard was soon redesignated Sonderkommando (Special Command) Berlin, reinforced by two other similar units in June 1933. Shortly afterward the Sonderkommando was housed in the famous Lichterfelde barracks in Berlin. Recruited mainly from the SS and SA, the new guard grew to around 800 men, receiving three months of basic training from the army. Hitler conceived the Sonderkommando as his own special unit, separate from the army and police and semi-independent from the rest of the SS. Dietrich zealously maintained this latter distinction, much to Himmler's irritation.

Hitler confirmed the Sonderkommando's special position by upgrading it as the Adolf Hitler Standarte (Regiment) in September 1933. On November 9—the tenth anniversary of the Beer Hall Putsch—the regiment was assembled in front of Hitler at the Feldherrnhalle in Munich, where the failed coup had been brought to its bloody conclusion. At midnight, under flaming torches, the Führer's guard was formally redesignated Leibstandarte SS "Adolf Hitler," a name that referred back to the imperial lifeguards of Prussia and Imperial Germany. More significantly, the assembled soldiers swore an oath of allegiance, not to the German state but directly to their leader: "We swear to you, Adolf Hitler, loyalty and bravery. We pledge to you, and to the superiors appointed by you, obedience unto death—so help us God."

LEIBSTANDARTE WAS JUST the first of three militarized elements that were separate from other sections of the SS and that eventually came together to create the Waffen-SS (although the term was not used until 1940). Those SS men not part of the armed SS (or any other specific SS organization) were lumped together as the Allgemeine (General) SS. Many of these were part-timers, and with the outbreak of war in 1939 the influence and numerical size of the black-uniformed Allgemeine-SS would rapidly decline.

In Germany's major towns and cities, specially selected SS members were assembled into the full-time SS Verfügungstruppe, or SS-VT (roughly translated as "Troops at the Führer's Disposal"). Their duties took on an increasingly paramilitary nature, and they would become the second strand of the armed SS. Originally consisting of small groups scattered across Germany, they coalesced into two Standarten (regiments): "Deutschland" in Munich and "Germania" in Hamburg. They took the organizational form of a German Army infantry regiment, each Standarten comprising three battalions of infantry. For administrative purposes, Leibstandarte was considered a constituent part of the SS-VT, even though Dietrich and his fellow Leibstandarte soldiers considered themselves a separate entity.

The third armed element comprised the SS Totenkopfverbände (SS-TV), units of prison guards recruited to contain the internal enemies of Nazi Germany, now housed in SS-run prisons and concentration camps. The first of these camps was situated at Dachau, a rail stop away from Munich. Its inmates were predominantly communists, socialists, trade unionists, and the more vociferous liberal democrats, soon to be joined by increasing numbers of Jews.

The Dachau camp was badly run, and after a series of scandals it attracted strong criticism from the police, at this time not under full Nazi control. Himmler was sufficiently alarmed by the criticism that in June 1933 he replaced the camp commandant, Hilmar Wäckerle, with one of his protégés, Theodor Eicke. Wäckerle's career was not harmed, however: the bullwhip-wielding sadist[8] transferred to the SS-VT, where he was commissioned as an officer.

Eicke was born in Alsace in 1892, the son of railroad stationmaster, and after an indifferent schooling he enlisted in the German Army at the age of seventeen. Although winning an Iron Cross (2nd Class) on the outbreak of war, he spent most of the conflict behind the lines as a regimental paymaster. In the uncertain post-1918 world he sought a variety of jobs, variously as a policeman, salesman, and security officer. But his restless nature and violently expressed opposition to the Weimar government made any time holding an official position necessarily short.

In 1928 he joined the Nazi Party, an organization that closely accorded with his virulent right-wing views, and two years later entered
the SS. Eicke was a rough-hewn thug who possessed the ability to get
things done and had no scruples in how this might be achieved. In many
ways his background and approach mirrored that of Sepp Dietrich, but
Eicke differed from Dietrich in his unbounded hatred for those he saw
as enemies of the Nazi cause. His violent and quarrelsome nature caused
problems for Himmler. At one point he was briefly incarcerated in a
mental hospital during 1933 for attacking a fellow Nazi dignitary. But
after entreaties from his psychiatrist pleading that Eicke was, in fact, sane,
Himmler allowed him to leave the hospital to take command of the concentration camp at Dachau.

Once out of the asylum, Eicke went from strength to strength. He put
the camp on a sound footing, replacing corrupt and incompetent guards
with more capable men dedicated to the Nazi cause. There was no letup
in the camp's brutal discipline, but with Eicke at the helm the applica-
tion of violence was orderly rather than arbitrary. The poor unfortunates
in Dachau may have seen little or no amelioration in their suffering, but
Himmler was impressed with Eicke's skills in prison management.

Rudolf Hoess, who subsequently achieved infamy as the commandant of Auschwitz, worked alongside Eicke at the time. He described
Eicke's methods: "The prisoners were sworn enemies of the state, who
were treated with great severity and destroyed if they showed resistance.
He installed this attitude of mind into his officers and men." Eicke issued this stark warning to his guards: "Behind the wire lurks the enemy,
watching everything you do, so he can he use your weaknesses for his
own advantage. Anyone who displays the slightest sympathy with these
enemies of the state must vanish from our ranks. My SS men must be
tough and ready for all eventualities, and there is no room among us
for weaklings."[9]

Himmler encouraged Eicke to develop the methods achieved in
Dachau as a template for other concentration camps now under construction. Himmler agreed with Eicke that the camp guards should be more
than simple turnkeys; they were to receive military training and take their
place on the front line against the state's enemies outside the confines of

the camps. According to camp regulations, they were to adopt a military bearing at all times: "A guard who shelters from the rain becomes a figure of fun and does not behave like a soldier. The SS man must show pride and dignity."[10] During 1934 the first Totenkopf units were raised to become a constituent part of the armed SS.

As HITLER CONSOLIDATED his position during 1934, he faced a growing problem with the SA and its leader, Ernst Röhm. The storm troopers of the SA had acted as the vanguard in Hitler's rise to power, but now that Hitler had achieved this goal their role was largely redundant. With around 3 million members, many in the SA believed that the National Socialist revolution they had fought for had failed them. As they saw it, Hitler was making deals with industrialists, the army, and other sections of the German establishment at the expense of the SA foot soldiers, many still unemployed or in the most menial of occupations.

In attempting to find a new role for his followers, Röhm loudly and persistently argued that the German Army should be integrated into the SA as a "People's Army"—under his command. The army was unsurprisingly horrified at the prospect of losing its vaunted position to an ill-disciplined rabble and repeatedly petitioned Hitler to restrain Röhm's demands. Although suspicious of the army, Hitler needed it to back his future foreign-policy ambitions, and, encouraged by Himmler and Hermann Göring, he decided to eliminate Röhm and the SA leadership. The SS was chosen for the operation, to be conducted with the utmost secrecy.[11]

During the last week of June 1934, the SS made preparations to destroy its rival. Reinhard Heydrich—head of the SS Security Service—drew up bogus legal charges against Röhm, while Dietrich's Leibstandarte was entrusted to take the lead in apprehending and killing the chosen SA victims. Röhm and several senior SA officers were known to be vacationing in the Alpine resort of Bad Wiessee, to the south of Munich. On 29 June Hitler ordered Dietrich to send two companies of Leibstandarte to arrest the SA men. While the Leibstandarte contingent traveled by train from Berlin to Munich, Dietrich rendezvoused with Hitler to await his direct orders.

On the evening of the twenty-ninth, a visibly strained Hitler took matters into his own hands. He flew to Munich in a Ju-52 and then with a few personal bodyguards drove to Bad Wiessee. It was a potentially rash move, as the Leibstandarte soldiers had yet to arrive. Hitler's entourage could easily have been overcome by Röhm's own guards, but Hitler was determined to deal with the matter without delay.

Hitler and his bodyguards arrived at Röhm's hotel at 6:30 A.M. and took the SA men completely by surprise. Offering no resistance, they were arrested and taken to Munich's Stadelheim prison. Röhm was kept in custody, while Hitler instructed Dietrich to have six of the SA leaders shot without delay. As Hitler returned to Berlin, Dietrich reluctantly assembled a firing squad from the waiting Leibstandarte. It was a difficult assignment, especially as he knew some of the condemned men as old comrades in the struggle for power. By the evening, however, the order had been carried out.

Hitler's own bonds of friendship with Röhm caused him qualms, and it was only on the following day, after promptings from Göring and Himmler, that he gave the order for the execution. Theodor Eicke was personally chosen to carry out the killing, although Hitler insisted that Röhm should be given a prior opportunity to commit suicide. Eicke, along with SS aides Michael Lippert and Heinrich Schmauser, drove the short distance from Dachau to Stadelheim. On entering Röhm's cell, Eicke exclaimed, "You have forfeited your life! The Führer gives you a last chance to avoid the consequences."[12] Eicke then placed a revolver on the prison-cell table and before leaving the cell told Röhm that he had ten minutes to make good on Hitler's offer. After waiting for a quarter of an hour without hearing any sound from the cell, Eicke and Lippert marched in and shot Röhm at point-blank range.

While the operation in Bavaria was underway, the order for action in Berlin was issued. As well as the arrest of SA leaders, old scores were settled, with both armed SS and Gestapo prominent in a series of gangster-style killings. These included Hitler's old enemy Gregor Strasser (leader of the left-wing faction of the Nazi Party), conservative anti-Nazi politicians such as former chancellor Kurt von Schleicher, and Gustav von Kahr, the man who had suppressed the Munich Beer Hall Putsch.

In Dietrich's absence, Sturmbannführer Martin Kohlroser was responsible for assembling the execution squads in the regiment's Lichterfelde barracks. How many were killed in the purge was never revealed. A minimum number of eighty-three murders was recorded, but the figure was possibly several times higher.

Concerned by potential criticism from home and abroad, Nazi leaders covered their tracks: official records were destroyed, and those involved were sworn to secrecy. The Nazi-dominated German cabinet gave a spurious legal cover to the killings: to "suppress treasonable activities . . . taken in emergency defense of the state." At a speech delivered to senior SS officers in 1943, Himmler declared: "We did not hesitate on June 30, 1934, to do the duty we were bidden and stand comrades who had lapsed up against the wall and shoot them. We have never discussed it among ourselves. It appalled everyone, and yet everyone was certain that if it is necessary and such orders are issued, we will do it again."[13]

What would be called the "Night of the Long Knives" marked the end of the SA's involvement in German political life. Röhm was replaced by Victor Lutz, who owed his position to Hitler and was persuaded to accept the new settlement. The army congratulated Hitler for removing the SA threat and extended thanks to the SS for carrying out the dirty work in the purge. The SS was the clear winner in this affair, and with the SA in the background it was now the prime arbiter of violence in Nazi Germany. The SS had demonstrated both unquestioning obedience and efficiency in carrying out the Führer's orders. A grateful Hitler declared it to be a completely independent organization within the Nazi Party and agreed to its immediate expansion.

Hitler rewarded Dietrich by promoting him to Obergruppenführer, with Himmler awarding him one of his most coveted ceremonial daggers. That Eicke had been chosen by Hitler to carry out the difficult task of killing Röhm reflected his faith in the man, who was promoted to the rank of Gruppenführer. He was also appointed as inspector of concentration camps and leader of SS guard formations. The SS was now the coming force in Nazi Germany.

Chapter 2

CREATING AN ELITE

THE DESTRUCTION OF the SA leadership on the Night of the Long Knives cleared the way for the expansion of the SS-Verfügungstruppe (SS-VT). Yet Himmler faced a quandary: Who would train these men to the standards necessary for a genuine elite? Dietrich and Eicke were hardened street fighters, but if the armed SS was to become an effective force, Himmler would need men with greater military knowledge. Inevitably, if somewhat reluctantly, he turned to former officers from the German Army.

In November 1934 Himmler persuaded Paul Hausser, a recently retired army lieutenant general, to take command of the SS-VT. The lean, long-faced Hausser was a career officer, far removed from the likes of Dietrich and Eicke. Born into a Prussian military family, Hausser had entered the German General Staff in 1912, taking up various staff appointments on both Western and Eastern Fronts during World War I. After the war he had continued to serve in the new Reichswehr until retirement in 1932, when he joined the right-wing nationalist ex-soldiers association Stahlhelm. Hausser's career had been solid if unspectacular, but his steady hand and detailed military knowledge were exactly what Himmler required.

At the start of 1935 Hausser founded the SS Junkerschule (officer cadet school) at Braunschweig. He also developed the curriculum for the other cadet school at Bad Tölz in Bavaria. Hausser was no military radical, however, stating that "the SS force must be formed on the well-tried training regulations of the Reichswehr."[1]

Himmler accepted the necessity of his soldiers receiving sound military training, but he also had more ambitious aims, as he explained in an address to SS officers in January 1935: "Never forget that we have far greater tasks to perform than just to be troops. We are a volk, a tribe, clan, community, a knighthood from which one cannot resign, into which one has been accepted on the basis of blood, and within which we remain with body and soul as long as we walk the earth."[2]

Himmler's musing on the SS and race would have meant relatively little to Hausser, who primarily saw himself as a military technician, a trainer and leader of frontline soldiers. He looked around for a suitable staff, attracting a small group of gifted officers who included such future luminaries as Felix Steiner, Matthias Kleinheisterkamp, and Wilhelm Bittrich. They would establish a training regime that would become the foundation for the wartime Waffen-SS.

These officers, brought up in the Kaiser's Imperial Army and forged as soldiers in the trenches of World War I, were military professionals to the core. They were also keen supporters of the Nazi regime, even if they possessed limited understanding of the finer points of its ideology. They certainly found it difficult to embrace Himmler's own vision for the SS as a modern-day order of Teutonic Knights. From the outset they demonstrated surprisingly casual attitudes to SS rules and regulations, which included their use of army ranks instead of the prescribed SS system, their refusal to formally renounce religious affiliations, as well as an often barely concealed disregard for the Reichsführer himself. Himmler, however, was sufficiently in their debt to overlook such shortcomings.

As for the lower ranks of the armed SS, Himmler had no difficulty in attracting recruits. Very much in the vanguard of the Nazi movement, the armed SS acquired a glamorous aura, priding itself on its separateness from the other armed forces in Germany. The smart black uniforms of Leibstandarte SS "Adolf Hitler," complete with polished white leather accouterments, caught the eye of many a German schoolboy.[3] On a practical level, following the introduction of conscription in 1935, enlistment in the SS-VT (including Leibstandarte) counted as the fulfillment of universal military service.

Unlike the Wehrmacht—the combined armed forces of army, navy, and air force—the armed SS was a volunteer organization that set its own criteria for selection. Himmler decreed that he only wanted men with a confirmed Aryan pedigree and a high level of physical fitness. In Leib-standarte, with its ceremonial guard duties under constant public scrutiny, a minimum height was set at 180cm (5'11")—later raised to 184cm (6'½")—with well-chiseled Aryan features considered an asset. Racial purity for all volunteers was essential, proved by appropriate marriage and birth certificates dating back to at least the year 1800 (1750 for officers). This was followed by a visual assessment of the potential recruit. The tester—apparently an expert in divining racial characteristics—employed a five-point scale that ranged from the very acceptable "purely Nordic" down to the ominous "suspicion of extra-European blood mixtures."[4]

If the recruit had the appropriate racial ancestry, Himmler argued, then he would also display the correct political outlook. Membership in the Nazi Party was by no means essential but nonetheless demonstrated dedication to the cause. More important was to bar those who had erred through membership in communist or left-wing organizations, as well as former Freemasons or members of the clergy. In the main, however, recruits came naturally from such suitable organizations as the Allgemeine-SS, the Hitler Youth, the Reich Labor Service, and the SA. This helped make the ideological transition from civilian to SS soldier a relatively seamless process.

Himmler placed little store in educational qualifications, once again believing in race as the ultimate determinant of ability, military or otherwise. This belief extended to SS officer recruitment, so that in contrast to the army the right social or educational background counted for little. Until 1938 some 40 percent of officer candidates possessed only a basic education without any formal academic qualifications.[5] This had the advantage of opening up the officer corps to a wider social group, allowing such rough diamonds as Kurt Meyer to flourish in a way impossible in the more socially stratified army. Yet this otherwise enlightened approach was subsequently to fail in the rigorous test of combat, with far too many cadets unable to master the technical aspects of military command. From 1940 onward, more stringent educational qualifications were introduced.

Whatever the selection criteria chosen for entry into the officer cadet schools at Bad Tölz and Braunschweig, the recruit was immediately made aware that he was part of an elite institution whose aim was to produce

a vanguard of political soldiers for the Nazi cause. The move of the Bad
Tölz cadet school to Bavaria in October 1937 underlined Himmler's
commitment to the armed SS. The finely proportioned, castle-like main
building was set at the foot of the Bavarian Alps, a suitably Wagnerian
setting with peaks rising to 6,000 feet in the background.

No expense was spared in providing the finest facilities for the officer
cadets, with an Olympic-size indoor swimming pool, a large athletics field
that included an electric scoreboard, and a 400-seat theater with a de-
scending film screen. Servants were supplied by inmates from the nearby
Dachau concentration camp, quartered in cells underneath the barracks.[6]
New arrivals would typically have served for two years as an enlisted soldier within the SS. They would then spend the next ten months undergoing an intense ideological and military education.

Postwar apologists for the Waffen-SS—notably Hausser and Steiner—
made a point of downplaying the ideological aspects of the cadet training
programs. Initially, political indoctrination was carried out by specialists from the SS Schulungsamt (education office). They instructed their
charges in the fundamental tenets of National Socialism, concentrating
on what they saw as the multiple evils of Judaism, Bolshevism, Christianity, and Western liberalism, and the violent struggle to be waged by the
German people to overcome these evils, before establishing their rightful
supremacy over Europe. But the instruction was heavy-handed, boring
the students and irritating the military trainers.

From 1936 onward, instruction in ideological matters began to be reassigned to the unit commanders. They displayed a lighter touch that was
welcomed by the students, helping develop their already authoritarian
beliefs toward a more structured Nazi worldview. Indeed, formal lectures
played a relatively small part in the ideological conditioning of the SS
officer cadet; more important was the largely unnoticed socialization of
the recruit through shared experience, adroitly shaped by Nazism from
childhood onward.

Military training was based squarely on the model established by the
Army War College in Munich. Much has been made of the uniqueness of
the Waffen-SS approach to war, but the differences between army and SS
were confined to specific areas and were largely matters of degree. It could

hardly have been otherwise, as most SS instructors were former army officers. And it would have been perverse to have rejected the existing system out of hand, given that it produced Europe's best-trained armed forces.

SS officer training emphasized an aggressive "can-do" approach, with the more academic or theoretical subjects that might be studied at West Point or Sandhurst discounted in favor of straightforward problem-solving exercises. Sports and physical exercise played a larger part in the officer's development than was customary in the Wehrmacht. As well as the traditional track and field sports, the cadet was encouraged to engage in horse riding, sailing, skiing, fencing, boxing, and swimming. This was not only to improve physical fitness but also to encourage teamwork among the cadets.

During the war, new cadet schools were established to meet increased demand, so that by 1945 more than 15,000 men had graduated as Waffen-SS officers. While the higher ranks were staffed by older officers originally commissioned into the army, the graduates from the cadet schools would provide the vital core of field-officer leadership throughout war.

———————

THE BASIC TRAINING of the ordinary soldier followed the pattern set in the officer cadet schools, physical fitness being central to the program. The distinctions that existed between officers, noncommissioned officers (NCOs), and enlisted men in the German Army had little place in the armed SS. All ranks played sports together to encourage both competition and comradeship, and, most significantly, they ate at the same communal tables. Differences in rank were deemed as meritocratic rather than class based, with the lowliest recruit made aware of the SS as a career open to talent. Indicative of this approach was the way an SS man addressed a superior: instead of the traditional "sir," he called him by his rank and name.

As the recruits were all volunteers, trainers could work them harder than the potentially less committed army conscripts, although it would seem that even if the training was tough it was not unduly harsh by the standards of the day. Hans-Gerhard Stack, subsequently an Oberscharführer in Leibstandarte, wrote of his early experiences:

The days spent in training were long and hard. The training was always intense and repetitive, and very realistic. It was repeated until everything was done almost automatically, but I think that helped save many lives when we were in combat. We were all good at sports, but the instructors always pushed us to the limits of our endurance and gave us tasks to prove our steadfastness. One day, for example, we were taken on a march carrying full kit. We reached a large pool with water around 180cm deep. We were ordered to march on, straight into the water, singing all the while. Nobody faltered. Then when the water reached our necks we were, at last, ordered to turn back. We returned to barracks soaking wet, at the double.[7]

Central to SS training—as in all military elites—was the ability to cover long distances over rough terrain and then be fit enough to fight at the end of the march. The two other essentials of traditional elite training were a comprehensive knowledge of the weapons they would use in combat and an ultra-attentive detail to cleanliness and tidiness, which extended to the recruits, their uniforms, and their barrack rooms.

Dutch volunteer Jan Munck described the latter process: "On a Saturday morning we usually had our major cleaning exercise. It started with all the lads on hands and knees scrubbing the long stone corridors and stairs. That done (and to get it to their satisfaction could mean doing it two three times over) we started on our own rooms, moving beds and wardrobes, scrubbing the floor and dusting every ledge or shelf. After that—the inspection."[8]

Munck described the consequences of one failed inspection, when a single matchstick was discovered behind a wardrobe:

Nothing was said at the time, but that night at about 2300 hours, when we were all fast asleep, there was a call-out with full pack. We were ordered to bring one blanket as well. When we were assembled and ready, four men were ordered to carry the blanket, one at each corner with the match in the center. We then marched for about an hour, and then we had to dig a hole exactly one meter by one meter and bury the match. Next morning it was back to normal as if nothing had happened.[9]

Sleep deprivation was also factored into the training, reflecting real battlefield conditions where sleep is a luxury. Werner Volkner, a future Flak gunner in the Totenkopf Division, recalled one form of torture known to the training staff as the "masked ball":

> This would always happen in the middle of the night, the squad, platoon or even the whole company would be called out and then told we had three minutes to report in full sports kit. The first three were allowed to return to their beds. The remainder, however, were told they had six minutes to get changed into full battle dress and report back again, the first three back would also be allowed to return to their beds. As we had about six different uniforms it could go on all night. Of course it did create the spirit of competition and harden us, making us determined not to let the instructors break our spirits, and so in the end it was a useful exercise.[10]

Having completed his basic training the SS soldier would be sent to one of the three SS-VT regiments: the 1st Regiment "Deutschland" (based in Munich), the 2nd Regiment "Germania" (Hamburg), or Leibstandarte "Adolf Hitler" (Berlin).

ON 1 OCTOBER 1936, Himmler promoted Hausser to Brigadeführer and appointed him as inspector of the SS-VT. Hausser and his small staff were to oversee the training and equipment of the armed SS and ensure appropriate military standards were maintained throughout—a task that would prove more difficult than anticipated.

While Hausser was responsible for overall direction of the armed SS, much of its tactical development came under the charge of Felix Steiner, a battalion commander within "Deutschland" who took overall regimental command in July 1936. The Prussian-born Steiner had joined the German Army as an officer cadet on the outbreak of war in 1914. He was severely wounded in 1915 but returned to active service as leader of a machine-gun detachment in a storm-troop battalion. These elite soldiers were organized in combat groups whose responsibility was to break through the enemy front line, employing speed, aggression, and initiative. The battlefield success of the storm-troop units in the final battles of World War I convinced Steiner that in this lay the future of land warfare.

Post-1918, Steiner remained in the army but was frustrated by the lack of interest in his ideas from what he considered a hidebound military establishment. Leaving the army, Steiner was attracted to the SA as an avenue to develop his storm-troop concepts but prudently transferred over to the SS, where Hausser gave him his chance with "Deutschland." Steiner adopted the armed SS's more relaxed attitudes toward discipline, which fostered unity of purpose and good fellowship within all ranks.

In his own words, Steiner wished to create a "supple adaptable type of soldier, athletic of bearing, capable of more than average endurance on the march and in combat."[11] In this he succeeded, his troops able to march three kilometers in just twenty minutes. Once his men had completed their basic training, he introduced them to live-firing range exercises, which attempted to replicate combat conditions with preplanned explosions and machine guns firing from fixed positions over the heads of the advancing infantry. Steiner insisted that his infantrymen must be aggressively proactive in the hostile conditions encountered on the battlefield.

Steiner also played his part in the introduction of camouflage uniforms. Although the army had made some tentative experiments with camouflage patterns, it was Steiner who in 1935 took up a suggestion for camouflaged uniforms made by an SS officer with an engineering background, Dr. Wilhelm Brandt. Working with Professor Otto Schick, Brandt developed a series of tree-based patterns that led to the introduction of a camouflage smock and helmet cover. In 1937 the camouflage items were used by the "Germania" Regiment, the first stage in a general issue to all armed SS units. Having proved its worth in combat, the Wehrmacht subsequently took up the idea.

By 1938 "Deutschland" was the showpiece unit of the armed SS. Himmler—despite misgivings over Steiner's lack of Nazi zeal—was certainly impressed. A little sourly, Hausser noted that Steiner was "definitely his favorite baby."[12] Yet Steiner's work with "Deutschland" and other SS units was not as revolutionary as has often been supposed, nor was the German Army as conservative as some SS officers claimed. In the new panzer and mechanized light divisions, for example, ideas similar to those of Steiner had already been introduced. Steiner was just one of many able and thoughtful German officers looking to transcend the tactical restraints of the attritional warfare of 1914–1918.

Understandably, SS staff took every opportunity to proclaim the uniqueness of the armed SS and its superiority to the Wehrmacht. The first step in creating an elite force is constantly to drum into its members that it is indeed an elite force. SS recruits were encouraged to develop an aggressive sense of ascendancy over the army, which at times boiled over into garrison-town street fights.

The head of the army, General von Fritsch, was sufficiently annoyed to complain that the attitude of the SS-VT was "frigid, if not hostile. One cannot avoid the impression that this hostile attitude is deliberately cultivated."[13] Friedrich-Karl Wacker, later of the 16th SS Panzergrenadier Division, would have probably agreed: "Our confidence was overwhelming. We had an arrogant pride in ourselves, and immense esprit de corps. I always felt better than any Wehrmacht soldier. I wasn't, of course, but I felt that I was."[14]

What made the armed SS unique was its intense level of comradeship, even in peacetime. Accounts from former SS troops repeatedly speak of this sense of togetherness. Heinz Köhne, subsequently a Leibstandarte staff sergeant, recalled how "the comradeship of the Waffen-SS was based on the test of 'all for one and one for all.' Throughout training great emphasis was put on this to ensure the principle would be adhered to."[15] Herbert Walther, also from Leibstandarte, explained further: "In the Waffen-SS we left our lockers open all the time. Stealing from your comrades was an offense that would be very heavily punished. You had to learn to trust, to depend on your comrades, and to share. This all helped in the formation of the sense of comradeship that went right through the Waffen-SS."[16] Even before a shot had been fired in anger, the training staff had created an elite ethos within their students.

By the end of 1936 Hausser was pleased with the progress made by "Deutschland." The "Germania" Regiment had also performed to a generally high standard, with capable officers, such as Walter Krüger and

Herbert Gille, advancing through its ranks. Based around Hamburg, it
did, however, experience some disciplinary problems when its III Battalion was separated from the rest of the regiment and stationed on Lake
Constance near the Swiss border.

The commander of "Germania," Karl-Maria Demelhuber, followed
a path taken by several successful SS commanders: after frontline service in World War I, he transferred to the police before joining the SS.
Demelhuber—a Bavarian who cultivated a thickly bristled toothbrush
mustache—was an early convert to the Nazism and had a close relationship with Himmler. He had little of Steiner's obsession with military
improvement, however. Like many German men of the period, Demelhuber was a regular user of cologne as an aftershave, sufficiently so for
him to be nicknamed "Tosca," after his favorite brand. Himmler even
quipped to him: "You may not be my best general, but you are certainly
my sweetest!"[17]

Hausser, meanwhile, was exasperated in his dealings with the other
regiment of the SS-VT, Leibstandarte SS "Adolf Hitler." Leibstandarte
commander Sepp Dietrich considered his regiment a special unit within
the armed SS, its prime responsibility being the protection of the Führer.
As one of Hitler's old comrades, Dietrich was given remarkable latitude
in his dealings with both Hausser and Himmler. Confident in Hitler's
support, Dietrich paid little heed to orders from his superiors, determined
to carve out his own sphere of influence within the SS.

In 1934 Leibstandarte had taken over the Lichterfelde barracks in
Berlin, which Dietrich helped develop into a first-rate military complex,
the equal of the cadet schools at Bad Tölz and Braunschweig. In an expansive moment, Dietrich took a journalist on a tour of the barracks.[18]
After passing through the main gate, guarded by two massive, heroically
carved stone statues of German soldiers, the newspaperman was guided
through the parade ground into the main instructional area, bounded by
four huge dormitory blocks.

Once inside the barracks, Dietrich proudly displayed the enormous
mess hall, capable of feeding 1,700 men at one sitting and adorned with
paintings depicting the Nazi rise to power. Beyond that was the officers'
quarters, complete with a dining hall dominated by a painting of Hitler

and an oak-paneled reception area with one of its walls inscribed with silver Nordic runes. There was no shortage of space outside. Alongside the barracks were several playing fields, a riding stables, an indoor swimming pool, a 200-meter underground shooting range, and a vast garage capable of holding the vehicles of a motorized regiment.

The journalist noted the enthusiasm of the recruits when Dietrich was present. The five-foot-seven balding, barrel-chested Dietrich was not much of a physical specimen when compared to the soldiers under his command, but he possessed that most vital of military attributes: men wanted to follow him into action. He also displayed a genuine concern for their welfare that was reciprocated.

Military instruction for Leibstandarte had been provided by the army's Berlin-based 9th Infantry Regiment. The training was rudimentary but involved parade-ground drill, an essential requirement for the conduct of Leibstandarte's ceremonial duties, which included escorting the Führer and providing guards at the Reich Chancellery. Looking back to the traditions of the Prussian Guard, the Leibstandarte soldiers achieved an enviable reputation for the smartness of their appearance and the crispness of their drill, well recorded in Nazi propaganda photographs and newsreels. But this concentration on the parade ground took time and resources away from field training, so much so that other SS units gave Leibstandarte the derisory nickname of the "Asphalt Soldiers."

Leibstandarte typically waved away criticisms of this nature, although one NCO provided this unusually candid assessment of his regiment in 1936: "The men can handle a rifle all right, but little else. If you told them to assault a strong point they would probably bunch together and run at it hoping that the combination of noise and numbers would suffice. Some have never practiced fire and movement. We are smart enough and tough enough, but there's a long way to go."[19]

Hausser's attempts to bring Dietrich and Leibstandarte into line were simply ignored. Himmler, too, seemed unable to contain his unruly subordinate. In a plaintive letter to Dietrich in March 1938, he complained, "Your officers are good enough to recognize me personally; otherwise, however, Leibstandarte is a complete law unto itself; it does and allows anything it likes without taking the slightest notice of orders from above."[20]

Events came to head later in 1938, when an exasperated Hausser threatened to resign as inspector of the SS-VT, sarcastically informing Himmler that maybe Dietrich should take full command of the armed SS. At this point, under renewed pressure, Dietrich finally gave way, grudgingly accepting Hausser's authority and agreeing to an exchange of officers between his regiment and the rest of the SS-VT.

Among the officers sent to educate Leibstandarte in the latest tactical methods was Wilhelm Bittrich, then a company commander in "Deutschland." Bittrich, the son of a commercial traveler, had joined the Imperial Army just before the outbreak of war in 1914. While recovering from wounds suffered in the fighting along the Carpathians in 1915, he transferred to the flying corps and qualified as a pilot in the air force, where he remained for the rest of the war. As an air force was banned by the Versailles Treaty, he worked as a civilian flight instructor in the 1920s, all the while covertly supervising the training of German military pilots in the Soviet Union. On joining the SS in 1932 he returned to the infantry. A capable and well-educated officer, Bittrich held a poor opinion of his new commander. He later wrote, "I once spent an hour and a half trying to explain a situation to Sepp Dietrich with the aid of a map. It was quite useless. He understood nothing at all."[21]

Dietrich, for his part, resented the interference of outsiders in his regiment, which he believed a cut above the other units in the armed SS. Despite his lowly, provincial origins, his time in Berlin at Hitler's side had given him a rather superior outlook, so that at one occasion he dismissed a unit from the Bavarian-recruited "Deutschland" with a resigned wave of his hand: "Oh well—the peasant battalion."[22] Yet whatever the differences between Hausser and Dietrich, Leibstandarte was the beneficiary, acquiring a new and vital military edge. Leibstandarte would ultimately break away from the SS-VT as a separate formation, but the system of cross-posting capable officers to reinvigorate command positions continued into the war years.

The SS-VT would evolve into the fearsome Das Reich Panzer Division, and experienced officers were regularly dispatched from the division to take command of new formations. Bittrich's career provided a good example of the system in operation. Following his time with Leibstandarte, he returned to command "Deutschland" and briefly Das Reich Division itself. After recovering from wounds on the Eastern Front, he was sent to lead the new SS Cavalry Division in May 1942 and then, in February 1943, to raise and command the Hohenstaufen Panzer Division, before taking charge of II SS Panzer Corps in 1944.

The SS-VT was also required to donate complete units to strengthen other formations. In October 1939 it provided an artillery battalion to the Totenkopf Division, while at the end of 1940 the entire "Germania" Regiment became the core around which the new Wiking Division was built. Thus, the SS-VT acted as a prime mover for the wartime expansion of the Waffen-SS, all the while maintaining a benchmark of excellence for others to follow.

Chapter 3

THE MARCH TO WAR

Iᴺ 1935 Hɪᴛʟᴇʀ publicly repudiated the military restrictions of the Versailles Treaty by introducing conscription, expanding the army to a force of thirty-six divisions and instigating a policy of comprehensive rearmament. The old Reichswehr was replaced by the Wehrmacht (armed forces) that included the German Army (Heer), Navy (Kriegsmarine), and the newly formed Air Force (Luftwaffe). The armed forces high command (Oberkommando der Wehrmacht [OKW]) was delighted to free itself from the shackles of Versailles. There was, however, some disquiet about the increase in size of the armed SS, which seemed to fly in the face of Hitler's promise that the Wehrmacht would be Germany's "sole bearer of arms."

Toward the end of 1934 Himmler urged Hitler to allow the armed SS to develop into a divisional formation, complete with artillery and supporting units. The army, which had previously looked favorably on the SS, vehemently opposed this suggestion. At this time, Hitler did not share's Himmler's empire-building enthusiasm for the SS and, not wishing to unduly alarm the army, held the Reichsführer-SS's ambitions in check.

In a secret decree of 2 February 1935, Hitler partially changed his mind and accepted in principle that the armed SS might expand to divisional size, but only at some point in the future. The decree also integrated the armed SS units within the army's mobilization plans. While the army would exercise control over the armed SS in time of war, the decree was also an official acknowledgment of the armed SS's legitimacy as a military force, with the army responsible for its training and equipment.

The army was justified in seeing the armed SS as a threat. It was appropriating precious resources—in terms of weapons and equipment as well as manpower—while lurking in the minds of the General Staff was a fear that the SS might ultimately prove as dangerous a foe as the SA, which had once openly boasted of its intention of replacing the army. Throughout the 1930s the army would fight a rearguard action against any further growth of the SS.

As Himmler was promoting the SS case for expansion, Hitler was experiencing more fundamental problems with his generals. Once safely in power, Hitler insisted that Germany must regain its pre-1914 territories and dominate central Europe. Field Marshal von Blomberg, the war minister, and his staff were in agreement with such a program but were concerned at the speed with which Hitler wanted to achieve his objectives, believing the army still unready to undertake what might become a full-scale European war. Hitler was profoundly frustrated by the army's attitude.

In 1938 events were to play into Hitler's hands as a result of the Blomberg-Fritsch affair. The widowed Blomberg had recently married a young woman, and Göring and Himmler discovered evidence that she had featured in a pornographic film and may have been involved in prostitution. The German high command—with an inflated sense of its own "honor"—considered the army to be tarnished by this revelation. Blomberg was forced to resign. His natural successor would have been the army commander in chief, General von Fritsch, but Himmler's secret intelligence chief, Reinhard Heydrich, concocted evidence that Fritsch had been involved in a homosexual relationship. This proved to be false, but the damage to Fritsch's reputation had been done. He too was removed from office.

Hitler then seized the moment, directly taking over as commander in chief of the Wehrmacht, sacking sixteen generals and transferring a further forty-four to other posts. They were replaced by senior officers more amenable to the Nazi worldview. Himmler exploited the affair as an opportunity to argue his case for a larger armed SS.

On 17 August 1938 Hitler issued a further secret decree to define the position of the SS within the wider armed forces and to minimize friction between the two organizations. Hitler made a formal distinction between the General (Allgemeine) SS and the armed SS. The General SS was defined as a political organization of the Nazi Party and was not to be armed or receive military training. He confirmed the already existing definition of the armed SS as the units of the SS-VT (including Leibstandarte), the SS Junkerschulen (officer training schools), and Eicke's SS Totenkopfverbände and their reserves. They were to receive military training and weapons from the army.

Hitler attempted to encourage better relations between the SS and army by suggesting mutual officer exchanges. He also accepted—for the time being—the army's refusal to allow membership of Totenkopf units to count against compulsory military service in the Wehrmacht. While the army was prepared to tolerate a modestly sized SS-VT as a military formation, it drew the line at accepting former concentration-camp guards as fellow soldiers. The Totenkopfverbände—ignored by the army and protected from its scrutiny—was allowed to develop largely unnoticed.

The small guard Eicke had assembled at Dachau in 1934 had grown to six battalions by March 1935, one for each of the major concentration camps then in Germany. Eicke was tireless in his transformation of the guards into a capable paramilitary force. Given that he was unable to impose the strict selection criteria of the SS-VT, this success was all the more remarkable. As part of a four-week cycle, one week was spent guarding the prisoners, the other three in training. The training duties were basic when compared to those of the SS-VT, comprising drill, marching, and weapon handling, but they were sufficient to fulfill Eicke's demand that his men be forged into a cohesive, obedient whole.

The training was deliberately tough, extolling the Nazi version of social Darwinism, that only the fittest should be allowed to survive, that pity and mercy were contemptible, while ruthlessness and hardness counted for all. Men who failed to adopt this philosophy were kicked out of the Totenkopfverbände. Set against this nihilistic doctrine, Eicke preached the virtues of comradeship. Rudolf Hoess described his boss's methods: "He punished any lapse on the part of the guard with great severity. Yet his men loved 'Papa Eicke,' as they called him. In the evenings he sat with them in the canteen or in their barracks. He spoke with them in their own language, and he went into all their troubles and worries, and taught them how to become what *he* wanted, hard, tough fellows who would shrink at nothing he ordered them to do." According to Hoess, Eicke made a point of speaking to the enlisted ranks without NCOs or officers present so that he could more accurately gauge their mood. He subsequently developed a system where letter boxes were set up in the camps to which he alone had the key. This gave all individuals a "means of communicating reports, complaints and denunciations direct to him. He also had his confidants among the prisoners in every camp, who, unknown to the others, informed him of everything that was worth knowing."[1]

Eicke ensured that his men received a comprehensive and well-structured ideological indoctrination, in contrast to the more halfhearted efforts of Hausser and Dietrich. The recruits were expected to know about the Nazi Party and its history, understand the central importance of race and Germanic racial superiority, and be aware of Germany's enemies. These, according to Eicke, were primarily Jews, Freemasons, communists, and Christians.[2]

Whereas most other senior officers in the armed SS took a fairly relaxed attitude toward the religious beliefs of their men, Eicke zealously followed official Nazi practice. His hatred of Christianity was enduring, and he persecuted those of his men who refused to renounce their beliefs. "Prayer books are things for women and for those who wear panties," he ranted. "We hate the stink of incense; it destroys the German soul as the Jews do the race."[3]

Whereas the minimum term of service for the SS-VT was four years, for the Totenkopfverbände (SS-TV) it was a daunting twelve years. But in the desperate economic conditions of the 1930s, Eicke managed to find sufficient men. One such early volunteer was Gustav Doren, subsequently a soldier in the Totenkopf Division:

> The job was quite arduous but the pay reasonable. Our uniform, food and quarters were provided free, we had warm huts with cots and good stoves. We were at Oranienburg, one of the camps formerly run by the

SA. I was taken on as a guard but we had no arms at that time except for a short rubber cudgel. Although we lived on camp we were allowed out in free time at the weekends, with one week's leave every six months. I signed a contract for twelve years; this I later saw as foolish, but at the time when I was out of work and with no particular trade it seemed a very good opportunity.[4]

According to Charles W. Sydnor, a historian of the Totenkopf Division, Eicke's achievement lay in "removing, in the minds of his men, the stigma of the SS-TV as jailers or prison guards." Eicke constantly bombarded his men with the belief that the camps held "the most dangerous political enemies of the State, and since the Führer had given the SS-TV—a racially select band of men—sole responsibility for guarding and running the camps, then the SS-TV constituted an elite within the elite structure."[5] Himmler congratulated Eicke on his work.

In 1937 the growing numbers of Totenkopf units were reorganized to reflect changes in concentration-camp organization, with the construction of much larger, if fewer, camps. The separate battalions were combined into three regiments (Standarten), each three battalions strong. Totenkopfstandarte I "Oberbayern" was stationed at Dachau (Munich), Totenkopfstandarte II "Brandenburg" at Sachsenhausen (Oranienburg), and Totenkopfstandarte III "Thuringen" at Buchenwald (Weimar).

In the lead-up to war in September 1939, other new Totenkopfstandarten were in the process of being raised. One of their functions was to provide a large reservoir of manpower for the armed SS as a whole, so that in time of war men from Totenkopf units could be used to replace losses in the SS-VT.

By the end of 1938 Totenkopf units had grown to a force of more than 10,000 men, while those of the SS-VT (including Leibstandarte and Junker schools) totaled 14,234.[6] These numbers clearly exceeded the requirement of the original mission of the armed SS, namely, to protect the Führer and other leading Nazis across Germany. Hitler and Himmler were deliberately vague about the future role of the armed SS.

The decree of 17 August 1938—intended to define the functions of the SS relative to the army—was, in fact, far from precise, with Hitler maintaining that the SS-VT was "a standing armed unit exclusively at my disposal."[7] Although Hitler did not elaborate on how he would "dispose" of the SS-VT, he and Himmler were agreed that a well-armed force (SS-VT and Totenkopfstandarten) was required to maintain internal order in time of war, both within Germany and in any occupied territories.

In light of the social unrest that swept through Germany during 1918–1919, Hitler placed little trust in his own people. His covert reason for the existence of the armed SS was that it would be sufficiently obedient to turn against its fellow countrymen if so ordered. In light of this, Hitler and Himmler insisted that the armed SS must take its part on the front line when war broke out. Himmler argued that through its own "blood sacrifice," the armed SS would earn the respect of the German people and, in his words, maintain "the moral right to shoot at malingerers and cowards on the home front."[8]

Hitler's ambivalent attitude toward the army encouraged him to develop the armed SS as a parallel military force. He never saw it as taking over from the army but wanted it to be a military vanguard for Nazi Germany, acting as an inspiration and guide for the Wehrmacht. At the same time, he was also reassured by the presence of a powerful and loyal counterweight to the army should the latter prove politically unreliable.

Himmler always had greater ambitions for the armed SS, although he kept his thoughts largely to his immediate circle. Even before the outbreak of war in 1939, he was showing a quiet interest in expanding the SS from a solely German institution to one that would transcend state boundaries and forge a Pan-European Aryan racial community.[9]

AT DAWN ON 7 March 1936 a company of Leibstandarte marched into the Rhineland, leading a German force that assumed authority over the formerly demilitarized area to the west of the River Rhine. While this action was a breach of the Versailles and Locarno Treaties, the Western powers did nothing to oppose Hitler's move. Although of seemingly little consequence at the time, the remilitarization of the Rhineland represented the first step in Germany's increasingly aggressive foreign policy that would lead to war in 1939.

Hitler's next target was the country of his birth. Austria was a sovereign state created at the end of World War I, yet on coming to power Hitler had tried to impose a union (Anschluss) on Germany and Austria. The takeover attempt in 1934 had been thwarted, but by 1938 Hitler felt sufficiently confident to force the issue. Pro-Nazi Austrians campaigned vociferously for union, supported by a significant minority of the population. The Austrian government rejected the idea—despite Hitler's bullying—although in 1938 it proposed a plebiscite to settle the issue either way. Fearing that a majority of Austrian voters would reject Anschluss, Hitler decided to invade Austria before the plebiscite could be held.

On 12 March 1938 mobile forces of General Guderian's XVI Army Corps crossed the border without resistance. Among them was Sepp Dietrich's motorized regiment, Leibstandarte SS "Adolf Hitler." To the relief of the Germans, not only was the advance unopposed, but Nazi supporters lined the route, cheering the advancing troops. The trucks of Leibstandarte entered Linz—the city of Hitler's youth—on the twelfth, and two days later they followed the remainder of XVI Corps in a triumphal entry into Vienna.

The SS-VT "Deutschland" Regiment crossed into Austria just behind the German Army motorized units, arriving at the town of Kufstein on the twelfth. For the regiment's II Battalion—formed from Austrian Nazis who had fled to Germany in 1934—it was an emotional reunion. The divisional history records how the regiment "marched into Kufstein among the roaring jubilation of enormous crowds" and how a "number of former Imperial Austrian officers reported to the regimental commander in their old, traditional uniforms and offered to be sworn into the German Reich."[10] Those who opposed Anschluss kept away.

The incorporation of Austria into the Nazi Reich as Ostmark supplied a new pool of manpower. An SS-VT regiment was raised without delay, receiving the title "Der Führer" in September. Commanded by Oberführer Georg Keppler, it was based around "Deutschland's" old Austrian battalion. The cadres for the other two battalions were supplied from the "Germania" Regiment and Leibstandarte, although Dietrich begrudged surrendering experienced officers and NCOs to the new unit. Inundated with local volunteers, "Der Führer" was soon up to strength.

Keppler, a former senior police officer from Hanover, made a point of emphasizing to his recruits the regiment's Imperial Austrian background, which included the adoption of the "Prinz Eugen" regimental march. Along with the other SS-VT units, "Der Führer" was upgraded as a motorized unit. In the words of the divisional history, "The horses were given up and the stables were rebuilt into garages."[11]

Theodor Eicke also made good use of the Reich's extra territory, establishing a concentration camp at Mauthausen, outside Linz, and raising a new regiment, Totenkopfstandarte IV "Ostmark," in September 1938.

While these new SS units were being formed, Hitler was already preparing the destruction of Czechoslovakia. Exploiting the grievances (real and imagined) of German-speaking Czechs in the Sudetenland region, Hitler demanded the incorporation of these border regions into Germany. In the ensuing Munich Agreement of October 1938, the Czech government was forced to accept the German ultimatum. The vehicles of the SS-VT successfully negotiated the mountain passes into the Sudetenland, the Czech Army withdrawing without a fight. In March 1939 the remainder of Czechoslovakia would fall to Hitler.

As Hitler became increasingly belligerent in his territorial demands over central Europe, so the armed SS moved toward an active military role in support of the army. But participation in the suppression of the Reich's internal enemies was not forgotten. During the attacks on German Jews and Jewish properties on 9 November 1938—"Kristallnacht"—at least one unit of the SS-VT was involved in the pogrom, as witnessed in this teleprinter report to Heydrich from SS headquarters in Vienna: "Mobile detachments of the Verfügungstruppe drove up to the synagogues and placed stocks of hand grenades in position preparatory to setting fire to the buildings."[12]

When Hitler turned his attention toward Poland in 1939—demanding the return of former German territory lost at Versailles—he was met by a stonewall refusal from the Polish government. War seemed inevitable, and the German armed forces prepared for action. Since 1938 relations between the army and armed SS had been improving, and with the prospect of serious fighting now an actuality, cooperation increased further, with the army freely supplying equipment and expertise. The SS-VT was developing into a fully motorized infantry division. As well as the three

infantry regiments—"Deutschland," "Germania," and "Der Führer"—
and the signals and pioneer battalion, new units were added. The old
motorcycle battalion was transformed into a powerful reconnaissance
battalion, joined by antitank and antiaircraft units.

The army's former opposition to an artillery regiment faded, so that in
May 1939 Major Peter Hansen and other army staff were transferred to
the SS to begin the formation of the regiment. Three battalions of light
artillery were established, with a heavy battalion to follow. Some 2,000
soldiers from the infantry-gun and machine-gun companies of Leibstandarte, "Deutschland," and "Germania" provided the regiment's manpower. Progress was rapid, sufficiently so for batteries to be committed to
action in September.

Leibstandarte—increasingly separate from the SS-VT—was aug-
mented by a fourth battalion, ready to fulfill ceremonial duties at the
Reich Chancellery and at Hitler's Alpine retreat, the Berghof. This left
the other three battalions and their support companies free for a purely
operational role.

On the eve of war, Leibstandarte and SS-VT had a strength of 18,000
soldiers, with a further 22,000 in the Totenkopfstandarte and other reserve units.[13] Although an impressive figure, it would grow further once
war was declared. Himmler drew upon his resources within the General
SS and the police to provide a reserve for the frontline units.

The post-1918 loss of German territory to Poland—notably the "Polish Corridor" that separated East Prussia from the rest of Germany—
rankled most Germans. The German high command considered it a
personal affront and was determined to exact revenge. But this war would
not be a simple military operation to restore the 1914 boundaries—as
Hitler publicly proclaimed in justification of his demands—but was, instead, a racial war against the Slavic population of Poland. The Polish
state would be eliminated, its elites destroyed, its people enslaved. General Franz Halder, the army chief of staff, echoed the Führer's views when
he told fellow officers that "Poland must not only be struck down, but
liquidated as quickly as possible."[14]

The attack on Poland provided new opportunities for all elements of
the SS, which Himmler was determined to exploit. Leibstandarte and
SS-VT were to operate alongside the army at the head of the invasion

force, while Totenkopf units would follow and be responsible for behind-the-lines security. They would be assisted by Heydrich's secret security service and Gestapo, along with other police units deployed in Einsatz-gruppen (deployment groups).

During the summer of 1939 Heydrich and his officers dutifully assembled a wanted-persons list (Sonderfahndungsliste) that totaled 61,000 Polish individuals. These consisted of known or presumed enemies of Germany and included military officers, Catholic clergy, intelligentsia, nobility, and other leading members of the establishment. Poland's large Jewish population was also a target. When discovered, those on the list were to be arrested or killed.

In order to justify the invasion of Poland, a series of "provocations" along the border were set in motion on 31 August, immediately before Hitler's order to attack Poland was given. Agents donned Polish uniforms and "seized" a German radio station at Gleiwitz to broadcast—in heavy Polish accents—that Germany was being invaded. Elsewhere, six corpses in Polish uniforms were dumped at a customs post, the victims helpfully supplied by Eicke from the Sachsenhausen concentration camp. Another sham attack was made on a border forestry station, complete with pools of ox blood. Hitler then broadcast to the world that Germany was in danger and that military action against Poland was his only option.

Chapter 4

THE DESTRUCTION OF POLAND

O N 24 AUGUST 1939 Sepp Dietrich received orders to take Leib-standarte SS "Adolf Hitler" from Berlin to its assembly area just north of Bromberg on the Polish border. Any movement of Leibstandarte attracted attention, so deployment orders had been left to the last minute, with the invasion planned for 26 August. Standartenführer Felix Steiner's "Deutschland" Regiment experienced a more leisurely transit to the invasion zone, when in late July its troops and vehicles sailed from Stettin to the port of Königsberg in East Prussia, separated from the rest of Germany by the Polish Corridor.

Although on the verge of achieving divisional status, the units of the SS-VT were divided between the two army groups facing Poland. Army Group South, deployed along Germany's eastern border and in former Czechoslovakia, included Leibstandarte and "Germania" regiments, the latter very much in a support role. Army Group North, stationed in Pomerania and East Prussia, included the remaining SS-VT units (with the exception of the newly raised "Der Führer," held back in reserve in the West).

To improve its mobility, Third Army, based in East Prussia, formed an improvised armored division, named after its commander, Major-General Werner Kempf. The army's 7th Panzer Regiment was combined with the motorized infantry of "Deutschland," as well as the new SS artillery regiment, the SS reconnaissance battalion, and an SS antiaircraft unit. The remaining support units came from the army. For a formation

assembled in such haste, it was perhaps inevitable that Panzer Division
Kempf would undergo teething problems once in action.

The German plan of attack exploited the strategic advantage of surrounding Poland on three sides. It comprised a series of concentric thrusts
by the two army groups that would both surround the main Polish forces
in western Poland and encircle the capital, Warsaw, cutting it off from
the rest of the country. The German armed forces were far superior to
those of Poland, in terms of both quality and quantity. The Poles' already
desperate position was made hopeless by the terms of the secret non-
aggression pact signed between Germany and the Soviet Union on 23
August 1939, which, in the event of war, agreed to divide the Polish state
between the two powers.

In late August Panzer Division Kempf secretly moved up to the border, its troops hidden in nearby forests. The divisional staff covertly reconnoitered the Polish defenses on the far side of the line, General Kempf
and his senior staff officer even dressing up as hunters on a day's shoot to
disguise their presence from Polish border guards. The attack on 26 August was canceled as a consequence of last-minute diplomatic wrangling,
causing much confusion to the advancing troops who suddenly had to retreat back to their start lines in the hope that they hadn't been noticed by
the Poles. By the thirty-first Hitler felt sufficiently confident to send the
irrevocable order to attack. At 4:45 A.M. on 1 September 1939, German
forces crossed the Polish border.

Covered by the fire of 10.5cm howitzers, I and III Battalions of
"Deutschland" spearheaded the advance of Panzer Division Kempf. Opposition was light, and it was only when the advancing SS infantry were
several miles inside Polish territory that they came under sustained fire.
"Deutschland" had spent nearly six years training for such a moment, but
actual combat on the battlefield was far removed from practice on training grounds, no matter how realistic. Peter Zahnfeld, a junior officer in
"Deutschland," recalled his first engagement: "Several men went down as
we rushed forward in a great dash to capture some ruined homes where a
number of Poles had a set up a strong point. When we reached the ruins
we discovered several corpses. These were the first dead we had seen and
we were quite sickened by them, but soon pulled ourselves together."[1]

The men of "Deutschland" had successfully passed their first test of combat, and supported by artillery and Stuka dive-bombers they pressed forward through the Polish frontline defenses toward their objective for the day, the town of Mlawa. Although the Germans were aware that Mlawa was a Polish stronghold, they were caught out by the effectiveness of its defenses and the determination of the Poles to hold the position. A series of linked bunkers allowed the defenders to pour down well-directed fire against the Germans. By midday "Deutschland's" attack was losing momentum, the SS troops forced to dig for cover.

Bringing up reinforcements, the German corps commander ordered a renewed frontal attack for 3:00 P.M. To provide close fire support 7th Panzer Regiment moved up alongside the SS infantrymen, but the proposed tank advance had been poorly reconnoitered, and once the assault got under way the tanks blundered into a series of antitank obstacles. Unable to advance, they milled around hopelessly, allowing themselves to become targets for the Polish guns. Approximately forty tanks were either knocked out or severely damaged before the regiment was forced to retreat. The men of "Deutschland" pushed forward but were repulsed by withering fire from the seemingly unassailable Polish bunkers. At 10:00 P.M. the exposed infantry were ordered to retire under cover of darkness to take up a new security line, where they would remain throughout the following day.[2]

The failure to take Mlawa was no reflection on the capability of Steiner's troops but instead represented the weakness of corps and divisional commands to properly coordinate their various units. A frontal attack against a fortified position was always a hazardous operation, made worse by the inclusion of armored vehicles in a highly constricted environment. Elsewhere, German forces had broken through the Polish defenses, and on 3 September Panzer Division Kempf had to accept the ignominy of being withdrawn and redeployed to follow the units leading the breakthrough.

As THE GERMAN armies pushed into Poland, Adolf Hitler boarded his special train and steamed eastward from Berlin, regularly stopping off to inspect his forces and pose for propaganda newsreels. He kept a special interest in Leibstandarte; a marker on the war maps had "SEPP" written on it, charting the progress of the regiment.

Leibstandarte had been assigned to General Blaskowitz's Eighth Army, whose role was to act as a flank guard to the more powerful Tenth Army leading the drive toward Warsaw. As the only motorized unit in Eighth Army, Leibstandarte was expected to push ahead while maintaining a link with Tenth Army on its right flank. To give the regiment more firepower, it was loaned an artillery battalion from the army.

As the men of Leibstandarte approached the border they were greeted by Dietrich, a familiar and steadying presence for young troops without battlefield experience. Hidden by a light early-morning mist, the advance was unopposed until the armored cars of the reconnaissance company were hit by antitank shells from a concealed Polish defensive position by the village of Boleslawecz. Hauptsturmführer Kurt Meyer, commander of the antitank company, had gone forward to witness the reconnaissance troops in action. His dramatic account demonstrates the shock of combat for the first time:

> Round after round penetrated the vehicles; machine-gun bursts swept down the street, forcing us to take cover, we heard the cries from the *Panzeraufklärer* [armored recon crew] trapped in the armored cars and were forced to watch without being able to go to their aid. Each time a round penetrated the armored car's interior the shrieks of our mortally wounded comrades grew louder. The machine-gun fire mowed down the *Panzeraufklärer* who managed to get out of the armored cars. The moans in the vehicle grew weaker. Spellbound, I watched blood dripping from the fissures in the first vehicle. I was paralyzed. I had not seen a live Polish soldier, but my comrades were already lying dead, right in front of me.[3]

The Polish defense revealed serious shortcomings in Leibstandarte's tactical skills and leadership, from the divisional commander downward. A damning report from XIII Army Corps described the regiment's failings at Boleslawecz:

> There the unit suffered its first casualties and let itself get embroiled in frontal house-to-house combat with weak enemy forces but to which the

Leibstandarte was not equal in regard to infantry combat training. The bulk of the Leibstandarte was not put into action. The possibility of going around the enemy to the east of Boleslawecz was not exploited: the heavy artillery was used for shelling from house to house, and the unit only moved forward when all life appeared to have been destroyed. In this manner, the battle was only conducted with the foremost companies; the rest of the Standarte stayed right behind them. Actual leadership did not exist.[4]

The following day, to Leibstandarte's relief, the Poles fell back from Boleslawecz in the face of an assault by the German 17th Infantry Division. Linking up with the division, Leibstandarte marched toward the River Warta, which was to be bridged before the Poles could establish a defensive line.

AFTER ITS WITHDRAWAL from the Mlawa position, Panzer Division Kempf was transferred to General Wodrig's Special Purpose Corps and ordered to exploit the rupture in the Polish border defenses. To promote operational flexibility, the "teeth" elements of the panzer division were divided into three Kampfgruppen, or combat groups: Kampfgruppe Steiner, Kampfgruppe Kleinheisterkamp (commanding officer of III Battalion "Deutschland"), and Kampfgruppe Schmidt (CO of 7th Panzer Regiment). The combat groups comprised individual units of infantry, artillery, and tanks, plus supporting troops. Steiner's was the lead group, reinforced by the SS reconnaissance battalion. That a fundamental structural change could have been made at such short notice was a reflection of the inherent organizational flexibility of the German armed forces.

By nightfall on 3 September the German advance had completely outflanked the Mlawa position, and the SS men had the satisfaction of hearing that the Polish defenders were now fleeing from the town to avoid complete encirclement. Over the next few days Steiner led his forces deeper into Poland, engaging in skirmishes with retreating Polish troops. Yet progress was not as swift as he had hoped.

As well as the natural congestion of too many troops struggling along too few roads, the condition of the roads themselves was a problem. The divisional history noted that they "were in incredibly bad condition in comparison to our concept of a road. They were made up almost exclusively of pot holes."[5] At times the trucks were often forced to stay in first gear, less mobile than the Polish cavalry squadrons acting as a rearguard for their retreating infantry.

The unsurfaced roads and the unusual heat of an extended summer saw great clouds of dust rising into the air, making it hard to distinguish friend from foe, especially as the German Army was unfamiliar with the camouflage helmet covers and smocks worn by the SS. On at least one occasion German cavalry patrols fired on "Deutschland" troops in the belief they were Polish.[6]

By 5 September the Poles had fallen back across the River Narew. The mixed army-SS combat groups of Panzer Division Kempf were ordered to capture Rozan, a fortified town on the near bank of the Narew. The Germans had underestimated the strength of the Polish defenses. A mixed infantry-armor assault soon found itself in difficulty, unable to make any progress. A Polish counterattack then drove the infantry and remaining tanks back toward their start line. For the attacking forces the action seemed like a depressing repeat of Mlawa. The divisional history concluded, "This was one of the most difficult days of combat during the entire campaign for the tankers and the soldiers of II/Deutschland."[7]

The assault on Rozan had at least drawn in Polish reserves to help the German forces to cross the Narew on either side of the town, with the SS pioneers and reconnaissance battalion in the forefront of the crossing. To avoid encirclement, the defenders of Rozan then withdrew, allowing the bulk of Panzer Division Kempf an easy passage through the town. Once on the far side of the river, Steiner was ordered to swing northward to attack the rear of the Polish troops defending Lomza, already under threat from other German units.

Steiner's Combat Group, reinforced with SS and army artillery batteries and a battalion of tanks, advanced northward, fought a confused action against Polish forces that were falling back from Lomza on 10 September. As Steiner began reorganizing his troops after the battle, news arrived of another, very different, problem.

In the village of Goworowo a sergeant in the SS artillery regiment along with fellow SS gunners (and an army military policeman) had run amuck, killing fifty Jews from the village as well as preparing to set alight the local synagogue containing more Jews. Only the chance intervention of an army officer prevented the immolation of the synagogue captives.

Despite the brutality of the Wehrmacht's official policy regarding the people of Poland, it took exception to this atrocity. Major General Kempf referred the matter to his corps commander, who in turn alerted the commander of Third Army, General von Kückler. He demanded an investigation that led to the arrest and imprisonment of those involved (all subsequently released through Hitler's October amnesty order).[8]

This incident did nothing to aid the cause of the SS-VT units within Panzer Division Kempf, whose generally lackluster performance in the first week of combat had raised concerns within Oberkommando des Heeres (OKH), the army's high command. There had even been talk of disbanding the division to reallocate the panzer regiment as reinforcements for the 10th Panzer Division while sending the SS units back into Army Group North's general reserve.[9] Nothing came of this, however, and the reprieved Panzer Division Kempf continued to press the Poles back toward the River Bug.

THE PERFORMANCE OF Leibstandarte also incurred further army criticism. Leibstandarte has been assigned to XIII Corps (10th and 17th Infantry Divisions), which was to earn a reputation for the destructiveness of its advance through western Poland.[10] The town of Zloczew suffered particularly heavily, with almost 200 civilians being killed by soldiers from Leibstandarte and the 95th Infantry Regiment.[11]

Major General Loch, commander of the 17th Infantry Division, complained of Leibstandarte's tendency for "wild shooting and burning of villages" during the advance.[12] Given the widespread involvement of his own troops in these actions, Loch's criticisms appear hypocritical, but his reprimand was based not on moral concerns but on operational requirements. Such behavior undermined discipline and slowed the advance. It was this latter point that formed the crux of the army's displeasure with Leibstandarte. It was only late in the day on 4 September that SS troops reached the River Warta, which had already been crossed by Tenth Army. As a consequence, Eighth Army commander General Blaskowitz faced potential censure for not keeping up with Reichenau, and with Leibstandarte his only effective mobile unit he expected it to be in touch with Tenth Army.

Once over the Warta, Leibstandarte was ordered to race toward the city of Łodz as part of a maneuver to trap Polish forces in what would eventually become the Bzura pocket. Speed was of the essence, but the SS regiment's advance was sluggish, slowed by the loose, sandy soil that at times reduced movement to little more than a walking pace. Dietrich blamed the inadequacy of his vehicles for his tardy progress, but whatever the reason the motorized regiment got in the way of the two hard-marching infantry divisions following behind.

On 7 September XIII Corps reached the town of Pabiance, to the southwest of Łodz, and encountered stiff Polish resistance. Leibstandarte's I Battalion and armored vehicles from the 23rd Panzer Regiment opened the assault but were repulsed with heavy losses, the thin armor of the German light tanks fatally vulnerable to Polish antitank rifles. Leibstandarte's other two battalions were then thrown into the attack but fared little better.

A Polish counterattack caused a moment of crisis, with the regiment virtually surrounded and Dietrich's command post under threat. Fortunately for Dietrich's beleaguered soldiers, a regiment from the 10th Infantry Division came to their rescue and beat back the Polish attack.[13] Fighting for Pabiance continued into the night; by dawn on the eighth the town was in German hands.

The ensuing attack on Łodz was conducted by XIII Corps without Leibstandarte, which was held back for security operations to the south of the city. On 9 September it ended its unhappy tenure with XIII Corps and was transferred to Lieutenant General Reinhardt's 4th Panzer Division, part of Tenth Army.

The southward advance of Army Group North had squeezed as many as 170,000 Polish troops into a small area to the west of Warsaw, bounded to the south by the River Bzura. OKH sensed the possibility of a vast encirclement maneuver and directed forces from Army Group South to complete the ring around the beleaguered enemy. Virtually surrounded, the Poles attempted to break eastward toward Warsaw, only to encounter the blocking force provided by Tenth Army.

Driven by desperation, the Polish forces threw themselves at the German lines. On the night of 12–13 September, Leibstandarte fought a ferocious defensive action. The II Battalion's 6th Company was briefly overrun in one attack and its commander killed, but, ultimately, the Polish efforts were doomed. Kurt Meyer recalled the enemy's bravery: "The Poles attacked with great stubbornness and proved repeatedly that they knew how to die. The fighting on the Bzura was desperate and intense. The best Polish blood was mixed with the river water."[14]

Further Polish attempts to break out of the pocket were again repulsed with heavy losses, allowing the surrounding Germans to go over to the offensive, squeezing the Poles into an ever-smaller area. On 17 September Polish defenses began to collapse. The only troops to escape were individuals or small groups, slipping through the cover provided by the Kampinos Forest. The German Army now turned its attention toward Warsaw, pounding it with artillery, while the Luftwaffe bombed it from the air. This marked the end of Leibstandarte's active involvement in the campaign, the regiment held back in reserve thereafter. A company of Leibstandarte provided an honor guard for Hitler when he visited Eighth and Tenth Armies on 25 September.

While Leibstandarte was fighting along the Bzura, Panzer Division Kempf was pushing southward to the River Bug. On 10 September engineers of Combat Group Kleinheisterkamp constructed an improvised bridge over the river at Brok (due east of Warsaw). As the senior officers of "Deutschland" crossed the Bug, they realized that the tide of the fighting was turning in their favor. Organized Polish resistance withered away; the remnants of the Polish Army were now retreating to the southwest of Poland in an attempt to form a "Romanian bridgehead." Panzer Division Kempf was ordered to form a defensive line to block Polish attempts to break out from the Bzura pocket and Warsaw.

Any hopes the Poles had for continuing the war were dashed on 17 September when Soviet mechanized forces invaded the country from the east, in accordance with the agreement reached in the Soviet-German pact. Any Polish units still in existence were instructed to escape to Hungary or Romania.

As Panzer Division Kempf continued its advance, it became increasingly dispersed, fighting a succession of small actions against the fleeing Polish troops. Resupply became a problem, especially a serious shortage of fuel that was beginning to render the mechanized division immobile. Help came from the air, when on 14 September a flight of a Ju-52 transport aircraft landed near Steiner's blocking position at Zelechov.[15] The barrels of precious gasoline were swiftly unloaded, and the aircraft flew back to Germany with the division's more seriously wounded—an excellent example of interservice cooperation then unknown in other armed forces.

With the reduction of the Bzura pocket on 17 September, the two remaining areas of serious Polish resistance were Warsaw and the nearby fortress of Modlin. The Polish capital was remorselessly pounded into submission, its inhabitants without food and drinkable water. Panzer Division Kempf (minus its panzer regiment) was assigned to the assault on Modlin, arriving on 20 September.

Under the command of Haupsturmführer Fritz Witt, three fighting patrols were dispatched to conduct a reconnaissance in force toward the fort complex. They soon came under heavy fire from previously concealed machine guns. "Eleven heavy and light machine guns were discovered," wrote the divisional history, "thus fulfilling the purpose of the reconnaissance in force."[16] During the operation one of the company runners was shot in the throat. Witt calmly lifted him onto his shoulders and carried him to safety, all the while under machine-gun fire. Witt was the first soldier in the SS-VT to receive the Iron Cross (1st Class).

The Polish defenses were repeatedly attacked by Stuka dive-bombers as the Germans prepared their assault. At dawn on 28 September the soldiers of "Deutschland" went forward, their initial advance protected by a heavy artillery barrage. But as the SS troops closed on the forts, intelligence arrived that the Poles had accepted a German surrender offer. White flags began to appear, and the firing died down.

Warsaw had surrendered the previous day, so the capture of Modlin effectively brought the military side of the German invasion of Poland to a close. Leibstandarte was redeployed to Prague, receiving an enthusiastic welcome from ethnic Germans in the city. The SS-VT units were also sent to the former Czechoslovakia, where they would be reformed as a motorized infantry division.

THE DESTRUCTION OF Poland's armed forces by the Wehrmacht was only the first step in the elimination of the Polish state in which the various organs of the SS would play a leading role. Heydrich dispatched seven Einsatzgruppen to begin the work, and operating alongside them were the three original Totenkopfstandarten—"Oberbayern," "Branden-burg," and "Thuringen"—under Theodor Eicke's direct command. Their function was to confiscate Polish goods and follow Heydrich's directive to kill intellectuals, officers, priests, and Jews and terrorize the remainder of the population.

In early October the three Totenkopfstandarten were withdrawn from Poland to become the nucleus of the future Totenkopf Division. Their work was continued by the recently raised independent Totenkopf units. Among them was the 12th Standarte, one of whose units spent nearly a month steadily killing more than 1,000 patients from a psychiatric hospital at Owinsk. The 11th Standarte was responsible for security in the Warsaw-Radom area and earned the special ire of General Blaskowitz for its overt displays of savagery against Poles and Jews, combined with repeated acts of drunkenness and looting.[17] This unit would replace the "Germania" Regiment in the SS-V Division in December 1940.

The army's criticism of the SS was that it flouted its authority in the for-ward zone. A case in point was the killing of fifty Jews on the authority of Leibstandarte music director Hermann Muller-John at Blonie on the night of 18–19 September. This infuriated General von Reichenau, who ordered Muller-John's court-martial (subsequently abandoned). Reichenau—an ardent Nazi—did not publicly express regret over the killings but was ex-asperated that they took place without army sanction. During the course of the Polish campaign more than 16,000 Polish citizens were shot by the army—but under its orders.[18]

The army's strictures on the behavior of the SS in Poland had little effect on the Nazi leadership. Himmler, in fact, persuaded the Führer to remove SS personnel in military areas from army jurisdiction. The decree of 17 October 1939 stated that SS men charged with crimes would not be subject to army courts-martial but instead were to be tried by special SS courts whose members were nominated by Hitler and Himmler.

More serious for the future development of the SS were the criticisms of its military performance. The army specifically argued that armed SS units had taken unnecessarily high casualties as a consequence of the inadequate training of its officers. Leibstandarte had certainly got off to a poor start during the opening phase of the campaign but had largely recovered during the fighting along the Bzura. Leibstandarte casualties included 432 killed, missing, and wounded, admittedly a relatively high figure for the amount of fighting conducted by the regiment.[19] Casualty figures for the SS-VT within Panzer Division Kempf were embedded with those from other army units but were not especially high.[20] Any shortcomings of performance on the part of "Deutschland" and associated SS units were in large part a consequence of army leadership failings. Kempf had not proved himself a capable general in Poland, and the SS troops under his command had suffered accordingly.

Overall, the Polish campaign was an invaluable training tool for the armed SS, enabling lessons to be learned in the months of peace that followed. And from Hausser's perspective, once SS troops were removed from the constraints of army command they would reveal their true potential.

Chapter 5

DEPLOYMENT IN THE WEST

EVEN AS LEIBSTANDARTE was repelling Polish counterattacks along the River Bzura, Hitler was preparing for the confrontation with the French and British in the West. On 27 September 1939 he summoned his three service chiefs to the Chancellery in Berlin and instructed them to prepare an invasion plan, to be launched by the end of November. Taken by surprise, the generals procrastinated, arguing that their forces were unready for such a swift redeployment. And with the onset of a particularly harsh winter, the invasion was repeatedly postponed. These delays worked in the favor of the armed SS, most of whose units were still in the process of forming up.

Once the fighting in Poland was over, the creation of the motorized infantry division from the SS-VT took place at its new training grounds in the Protectorate of Bohemia and Moravia. Designated as the SS-Verfugüngs (SS-V) Division, it was the cutting edge of the armed SS. During the Polish campaign Paul Hausser had spent an uncomfortable few weeks as an observer on Major General Kempf's staff, a frustrating role for an officer determined to lead his men into action. Now master in his own house, Hausser was ably assisted by Sturmbannführer Werner Ostendorff, the division's chief of staff or chief operational officer, a former Luftwaffe airman who been plucked from the SS antiaircraft unit to fill this vital staff position.

For the first time, the three infantry regiments were brought together with their own artillery. "Deutschland" had proved itself an effective

57

fighting unit in Poland and would act as the division's lead regiment. "Germania"—under the command of Karl-Maria Demelhuber—had gained basic combat experience supporting the German advance into southern Poland. "Tosca" Demelhuber, however, lacked the seriousness demanded of the SS-V Division. Excluded from the division's inner circle, he was transferred to a post in occupied Poland in November 1940. The Austrian "Der Führer" Regiment had not taken part in the Polish invasion due to the relative inexperience of its troops. The regiment's commander, Georg Keppler, a former battalion CO in "Deutschland," was a capable officer and a first-rate trainer of infantry.

Peter Hansen, the division's senior artillery officer, had been a member of the General SS and an army major before accepting a promotion to Obersturmbannführer in the SS-VT in 1938. He would subsequently become the inspector for artillery in the Waffen-SS. The regiment was still short of its heavy howitzers, however, while the II Battalion was transferred to bolster the new Totenkopf Division. The remaining batteries gained valuable experience training with their own infantry.

Supporting the infantry and artillery were the signals, pioneer, and reconnaissance battalions, plus antitank and antiaircraft units. Wim Brandt, a doctor of engineering and the officer behind the Waffen-SS camouflage experiment, led the reconnaissance battalion. Equipped with motorcycles, motorcycle combinations, and armored cars, it was a formidable force that was expected not only to scout for intelligence but to fight for it as well. The more daring officers eagerly sought positions in a unit that was always in the lead as the division advanced into combat.

Equally vital, if more mundane, were the support services that kept the 20,000-plus troops of the division working effectively. They included ammunition, fuel, and transport columns, along with a bakery company, butcher platoon, reinforced military-police company, field post office, and a medical battalion of three ambulance platoons and a field hospital.

The SS-V Division was based on the triangular system (three infantry regiments) developed during World War I. In its motorized format, however, the whole division had become too cumbersome, as the divisional historian remarked: "The length of its march columns prevented the movement of the entire division in one day. It needed two routes of march, which was rarely possible when operating within a larger unit."[1] After the experience of the Polish campaign, the army changed to a simpler twin infantry-regiment system, although the armed SS persisted with the triangular system until after the invasion of the Soviet Union. All divisions of this early period of the war (1939–1941) were unbalanced in having too large an infantry component and insufficient heavy firepower from its artillery, antitank, and antiaircraft units.

On 28 November 1939 the SS-V Division began its redeployment to the West, assigned to General von Küchler's Eighteenth Army, stationed close to the border with the Netherlands—a target in Germany's invasion plan. To make the division less unwieldy, "Der Führer" (plus a battalion of artillery, a pioneer company, and supply column) was detached from the SS-V Division to Eighteenth Army's X Corps.

Sepp Dietrich's Leibstandarte SS "Adolf Hitler" also left Czechoslovakia in November for transfer to the West. Assigned to Guderian's XIX Panzer Corps—which had been so successful in Poland—the men of Leibstandarte were quartered around Koblenz. Hitler visited his guard at Christmas, and at a celebration in Bad Emms he told the assembled officers, "It is for you, who are honored to carry my name, to stand at the forefront of the struggle."[2] Demonstrating his troops' devotion to the Führer, Dietrich proclaimed in response, "We will always be his most loyal soldiers."[3] As Christmas gifts, each soldier received cake, cigarettes or tobacco, and a bottle of wine.

More useful presents for Leibstandarte included the arrival of a second infantry gun company, an engineer platoon, and an assault-gun battery. This latter unit was equipped with six of the new Sturmgeschütz III assault guns, built on the Panzer Mark III tank chassis and armed with a low-velocity 7.5cm gun. This was followed by the arrival of an SS artillery battalion, comprising three batteries of 10.5cm field howitzers. While still designated as a reinforced motorized infantry regiment, Leibstandarte was evolving into a miniaturized all-arms division.

In February 1940, to the disappointment of Leibstandarte officers hoping to fight with Guderian's panzers, the regiment was transferred, like the SS-VT, to join Küchler's Eighteenth Army. Throughout the spring of 1940, SS soldiers rehearsed the intricacies of seizing bridges and conducting river and canal crossings under enemy fire. Assigned to the 227th Infantry Division, Leibstandarte would act as the mobile spearhead of the division's assault into the Netherlands, to seize the road and river crossings as far as the River IJssel.

AT THE CONCLUSION of the Polish campaign, the SS and army were once again locked in conflict over the future of the armed SS. The army tolerated the formation of Leibstandarte and SS-VT units as special troops under Hitler's express direction, but resisted attempts at further expansion. During this period, Hitler was prepared to accept a limited increase in armed SS numbers but was mindful of the army's misgivings. Hitler also saw the armed SS as an elite guard and did not favor diluting its special character through mass recruitment. Himmler, by contrast, had untrammeled ambitions for the SS; the advent of war had made a powerful armed SS all the more important.

To achieve these ambitions Himmler found a vital supporter and ally in Gottlob Berger, his head of recruitment. The son of a carpenter and sawmill owner from the old duchy of Swabia in southwest Germany, Berger fought in the 1914–1918 war and was wounded on four occasions. He reentered civilian life in January 1919 with an Iron Cross (1st Class) and a 70 percent war-disability pension. Berger then trained as a gymnastics teacher, joining the SA in 1930. Argumentative and loudmouthed, Berger fell out with the local SA leadership, one SA man rather primly condemning him for his "deplorable lack of self-criticism and soldierly modesty."[4]

Joining the SS in 1936, Berger served in a number of relatively minor administrative posts, until 1 August 1938 when he was appointed chief of recruitment in the SS Main Office (Hauptamt). There he came to the attention of Himmler, who made him chief of the Main Office in April 1940. Journalist and SS historian Heinz Höhne called Berger "the real founder of the Waffen-SS," and although this may be something of an exaggeration he was nonetheless central to its development.[5]

Berger became one of Himmler's most loyal supporters, sharing his superior's belief in an ever-larger SS. He soon earned the dislike of the

Waffen-SS field commanders who feared such a rapid expansion of the armed SS; they also correctly believed him to be an informant, reporting back their rebellious gossip to the Reichsführer-SS. In the period after 1945 his contribution was written out of the semiofficial Waffen-SS record. The haughty Prussian Felix Steiner sarcastically dismissed him as the "Duke of Swabia" and claimed he had "had nothing to do with the Waffen-SS." Wilhelm Bittrich called him a "swindler."[6] Bittrich was right to denounce Berger as a swindler, but he did so in the SS cause. Although physically ponderous, Berger had a nimble and resourceful mind, and from the outset he schemed against Wehrmacht restraints.

Hitler had accepted Himmler's request for concentration-camp Totenkopfstandarten and units from the Order Police (Ordnungspolizei) to become division-strength military formations. The concentration-camp guards and police were all part of Himmler's SS empire and outside Wehrmacht control. Berger's plan was to convert sufficient numbers of these men to make up the two new divisions and then to recruit their replacements from the civilian population. While the Wehrmacht could prevent potential recruits from being signed up to an SS military unit, they could not stop men from becoming "civil servants" in the concentration-camp and police forces. The growth of the independent Totenkopfstandarten—largely concealed from the army—had been rapid during 1939–1940. By the end of June 1940 there were fourteen Totenkopfstandarten, plus two Totenkopf cavalry regiments and support units, totaling 34,325 men.[7]

By this sleight of hand, Berger had effectively doubled the size of the armed SS. He did not stop there, however, and in December 1939 set up a series of recruitment centers across Germany that paralleled those of the Wehrmacht itself. At this stage in the war, Berger's recruitment offices were for volunteers only, and these might still be denied entry into the armed SS if they exceeded Wehrmacht quotas.

During the winter of 1939–1940 Berger and Himmler negotiated with OKW to place the armed SS on a more secure footing. Among many areas of dispute, two points were bitterly contested without resolution. Berger attempted to persuade OKW to accept service in the Totenkopfstandarten as compulsory military service (as it was in Leibstandarte and SS-VT) and to establish an independent peacetime military reserve, vital for the maintenance of units in wartime. The army refused both requests on the basis that they would have no control over them. When Himmler learned that Hitler had supported OKW on these matters, he reluctantly accepted defeat—albeit temporarily.

One area of agreement that was reached was the official designation of the militarized SS as the Waffen (armed) SS, along with a definition of what units and formations it would contain. The expression *Waffen-SS* was first used within the SS in November 1939, and by March 1940 it was recognized by other agencies, including the German armed forces. The official name removed the ambiguity of classification existing between the old armed SS units and the newer formations. In addition to Leibstandarte and SS-V Division, it was accepted that the Waffen-SS now included the Totenkopf and Polizei Divisions as well as the individual Totenkopfstandarten and the two SS Junker cadet schools, plus associated administrative organizations.[8] This represented another step in legitimizing the Waffen-SS as a military force in its own right, in what the SS would subsequently call "the fourth branch of the Wehrmacht."

Not all Waffen-SS commanders welcomed this official inclusion of soldiers who had not gone through the rigorous selection methods of the SS-VT. As leader of the old guard, Hausser lamented "this infusion of inferior material." After the war he wrote that "thousands of men were thrown at us who had not been selected and would never have been in normal circumstances, by which I mean if we had been left to our own devices."[9]

From a purely military perspective, there was little point in the raising of the Totenkopf and Polizei Divisions, but Himmler was looking beyond simple military considerations. Such was his determination to increase Waffen-SS numbers that he was prepared to lower not only general selection criteria but those of race as well. This was especially true of the Polizei Division, although this caused him some qualms, which he attempted to assuage by declaring that because of wartime circumstances, "not everybody in the Ordnungspolizei can be an SS man."[10] To reflect this distinction, until February 1942 men of the Polizei Division wore police/army insignia.

In contrast to the police in the United States or Britain, those of continental Europe had substantial paramilitary elements, especially so in

Germany. The order or regular police (Ordnungspolizei) performed the usual police duties, but most possessed basic military knowledge. This made the transition from the civilian to the military world somewhat easier, but they remained, at best, semitrained infantrymen.

The division—which subsequently became 4th SS Polizei Panzergrenadier Division—was established in October 1939 and commanded by Karl Pfeffer-Wildenbruch, a career policeman who had served as an army staff officer during World War I. The Polizei Division was a purely infantry formation, whose men marched on foot, their vehicles and artillery drawn by horse. To speed up its expansion to divisional level, the army temporarily supplied a full artillery regiment and a signals battalion. The division was ordered to begin training as part of Army Group C, holding a defensive position in the Black Forest opposite the French-held Maginot Line.

If Pfeffer-Wildenbruch accepted the lowly status of the Polizei Division, Theodor Eicke bristled at the idea that his Totenkopf not be included in Germany's military vanguard. Also established in October 1939, the Totenkopf Division had at its core the three original Totenkopfstandarten ("Oberbayern," "Brandenburg," and "Thuringen") that now became Infantry Regiments 1, 2, and 3, respectively. They were reinforced with some experienced troops transferred from the SS-V Division, including a complete artillery battalion. The remaining manpower was supplied by police and General-SS reservists.

Through dogged willpower Eicke had built up his concentration camp guards into an effective paramilitary force. A far harder task now awaited him: to combine these separate units into the complex formation of a motorized infantry division. As the army was reluctant to provide practical assistance, Eicke was forced to improvise. The camp at Dachau became the division's first training ground, the inmates temporarily dispersed to other camps.

Eicke was supported in his mission by a band of lieutenants, most drawn from the camp system.[11] Of these, Standartenführer Max Simon—assigned to lead the 1st Infantry Regiment—was Eicke's closest confidant. Simon had been recruited into a German cavalry regiment in World War I and served on the Western Front and in Macedonia. After periods with a Freikorps unit and the Reichswehr, he joined the General SS, where he came to Eicke's attention. Promotion was rapid, as Simon headed the guard unit at the Sachsenburg concentration camp before rising to regimental commander of the "Oberbayern" Standarte.

Eicke's officers lacked one vital ingredient: military knowledge at a higher level. This was supplied from an unlikely source: Baron Cassius von Montigny, an aristocratic naval officer who had been a U-boat commander during World War I. In the postwar period he fought with the Freikorps and served in the police and army before joining the SS. His military experience and able mind were swiftly utilized by Himmler, who assigned him to the Bad Tölz Junkerschule. On the formation of the Totenkopf Division, Himmler offered Montigny the position of chief operational officer.

The army's antipathy toward the Totenkopf Division was expressed in its refusal to allocate it uniforms, military equipment, and weapons. The rapid expansion of the German armed forces made intense demands on German industry, and the army insisted that its own troops must be supplied first. Eicke badgered both Himmler and the SS Main Office for access to the necessary supplies but when this was not forthcoming he looked elsewhere. Vehicles, small arms, and ammunition were requisitioned from concentration-camp guard units, while heavier weapons and equipment were pilfered from SS-VT stocks, which included a consignment of radio equipment destined for the signals battalion of the SS-V Division.

These still proved insufficient for the needs of a 20,000-strong formation, and as a gesture of goodwill the army provided Czech small arms impounded during the German takeover of Czechoslovakia in March 1939. Although a logistical nuisance, the Czech weapons were of a high standard and armed Totenkopf throughout the 1940 campaign. But to Eicke's intense frustration, the army refused to release essential medium and heavy artillery pieces built in the Czech Skoda works, guns and howitzers that he could not secure from other sources.

Eicke and Montigny instituted an intensive training regime during the autumn of 1939, although the program was interrupted at the beginning of December with orders for Totenkopf to move westward to the area around Ludwigsburg and Heilbronn, where it would come under army command. Of all the SS barons, Eicke was the most determined in protecting his fiefdom from outside interference. Army supervision did, however, bring advantages in the form of improved training facilities and, from March 1940 onward, a growing supply of arms and equipment. By this time the army had equipped most its frontline divisions and was more generous in listening to requests from the Waffen-SS.

All the while the division worked hard to improve its efficiency, although hampered by the poor weather of the extremely cold winter of 1939–1940 and repeated cases of ill-discipline centered around drunkenness, fighting, and theft. Eicke returned offenders to the concentration camps as guards, and for the most serious crimes the men were dismissed from the SS and sent back as inmates.

At the end of February the Totenkopf Division was assigned to General von Weichs's Second Army, acting in reserve. Eicke protested that his men should be deployed on the front line, but the army wisely decided that the SS division was not yet ready for such a testing role. Weichs, initially suspicious of Totenkopf, inspected it on 2 April. He came away from his day with the division pleasantly surprised, noting that it had "select troops, rare élan and a great deal of discipline."[12] And, as his only motorized formation, Totenkopf was a useful addition to Second Army's mobile forces. He even looked favorably on Eicke's request to supply the 15cm heavy howitzers the division still lacked.

THE GERMANS DEPLOYED three army groups for the attack in the West, with 135 divisions (including reserves) spread out along a 400-mile front from Switzerland to the North Sea. The original German plan was for General von Bock's Army Group B (in the North) to invade neutral Belgium and the Netherlands and then outflank and divide the Anglo-French forces in northern France. Hitler was never happy with the plan, and in the spring of 1940 he adopted a more daring proposal suggested by Lieutenant General von Manstein, the chief of staff of General von Rundstedt's Army Group A, deployed in the center of the German line.

Manstein's plan called for the main German thrust to be conducted by Army Group A, which would be assigned most of the panzer and motorized divisions. The initial assault would be directed through the hilly, wooded Ardennes region, lightly defended by the French, who believed it unsuitable for armored warfare. Once through the French defenses, the massed armor of Army Group A would drive straight toward the English Channel, cutting the Allies in two. Army Group B—which contained the SS-V Division and Leibstandarte—was still vital to the success of the operation, as its advance would draw large numbers of British and French divisions into northern Belgium and away from the main blow being struck by Army Group A in the South.

On 9 May 1940 the message for the invasion in the West was issued to all German units. The Polizei Division held its position around Tübingen—as part of Army Group C facing the Maginot Line—while Eicke fretted at the rearward deployment of Totenkopf in the general reserve. It was a different matter for the SS-V Division and Leibstandarte, both preparing to attack the Netherlands.

Chapter 6

INVADING THE NETHERLANDS

O N THE EVENING of 9 May 1940, the three battalions of the "Der Führer" Regiment silently took up position around the German village of Elten, a short distance from the border with the Netherlands. The regiment—commanded by Oberführer Georg Keppler and reinforced by an SS artillery battalion and support troops—was to be the cutting edge of the 207th Infantry Division, tasked with the immediate capture of the crossing over the River IJssel. In the early hours of 10 May radio reports of aerial bombing far to the west reached the "Der Führer" headquarters, situated in a house just 500 feet from Dutch soil. An SS officer remembered the calm atmosphere at the headquarters, the silence broken only by the ticking of a clock in the adjoining dispatch rider's room.[1] The bespectacled Keppler looked an unlikely commander of an elite infantry regiment, his studious appearance suggesting a university academic, but he and his Austrian troops would experience some of the campaign's toughest fighting.

"Der Führer's" III Battalion launched the assault at 5:30 A.M., easily overpowering the border guards at the customs post at Babberik. Supported by armored cars and a platoon of motorcyclists, the battalion pushed aside what little opposition there was to reach the IJssel by 7:20 A.M. There they would encounter the Netherlands Army, holding a defensive position in Fort Westervoort on the far side of the river.

Lacking the military resources to guard its long frontier with Germany, the Dutch had built a series of defensive lines behind its many rivers and canals, ready to blow vital bridges and flood low-lying areas to delay any invading force. The final defensive line—Fortress Holland—acted as a ring around the key cities of Rotterdam, The Hague, and Amsterdam. Although a neutral country, the Netherlands, like Belgium, feared a possible German invasion. Both countries had entered into secret talks with France and Britain, so that in the event of war they would allow Anglo-French forces to enter their countries to help repel a German assault. In May 1940 the Netherlands government hoped its troops could hold off the Germans long enough for the arrival of Allied reinforcements.

Wehrmacht strategy on the Western Front was committed to a main assault through the Ardennes region of southern Belgium. The Netherlands—with its small underresourced army—was a subsidiary theater, and OKW assumed it would offer only minimal resistance. General von Küchler's Eighteenth Army comprised second-rate infantry divisions and just one armored formation, 9th Panzer Division (mainly equipped with obsolete Mark I and II light tanks).

To prevent the Dutch from falling back behind the defenses of Fortress Holland, the Germans deployed their trump card: the paratroopers of General Kurt Student's 7th Airborne Division and the glider-borne infantry of 22nd Air Landing Division. Dropped deep inside the Netherlands, they were to capture key installations—bridges, airfields, government buildings—around Rotterdam and The Hague. Unable to hold out indefinitely, the airborne forces would await the swift arrival of German ground units. This gave the Waffen-SS a special importance in the campaign, as apart from 9th Panzer Division the Leibstandarte and SS-V Divisions were the only motorized formations in Küchler's otherwise all-infantry army.

Speed was of the essence for the German ground troops. The airborne forces experienced mixed fortunes during the morning of 10 May: the bridge at Moerdijk that opened the way to Rotterdam had been successfully captured, but elsewhere the attacks on The Hague had largely failed, with isolated groups of airborne soldiers now fighting for their survival.

The commander of III Battalion "Der Führer," Obersturmbannführer Hilmar Wäckerle, was aware that nothing must delay the advance. Wäckerle, the original commandant of the Dachau concentration camp, had

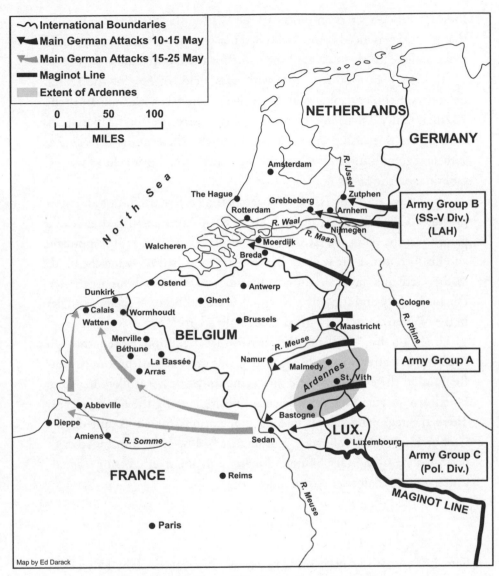

German Blitzkrieg: The Low Countries, 1940

forged a new career as an officer in the Waffen-SS. He was determined
that his inexperienced troops, who had not seen action in Poland, would
make a name for themselves in the battle for the Netherlands.

The IJssel was 500 feet wide with clear fields of fire for the Dutch
defenders. Keppler deployed an SS artillery battery—with units from the
207th Infantry Division—to provide suppressive fire for III Battalion,
crossing the river using inflatable rubber boats. The ensuing barrage was
sufficient to minimize Dutch return fire, and a small bridgehead was established on the far bank.

The bridge over the IJssel had been partially destroyed, but an enterprising NCO, Oberscharführer Ludwig Kepplinger, managed to lead a
patrol over the damaged crossing. The surprise appearance of Kepplinger
and his men under the walls of Fort Westervoort helped swing the battle
in the Germans' favor, leading to the surrender of the Dutch garrison.
For his bravery and initiative, Kepplinger would become the first soldier
in the Waffen-SS to be awarded the Knight's Cross.

Urged on by Wäckerle, the men of III Battalion passed through
Arnhem and after a swift firefight at Heelsum reached the woods near
Renkum in the evening, where they came under heavy artillery fire from
Dutch troops guarding a key defensive position along the River Grebbe.
There the regiment halted, making preparations for an assault on the
Grebbe Line on the following morning. It had been an impressive day's
performance from "Der Führer," forcing a major river crossing and ad-
vancing more than twenty-five miles.

———

Sepp Dietrich's Leibstandarte was also in the thick of the action from
the outset. Deployed just to the north of "Der Führer," Leibstandarte was
divided into two Kampfgruppen (battle groups) that swiftly overwhelmed
the border guards at De Poppe and drove deep into enemy territory. The
reconnaissance company, now under the leadership of Hauptsturmführer
Kurt Meyer, headed the northern group, and by 2:00 P.M. it had reached
Zwolle on the IJssel. The defenders, totally unaware of the German advance, were sunning themselves as Meyer's motorcycles roared into the

town, which fell to the Germans without a fight. But the bridges over the river had been destroyed earlier in the morning, forcing Meyer's troops to move due south to Zutphen and join the other Kampfgruppe in an attempt to cross the river.

Not all of Leibstandarte was fully motorized, and one company on the road to Zutphen found itself without motor transport. Not wishing to be left behind, the troops commandeered all the bicycles they could find. Within two hours the company was fully mounted, although it was found that two men had never ridden a bicycle before. A swift ten-minute training session provided them with the necessary skills to pedal to Zutphen. War correspondent Walter Krüger was especially pleased with his bicycle, which he considered "very chic, with chrome wheels, dual caliper brakes, pennants and saddlebags."[2]

The bridges at Zutphen had also been blown, but men of Leibstandarte's III Battalion, supported by artillery, managed to cross the river farther downstream later in the day. Despite this success, General von Bock, the Army Group commander, considered the advance stalled. During the night of 10–11 May he ordered Leibstandarte to withdraw and support the main drive on Rotterdam, spearheaded by 9th Panzer Division.

The panzer division's advance to Rotterdam was made through the southern Netherlands, and almost immediately it encountered the barrier of the River Maas. A few crossings were made, but they were insufficient to allow the swift passage of the German armored units, leading to enormous traffic jams. Following behind the panzers was Hausser's SS-V Division (minus "Der Führer"). During 10 May the division crawled toward the border, and, to Hausser's immense frustration, the following day's advance was similarly slow.

The division's chief operational officer, Werner Ostendorff, tried fruitlessly to get the division onto the far side of the Maas. Hausser considered Demelhuber's "Germania" Regiment to be especially remiss, with units hopelessly confused and in the wrong advance order. When Demelhuber reported to divisional headquarters on the evening of the eleventh, Hausser, who was well known for his heavy-handed sarcastic tongue, greeted him accordingly: "I thought you intended to open operations with the [supply] train. They've been here for some time."[3]

On 12 May the SS-V Division was finally able to cross the river, but progress remained sluggish, prompting the divisional history to complain: "The character of the marches throughout the following days is always the same: hours of waiting in front of destroyed bridges or long, difficult detours along poor, quickly ruined secondary routes. The division's motorization, its quick mobility, has no effect whatsoever here."[4]

The SS-V Division was divided into two Kampfgruppen based around "Germania" and Steiner's "Deutschland." Their twofold responsibilities included mopping up Dutch resistance behind 9th Panzer Division's advance and guarding the German left flank against any Allied forces pushing up through Belgium.

Once past the defenses of the Peel Line—a southerly extension of the Grebbe Line—the German panzers and SS-V Division began to make good progress through the open terrain of the southern Netherlands, their objective to relieve Student's paratroopers holding the bridge at Moerdijk before pushing on to Rotterdam. A short distance behind was Leibstandarte.

Hausser had been informed on 12 May that lead elements of a French mechanized division had crossed through Belgium into the Netherlands. The SS-V Division and half of 9th Panzer Division then turned to face the French, who had occupied the Dutch city of Breda and landed troops on the island of Walcheren. Supported by massed aerial attacks from the Luftwaffe, the German panzers and SS motorized infantry repulsed the French advance (which had not been made with any great determination). On 13 May the French retreated back into Belgium, and while its force on Walcheren remained in place, the Netherlands was effectively on its own, isolated from Allied assistance.

––––––––––

WHILE THE MAIN German thrust through the southern Netherlands appeared to be back on track, farther north Keppler's reinforced "Der Führer" Regiment faced a difficult test in breaking through the Grebbe Line. As the slower-moving units of the 207th Infantry Division had not yet arrived on the battlefield, Keppler ordered an immediate attack on the morning of 11 May in the hopes of exploiting the confusion caused by the previous day's rapid advance.[5]

The II and III Battalions of "Der Führer" were used for the attack on the Grebbeberg, but their advance was broken up by small groups of Dutch troops using the many hedgerows and orchards to good effect. After a full day's fighting the Germans had managed only to breach the enemy outpost line. An SS night attack was also repulsed by the defenders.

Keppler was forced to admit he had made a mistake in throwing his infantry against a well-defended position without supporting fire. But with the arrival of the SS artillery battalion and the various batteries of the 207th Infantry Division, Keppler renewed the attack on 12 May. At 2:00 P.M. the guns opened fire; smoke shells were combined with high explosive to provide concealment for the advancing infantry.

Attacking with their customary aggression, the SS troops used submachine guns and grenades to clear the defenders from their bunkers, who by late afternoon were forced back to the summit of the Grebbeberg. Keppler then came forward to discuss the next stage of the attack with Wäckerle, who believed that the time was right for a further push to break through the last line of Dutch defenses. Keppler agreed and ordered the III Battalion to form into three attack groups and open the assault at 10:00 P.M., with the other two battalions in support.

The strain and excitement of the battle had clearly gotten to Wäckerle, who abandoned his command post to lead one of the assault groups. The battalion broke into the Dutch lines, and urged on by an intemperate Wäckerle his group rushed toward their final objective, the railway line near the town of Rhenen. It proved a precipitate advance, however, as Wäckerle's troops were without support, and when the Dutch rallied the Germans were surrounded. Wäckerle was wounded in the arm and back; he ordered Hauptsturmführer Otto Kumm to crawl back to German lines to organize a rescue.

As dawn broke on 13 May General von Tiedemann, commander of the 207th Infantry Division, sent an infantry regiment to support the SS troops still closely engaged with the Dutch. Already pounded by withering fire from German artillery and Ju-87 Stuka dive-bombers, the arrival of German reinforcements proved too much for the defenders, who retreated off the Grebbeberg. A unit commanded by Kumm fought its way forward to rescue Wäckerle.

By the end of the day's fighting the Grebbe Line had been breached. "Der Führer" had suffered total casualties of 364 men killed, wounded, and missing, testimony to the determination of the Dutch defense.[6] On the following day, the regiment reorganized itself in preparation for the next phase of the campaign, the assault on Fortress Holland. But by the evening of 14 May, events elsewhere had rendered the action unnecessary.

IN THE SOUTHERN Netherlands, the SS-V Division continued to guard the German open flank against interference from Allied forces in Belgium. Meanwhile, on 12 May tanks of 9th Panzer Division had reached the vital road and rail bridges over the Maas at Moerdijk, held intact by Student's paratroopers. The panzers advanced over the bridge in readiness for the assault on Rotterdam, which, following the arrival of Dietrich's Leibstandarte, was to be launched on the fourteenth.

The continuing resistance of the Dutch Army was causing growing disquiet at OKW, which wanted a speedy conclusion to the campaign in the Netherlands so that its mobile forces could be redeployed to join the main battle against France. The Germans had opened negotiations with the Dutch commander of Rotterdam for its surrender, but Hitler and Göring decided to force the issue and ordered the Luftwaffe to bomb the city into submission. During the afternoon of 14 May negotiations between the two sides continued, and following a German threat to bomb Rotterdam the Dutch commander conceded to German demands. As the agreement was reached, however, squadrons of Heinkel He-III bombers closed on the city. German attempts to abort the mission failed, and the first bombs fell at around 3:30 P.M. The bombardment produced a massive conflagration, which killed more than 800 civilians and left many thousands homeless.[7]

Dietrich had already been given orders to lead his regiment through or around Rotterdam toward The Hague, to rescue German airborne forces who were still surrounded by the Dutch. With Kurt Meyer's motorcycle company to the fore, Leibstandarte advanced through the city, much of it now on fire. "People were fleeing towards the port area to escape the flames," Meyer wrote. "My motorcyclists were moving through the narrow streets as if possessed by the devil. Shop windows exploded about our ears. Burning decorations and clothed mannequins presented an unearthly picture."[8]

In this confused situation Leibstandarte infantrymen fired on a group of Dutch soldiers. Unknown to the SS troops, they were preparing to lay down their arms as part of the surrender negotiations being supervised by General Student. On hearing the commotion, Student looked out from his command post and was hit in the head by a stray bullet and severely wounded. Although Student subsequently recovered, Leibstandarte had nearly killed the founder of Germany's elite airborne army. The SS soldiers, unaware of the incident, continued to race on through the burning city toward The Hague. They successfully rendezvoused with the airborne soldiers at the end of the day, although by then the fighting was drawing to a close as the Dutch opened negotiations to cease all hostilities. The following morning the Netherlands government surrendered.

Immediately after the surrender, the Leibstandarte and 9th Panzer Divisions took part in a ceremonial drive through Amsterdam and other major cities to impress upon the Dutch the power of the German armed forces. On 18 May the German column crossed the Belgian border to resume hostilities against the Allies.

As LEIBSTANDARTE WAS moving to attack Rotterdam on 14 May, the SS-V Division was continuing to defend German positions from French interference and preparing to advance into the coastal province of Zeeland. Demelhuber's "Germania" was assigned the responsibility of containing the French and forcing them back toward Antwerp. The remainder of the division would attack the strong Franco-Dutch force in Zeeland, concentrated in South Beveland and the adjoining island of Walcheren. Steiner's "Deutschland" would lead the assault, supported by the division's artillery and pioneers. For greater tactical effectiveness,

"Deutschland" was divided into two reinforced Kampfgruppen based around Witt's I Battalion and Kleinheisterkamp's III Battalion.

On 15 May the SS troops advanced along the isthmus connecting the mainland to South Beveland before encountering their first major obstacle, the South Beveland Canal. It was a formidable barrier, more than one hundred yards wide in places and with good fields of fire for the defenders. It was, however, defended along its five-mile length by just two battalions of French infantry.

During the night of the fifteenth, artillery was brought forward for a prepared assault at 10:00 A.M. the following day. As the German shells hit home, Steiner ordered Kampfgruppe Witt and a company of pioneers to launch their rubber assault boats without delay. By midday a lodgment over the canal had been established. The defenders began to retreat, allowing Kleinheisterkamp's infantry to cross farther north against minimal opposition. Once over the canal the SS raced through South Beveland, capturing 2,000 prisoners before reaching the narrow causeway that separated it from Walcheren.

Following the Dutch surrender on 15 May, the French began the evacuation of Walcheren, but the process was far from complete when the Germans arrived at the causeway on the evening of the sixteenth. To cover the final stages of the withdrawal, a strong French rear guard was established on their side of the causeway

Led by "Deutschland's" 9th Company, the German attack went in on 17 May, but for the SS troops a daunting 1,600 yards of open ground separated them from the French defenses. Despite heavy suppressive fire from artillery and the Luftwaffe, the attack faltered, with the SS troops forced to go to ground, as described by infantryman Paul Schürmann:

The ground trembles perpetually from the bursting shells. A comrade rushes past my position to the rear, his shirt ripped from his shoulders and a gaping hole in his back. I see the rapid pulsing of his lungs. To the left goes another, walking upright in an almost festive manner, paying no attention to death while shots whistle around him. His neck and chest have been quickly bandaged. The bandages are already soaked with blood. He looks past me with large, open eyes. His face is gray. The Ninth is pulled out of combat. We move back slowly, unit by unit.[9]

After this failure, Steiner regrouped and called upon the Luftwaffe for extra effort. Under the protection of a fierce Stuka bombardment, the 10th Company of Kleinheisterkamp's Kampfgruppe managed to secure a position on the far side of the causeway, swiftly followed by the rest of the battle group. By 7:15 P.M. Witt's men had also crossed over, with the French rear guard falling back to the port of Vlissingen. As they arrived in the port, the Germans were able to see the last French destroyers sailing out to sea.

The SS-V Division was given just a day to recuperate, with "Der Führer" rejoining the division for the first time in the campaign. On 20 May it combined forces with Leibstandarte, both coming under the control of Colonel-General von Kluge's Fourth Army, which was already exploiting the gains made by the German panzer attack through the Ardennes.

Chapter 7

THE ASSAULT ON FRANCE

A S THE PANZERS of Army Group A crashed through the flimsy Allied defenses in the Ardennes, the Totenkopf Division stood idle as part of the general reserve. The impatience felt by Theodor Eicke at this lack of action briefly lifted on the afternoon of 12 May when he was instructed to move his division to the Belgian border. But to Eicke's continuing frustration, the division spent the next four days waiting for further orders. Finally, on 17 May Totenkopf was ordered to reinforce 5th and 7th Panzer Divisions of General Hermann Hoth's XV Panzer Corps.

The extraordinary success of the armored thrust had caught even the German high command by surprise. On 15 May the panzers had emerged from the hills of the Ardennes and in what became known as the "race to the sea" drove straight for the English Channel, reached just five days later. The Allies were now split in two, the northern half—forty-five French, British, and Belgian divisions comprising nearly 1 million men—was separated from the remainder of the French Army to the south.

Although a brilliant feat of arms, the extended panzer corridor was vulnerable to Allied counterattack. The German planners had correctly gambled that the Allies would be slow to react, but the need for infantry to protect the corridor remained paramount. Accordingly, as one of the few uncommitted motorized formations, Totenkopf was rushed to the front.

Despite the need for alacrity, Totenkopf—slightly over strength with 21,000 officers and men—found itself held up by the infantry of Army

Group B, advancing into Belgium across the SS division's line of march. Karl Ullrich, a Totenkopf officer, complained that the "roads were often jammed by undisciplined individual vehicles, creating double and triple traffic in some spots. Traffic control by Army Group B at junctions and intersections was insufficient and flawed."[1] Despite the best efforts of Totenkopf's chief operational officer, Oberführer Montigny, to clear the congestion, it was only on the evening of 19 May that the rear echelons of the division finally shook themselves free of the army columns and found clear roads into France. From that point on the division entered the battle zone.

At the head of the Totenkopf Division, Standartenführer Max Simon's 1st Regiment was engaged by French colonial troops on the morning of 20 May, but after a fierce firefight the French were driven off. This action was merely a foretaste of what was to come the following day. Eicke had been ordered to support Major General Erwin Rommel's 7th Panzer Division, driving westward past the town of Arras. It was at this point that the Allies finally mounted a counterattack in an attempt to break into the panzer corridor. The attack was intended to be launched from both the north and the south of the corridor, but due to Allied failures of command and coordination, only the northern assault took place, and this was marred by poor Anglo-French cooperation. Nonetheless, it threw the Germans into temporary disarray.

Just after 2:30 P.M. three British tank columns caught the advancing Germans in the flank as they marched in an arc around Arras. Two of the columns engaged Rommel's 7th Panzer Division, while the third hit Totenkopf, which also had to contend with a French attack later in the afternoon. Surprised by the British intervention, some troops from both German formations broke and ran, causing an atmosphere of panic. But they were soon rallied, with Rommel himself running between frontline units in his own division to restore order. Totenkopf was more dispersed than the panzer division, and Eicke lacked the sure tactical instincts of Rommel to be at the right place at the right time. Consequently, it was left to individual SS commanders to repel the Allies.

Although the Totenkopf antitank battalion was at the fore of the battle against the British tanks, the light 3.7cm rounds of its guns were no match for the frontal armor of the British Matilda II tanks bearing down on them. The gun was contemptuously nicknamed the "door knocker" by its crews and was effective only against the Matilda's tracks or side and rear armor, and then only at short range.

The SS troops hung on to their battered defensive line, sufficiently long for the British advance to lose momentum. The fighting became increasingly confused as the British tanks—lacking sufficient infantry support—fought a cat-and-mouse battle with the Totenkopf antitank guns and infantry. Hein Schlect, operating with Totenkopf gunners, described an encounter with Allied armor in the village of Berneville:

> There was a lone, friendly anti-tank gun firing on the main street. The men were holding out in spite of the heavy pace of fire. Then a direct hit struck the gun. The gun's shattered armored shield split open the main gunner's skull and he fell to the pavement dead. At that moment, the platoon leader jumped through the smoke to take up the dead man's position at the gun. It fired and continued to fire [but] another wave of fire and smoke foamed over the gun, and steel shards smashed the lead gunner's face. Nothing worked, and the anti-tank men tried to find a way out of their desperate situation. Help arrived after three hours when an infantry assault team fought its way into the village.[2]

Although the defense by the antitank gunners slowed the Allied advance, the turning point in the action came with involvement of Totenkopf's artillery—including 8.8cm Flak guns—firing over open sights at the enemy tanks. Around the hotly contested village of Mercatel, twenty-three out of twenty-five British tanks were knocked out by German artillery at ranges of 2,200 yards or less.

At around 6:00 P.M. the SS soldiers heard the distinctive howl of Stuka dive-bombers going into the attack, forcing what remained of the Allied armor into a full retreat. The action had cost the Totenkopf Division just over 100 men killed, wounded, and missing, and apart from a few minor instances of panic, the division had fought with commendable resolve in repelling the Allied assault. Rommel would subsequently take the credit for the victory, but it was very much a combined Waffen-SS and army effort.

The fighting on 21 May initiated or certainly coincided with a series of massacres by Totenkopf troops against the local civilian population, which included the burning of houses and farms as well as numerous executions and random killings. The first took place in Mercatel immediately after the end of the fighting, with six civilians shot by Totenkopf soldiers.[3] More killings followed in the village of Simencourt, also the scene of fierce fighting, with 24 civilians executed. The soldiers' ugly mood continued, culminating in the atrocity in the village of Aubigny-en-Artois. Some 30 people had been killed on the twenty-first, and on the following day 64 civilians were rounded up and taken to a nearby quarry, where they were mown down by machine-gun fire.

It would seem that frustration caused by Totenkopf's slow progress was a key motive for these atrocities, combined with the naturally violent attitudes toward the enemy encouraged by Eicke and his officers. Some insight into the violent behavior of Totenkopf soldiers can be discerned from the testimony of one of the survivors, Madame Sternicki. Rounded up by SS soldiers after one massacre, she asked the officer in charge why it had happened and why they had killed her husband. He simply replied, "This is war." She then protested that they were merely unfortunate refugees, to which he countered, "Since there are no soldiers here, we make war on civilians."[4] As Totenkopf marched due north in pursuit of the retreating Allies, the killings continued, with a total of 264 civilian fatalities recorded against Totenkopf by 28 May.[5] By this time the division was hotly engaged with the British rear guard holding the La Bassée Canal.

AFTER THEIR SUCCESS in the Netherlands, the SS-V Division and Leibstandarte joined the vast traffic jam that followed the panzer breakthrough into France. As the most disciplined of the Waffen-SS formations, the SS-V was able to thread its way through the congested roads better than most. Much of the division's movement was carried out under cover of darkness, making progress especially difficult for a mechanized formation of its size. In the early hours of 21 May it crossed the border from Belgium to France, northeast of Hirson. The divisional history described some of the problems of an advance in the dark: "The night march to Hirson is particularly strenuous and nerve wracking. The road is continuously congested. Enemy aircraft search for opportune targets by the light of their parachute flares, which hang in the sky endlessly, and drop their bombs but cause no damage. Adding further difficulty are a pitch-black night, driving without lights in thick clouds of dust, rear-end collisions, individual vehicles becoming separated and lost, constant turning around and renewed congestion."[6]

On 21 May—as Totenkopf was holding the Allied counterattack around Arras—the SS-V Division advanced deeper into France. The German high command had made the decision to adopt a defensive posture on the southern flank of the panzer corridor while committing all mobile divisions to drive northward to trap and then destroy the Anglo-French-Belgian armies.

Faced by this threat, the Allied command set up a series of defensive lines to slow the German advance. Initially, they hoped this might be a means of stabilizing the front, but as the Germans pushed farther into France they became stop lines for rearguard actions, to buy time for a mass evacuation from the port of Dunkirk. On the eastern side of the steadily shrinking Allied pocket was an ad hoc position built on a series of canals and canalized rivers stretching from the coast to Béthune, much of it utilizing the La Bassée Canal. Known as the Canal Line, it was held primarily by British troops, and it was here that all three Waffen-SS formations would be severely tested.

After crossing into France with the SS-V Division, Leibstandarte was dispatched to join Guderian's XIX Panzer Corps, driving toward the northern section of the Canal Line, opposite the town of Watten. To the south of the line, Totenkopf—reorganized following its action at Arras—marched on British positions around Béthune. Deployed between Leibstandarte and Totenkopf, the SS-V Division moved swiftly to capture Aire, at the junction of the La Bassée and Lys Canals. Led by Keppler's "Der Führer" Regiment, forward units reached Aire on the evening of 22 May, well ahead of the rest of the German advance.

While preparing to establish bridgeheads across the Canal Line for the following morning, the Germans were unaware of the presence of a strong French armored force. In the early hours of 23 May the French struck, tank columns advancing through the dispersed German lines. "Der Führer's" III Battalion (now under Otto Kumm) found itself heavily engaged.

Although the battalion had never faced tanks before, there was no panic among the troops, even when they discovered that their 3.7cm "door knockers" were all but useless in fending off frontal assaults by the French tanks. In one instance the crew of an antitank gun waited until the tank was only twenty yards away before opening fire, bringing its progress to a halt at only five yards' range. The infantry had their own methods to deal with the enemy armor. They formed bundles from their "potato-masher" grenades, rushing from cover to jam them into the tanks' road wheels or under their hulls to bring them to a halt, before throwing further grenades into any open tank hatches.

The French armored charge was based on desperation, with no seeming objective in mind. During the afternoon, "Germania" moved up to support "Der Führer," bringing the attack to a halt; fifty-four French tanks and other armored vehicles were destroyed and more than 3,500 soldiers captured.[7] Among the booty taken from the French were the instruments from a marching band, subsequently played by the men of the reconnaissance battalion, loudly and tunelessly. Later in the day the Luftwaffe made an appearance, and as well as strafing the retreating French the aircraft managed to attack both "Der Führer" and "Germania" before disappearing back to their bases. With the repulse of the French tanks, the entire SS-V Division was in place, ready to initiate a planned assault across the Canal Line on the twenty-fourth.

Allied defenses opposite the SS-V Division were not organized when two battalions of the "Germania" Regiment crossed the La Bassée Canal at dawn on 24 May. They faced little opposition and established a bridgehead at St. Venant before pushing forward to the banks of the Lys Canal.

Farther south, Eicke's Totenkopf Division had reached Béthune and the Canal Line late on the evening of 23 May. Without waiting to assess the situation, Eicke ordered an immediate attack, but this was easily thrown back by the British. On the following morning, Eicke, waving his pistol aloft, personally led the 1st Totenkopf Infantry Regiment across the canal. Although coming under heavy fire, Eicke and his men established a bridgehead, which they expanded over the course of the day as more units crossed over to their side. But to Eicke's bewilderment and dismay, he then received a surprise order to cease the action and withdraw back across the canal. The retreat proved a difficult task, and as British small-arms fire increased the last Totenkopf units were forced to throw away their heavy gear and swim across the canal to gain cover on the south bank.

Eicke was understandably furious at the order, which put his troops back at square one for the loss of 168 casualties. He had a stand-up row with his corps commander, General Erich Hoepner, who had arrived at Béthune to oversee the operation. Hoepner, who held a poor view of the Waffen-SS, openly berated Eicke for his conduct and for challenging the order, calling him "a butcher and no soldier."[8]

Hoepner's order had, in fact, come from General von Rundstedt, the Army Group A commander. Rundstedt wanted to rest and refit his panzer divisions for the forthcoming battle with the main French Army to the south, and on 24 May he began to put the brakes on his army group's advance. Hitler held similar views, and in the late afternoon he issued the stop order that halted Army Group A along the Canal Line. Bock's Army Group B would now act as the main hammer to Army Group A's anvil. Hitler's decision was also influenced by Göring's promise that his Luftwaffe would destroy the remnants of the Allied armies as they tried to embark from Dunkirk.

The commanders in the field were mystified by the order, believing the Allies to be on the point of collapse. General Guderian, whose XIX Panzer Corps was opposite the Aa Canal at the north of the line, accepted the order with the greatest reluctance. Early on the twenty-fifth he recalled motoring over to Leibstandarte's headquarters to ensure that they too were following Hitler's directive:

When I arrived there I found the Leibstandarte engaged in crossing the Aa. On the far bank was Mont Watten, a height of only some 235 feet, but that was enough in this flat marshland to dominate the whole surrounding countryside. On top of the hillock, among the ruins of an old castle, I found the divisional commander, Sepp Dietrich. When I asked why he was disobeying orders, he replied that the enemy on Mont Watten could "look right down the throat" of anybody on the far bank of the canal. Sepp Dietrich had therefore decided on the 24 May to take it on his own initiative. In view of the success they were having I approved the decision taken by the commander on the spot.[9]

As the German panzers waited along the Canal Line, the Allies proceeded with the withdrawal toward Dunkirk, their rear guards on the eastern side of the pocket just sufficient to hold the infantry of Army Group B. The truth then began to dawn on Hitler and his senior Wehrmacht commanders that the Allies might escape the German trap. Accordingly, the stop order was revoked on the evening of 26 May, with operations to begin in earnest the following morning.

In the SS-V Division, Hausser was instructed to cross the canal and attack the British defending the Nieppe Forest, although Steiner's "Deutschland" Regiment was assigned to assist the advance of the 3rd Panzer Division against St. Venant and Merville. In the attack through the Nieppe Forest, the Kampfgruppe (battle group) based around "Der Führer" made some progress on the forest's more open left flank, but the "Germania" Kampfgruppe became hopelessly bogged down, with the British infantry stubbornly contesting every yard. As night fell the SS-V had advanced only a few miles, with at least half of the forest still in British hands.

Supported by the tanks of the 3rd Panzer Division, "Deutschland" had more success, forcing the British back to the Lys Canal. This relatively narrow water barrier was breached in several places during the evening, but the SS infantry faced repeated counterattacks from French and British armor. The Allied tanks were eventually driven off, and Merville was reached at the end of the day. During the night, the soldiers of "Deutschland" wrested control of the village from its British defenders.

For the Totenkopf Division, farther south along the Canal Line, 27 May would be a day of sustained combat. In anticipation of the resumption of offensive operations, Eicke had infiltrated patrols across the La Bassée Canal on the evening of the twenty-sixth, SS combat pioneers working through the night to build pontoon bridges over the waterway. The division was to advance due north of Béthune and meet up with Steiner's "Deutschland" regiment on the Lys between Merville and Estaires.

Totenkopf's British opponents had been instructed to hold the Canal Line before slowly falling back to the new defensive position along the Lys a few miles farther north. The infantry of Totenkopf were able to cross the canal, but to their dismay this was not the easy victory they anticipated, as the flexible British defense remained unbroken, continuing to inflict casualties on the SS.

The 2nd Totenkopf Infantry Regiment, commanded by Standartenführer Bertling, crashed into the British lines but was caught in heavy cross fire, its advance brought to a standstill. Radio contact with divisional HQ was lost, and to Eicke, at least, it seemed that the regiment was on the point of destruction. Fearing the worst, Eicke ordered a halt to the divisional attack and around midday instructed Standartenführer Götze, commander of the 3rd Totenkopf Infantry Regiment, to break off his northward advance and come to Bertling's aid.

The confusion that reigned in Eicke's headquarters was made worse by the sudden collapse of Montigny, the division's capable chief operational officer. Diagnosed with a hemorrhaging stomach ulcer, Montigny was evacuated back to Germany, removing in one stroke the coolest head in the division.[10] Götze, meanwhile, had detached a battalion from his regiment, which he personally led toward the British holding the hamlet of Le Paradis. In the ensuing attack the British were forced backward, but in the process Götze was killed by a rifle bullet.

The last British resistance was maintained in a farmhouse at Le Paradis, held by around 100 men of the 2nd Norfolk Regiment. Completely surrounded and out of ammunition, the men of the Norfolks eventually surrendered to the 14th Company of the 2nd Totenkopf Infantry Regiment, commanded by Obersturmführer Fritz Knöchlein. After the Norfolks' surrender, the men were kicked and hit with rifle butts and then lined up against a wall by the farmhouse. Facing them were two tripod-mounted machine guns that opened fire without warning. The men collapsed in a long heap. Knöchlein instructed his men to finish off anyone showing signs of life with bayonet thrusts or shots to the head.

The whole action took over an hour, and when Knöchlein was satisfied that there were no survivors, he ordered his troops to join the main advance toward Estaires and the Lys Canal. Despite the best efforts of the SS killers, two badly wounded British soldiers survived, tended by French civilians and then picked up by a German Army unit. The two men would later provide testimony that led to Knöchlein's postwar trial, where he was found guilty and hanged.[11]

Totenkopf casualties for the twenty-seventh—just under 700 men killed, wounded, and missing—reflected the intensity of the combat.[12] The Waffen-SS formations involved in the canal battles attested to the tenacity of their opponents. Of the fighting on 27 May, the SS-V divisional history wrote: "The British showed on that day that they could fight extremely hard and with great determination. The young soldiers in the elite British regiments all fought with exceptional bravery."[13] Even Eicke acknowledged that his British opponents "fought magnificently and grimly to the death."[14]

After the hard fighting of 27 May, both the SS-V and Totenkopf proceeded more cautiously on the following day. The bulk of Hausser's division slowly pushed its way through the Nieppe Forest, while the detached "Deutschland" regiment remained in position along the Lys. Totenkopf was ordered to cross the Lys on the twenty-eighth, but the effect of exhaustion and heavy casualties saw a lackluster performance from the SS division: all attempts to break the line were driven off by artillery fire and a series of British counterattacks. General Hoepner, exasperated at the division's failure, telephoned Eicke in the evening and demanded a continuation of the offensive the following morning. Eicke was saved from further embarrassment when the British rear guard, having achieved its objective, began to fall back to the Dunkirk perimeter.

FARTHER NORTH ON the Canal Line, Leibstandarte prepared to resume offensive action from its jumping-off point on the heights above Watten on 27 May. Progress was slow, however, and even with direct support from a unit of army panzers, the regiment's objective for the day—the village of Wormhoudt—was not reached. On 28 May the advance continued but again was held up by determined resistance. Anxious at this failure, Dietrich, along with his adjutant Max Wünsche, drove forward in their Mercedes staff car to reinvigorate the attack. General Guderian recounted the subsequent events:

> Dietrich, while driving from the front, came under fire from a party of Englishmen who were still holding out in a solitary house behind our lines. They set his car on fire and compelled him and his companions to take shelter in the ditch. Dietrich and his adjutant crawled into a large drain pipe, where the ditch ran under a cross road, and in order to protect himself from the burning petrol of his car covered his face and hands with damp mud. A wireless truck following his command car signaled for help and we were able to send part of the 3rd Panzer Regiment to get him out of his unpleasant predicament. He soon appeared at my headquarters covered from head to toe in mud and had to accept some very ribald comments on our part.[15]

It was only in the midafternoon that Leibstandarte infantry reached Wormhoudt, and the rest of the day was spent in bitter hand-to-hand combat before the village fell to the Germans at around 10:00 P.M. Substantial numbers of Allied soldiers were captured by Leibstandarte. The ferocity of the fighting and the casualties suffered by Leibstandarte's II Battalion, commanded by Hauptsturmführer Wilhelm Mohnke, led to several incidents where captured British soldiers were killed, culminating in a further massacre of Allied prisoners, most from the 2nd Royal Warwickshire Regiment under the command of Captain James Lynn-Allen. The Warwickshires' regimental history described the prisoners' fate:

> They were double-marched to the barn, and thrust at with bayonets on the way. Wounded and unwounded alike were then herded into the barn. Captain Lynn-Allen immediately protested. He was answered with taunts, and several hand grenades were thrown among the crowded troops, killing and wounding many of them. Survivors were then taken outside to be shot, in batches of five. After this had happened twice, those left behind

refused to come out; whereupon the Germans fired indiscriminately into the barn until they had judged that none were left alive.[16]

Out of the approximately 95 men imprisoned in the barn, 15 individuals survived and were subsequently treated for their wounds by German Army units and then imprisoned. A British inquiry was held after the war, but Mohnke was then in Soviet captivity, and after his release in 1955 it was deemed there was insufficient evidence to mount a prosecution against him or any other individual.[17]

After the fall of Wormhoudt, Leibstandarte slowly pushed forward against the perimeter defenses established by the Allies around Dunkirk, but the staff of Army Group A once again returned to the continuing battle with the French to the south. The remainder of the campaign in Flanders was left to the infantry of Army Group B, confirmed by the removal of the elite German panzer and mechanized divisions from the Dunkirk area at the end of May.

Soldiers from "Der Führer" had advanced as far as the hilltop town of Cassel, and they looked down across the flat plain toward Dunkirk. They could clearly see British soldiers retreating toward the port and the long columns of black smoke that marked the Luftwaffe's bombing of the port installations. The Allied rear guards (primarily French) were sufficient, however, to hold the advancing German infantry, while the aerial bombardment proved less effective than Göring had promised. When the Germans marched into Dunkirk on 4 June, 338,000 Allied troops (including 110,000 French) had been rescued from German captivity.

Chapter 8

FRANCE DEFEATED

T HE END OF hostilities in Flanders afforded the Wehrmacht a brief and necessary opportunity to rest and refit. Twenty days of combat and maneuver had taken its toll on the vast array of vehicles deployed by the mechanized formations; maintenance and replacement became a priority. The exhausted troops also found an opportunity to rest. For the officers, the pause was a chance to restore the order and discipline that inevitably slipped while on campaign. This was especially true of the soldiers' appearance. Even in Leibstandarte, improvements in soldierly bearing were called for. According to one history of the formation, "The men were ordered to cease wearing civilian business suits, which some had apparently 'liberated,' and to banish dogs, dolls, and stuffed animals from their vehicles, which in Dietrich's words had taken on a 'gypsy like appearance.'"[1]

Totenkopf underwent a similar overhaul, its commander, Theodor Eicke, issuing an order of the day to "re-establish good order and discipline." Eicke warned his men that they were not to be caught looting from the civilian population: "We are currently subject to sharp criticism from all quarters and are thus obligated to ensure that we show no weakness or give cause for such criticism. Two wrongs don't make a right! Experience in the last few days has shown that through the small mistakes of isolated individuals, incidents have been ascribed to our division that are not reflective of the facts."[2]

The "sharp criticism" referred to by Eicke had been made by his immediate superior, General Hoepner, and by the Reichsführer-SS himself.

The war diary of Hoepner's XVI Corps, while acknowledging the bravery of SS officers, contained this admonishment: "Higher level commanders and company commanders were not capable of leading their men by means of clearly stated combat orders."[3]

Hoepner's already poor opinion of Eicke fell even further when rumors of the Le Paradis massacre reached him. Outraged, he ordered a full investigation of the incident, although Himmler and the SS administration made sure the whole matter was swept under the carpet. Fritz Knöchlein, the chief suspect, continued his successful career within the Waffen-SS, which would include the award of a Knight's Cross in 1944.

On 30 May 1940 Himmler arrived in northern France to inspect the division, calling Eicke to a conference at Bailleul. Although no record of the interview remains, from associated correspondence it seems fairly clear that Eicke received a severe dressing-down.[4] As well as the bad publicity engendered by the Le Paradis massacre—the killings of civilians earlier in the campaign seemed not to figure in the reprimand—Himmler was primarily concerned at the substantial losses in men and materials incurred by the division. Most serious was the disproportionate loss of officers: out of 1,140 total casualties, an extraordinary figure of around 300 were officers.[5] They were impossible to replace through the normal reserve system, forcing Himmler to draw upon partially trained cadets from the two officer training schools at Braunschweig and Bad Tölz.

Himmler was also determined to rein in Eicke's independence and bring the division fully back within the SS system. As part of this process, he personally nominated Brigadeführer Kurt Knoblauch as Montigny's successor. Knoblauch was Himmler's man, however, and a suspicious Eicke studiously kept him at arm's length. Another unwelcome intrusion was the arrival of Oberführer Matthias Kleinheisterkamp to replace the deceased Götze as commander of the 3rd Totenkopf Infantry Regiment. Although a promotion for Kleinheisterkamp, the transfer from a battalion command in the crack "Deutschland" to a Totenkopf regiment was something of a poisoned chalice.

On 6 June Totenkopf departed its base in the coastal town of Boulogne to begin a leisurely move southward to St. Omer and then to Peronne, which was reached on the twelfth. There it acted as part of a general reserve before commitment to active operations on the fourteenth.

No such luxury of time was given to Hausser's SS-V Division. On the evening of 1 June, its units were ordered to take up position for the proposed assault against the French, now holding a new position along the Somme and Aisne Rivers. Dietrich's Leibstandarte followed in the wake of the SS-V. The balance of power now lay firmly in Germany's favor, some 104 divisions set against the 60 or so French formations on the Somme-Aisne line.

On 5 June Panzer Group Kleist opened its offensive against the French holding the south bank of the River Somme. The artillery of the SS-V Division supported the German attack, and on the following day the panzers broke through the French defenses with the SS troops following in support. The seemingly easy advance came to a halt on the seventh when the SS-V infantry hit the main French defensive line along the River Avre.

Preparations were made for a continuation of the assault for 8 June, to expand the bridgehead and then drive on through the French defenses. But at 9:20 A.M. the attack was suddenly canceled and the SS-V Division ordered on the defensive. The reason for this abrupt halt lay in General von Bock's concern that Panzer Group Kleist was becoming bogged down in this sector. German attacks elsewhere were making better progress, and Bock decided to redeploy Kleist's mobile forces farther east.

In the early hours of 9 June the men of "Der Führer" wearily returned over the Avre, rejoining the division that was now swinging east to support the breakthrough already achieved in the Aisne-Oise area. Leibstandarte was also part of this transfer, and on 12 June it joined other German forces in bridging the Marne; two days later it reached the Seine. The Totenkopf Division—released from the reserve—joined the SS-V and Leibstandarte as part of an increasingly powerful Panzer Group Kleist.

German success on the battlefield was mirrored by encouraging developments in the political sphere. On 10 June the French government fled Paris for Bordeaux, declaring it an open city two days later, so that on 14 June the Germans entered the French capital unopposed. When troops of Leibstandarte heard the news, they rang the bells in a local church to celebrate. French resistance began to crumble, the German breakthrough turning into a pursuit. The motorized troops of the Waffen-SS drove at speed across the rolling French countryside.

In order to prevent the French Army from having any chance of recovery, Hitler and OKW ordered the pursuit to continue deep into the French heartland. While the German infantry trudged through central France, the mobile formations were given free hand to chase the enemy. Kurt Meyer, leading Leibstandarte's motorcycle company, described their hectic progress: "At dawn, my advance guard was moving through the tree-dotted, undulating landscape, clearing the road with gunfire. The fleeing French units repeatedly tried to form lines of resistance to gain time and space for their retreat. These attempts didn't bother us anymore. We had only one aim: to gain ground to the south. The flanks had become unimportant. We moved down the roads like a fire-spitting dragon. Halting was taboo. Firing was only conducted from moving vehicles. The advance was beginning to look like a wild hunt."[6]

As the mechanized formations of the Waffen-SS drove through France, they were followed by the foot-slogging, horse-drawn Polizei Division. Under the command of Obergruppenführer Karl Pfeffer-Wildenbruch, it had crossed into France and by 9 June was ready to participate in the assault across the Aisne River and Ardennes Canal. On the ninth, the army's 26th Infantry Division had waged a fierce battle against the French defenders along the Ardennes Canal, the Germans making little progress.

On the tenth the Polizei Division was ordered into the battle. The 1st Polizei Infantry Regiment crossed the canal and advanced toward the wooded high ground to the west of Voncq, only to find itself repeatedly counterattacked by the French. A seesaw battle continued throughout the day, until the 2nd Police Infantry Regiment captured the town and forced the French to retire to avoid encirclement.

The Polizei Division then took part in the advance into the Argonne Forest, harrying retreating French rear guards. A final engagement took place at Les Islettes on 14 June, when the French made a stand against the Germans. According to Pfeffer-Wildenbruch, they "defended themselves with the same toughness and skill as the French troops at Voncq."[7] But in scenes of close-quarters combat, the SS troops eventually overwhelmed the enemy. This marked the end of the division's involvement in the campaign in the West; on 20 June it was withdrawn to Germany.

THE GERMAN ADVANCE into the Argonne was part of a wider strategy to encircle the French holding the Maginot Line. On 14 June Army Group C had begun its assault on the much-vaunted French defenses, and two breaches were made at Saarbrucken and Colmar. The French fell back from the Maginot Line and the Vosges region in an attempt to link up with what remained of the main French Army in the southwestern area of the country. The SS-V Division was one of a number of German formations ordered to contain the French breakout attempt.

The main fighting took place on 16 and 17 June, the SS-V colliding with French units trying to escape from the fast-closing encirclement. After a few sharp actions, the SS soldiers became aware that the fight was going out of their opponents. Hauptsturmführer Christian Tychsen, an officer in the reconnaissance battalion, recalled his experiences when his company neared Mussy-sur-Seine on the seventeenth: "We entered villages and towns with bravado, capturing countless prisoners. Artillery pieces with horses still in harness stood by the road. Everyone surrendered without a fight as we continued still further. French approached us from out of a small forest. Hundreds. An interpreter came up to the front. It was useless to explain to the French that we would shoot if they tried to escape. They were all happy that the war was over for them."[8]

There was little more fighting for the SS-V Division after 17 June; from then on it was a case of collecting and disarming French troops whenever they came upon them. Hausser was able to announce that the division had captured approximately 30,000 French soldiers in just ten days of campaigning.[9]

On the right flank of Panzer Group Kleist's advance, Totenkopf had even less to do. Although the pursuit across France was undoubtedly exhilarating, it had one disadvantage, as one officer grumbled: "The quick pace of the advance prevented the division from collecting up the captured booty, and it had to be left where found."[10] Eicke always maintained his interest in accruing material resources for the division, regardless of where or how this might be achieved.

The only real action experienced by the division took place on 18–19 June at Tarare and L'Arbresle, where Totenkopf infantry were involved in two fierce clashes with French Moroccan troops. Of the L'Arbresle action Charles Sydnor writes, "In clearing out this rearguard position, the SS men refused to take any prisoners and killed every one of the 30 Moroccan soldiers involved in the skirmish."[11] The implication that these men were massacred was refuted by Totenkopf officer Karl Ullrich: "That more whites than blacks were captured is due to the fact that the Moroccans defended themselves with an unbelievable sense of death defiance and hatred."[12]

The German armed forces as a whole had been strongly imbued with a sense of the racial inferiority of Africans, and during the 1940 campaign there were several well-recorded instances of Wehrmacht troops killing surrendered African soldiers.[13] Given this tendency and the fact that the division had only recently massacred British prisoners and French civilians, these unauthorized killings seem quite probable. And within the Wehrmacht, reports of Totenkopf killing African prisoners were commonplace. A Luftwaffe crewman described how a friend in the division told him that "in the campaign in the West they took no colored prisoners whatever. They simply put up a machine gun and mowed them all down."[14]

LEIBSTANDARTE CONTINUED ITS march into east-central France, reaching Riom and then Clermont-Ferrand on 20 June. At this point, the French had opened discussions with the Germans for an armistice, but while talks were ongoing the drive continued. A final push was made toward St. Étienne on 24 June, and it was just north of the town, in the village of La Fouillouse, that Leibstandarte fought its last action of 1940. To their surprise, the SS infantry found themselves faced by several French tanks of World War I vintage, slowly lumbering toward them along the main street. A soldier from the 10th Company witnessed a duel between one of these tanks and a 3.7cm antitank gun:

> There is an alarm of gunfire in the street. At only 20 meters distance the French tank and the anti-tank gun face each other. The anti-tank gun fires first, and we hear the shrill whistle of the shell ricocheting off the tank. A second round also fails. The steel plates are too strong for the 3.7cm

rounds. We now see the tank fire directly on the gun, scoring a direct hit. Fortunately the tank retreats, its turret jammed. The 10th Company platoon commander shouts back to bring forward the 15cm infantry guns. The guns force the tanks to withdraw.[15]

On 25 June Leibstandarte took St. Étienne, marking the deepest penetration by German forces during the entire battle for France. In the evening, Dietrich was informed that the armistice had come into effect and the war in the West was over.

On 21 June, while armistice negotiations were still ongoing, a substantial portion of Panzer Group Kleist was ordered to drive along the Loire Valley and then advance south toward Bordeaux. France was to be divided in two: a German-occupied zone comprising northern and western France and a zone administered by a puppet French government in the south. The SS-V and Totenkopf joined 9th and 10th Panzer Divisions in a dash to take control of what would become the German-occupied zone that ran along the Atlantic coast. Although there was little fighting, the two countries were still in a state of war, so a resolute display of German military might was the order of the day. On 24 June the SS-V Division raced through the Angouléme, to the surprise and dismay of the local civilians, as described by one officer: "Without firing a shot the armored spearhead pushed into the town, which crawled with armed French soldiers and refugees. It was a picture of unholy disorder. The surprise occupation of the city by German troops took place in front of the populace, who stood along the road with questioning, astonished, confused or frightened looks on their faces. Several times the frightened and bewildered cry of 'Mon Dieu—les Allemande!' rang from the roadside."[16]

On 27 June, the reconnaissance battalion pushed on past Bordeaux (then the seat of what remained of the French government) and on to the coastal resort of Biarritz and the Spanish border. They received a friendly welcome from the Spanish border guards, who threw open the barriers to welcome the SS men into Bidassoa. They were given an official reception by the local Spanish commander, with much mutual congratulation. For the next few days the men of both the SS-V and Totenkopf Divisions were allowed to rest, swimming in the Atlantic and basking in the warm sun. "They were dream-like days," recorded the SS-V divisional history, "during which we almost forgot the past battles and hardships of the Western Campaign."[17]

———————

THE WEHRMACHT HAD won a stupendous victory against the combined forces of France, Britain, Belgium, and Holland, the Austrian corporal achieving in six weeks what the Kaiser's generals had failed to do in four years. The contribution of the Waffen-SS was necessarily small in terms of securing overall victory, but it had, for the most part, acquitted itself well.

The SS-V Division and Leibstandarte had demonstrated the aggressive fighting qualities and tactical acumen that would become the hallmark of the best Waffen-SS formations in the years to come. The performance of the Totenkopf Division was mixed, its clumsy battlefield skills set against its undoubted determination. Not much had been expected of the Polizei Division, but given the indifferent quality of its manpower and lack of training and equipment, it had performed creditably enough. Himmler wasted no time in providing his master with stories of his soldiers' triumphs, which Hitler readily acknowledged in his speech to the Reichstag on 19 July 1940, singling out the Waffen-SS for special praise.

Rewards for the SS soldiers' performance in 1940 included a wide distribution of Iron Crosses (both 1st and 2nd Classes) and the award of the totemic Knight's Cross of the Iron Cross to six recipients. Dietrich was unsurprisingly one of those rewarded, although Hausser missed out in this round of awards in favor of two of his regimental commanders, Felix Steiner and Georg Keppler. The other three medals were awarded to Ludwig Kepplinger, Fritz Vogt, and Fritz Witt, all from the SS-V Division.

The award of the Knight's Cross to officers and men would become increasingly important as the war went on. For an officer, to have a "tin collar" was the sign of combat success, bringing the wearer the respect of his fellow soldiers and the slavish admiration of the public. When a photographer was present, the Knight's Cross holder would make sure the medal was prominently on display, while in the civilian world the mere sight of the award would ensure the best seats in a restaurant or free tickets to a theater performance. Otto Weidinger—Knight's Cross holder in Das Reich—enjoyed the perks the medal afforded him, but on one occasion he became embarrassed by the preferential treatment accorded him: "I found a seat in a fully occupied train and wanted to offer it to a woman and child, who had boarded the train after me, and absolutely refused to accept it. Only after an energetic talking to could I convince her to do so."[18]

In total, 448 officers and enlisted men of the Waffen-SS would be awarded the Knight's Cross (see Appendix B for awards by division).[19] There was some grumbling in the Wehrmacht that the Waffen-SS received more than its fair share of Knight's Crosses, so that, for example, one naval lieutenant complained that the "SS get their badges not for what they've done but for their political and moral attitudes."[20] Yet a detailed examination of the award system saw the Waffen-SS receiving the decoration at broadly the same rate as other ground soldiers in both the army and the Luftwaffe.[21]

Some awards of the Knight's Cross were undoubtedly given for political or other nonmilitary reasons, but insomuch as this was true of the Waffen-SS, it was equally so of other service arms. If there was any marked unfairness in the system, it would have to be directed at the Luftwaffe's airmen and the Navy's U-boat commanders, where medals were routinely dispensed for exaggerated figures claimed in enemy aircraft shot down and ships sunk.[22]

WHILE THE WAFFEN-SS had proved itself in combat, there was its other, darker, side to consider. The Waffen-SS atrocities in the 1940 campaign were as surprising as they were shocking, committed against Western opponents where it was customary to follow the rules of war as laid out in The Hague and Geneva Conventions. Despite its many and increasingly hollow protestations as to its honor, the Wehrmacht had been fatally compromised by its association with National Socialism. The German Army was increasingly becoming Hitler's army, with an attendant blurring of moral boundaries. The men of the Waffen-SS, as Hitler's standard-bearers, were even more compromised.

This is, of course, not to say that Waffen-SS soldiers were incapable of behaving in an honorable and humane fashion. After the civilian massacres at Aubigny carried out by Totenkopf troops, other men from the division separately came forward to help the victims, providing food and medical assistance.[23] Yet at the same time, if Waffen-SS troops committed atrocities, they faced no effective legal sanction. This had proved to be the case in Poland and was also true in the West. Soldiers understandably took their lead from their superiors, and when senior officers such as Eicke made it clear that moral qualms were for the weak, it was hardly surprising that in times of extreme tension their subordinates crossed the line into barbarity.

ONCE THE ARMISTICE with France was in place and the Atlantic Seaboard secured by second-rank infantry units, the SS-V and Totenkopf Divisions withdrew from the Franco-Spanish border, the former to the Netherlands to supervise the disarmament of the Dutch Army and the latter to new positions in German-occupied France. Leibstandarte had originally been promised a victory parade in Paris under the gaze of the Führer, but when Hitler decided on a more low-key sightseeing trip of the French capital, the regiment was diverted to take up garrison duties in the Alsatian city of Metz. At the time, there was talk of peace and disarmament, but this would not last long.

Chapter 9

TRANSITION AND EXPANSION

DURING THE LATE summer and early autumn of 1940, the Wehrmacht prepared for Operation Sealion, the invasion of Britain. While the Luftwaffe fought the Royal Air Force (RAF) for supremacy in the skies over southern England, the German Navy and Army rehearsed amphibious landings. Both Leibstandarte and the SS-V Division took part in the preparations, acquainting themselves with the use of life jackets and conducting disembarkation drills on the Moselle and other European waterways. Yet neither the navy nor the army demonstrated much enthusiasm for the operation, especially while Britain remained undefeated in the air.

The lack of confidence felt by the Wehrmacht's senior commanders filtered down through the ranks, and the comments of Obersturmführer Peter Zahnfeld were not untypical: "There followed a certain amount of half-hearted preparation as barges were readied and landings practiced. It was all very experimental. We were in no way ready for such an operation over the sea. For myself I was very relieved when it all fizzled out."[1]

Hitler's interest in Sealion wavered. On the basis of his success in France, he had hoped to force Britain to accept a diplomatic resolution to the conflict, but his overtures were firmly rebuffed. Even while the air battles were ongoing, Hitler returned to the project that mattered to him most, the destruction of the Soviet Union and the creation of a German empire in central and eastern Europe. As early as 31 July 1940 he had informed his generals that they must prepare for an invasion of Soviet Russia. On 17 September Sealion was postponed indefinitely.

During 1940 the Waffen-SS made fundamental changes to its command structure. Gottlob Berger's promotion to lead the SS Main Office (SS Hauptamt) on 1 June made him the most important figure in the Waffen-SS administration. This preeminence was not to last long, however, when on 15 August Himmler ordered the formation of the SS Leadership Main Office (SS Führungshauptamt). With Brigadeführer Hans Jütttner as its chief of staff (and effective head), the SS Leadership Main Office took over and developed the responsibilities of Hausser's old SS-VT Inspectorate. It was also a statement of intent by Himmler that his military force required its own command headquarters in the same way that OKH acted for the German Army.

Berger's Main Office was still crucial to Waffen-SS development, as its responsibilities included education, indoctrination, and, above all, the recruitment and replacement of all personnel. Thus, Berger remained in his position as Himmler's chief recruiting sergeant. Jüttner was the classic Nazi bureaucrat, seemingly without personality, efficient and ruthless, and quite distinct from the garrulous, overbearing Berger. Himmler had set up these two separate main offices so that Jüttner and Berger worked in competition with each other for his favor.

Despite the rivalries between the two men, they were at least united in their determination to curtail the influence and activities of Theodor Eicke and his burgeoning Totenkopf empire. After taking command of the Totenkopf Division, Eicke continued his relationship with the concentration-camp system, illegally siphoning off men, vehicles, and other equipment from the camps for the use of his own division. Eicke refused to accept the authority of Jüttner and Berger, claiming that his rank and experience made him answerable to the Reichsführer-SS alone.

Himmler tended to indulge Eicke, but eventually his patience was tested to the breaking point, especially when he discovered that Eicke was publicly naming and shaming officers. They even included senior officers such as Standartenführer Kleinheisterkamp—a bête noire of Eicke's—who had been confined to quarters for apparently failing to carry out a divisional order.[2] At the end of January 1941 Himmler wrote to Eicke in a letter that rebuked his behavior, as well as casting doubts on his sanity and fitness to command. This was followed by a series of reforms initiated by Jüttner, which formally took away control of the camps and the separate Totenkopf regiments from Eicke. He also removed Eicke's old concentration-camp cronies from positions of authority, replacing them with his own subordinates.

Eicke never gave up his belief in his authority transcending that of a divisional commander, but while continuing to fight the SS high command he worked hard to improve Totenkopf as a fighting formation. Ideological indoctrination was not skimped, either, with a comprehensive Nazi curriculum codified into a two-volume reference guide entitled *Schwert und Plug* (Sword and Plough). Despite his mistrust of outside institutions, Eicke took up an army offer of training assistance in matters such as artillery support and air-ground cooperation. He also threw himself into improving his own military knowledge. Heinz Höhne retold the story of how he "shut himself up in his billet for days at a time, cut the tactical signs out of the situation maps and played a war game with them on the floor of his room—all in deadly secret lest his senior general staff officer notice his suddenly acquired taste for military matters."[3]

Fortunately for Eicke, his senior staff officer, the unpopular Kurt Knoblauch, was transferred to work directly for Himmler. Eicke was allowed to choose his replacement: Sturmbannführer Heinz Lammerding, commander of the Totenkopf engineer battalion. Before joining the SS in 1935, Lammerding had been a construction engineer, and his talents were put to good use by Eicke, who swiftly appointed him as engineer officer within the concentration-camp inspectorate. In 1939 Lammerding transferred to the Totenkopf Division, proving an able and loyal lieutenant. He would go on to lead Das Reich in France during 1944.

———

Leibstandarte SS "Adolf Hitler" was officially upgraded from a reinforced regiment to a powerful motorized infantry brigade; its artillery battalion was increased to regimental size, along with an armored car company, Flak company, and a battalion each of engineers and signals.

But in a case of Peter robbing Paul, the extra artillery came from the Totenkopf and SS-V Divisions.

The drain on Hausser's SS-V Division did not stop there. At the end of 1940, it became the "mother" formation for the Wiking Division, commanded by the recently promoted Brigadeführer Felix Steiner. The entire "Germania" Regiment was transferred to the new formation, its chief, Karl-Maria Demelhuber, leaving the regiment to take up an administrative post in the Netherlands. Other units transferred from the SS-V to Wiking included an artillery battalion, reconnaissance and anti-tank battalions, as well as maintenance and medical units.[4]

The gap left by "Germania's" departure from the SS-V was filled by the 11th Totenkopf Standarte, a former concentration-camp guard unit that had gained an infamous reputation for ill-disciplined brutality in Poland. Its new commander, Obersturmbannführer Brandt—formerly of the reconnaissance battalion—faced a serious challenge in bringing these troops to a standard close to that of the rest of the division. The other departed units were replaced from within the division.

In December the division was renamed Deutschland, but shortly afterward, to avoid confusion with the "Deutschland" Regiment, it was changed to Reich (later Das Reich). The new Reich Division was then ordered to leave the Netherlands for deployment in Vesoul, in France's Haute Saone area. Once in France, training continued with renewed vigor. To improve mobile firepower, an assault-gun battery was formed in February 1941, followed by the creation of a motorcycle battalion. In March, a consignment of nine 5cm Pak 38 antitank guns arrived, the first stage in replacing the old 3.7cm "door knockers" that had proved so ineffectual during the 1940 campaign.

DURING GERMANY'S CONQUEST of Norway in 1940, Hitler ordered Himmler to send SS troops to act as a garrison for the settlement of Kirkenes in the far northern part of the country. The assembled battalion was dispatched to Norway at the end of June 1940. Further troops arrived in October to form SS Infantry Regiment 9. In the spring of 1941 two

Totenkopfstandarten (redesignated as SS Infantry Regiments 6 and 7) were also sent north, and after reinforcement with artillery and ancillary units they formed Kampfgruppe Nord—the first step in the development of 6th SS Mountain (Gebirgs) Division Nord.

After the disbandment of three more Totenkopfstandarten, through personnel shortages, Himmler was determined to hold on to the units still under his personal control. This was not only for reason of power and prestige but also to conduct antipartisan and anti-Jewish operations once the Soviet Union was invaded. In May 1941 he formed his own Reichsführer-SS Headquarters Staff (Kommando Stab des Reichsführer-SS), appointing Kurt Knoblauch from the Totenkopf Division as his chief of staff. The 8th and 10th Standarten were formed into the motorized 1st SS Infantry Brigade, while 4th and 5th Standarten became the motorized 2nd SS Infantry Brigade. A final Standarte retained its independent role as SS Infantry Regiment 5.

Mounted troops still had a useful role to play in antipartisan operations in eastern Europe and the Balkans. Accordingly, in 1939 Himmler had ordered the raising of a cavalry regiment, the SS Totenkopf Reiterstandarte, commanded by Hermann Fegelein.[5] The son of a Bavarian horse master, Fegelein was a keen and capable horseman with many influential Nazi friends. He had enrolled as a cadet in the Bavarian state police, although he was expelled for stealing exam-paper answers. Unscrupulous and intensely ambitious, he soon came to the attention of Himmler, who encouraged him to expand the riding schools and clubs under SA or SS control.

The SS Cavalry Regiment underwent rapid expansion in Poland, to include thirteen mounted squadrons and two batteries of artillery. The regiment's prime function was to provide mobile support for police operations in rounding up and killing Jews and other perceived troublemakers. Many of the early volunteers had only joined the regiment through their love of horse riding and were unsuited to the rigors of paramilitary operations, leading to a high dropout rate. Doubts grew as to Himmler's wisdom in forming such a unit, especially when charges of corruption were leveled at Fegelein and his officers.

As Fegelein enjoyed Himmler's protection, he was able to shrug off these charges with relative ease. He repaid the trust of the Reichsführer-SS

with his determination for getting rid of undesirables. In one instance, on
8 April 1940, the regiment killed 250 Polish men from villages close to
where partisans had been operating. Fegelein was highly satisfied with
the conduct of his men: "The set tasks of burning down villages and ex-
ecuting sinister elements were completed in such a clean and SS-worthy
way that every doubt about the troops' strength of character had to be
eliminated."[6] Recruitment of SS cavalrymen began to improve, allowing
the formation of a second regiment in May 1940. One the eve of the
invasion of the Soviet Union, the two regiments would be combined as
an SS cavalry brigade.

One other unit under Himmler's control was not formally part of
the Waffen-SS until its incorporation as the 36th Grenadier Division
in 1945. This was Sonderkommando (Special Command) Dirlewanger,
commanded by Oskar Dirlewanger, a former Great War comrade of
Gottlob Berger. An alcoholic and vicious sexual deviant, Dirlewanger
acquired a string of convictions for possession of illegal arms and em-
bezzlement before being sentenced to two years' imprisonment for the
statutory rape of a fourteen-year-old girl. Kicked out of the SS, he was
reinstated through Berger's direct intervention. After the outbreak of war
in 1939, Dirlewanger was given command of a battalion recruited from
ex-criminals, many of them former poachers who, Hitler and Himmler
believed, would make good soldiers in antipartisan operations. The
Sonderkommando Dirlewanger terrorized the civilian population of occupied Poland before wreaking havoc on the Eastern Front.

These units became Himmler's private army, to use as he saw fit. But
as the war in the East intensified, they would progressively come under
Wehrmacht control, leaving Himmler distanced from the fighting elements of the Waffen-SS.

BY THE SUMMER of 1940, the army began to realize that it had been
hoodwinked by Berger. Alarmed by the expansionist ambitions of the
Waffen-SS, the army exercised its right to put the brakes on new induction. In June Berger bitterly complained to Himmler that 15,000 recruits
due to join the Waffen-SS had not been released by Wehrmacht district

commands. The army continued its investigations into the practices of the SS Main Office, forcing a degree of circumspection on Berger's recruiting practices.

Berger also recognized that in wartime he would have difficulty finding sufficient replacements to keep existing formations in being. A proper reserve organization, where trained recruits flowed through the system to the front line when required—and where wounded men could be rehabilitated and returned to battle—was vital if a unit was to remain an effective fighting entity. The Waffen-SS in 1940 was still in the early stages of organizing a reserve system, which the army was undermining by limiting the release of reinforcements.

There were, however, two other sources of previously untapped manpower that lay beyond the reaches of Wehrmacht control. First were the large numbers of people of German descent who had spread throughout Europe, these supposedly ethnic Germans termed Volksdeutsche by the Nazis. Second were non-Germans of "Nordic blood" who qualified as Germanics (Germanen). They included the peoples of Denmark, Norway, Sweden, Finland, the Netherlands, the Flemish part of Belgium, and the German-speaking cantons of Switzerland. A handful of Germanic volunteers had been accepted into the Waffen-SS before the campaign in the West had begun. Now that many of these countries lay under German control, the Waffen-SS would have easier access to recruit men to the Nazi cause.

While it would seem that Berger's chief interest in these two sources of manpower was to make up the numbers, Himmler took a rather different position: the inclusion of Volksdeutsche and Germanics was not merely acceptable but positively desirable. Hitler was always an old-style nationalist, with Germany firmly at the center of his worldview. Possibly because of his Austrian ancestry, he maintained suspicions about the racial suitability of ethnic Germans from outside the Austro-German community, while Germanics would never be more than useful allies to be exploited in German interests. The more radical Himmler, by contrast, considered race to be of greater importance than nationality.

Himmler envisioned Germany as the driving force behind a vast Aryan racial struggle for mastery of Europe. He expounded this idea well before the onset of war, as evidenced in this extract from a speech to senior SS leaders on 8 November 1938: "We must have no illusions about facing unparalleled conflicts of the most critical nature in the next ten years. It will not only be a struggle of the nations, which will be the excuse of our opponents, but it will be the ideological struggle with all Jewry, the freemasons, Marxists and churchmen of the world."[7] The induction of racially suitable people into the ranks of the Waffen-SS was more than just a military measure; it was part of a wider long-term strategy to increase the power of the SS over other Nazi organizations and, in a postwar future, to encourage the assimilation of other countries into a Greater Germanic Reich.[8]

Himmler's interest in recruiting Volksdeutsche and Germanics into the Waffen-SS also predated the outbreak of war. In the same November speech he had said, "I really have the intention to gather Germanic blood from all over the world, to plunder and steal it where I can. The Standarte 'Germania' didn't get its name for nothing. Within no more than two years I have set myself the goal to have the Standarte 'Germania' consist entirely of non-German Teutons."[9] In the event, "Germania" remained a unit of Reich Germans, although it was joined in the Wiking Division by two other regiments that included men from the Netherlands and Scandinavia.

Himmler's early interest in Germanics was confirmed in a letter sent to a Nazi politician in March 1939 when he wrote that his intention was "to win over men of Nordic blood for the active regiments of the SS from all Germanic-type nations with the exception of the Anglo-Saxons."[10] The concept of "blood sacrifice" had an almost sacramental importance to Himmler, and allied to this idea was the belief that the winnowing fires of combat would help overcome national and linguistic differences to forge a new Pan-Germanic community.

Even though Himmler had planned in advance for the inclusion of Germanics into the Waffen-SS, the speed with which Berger's Main Office moved to secure new recruits was surprisingly quick: the first recruiting centers were open by June 1940. The process was facilitated by the good contacts Berger had previously established with right-wing groups in supposedly Germanic countries. The SS "Nordland" Regiment established offices in Oslo and Copenhagen to recruit Norwegians and Danes, while the SS "Westland" Regiment followed suit in The Hague and Antwerp for Dutch and Flemish recruits. In the neutral countries of Sweden and Switzerland, German embassies and local Far Right parties discreetly encouraged volunteers to come forward.

Himmler and Berger were overoptimistic in the appeal of their Germanic philosophy, expecting young men to suddenly renounce their own national affiliations and join the armed forces of the German state. Those men who crossed the line and volunteered for the Waffen-SS were treated as collaborators by the majority of the people in their homeland. Unsurprisingly, the take up of Nordic volunteers was minimal in the first year of recruitment, before the stimulus created by the invasion of the Soviet Union made itself felt. In this initial recruitment phase, German staff were sometimes less than truthful in what volunteering actually entailed. In one extreme case, a group of Danish recruits was unaware that they had signed up for military service at all, believing they were going to Germany for athletic and political training.[11]

The motivations of those who did volunteer were mixed: some were ardent Germanophiles or Nazi sympathizers; others felt let down by their own governments and placed their faith in the Nazi New Order. Still others looked for adventure and an escape from the drab existence of life in a defeated and occupied country. And more than a few, at the bottom of the economic ladder, were content to be housed and fed in exchange for military service.[12]

The selection standards for these foreign volunteers were the same as for Reich Germans, with the usual emphasis on a visible and certifiable Aryan racial background, good health, and a strong physique. In March 1941 Berger set up the German Guidance Office (Germanische Leitstelle) to organize the recruitment and training of the Germanics. It set up a training camp for new recruits at Sennheim in Alsace. Once there, the recruits from many nations encountered hardened German NCOs for the first time. The instructing staff in this initial phase lacked the flexibility to handle people whose backgrounds were very different from that of the average German recruit, who had already gained valuable experience from service in paramilitary and labor organizations. Norwegian volunteer Ole Brunaes summarized the training regime and its instructors: "They had

self-confidence, well skilled with a dynamic efficiency and were remarkably proud of their famous German military traditions. We Norwegians,
coming from a country where national defense had been neglected, the
military professions ridiculed and any tradition nearly ruined, had a lesson to learn with regard to accuracy, toughness, discipline, cleanliness—
physically as well as morally (fingernails being examined before eating,
the locking of wardrobes strictly forbidden, thefts from comrades punished hard)."[13]

There were many complaints from recruits about their treatment, not
so much regarding the physical severity of the training but because of the
dismissive and insulting attitudes shown by the instructors toward their
homelands. When made aware of these protests, Steiner and a few other
progressive officers intervened in an attempt to encourage the training
staff to show a more enlightened approach to the men under their charge.
Yet, despite their efforts, the national and ethnic abuse of foreign volunteers continued.

The overall shortage of volunteers and the strict selection and training
process made it impossible for the Wiking Division to become the Scandinavian formation that its name implied. As the division moved east for
Operation Barbarossa—the invasion of the Soviet Union—out of a total
manpower strength of 19,377, only 1,554 were foreign volunteers. Of
this figure, the separate national contributions were as follows:[14]

Dutch	621
Finns	421
Norwegians	294
Danes	216
Swedes	1
Swiss	1

In fact, throughout its history, Wiking would remain a predominantly
German Reich formation, supplemented by fluctuating numbers of
Volksdeutsche, Germanics, Finns, and Estonians. The majority of Ger-
manics would be assigned to other formations.

After Demelhuber's departure from "Germania," his replacement was
Standartenführer Karl Reichsritter von Oberkamp, a cavalry officer from

World War I and mountain warfare specialist in the interwar years. Differences with Steiner would lead to his removal from the Wiking Division in June 1942, to be replaced by Standartenführer Jürgen Wagner. Oberkamp and Wagner would go on to command divisions of their own, and both would share the same fate of being executed in 1947 by the Yugoslav government for war crimes.

The "Nordland" Regiment was assigned to Standartenführer Fritz von Scholz, a former officer in the Austro-Hungarian Army. Standartenführer Hilmar Wäckerle—the scourge of the Dutch Army on the Grebbeberg—commanded the "Westland" Regiment until his death in the first phase of Operation Barbarossa, when he was replaced by former Romanian general Artur Phleps. The Wiking Artillery Regiment was handed to Herbert Gille, a veteran SS-V artillery officer.

———

THE 10 MILLION or so ethnic Germans, or Volksdeutsche,[15] scattered across Europe represented the best hope for a mass army. By the end of the war, some 310,000 Volksdeutsche had entered the Waffen-SS, a triumph for Berger's recruitment measures.[16] As well as serving in their own ethnically organized units, they acted as a reinforcement pool for all other Waffen-SS formations.

Although groups of ethnic Germans were to be found throughout the Continent, the largest concentrations were in the Balkans and central and Eastern Europe. The origins of German settlement outside the homeland dated back before the twelfth century, when Germans had emigrated down the Danube into what would become Hungary, Yugoslavia, and Romania. Some groups had lost much of their connection with Germany, while others maintained a strong sense of attachment to the fatherland. Relationships between the Volksdeutsche and their host countries varied considerably from country to country, but the thrifty and industrious Germans were generally welcomed by host governments—who had often encouraged their emigration—and coexisted peacefully with the indigenous populations.

The Nazi regime, with its belief in the centrality of race and Volk (folk), demonstrated an interest in Europe's ethnic Germans from 1933 onward. This led to the formation of the Hauptamt Volksdeutsche Mittelstelle (Main Welfare Office for Ethnic Germans) in 1935, abbreviated to VoMi. The functions of VoMi were to look after the interests of Volksdeutsche and promote Nazi ideology within ethnic communities and to ultimately organize their return to the German Reich.

After the conquest of Poland, VoMi also encouraged newly arrived Volksdeutsche to take over farms seized from local Poles. Once settled in the German Reich, however, Volksdeutsche became liable for military service, and here the Waffen-SS was given first pick of the recruits ahead of the Wehrmacht. Although service in the Waffen-SS remained voluntary in theory, the pressure put on young ethnic German men to sign up was extreme, often to the point of physical coercion. Thus, from as early as 1940, the Waffen-SS began to lose its exclusively voluntary nature.

While Nazi propaganda liked the world to see the Volksdeutsche as a homogenous racial entity, comprising solid German stock with a heartfelt desire for a return to the homeland, the actual situation was rather more complex. Not least were the doubts expressed by Nazi racial "experts" as to the ethnic suitability of some Volksdeutsche for inclusion within the German Reich. Field studies by these officials suggested that for substantial numbers, the German racial line had been diluted by intermixing with their Slav hosts. But of greater concern was evidence of "interbreeding" with Jewish communities similarly scattered across central and Eastern Europe. As a consequence, all Volksdeutsche were ordered to be rigorously screened and their racial suitability classified prior to acceptance. And for many Reich Germans, the Volksdeutsche, with their strange accents and stranger dialects, remained less than properly German and were treated with varying degrees of disdain.

Among the ethnic Germans themselves, Nazi interest in their affairs could be disturbing and unsettling, especially for those not on the political Right. But for many without such political qualms, Nazi Germany represented a dynamic new force, and they were inspired and flattered by this interest shown in them by the fatherland. There were also cultural affinities that bonded the two sides. As VoMi historian Valdis Lumans points out, many Volksdeutsche were attached to Nazism because of its *Volkish* nature: "The Nazi obsession with the peasantry and the soil was better attuned to the mostly rural Volksdeutsche than to the predominantly urban Reich Germans."[17] During the 1930s VoMi encouraged the growth of pro-Nazi political groups and parties within Volksdeutsche communities.

Berger regarded the Balkans as a fertile recruiting ground, with Romania his first experiment. He knew the country well, as his daughter had married right-wing Romanian Volksdeutsche politician Andreas Schmidt. In June 1940, with Schmidt's help, Berger spirited away 1,060 Romanian Volksdeutsche. They traveled by boat up the Danube, nominally as agricultural laborers, but on reaching Germany they were medically screened with 700 joining the Waffen-SS.[18] Despite the success of this coup, Berger still had to tread warily. The Balkan governments may have feared Hitler, but they still drew the line at their citizens—regardless of ethnicity—being "kidnapped" by the SS.

In the spring of 1941, Himmler and Berger could take satisfaction that their plans for the mass expansion of the Waffen-SS were starting to bear fruit. Although the numbers of Germanics and Volksdeutsche within the ranks were still small, the beginnings of a Europe-wide recruiting system had been established. And it was this structure that would provide essential manpower for the war against the Bolshevik enemy to the east.

Chapter 10

BALKAN DIVERSION

AMID FINAL PREPARATIONS for the invasion of the Soviet Union, Hitler was distracted by the antics of his ally Benito Mussolini. The Italian dictator had long harbored dreams of creating his own empire in the Mediterranean and Balkans, and jealous of Germany's repeated military successes he decided to take action on his own—but with unfortunate results. In North Africa, an attempt to seize Egypt from the British ended in ignominious failure. Of more significance, however, was Mussolini's invasion of Greece in October 1940. Although outnumbered, the Greeks inflicted a costly and humiliating defeat on the Italian Army, which then retreated back into Italian-held Albania.

During the fighting, Britain and Greece came to an agreement that British forces would be deployed in Greece. This news worried Hitler as Germany relied heavily on Romania's Ploesti oil fields, which were now vulnerable to attack from RAF bombers flying out of Greek airfields. Before the invasion of the Soviet Union went ahead, Hitler decided to solve the problem by launching a full-scale assault on Greece.

Germany already dominated the Balkans, and its troops would be given free passage to Greece by the governments of Hungary, Romania, and Bulgaria, which had all signed up to the Axis Tripartite Pact. Field Marshal Wilhelm List's Twelfth Army, deployed in Bulgaria in preparation for the attack, comprised fifteen divisions (four of them armored), as well as Leibstandarte SS "Adolf Hitler." The Greek Army—plus a relatively small British and Commonwealth military contingent—could have little hope of fending off such a powerful force.

Yugoslavia—a fractious, newly formed state of Serbs, Slovenes, Croatians, Bosnians, and others—was eventually bullied into signing the pact on 25 March 1941. This was the final piece in the German strategic jigsaw; transit of German units through southern Yugoslavia was vital in outflanking the defenses of the Metaxas Line in northern Greece.

The surprise overthrow of the Yugoslav government on 27 March through a coup by Serb nationalists—and the country's withdrawal from the Tripartite Pact—temporarily threw German plans into disarray. A furious Hitler demanded the immediate destruction of Yugoslavia. The German high command readjusted its plans, with the German Second Army redeployed to invade northern and central Yugoslavia, while Twelfth Army's invasion plan was extended to include southern Yugoslavia.

Hostilities opened on 6 April as the Luftwaffe instigated a mass bombing campaign. The rebellious Serbs of Belgrade were the focus of Hitler's ire, and the city was bombed for three days and nights. Much of the city was destroyed, with at least 4,000 of its inhabitants killed. While the bombing was ongoing, German ground forces advanced into Yugoslavia.

At the beginning of April, the Reich Division, stationed in France, had been ordered to join General Reinhardt's XLI Army Corps in Hungary without delay. Crossing into Germany, the division passed through Munich and Vienna before driving over the border into Hungary on 5 April. Two days later it reached its assembly area at Temesvar, an advance of around 900 miles completed in a week.

Belgrade was the objective of the mechanized XLI Corps. The SS Reich Division was deployed alongside the German Army's elite "Grossdeutschland" Regiment. Both formations entered into an unofficial competition to see who would be first to reach the Yugoslav capital.[1] The advance of Reinhardt's corps was held back for a couple of days, allowing the Reich reconnaissance units a chance to survey the proposed line of attack. They discovered the ground was low-lying and that a sustained period of heavy rain had rendered it into a near-impassable swamp.

On 11 April Reinhardt ordered Hausser to open the offensive. The "Deutschland" and "Der Führer" Regiments led the attack, with the

11th Regiment held in reserve. Yugoslav resistance was light, the chief enemy being the waterlogged, marshy terrain. During the day increasing numbers of vehicles became mired in the mud, leaving the infantry to achieve the first day's objective alone. Reich's divisional history singled out Keppler's Austrians in "Der Führer" for special praise: "The attack was indescribably strenuous for the regiment's men. Only a person who has made a 50-kilometer march himself can imagine the enormous physical achievement it represents. The soldiers covered this distance carrying weapons, ammunition and equipment. They marched through deep mud, their boots sticking with every step. The athletically trained and physically fit men arrived in Seleuš thoroughly drained. This day brought the most strenuous march and attack for the Regiment 'Der Führer' that it had seen throughout the entire war."[2]

The "Grossdeutschland" Regiment—advancing over a slightly longer but far easier route—reached its objective just after the SS troops. For the next day's action, Reich was ordered to halt and await the arrival of its artillery and vehicles, which would travel behind "Grossdeutschland." Thus, it seemed inevitable that the army unit would win the race.

Reich's reconnaissance battalion—some way ahead of the division—was also ordered to hold position, but a motorcycle patrol of just ten men under Hauptsturmführer Fritz Klingenberg had apparently not received the order. Klingenberg, a former adjutant to Paul Hausser and a man with a reputation for audacity and for scrounging the best equipment and supplies for his men, reached the Danube later in the day. He sensed that the weakly held city might be taken by a coup de main. Although the bridges over the river were damaged or destroyed, one of his men found a small motorboat, and the patrol crossed over to Belgrade.

While marching through the streets of the city, they met a German official who guided them to the German consulate. With the consul's help, Klingenberg contacted the mayor of Belgrade and in a spectacular piece of bluffing managed to convince him that he was the advance guard of the main German Army and that if the city did not immediately surrender, it would be subject to a ferocious bombardment by artillery and Stukas. At 6:45 P.M. the mayor signed the terms of surrender—to a ten-man reconnaissance patrol. In a further display of bravado, Klingenberg ordered a nearby Serbian pioneer column to organize ferries across the Danube to collect waiting German troops at Pancevo on the far bank. Among them were units of "Grossdeutschland," now the losers in the race for the Yugoslav capital.

News of the raid was picked up by German propaganda units, soon to be broadcast across Europe. Hitler was also delighted and decorated Klingenberg with the Knight's Cross. The story had a less happy ending for the mayor: finding that he had been duped, he shot himself.

On 13 April German forces—including the rest of the Reich Division—entered Belgrade en masse, and five days later the remnants of the Yugoslavian government surrendered. Yugoslavia was broken up into its constituent parts: Serbia came under direct German control, with a fascist puppet state established in Croatia.

Hausser's division spent the next ten days acting as an occupation force, rounding up Yugoslav soldiers for dispatch to prison camps (an exception was made for ethnic Germans, released to their homes). As Reich prepared to leave Yugoslavia, a number of ethnic Volksdeutsche from the Banat region of northern Serbia were incorporated directly into the division. On 26 April a recruitment battalion for Romanian Volksdeutsche was established in the SS Schönbrunn barracks in Vienna, with Sturmbannführer Heinz Harmel as its commander.[3] This marked the beginning of the dilution of German Reich-raised divisions with ethnic Germans.

———————

ASSIGNED TO XL Corps in Bulgaria, Leibstandarte acted as a reserve for 9th Panzer Division as it crossed over the border into southern Yugoslavia on 6 April 1941. While the bulk of List's Twelfth Army advanced directly toward Greece, it was planned that XL Corps would overcome local Yugoslav resistance before pushing into northwestern Greece to outflank the main Greek defensive line. Yugoslav resistance was sporadic and ill-organized, although one congested Leibstandarte column was caught by Yugoslav bombers, seriously wounding Obersturmbannführer Wilhelm Mohnke, commander of the II Battalion.

Bypassing the city of Skopje, Leibstandarte and 9th Panzer Division drove toward the Monastir Gap and the Greek frontier. After a brief

skirmish to secure passage over the River Zrna, the Germans pushed
past Monastir and into Greece. Their advance threatened the left flank
of the Anglo-Greek defenses under the command of Lieutenant General
Sir Henry Wilson. If the Germans could penetrate the mountainous Klidi
Pass, then the whole Allied line would be in jeopardy.

Wilson ordered his troops to hold the pass for at least two days to
allow new positions to be organized farther to the rear. The pass itself was
held by British, Australians, and New Zealanders, who had been rushed
to Greece from North Africa. They were unprepared and ill-equipped,
not least for the terrible weather then sweeping the Balkans, where heavy
rain turned to swirling snowstorms in the mountains.

On 11 April the Germans pushed forward toward Klidi, only to be
rebuffed by the Allies holding the high ground on either side of the pass.
During the fighting Obersturmführer Fend of the 8.8cm Flak detachment
was captured by Australian troops, whose recent arrival was reflected in
their confusion as to what was happening and even where they were:
"I was taken back a few hundred meters along a railway embankment
and handed over to an enemy captain, whose troops were eating by their
vehicles. They seemed quite anxious as they did not know which way to
advance. During my short interrogation I got the impression that they
wanted to drive towards the [Greek-held] Klisura Pass. I told him that the
pass was already held by the Germans. Even more surprising, I was asked
if I knew a passable way to Athens!"[4]

Although the Germans sent outflanking columns on both sides of the
pass, a frontal assault was considered necessary if the momentum of the
advance was not to be lost. A Kampfgruppe based around Fritz Witt's I
Battalion would make the attack, scheduled for the twelfth.

Witt—recently transferred from Reich to Leibstandarte—was assigned powerful fire support. As well as most of the batteries from the
artillery regiment, including the heavy howitzers, his Kampfgruppe could
call upon the 3.7cm and 5cm guns of the antitank battalion, as well as
the antiaircraft battalion, whose high-velocity 8.8cm guns were ideal for
knocking out enemy bunkers and armor at longer ranges. The pioneer
battalion was also brought forward to clear the mines laid by the Allies
and to repair damage to the roads and paths leading to the pass. Finally,
Witt had the use of Leibstandarte's "heavy battalion." This included a

battery of six Sturmgeschütz III assault guns and the Panzerjäger company, now with nine modified Panzer Mark Is rearmed with Czech 4.7cm antitank guns.

The attack was spearheaded by Leibstandarte's 1st Company, the six-footers who formed the original SS staff guard that protected Hitler in Berlin. Commanded by Obersturmführer Gerd Pleiss, the 1st Company spent the day edging forward up the rocky slopes of the pass, all the while under intense machine-gun fire. One SS soldier, Johannes Bendixen, described the action: "The battle raged for several hours in the late morning, and never again during the long war did I experience such terrible moments. Everywhere one looked our young comrades were falling to the ground, killed or wounded."[5]

Dietrich and other senior Leibstandarte officers closely observed the progress of Witt's force, impressed by the ability of the tracked vehicles of the heavy battalion to crawl up the steep slopes of the pass and deliver suppressive fire on the enemy positions. All the while, SS pioneers calmly lifted mines amid the deafening barrage from both sides. As the day wore on, the men of 1st Company wrested control of the high ground, ejecting the British from the village of Klidi. A British armored counterattack in the late afternoon was repulsed, the Flak battalion's 88s knocking out eight tanks in the engagement. The following day Leibstandarte consolidated its position, fending off further enemy counterattacks. Obersturmführer Fend was released by Pleiss's men.

With Klidi Pass in German hands, the way was open to push on against the Anglo-Greek left flank, although the spirited Allied defense had given Wilson sufficient time to get his troops away from the threat of encirclement.

Dietrich recognized the key role played by 1st Company, as Bendixen recalled: "Gerd Pleiss and a dozen of his men formed up in front of Sepp Dietrich on an open country road. Sepp removed the Knight's Cross from his uniform and placed it on our company commander for the storming of the Klidi Pass. As well, six men received the Iron Cross, 1st Class. How proud we were in those moments."[6] Witt's enjoyment of the victory was tempered by news of the death of his younger brother Franz, an officer in the pioneer battalion killed while clearing mines on the road to Klidi.

While the battle for Klidi was still raging, Kurt Meyer and his reconnaissance battalion were ordered due west to take the nearby Klisura Pass. Guarded by Greek troops, the pass was another formidable defensive position, formed by a series of ridges that looked down on any attacking force. Supported by a Flak detachment with their formidable 8.8cm guns and a 15cm howitzer battery, Meyer's battalion made good progress on 13 April, although the attack came to a halt as darkness fell, leaving the push on the last and best-defended position for the following morning.

After spending a cold night shivering in a forward position, Meyer divided his forces to make a three-pronged attack, personally leading one of the assault groups. Born into a working-class family from Lower Saxony, Meyer had escaped from a succession of laboring jobs by joining the police in 1929, which led to entry into the SS and a commission in Leibstandarte. Of middling height, with a dark, sallow complexion and a piercing stare that was later to impress his Allied interrogators,[7] the rough-hewn Meyer was a dedicated Nazi, inspiring fierce devotion from the men under his command.

As Meyer's group closed with the enemy, heavy machine-gun fire forced him and his lead troops to take cover. In his own account of the action, Meyer realized the dangers of the attack losing momentum in what was a highly exposed position. He apparently adopted the unorthodox expedient of taking out the pin of a hand grenade and, after showing it to his comrades, dropping it into the hollow in which they were sheltering. As one, they all leaped out to escape the blast. "We grinned at each other," he recalled, "and dashed forward."[8] As Meyer's infantry neared the summit, the other two groups had begun to outflank the main position, forcing the Greeks to retreat.

In taking the pass, the reconnaissance battalion had captured 600 Greek troops. Reinforced by Leibstandarte's III Infantry Battalion, Meyer pushed hard toward the nearby town of Kastoria, captured after another hard fight on 15 April. The seizure of Kastoria cut off Greek troops retreating from the Italian front in Albania. Some 12,000 Greek soldiers ended up in captivity as a consequence, along with an impressive haul of weapons, equipment, and fuel, the latter especially welcomed by the gasoline-hungry vehicles of the motorized Leibstandarte.

Without delay, Leibstandarte and the remainder of XL Corps swept southward to transform tactical success into a strategic victory. Both the Greeks and the British were retreating at pace, the latter preparing for evacuation from Greece. On 18 April, Leibstandarte was suddenly diverted to the southeast to harry Greek forces falling back through the Pindus mountains. The II Battalion took the lead, and after an early-morning engagement with Greek troops on 20 April, a Kampfgruppe under the command of Hauptsturmführer Horstmann sent a surprise and rather garbled message to headquarters to the effect that the entire Greek Army wished to surrender.

This was to be Dietrich's finest hour. He drove along the winding, congested mountain roads, pushing aside German and Greek vehicles as he went. At 4:00 P.M. he saw the swastika flying over Horstmann's position at the summit of the Katara Pass.[9] After Dietrich had congratulated the men of II Battalion, Horstmann led him to the nearby Greek headquarters to meet General Georgios Tsolakoglou, commanding at least fourteen infantry divisions.

Tsolakoglou had decided that further resistance was pointless, and as well as surrendering his own substantial force he took it upon himself to surrender the entire Greek Army to the Germans and bring all hostilities to a close. Dietrich, although just a divisional commander, seized the initiative and instigated negotiations. A provisional document was drawn up and signed in less than two hours, with Dietrich offering generous terms to his defeated opponent: Greek soldiers were allowed to return to their homes, and officers were to keep their sidearms. During the short campaign the Germans had developed a respect for their tough Greek adversaries, while the Greeks, who despised and loathed the Italians, preferred to deal with the Germans. One of the terms of the surrender document was that the German Army would "place itself between the Italian and Greek forces."[10]

Dietrich immediately informed Field Marshal List of the surrender, who then relayed the news to OKW and Hitler. The only stumbling block was the Italian dictator, who was enraged at being so obviously sidelined from the proceedings. He immediately demanded Italian participation—it was *his* war, he insisted—and rescinded some of the terms, so that the long-suffering Greek soldiers were temporarily incarcerated in prison camps (many, however, had already slipped away to civilian life). Hitler was thrilled by Dietrich's success, although he felt forced to issue a friendly reprimand: "You are a good, brave soldier, but no diplomat, and still less a politician. You forgot that we still have a friend called Mussolini, and he is angry."[11]

IF THE WAR was over between Germany and Greece, there was still the possibility of preventing British and Commonwealth forces from escaping the Greek mainland to Crete and North Africa. Meyer and his reconnaissance battalion led the attempt to cut off the enemy evacuation. As Meyer drove his men forward, the previously hostile weather was suddenly transformed into a Mediterranean spring, the SS troopers looking enviously at demobilized Greek soldiers enjoying the sunshine. During one brief halt, Meyer allowed his men to fill their helmets with oranges, confirmation that they were at last in southern climes.

On 26 April the reconnaissance battalion reached the Gulf of Corinth, which all but divided the Peloponnese from the rest of Greece. Meyer looked across the five-mile stretch of water to see Stukas bombing the British evacuation from the port of Patras. He commandeered some fishing boats, loaded a patrol of motorcycle-sidecar combinations and a light antitank gun, and sent them across to the far side. As they returned, a relieved Meyer could see they contained British prisoners, proof that his seagoing patrol had been successful.

Meyer joined the next transfer, and on reaching the southern side of the gulf he commandeered any vehicles he could find to rendezvous with the main German assault through the Corinth isthmus. He recalled that "an elegant limousine towed an anti-tank gun and mortars stuck out of a sports car. The combat engineer platoon was in a bus."[12] The convoy of motley vehicles met German paratroopers close to Corinth, but by then the British had departed, leaving the Germans to mop up stragglers who had failed to arrive at the evacuation ports in time.

Leibstandarte enjoyed a few days of leisure. Motoring into Athens, Dietrich and his fellow officers wandered around the Acropolis and mused on what they saw as the legacy of ancient Greece. Medals were handed out and speeches made, while Himmler flew into Athens to congratulate the men of the Waffen-SS in person.

In the Greek campaign Leibstandarte had amply confirmed its status as an elite unit, demonstrating outstanding battlefield aggression and initiative. Meyer aptly summed up the regiment's tactical philosophy: "Everything we did was governed by speed. We had learned that only the swiftest will gain victory and that only the most agile soldier will survive the fight."[13] It would also appear that the regiment had fought a clean campaign, winning the respect of both Greek and British opponents. George Kennard, a British officer captured by Leibstandarte, left this revealing testimonial: "Over the entire fighting they had been brave, chivalrous and, towards the end, they would go out of their way, at considerable risk to themselves, to take prisoners rather than take lives."[14]

On 8 May Leibstandarte began the long drive back through Greece and Yugoslavia to Brno in Czech Moravia. There it would undergo a swift reorganization in preparation for the coming war in the East.

Part Two
THE GREATEST WAR IN HISTORY

We have only to kick in the door and the whole rotten structure will come crashing down.

—ADOLF HITLER

Chapter 11

OPERATION BARBAROSSA

A T 3:15 A.M. on 22 June 1941, Hitler launched his invasion of the Soviet Union. Artillery fire flashed across the horizon, German special forces overwhelmed Soviet border posts, and waves of aircraft flew over the frontier to destroy the Red Air Force on the ground. Although Stalin had received good intelligence from a multitude of sources that an invasion was imminent, he refused to believe it and take appropriate countermeasures. When Soviet frontline troops first telephoned news of the attack to their headquarters in the rear, they were openly disbelieved. Accordingly, the Soviet response to the German assault was slow and uncoordinated, allowing the German armies to surge forward into the Soviet Union against only local and confused resistance.

The initial experiences of Karl-Heinz Anold of the Wiking Division suggested an easy victory: "All went very well. Our artillery and air force were magnificent and we rushed into the Soviet zone, meeting very little organized opposition and seeing the first prisoners, who looked terrible. We were very encouraged. We were hot, tired and thirsty and had to wait for our ration trucks to catch up. There was no danger of a Russian attack, their armies were completely destroyed."[1]

Throughout the spring of 1941, vast numbers of German troops, tanks, artillery, and aircraft of all types had been covertly dispatched eastward to positions along the border with the Soviet Union. An estimated 17,000 separate trains were required to transport this array of military might to the railheads scattered through East Prussia, Poland, Slovakia,

Hungary, and Romania. Hitler had sent 3.2 million German soldiers in 148 divisions to the East. They were supported by sizable contingents from Romania and Finland, subsequently to be joined by troops from Hungary, Slovakia, Italy, and Spain.

All told, Axis forces for Barbarossa amounted to nearly 4 million men.[2] They were stretched along an 800-mile line that ran south from the Baltic to the Black Sea, soon to be stretched farther as the Germans drove deep into the Soviet Union. The Red Army deployed a little less than 3 million troops to face the German onslaught but could call upon substantial reserves once the fighting was underway. In no other theater of war were so many men and weapons engaged across so large a battlefield.

The war on the Eastern Front—nearly four years of unrelenting conflict—would be the greatest and most terrible in history. The dismal superlatives extended to the casualty figures, larger than in any other conflict: 5.5 million German and at least 20 million Soviet military and civilian dead,[3] with many more millions maimed and wounded.

The German invasion was the defining event of World War II, the ultimate test for Hitler's Nazi Germany against its ideological rival. It was a war of annihilation, as Germany sought to destroy Slav culture and carve out a new Teutonic empire in the East. The Waffen-SS would act as a military and political spearhead to guarantee the success of the German conquest.

THE GERMAN ARMY that invaded Russia was still predominantly an infantry force, although its mechanized element had been increased to nineteen panzer and twelve motorized infantry divisions. The army deployed 3,350 tanks, 7,184 artillery pieces, 600,000 trucks, and an equal number of horses. In support of ground operations, the Luftwaffe had more than 2,000 aircraft organized in three air fleets.[4]

The invasion of the Soviet Union was based around a broad-front strategy to be conducted by three army groups. Army Group North, commanded by Field Marshal von Leeb, comprised two armies and a panzer group, whose task was to advance through the Baltic States of Lithuania,

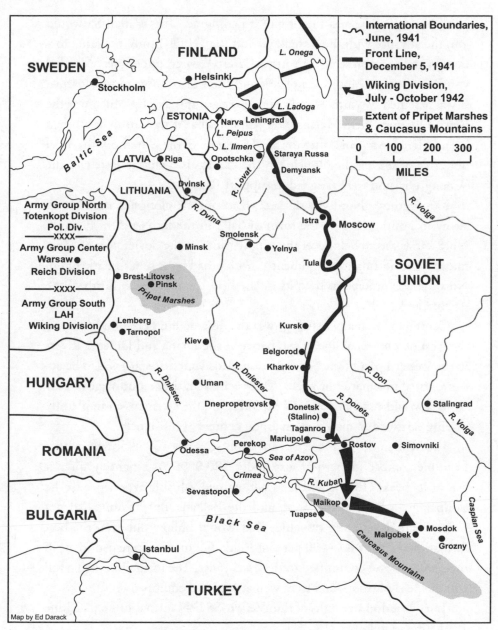

The Eastern Front, 1941–1942

Latvia, and Estonia and then capture Leningrad. The Waffen-SS would join the advance with the Totenkopf and Polizei Divisions, the latter formation acting in a reserve role. Army Group Center, under Field Marshal von Bock, was to capture Smolensk and then drive forward to Moscow. It was assigned two armies and two panzer groups, among which was the Reich Division. Field Marshal von Rundstedt's Army Group South had been ordered to advance into the fertile steppes of the Ukraine with a final objective of seizing the oil fields in the Caucasus. Leibstandarte and the Wiking Division were assigned to support Rundstedt.

Kampfgruppe Nord was dispatched to operate alongside the Finnish Army in positions facing the town of Salla in the far North of Finland. Nord's task was to help sever the supply route to the Soviet port of Murmansk. The SS Infantry Regiment 9, which had been sent to Kirkenes in Norway, was ordered to hold its isolated position someway north of the Arctic Circle.

Central to Germany's strategy was the destruction of the Red Army to the west of a notional line drawn between the Dvina and Dnieper Rivers in the western part of the Soviet Union. This vital first stage was to be accomplished in a matter of weeks. Once achieved, the second stage of Barbarossa would consist of a grand exploitation, the Germans triumphantly driving eastward to mop up remaining centers of resistance.

The Waffen-SS on the eve of invasion stood at 160,405 men, with a frontline combat strength of just under 100,000.[5] As a fighting force it was at its peak. Officers and men had gained valuable experience in the campaigns in Poland, the West, and the Balkans, but its units had not suffered the devastating casualties that would hollow out even the best formations. The troops—90 percent Reich Germans—were confident in their abilities and committed to the Nazi cause. The formations had a full complement of troops and were well armed and equipped.

The numerical strengths of the Waffen-SS field formations on 22 June 1941 were as follows:

Leibstandarte SS "Adolf Hitler"	10,796
Reich Division	19,021
Totenkopf Division	18,754

Polizei Division	17,347
Wiking Division	19,377
Kampfgruppe Nord	10,573
Kommandostab Reichsführer-SS	18,438

Leibstandarte and Kampfgruppe Nord would soon be upgraded to divisional status, with an attendant increase in personnel. The Kommandostab Reichsführer-SS organized Himmler's private army: two motorized SS infantry brigades and a brigade of SS cavalry. They came under his direct control rather than that of the army.

In addition to the field formations were various auxiliary and reserve units that were now an integral part of the Waffen-SS:

Administrative department	4,007
Reserve units	29,809
Inspectorate of Concentration Camps	7,200
SS guard battalions	2,159
SS garrison posts	992
SS officer and NCO schools	1,028
SS Volunteer Battalion "Nordost"	904

In April 1941, Himmler had quietly extended the definition of the term *Waffen-SS* to include administrative and concentration-camp personnel, thus muddying the waters for the postwar debate as to who was in the Waffen-SS. The "Nordost" battalion consisted of volunteers from Finland, who fought as a separate national unit, although with German NCOs and officers.

––––––

HITLER AND THE Wehrmacht justified the invasion of the Soviet Union on the grounds that it was, in fact, a preventative action, that the Red Army was set to invade Germany and enslave Europe under a communist yoke. This specious claim was readily taken up by Wehrmacht and Waffen-SS soldiers after the war. Hans Quassowski, from Leibstandarte's prestigious 1st Company, even went as far as to chastise those in the West who failed to applaud the German "intervention": "It does not bear thinking about how the war would have gone if the 'Russian Steamroller' had set itself in motion towards the West unhindered. It would surely not have stopped until it reached the Atlantic. Should not all of western Europe be grateful that the actions of the German armed services and their allies prevented the subjugation of all of Europe by the Soviet Union?"[6]

Stalin's aggressive foreign policy measures—the takeover of eastern Poland, the Baltic States, Bessarabia, and North Bukovina—were essentially defensive in nature, intended to protect the Soviet Union and reestablish its pre-1914 boundaries. The Winter War with Finland in 1939–1940 was designed to provide a buffer zone around the otherwise vulnerable Leningrad. Stalin's long-term foreign policy plans must remain a matter of debate, but in 1941 he had no intention of invading the West.[7]

The prime reason for the German invasion was Hitler's belief that Germany must have Lebensraum (living space) if it were to survive and prosper. The western portion of the Soviet Union would provide Germany with the vast agricultural and mineral resources to make this possible, so that Germany would be virtually self-sufficient in the economic sphere. At the back of Hitler's mind was the Allied blockade of 1914–1918, which had slowly but remorselessly reduced Germany to the point of starvation. Hitler was determined to avoid any similar outcome. The people of western Russia and Ukraine would be driven off their lands, killed, enslaved, or slowly starved to death. The "Hunger Plan" produced by SS bureaucrat Herbert Backe in May 1941, appropriating Ukrainian foodstuffs for the Wehrmacht, calmly accepted that "tens of millions of people will die of starvation."[8]

Traditional animosities between Germans and Slavs were raised to a fever pitch by the Nazis as war approached. For the Aryans to be a superior race, it necessarily meant that others must be inferior, and the Slavs of Eastern Europe were ideally placed for this role. Max Simon, a regimental commander in the Totenkopf Division in 1941, was still in thrall to such views long after the war had ended in Soviet victory. He wrote of the Red Army soldier: "All have in greater or lesser degree the Asiatic characteristics of frugality, cunning, cruelty, hatred of foreigners and indifference to death. The fact that, as Asiatics, they have little or no will of their own, indulging only in mass thinking, but at the same time can face mass death."[9]

Extreme racist attitudes permeated much of European society, and in Germany they were held by soldiers in the Wehrmacht as much as the Waffen-SS. Anti-Semitism was conflated with a hatred of Slavs and communism. The hyphenated "Jew-Bolshevik" was a constant of Nazi propaganda, hammering into German minds that somehow the two were indivisible, a Jew was a Bolshevik and a Bolshevik a Jew. Given the Nazis' belief in the Slavs' subhuman status and their perceived threat to Germany, it was an easy step to treat them with contempt and brutality. General Erich Hoepner, commander of the Fourth Panzer Group, was far from alone in his views when he gave this order: "The war with Russia is a vital part of the German people's fight for existence. It is the old fight of German against Slav, the defense of European culture against the Muscovite-Asiatic flood, and the repulse of Jewish Bolshevism. The war must have at its goal the destruction of today's Russia—and for this reason it must be conducted with unprecedented harshness. Every clash, from conception to execution, must be guided by an iron determination to annihilate the enemy completely and utterly."[10]

The Commissar Order, issued by OKW on 6 June 1941, demanded that Soviet political officers were to be summarily shot on capture and that any prisoners thought to be "Bolshevized" should also suffer the same fate. This gave German soldiers great latitude in who should be chosen for battlefield execution. In many postwar Wehrmacht and Waffen-SS accounts,[11] much has been made of frontline officers refusing to obey this order, but as German historian Jürgen Förster has revealed, this seldom occurred in practice.[12]

The war on the Eastern Front was from the start a war of atrocity. Both sides killed and mutilated prisoners, and German forces acted ruthlessly against the civilian population, killing, raping, and plundering as they advanced into the Soviet Union. The mass rapes committed on German women by Red Army troops in 1945 have been well documented, but it should also be remembered that Soviet female citizens suffered at the hands of the invaders, something studiously avoided in German memoirs

from the Eastern Front. An idea of the casual nature of sexual assaults on
Soviet women can be divined in a covert recording of German prisoners'
conversation in a British POW camp. One prisoner described his time in
the Ukraine: "Everywhere we saw women doing compulsory labor service. They were employed on road-making—extraordinarily lovely girls:
we drove past, simply pulled them into the armored car, raped them and
threw them out again. And did they curse!"[13]

The savagery of the fighting was not confined to the armed forces,
with national and ethnic rivalries exploding into violence among the
civilian population. The city of Lemberg (L'viv) in the western Ukraine
experienced an orgy of killing during the first two weeks of the invasion. Following news of the German assault, the People's Commissar-
iat of Internal Affairs (NKVD, Stalin's secret police) was ordered to kill
all 4,000 political prisoners in the city's crowded jails. As the Germans
closed on Lemberg at the end of June, the NKVD fled eastward, with
the city briefly coming under right-wing Ukrainian rule. Local Jews were
rounded up to remove the bodies from the prisons and prepare them for
burial. In the frenzied atmosphere of the period, a Ukrainian mob then
fell on the innocent Jews, the first stage in a vicious and bloody pogrom
against Jewish communities throughout the western Ukraine.

The arriving German forces also joined in the killings, with the Wiking
Division contributing to the bloodshed. According to Heinz Höhne, 600
Jews were killed by Wiking troops in Galicia, the village of Zborov being
the center for these massacres.[14] The death of Standartenführer Wäckerle,
commander of the "Westland" Regiment—apparently shot by a Soviet
straggler—was deemed a "justification" for these actions, although other
Wiking units joined in the killings. Norwegian Olav Tuff, a volunteer in
"Nordland," broke his silence as an old man to reveal his participation
in the atrocities: "The civilian population were driven like cattle into a
church. Soon after, soldiers from my unit poured gasoline on the church
and somewhere between 200 and 300 people were burned inside. I stood
guard, and no one came out. There was a lot of yelling and screaming,
and we could hardly believe what we were a part of. But there was little
we could do. We had to do what we were ordered." Tuff subsequently re-
gretted the incident, but with little sense of personal responsibility: "The

incident at the church was terrible, but it was still just one of many episodes. I have not felt guilty for it, because we could not do anything."[15] The deadly combination of indigenous rivalries and German racial ideology raised the levels of interethnic violence, not just in the Soviet Union but throughout Europe.

———

IN FEBRUARY 1941, while planning for the invasion was ongoing, Hitler famously exclaimed to his generals, "When Barbarossa commences, the world will hold its breath and make no comment!" The world of course did neither, but the consequences of Barbarossa spread across the globe, not least to make Britain and the Soviet Union wartime allies. Within Europe, what the Nazis dubbed as the fight against Bolshevism provoked massive interest, especially among the more vociferous right-wing groups in German-occupied countries who clamored to take part in the conflict.

The Germans responded to these requests with alacrity, and on 29 June—just a week after the opening of Barbarossa—Hitler sanctioned the formation of "national legions" to fight in the East. Given the previous experience of the Waffen-SS in recruiting foreign volunteers, it was assumed they would take over the whole operation, but during this period Himmler held strong reservations against including non-Germanics, so the legions were divided along "racial" lines between the army and SS. The army accepted volunteers from France, Croatia, Spain, and French-speaking Belgium (Walloons). The Waffen-SS organized legions from the Netherlands, Flemish-speaking Belgium (Flanders), Denmark, and Norway. The battalion of Finnish volunteers sent to reinforce the Wiking Division remained outside the national legion program.

The strict physical and racial recruiting standards of the Waffen-SS were relaxed for the national legions. As a result, they were not accorded full SS status—as was given to their compatriots in the Wiking Division—but were categorized as foreign soldiers in the service of Germany. Although they swore an oath of loyalty to Hitler and were given similar pay and benefits as Waffen-SS soldiers, they were not permitted to wear the SS runes and had, instead, their own national insignia. The recruits were informed that they would be able to speak their own languages and would be led, in the main, by their own NCOs and officers.

Right-wing nationalist parties in occupied Europe were enthusiastic supporters of the legions because they hoped that involvement in the "Crusade against Bolshevism" would raise their own status within Germany's New Order. Reimond Tollenaere, of the Flemish National Union Party, made this call for volunteers that was typical of right-wing parties within the "Germanic" states: "If we now prove in deed that we are prepared to take on the common European foe—Communism—we shall have our rightful say in building a new Europe. It is a matter of our people. It is a matter of saving Europe. It is a matter of our right to have our say in this era."[16] Tollenaere's hopes were not, however, shared by those who mattered: neither Hitler or Himmler had any genuine interest in promoting nationalist causes within occupied Europe.

In the first couple of weeks after the start of Barbarossa, there was a surge of volunteers from the Germanic countries, although this subsequently faded, with overall numbers failing to meet the hopes of the fascist parties sponsoring them. The reasons for joining the legions had a more ideological element than in the first phase of Germanic recruitment for the Wiking Division's "Westland" and "Nordland" Regiments. Olaf Krabbe, a company commander in the Danish Legion, considered the motivations for joining the Waffen-SS among the NCOs in his company and found that around 90 percent had joined up through their right-wing nationalist and anticommunist beliefs.[17] A more recent study of the backgrounds of Danish officers serving with the Germans maintains that they were "characterized by a high level of education, intellect and their strong mental character."[18]

A virulent strain of anti-Semitism also ran through the national legions, as can been seen in a diary entry of a Danish volunteer after arrival on the Eastern Front: "A Jew in a greasy Kaftan walks up to beg some bread, a couple of comrades get a hold on him and drag him behind a building and a moment later he comes to an end. There isn't any room for Jews in the new Europe, they've brought too much misery to the European people."[19]

In Denmark the Danish Nazi Party had contacted a Danish officer, Lieutenant-Colonel Christian Peder Kryssing, who agreed to lead a volunteer force that would be called Freikorps Danmark. The Danish government gave permission for its citizens, including those in the military, to volunteer for service in the Freikorps, which by August 1941 had a battalion strength of just over 1,000 men.[20] Kryssing handpicked most of the battalion's officers, former members of the Danish Army, prior to departure for basic training at the Langenhorn barracks in Hamburg.

Disputes soon arose between Kryssing and the SS staff overseeing the training. Kryssing was an old-school nationalist and resented outside interference in his battalion, while the SS instructors criticized him for not instilling a suitable National Socialist ideology among the men. The arguments continued throughout 1941, until Himmler lost patience and had Kryssing replaced by Hauptsturmführer Christian von Schalburg, a former Danish Army officer who had volunteered for the Wiking Division. A committed Nazi with frontline experience, Schalburg took over the command on 13 February 1942. He increased the tempo of training and integrated ten German officers into the battalion, which in turn led to replacement of Danish with German as the language of command. By May 1942 the battalion was considered ready for frontline service in the East.

In the Netherlands, Anton Mussert, leader of the National Socialist movement, prevailed upon a former chief of staff of the Dutch Army, General Hendrik Seyffardt, to act as a figurehead for the Legion Niederlande. Although some volunteers insisted on serving as part of a home-defense force only, there were sufficient recruits to form a standard three-battalion infantry regiment. The legion, however, relied upon a strong German input, so that out of a total strength of 2,937 men, 700 were German, the latter filling the technical and leadership positions.[21] As with the Danish experience, Seyffardt fought against the intrusion of the SS pushing the legion on a National Socialist course, while the ordinary recruits resented the heavy-handed methods of their instructors. Despite these issues, which were never properly resolved, the Netherlands Legion moved up to the Leningrad front at the end of 1941 to engage in behind-the-lines security duties.

In Flemish-speaking Belgium, right-wing nationalist parties had long advocated a split with the French-speaking Walloons in the southern part of the country, with some campaigning for a union with the Netherlands. The German authorities rejected any such idea, which would have flown in the face of their long-term secret plans for the Netherlands and Flanders to become part of a Greater Germany. Accordingly, they opposed associations between the two regions and encouraged the formation of a separate Legion Flandern. Sufficient volunteers came forward to form a motorized infantry battalion with an overall strength of nearly 1,000 men, the Germans providing a leadership cadre. After a hasty period of training, the Flemish Legion was dispatched to the Eastern Front, where it joined the 2nd SS Infantry Brigade in November 1941.

Himmler, with his sentimental attachment to Norway's Viking past, had high hopes for drawing in modern-day Norse warriors to the German cause. His interest was not reciprocated by many Norwegians, however, although a 1,000-strong infantry battalion was raised to form the Legion Norwegen under the command of Major Jorgen Bakke. Following basic training at a camp near Kiel, the Norwegians were transferred to the Leningrad front in early 1942.

Considerable levels of duress were used to find "volunteers." Jutte Olafsen, a teacher in a Norwegian school, claimed he faced the threat of deportation to Germany as forced labor: "But they offered an alternative, and this was to join the Legion Norwegen and assist in the anti-Bolshevik crusade, as they called it. I hated communism. So I decided that I would rather join this Legion than go to work in Germany."[22]

Olafsen's choice caused family disagreements. His father refused to speak to him, while his mother waved him off to war in tears: "They felt that while I was possibly following my convictions I was in a real sense a traitor to my own country and would have to pay some price eventually."[23] These conflicting emotions were true of most of the Germanic volunteers; they would indeed pay a price, whether on the battlefield or, if they survived, on their postwar homecoming.

Despite the best efforts of Berger and his recruiting teams, there were never enough volunteers to build an effective Germanic army backed by a working reserve system. After the war, the numbers of volunteers drawn from Germanic nations were inflated by Waffen-SS apologists. In his 1958 book, *Die Freiwilligen*, Steiner claimed that the Netherlands had supplied approximately 50,000 men, Flanders 20,000, and Denmark and Norway 6,000 each.[24] These figures were accepted by a number of historians of the Waffen-SS,[25] although more recent research has reduced them to a combined total of around 50,000. The Netherlands was still the largest group, with 23,000–25,000 recruits, followed by 10,000 from Flanders, 6,000 from Denmark, and 5,000 from Norway.[26]

THE SS NATIONAL legions would face a harsh baptism of fire on the Eastern Front in early 1942, as Stalin's armies confounded the boasts of Hitler and his generals that the war would be over in a matter of months. The easy victories in the West and the Nazis' racial contempt for the Soviet people had created a fatal complacency among the German high command.

Stalin's purges of the Soviet officer corps in the late 1930s and the poor showing of the Red Army during the Winter War against Finland in 1939–1940 indicated fundamental weaknesses within the Soviet armed forces. These included a rigidity in command and control and a reckless-ness in offensive operations that led to fearful casualties. Yet through poor intelligence and simple hubris, the German planners had failed to take into account the extraordinary resilience of the Red Army. Even if the situation was hopeless, sufficient numbers of Soviet troops would fight on to the end. The "Der Führer" regimental history made this comment on the Red Army soldier a few days after the opening of Barbarossa: "Con-cerning those first serious battles by the regiment in Russia it must be said that the toughness, stubbornness and skill of the Russian opponent came as a surprise."[27]

The German strategy was also undermined by a profound underes-timation of the logistical requirements demanded by such a vast under-taking and a failure to comprehend the nature of the terrain its forces would be fighting over. A comprehensive network of all-weather roads was essential for a successful blitzkrieg campaign, and such a network was noticeably absent in the Soviet Union. During the wet seasons in spring and autumn, vehicles simply sank into the mud. Even when the going was good, the Germans lacked sufficient numbers of motorized vehicles for the fast-paced offensive necessary for victory. Given the renowned expertise of the German General Staff—and the fact that many of its senior officers had fought in Russia during World War I—these failings were damning in the extreme.

The numerical strength of Hitler's armies seemed impressive, but they proved insufficient to the magnitude of the task facing them. The broad-front strategy—with separate objectives for the three army groups—was highly ambitious, stretching the Axis to the breaking point. During the opening phase of the campaign, these shortcomings were largely hidden, but when the Wehrmacht began to encounter more systematic resistance its meager general reserve of twenty (second-rate) divisions was soon exhausted. Thereafter, the Wehrmacht was dangerously exposed to any Soviet counteroffensive.

Chapter 12

ADVANCE ON LENINGRAD: ARMY GROUP NORTH

Field Marshal von Leeb's Army Group North—tasked with the capture of the Baltic States and Leningrad—was directed to advance over a relatively narrow front against Soviet forces deployed in depth. As a consequence, Leeb would rely less on maneuver skills and more on the sheer speed and power of General Hoepner's Fourth Panzer Group. Leading the panzer charge were General Reinhardt's XXXXI Panzer Corps and the LVI Panzer Corps, commanded by the German Army's rising star, General Erich von Manstein.

The motorized Totenkopf Division was held back in Hoepner's panzer reserve. As a consequence of the bad feelings engendered between Hoepner and Eicke in France during 1940, the assignment of Totenkopf to the Fourth Panzer Group seemed an unfortunate decision, yet over the course of the campaign relations between the two commanders improved, sufficiently so for Hoepner to use a squad of Totenkopf troops as his personal bodyguard.[1] For Eicke, the attack on the Soviet Union was the culmination of his military and political career. He impressed upon his troops that this was to be a war of unrelenting savagery, and unlike some of his more fastidious colleagues he openly promoted the Commissar Order.

The first German success of Army Group North's campaign was achieved by Manstein's LVI Panzer Corps. In an exceptional cross-country dash, Manstein advanced nearly 200 miles in just four days, reaching the Latvian city of Dvinsk (Daugavpils) on 26 June. The city was situated on the Dvina River, a strategic barrier running across the path of the German advance. The Russians were so surprised by the sudden German arrival that they failed to blow the bridges, allowing the Germans to establish a bridgehead on the far bank. With this line crossed, Manstein waited impatiently for the arrival of the slow-moving infantry. In this situation, motorized formations like Totenkopf were invaluable, able to close the gap between panzers and foot soldiers. Eicke's troops had begun to move eastward on the twenty-fourth, and with the capture of Dvinsk they were ordered to follow in the wake of LVI Corps.

As Manstein's armored vehicles were carving their way through the ranks of the Red Army, Totenkopf mopped up Soviet troops bypassed in the panzer advance. On 1 July the division encountered its first really organized resistance. Standartenführer Max Simon's 1st Infantry Regiment fought its way into Kraslau, although poor discipline and a failure to exploit the success brought censure from adjoining army formations. Major General Lancelle of the 121st Infantry Division lodged an official complaint with LVI Corps. According to the report, he "had to enter Kraslau on foot to untangle an enormous traffic jam of SS vehicles and to prod the resumption of an SS attack that had become chaotic and disorganized." In the town center he was shocked to find "a group of SS soldiers gathered in the main street trying fruitlessly to make an ancient Russian gramophone play while other groups of SS infantrymen shattered windows, looted shops, and loaded all available vehicles with booty of every description."[2] In the Totenkopf Division, old habits died hard.

The next objective was the Stalin Line, a defensive system that stretched across the western Soviet Union from north to south. In many places the defenses existed on paper only, but Eicke's men faced a well-prepared series of bunkers, trenches, minefields, and camouflaged artillery and machine-gun positions.

Fortifications around the town of Sebesh formed the first barrier. The attack was launched just before dawn on 6 July and came to an almost immediate halt as the Red Army held its positions to the end. Hauptsturmführer Friedrich, a divisional liaison officer, was with Eicke in his command vehicle when the initial assault was made: "Heavy artillery fire—off and away at high speed! In the infantry gun position, the men fire magnificently. The division commander calls out: 'Well done, men! Good shooting!' Smiling faces, joy. Then enemy counter-battery fire—direct hit, everybody is dead."[3]

The deadlock was broken by the arrival of StuG III assault guns from an adjoining army unit, their extra firepower forcing the remaining Russian survivors back to Opotschka, the linchpin in this section of the Stalin Line. There then followed three days of continuous battle as the SS infantry hacked their way through the Soviet defenses using submachine guns, flamethrowers, grenades, and, at times, bayonets, knives, and sharpened entrenching tools. They were supported by combat engineers, placing high-explosive charges to blow apart the most fiercely defended concrete bunkers.

Obersturmführer Klinter was in the forefront of the attack. Advancing toward a hill held by the enemy, he turned around to find no one following him—his platoon had gone to ground. They were roughly pushed back into action:

> I finally got them to the foot of the high ground. Then we could make out the enemy after all. I could see his positions, make out the machine guns, and could bring our own mortars into action. The artillery forward observer, who had come with us, had already established radio contact—friendly artillery fire really pounded the enemy positions! It was nice to hear the rush of our own artillery rounds fly overhead and watch the mushrooms of dirt, debris, stone and wood fly in the air. Yes—they had stopped firing at us. Over the top and no more waiting, Go! Go![4]

Klinter's troops gained the enemy crest and captured the few Soviet soldiers who remained. The fighting for Opotschka swung back and forth, but with grim determination Totenkopf soldiers finally overcame the defenders. "Opotschka is an unforgettable name," wrote Friedrich. "We fought over the city for three days. Once we captured it, we stood on a heap of rubble."[5]

Combined losses among the division were heavy, amounting to 88 officers and 1,777 NCOs and enlisted men in this opening phase.[6] Among the casualties was Eicke himself: his command car drove over a mine on 6 July, causing him serious leg injuries. Eicke was evacuated for surgery, with Kleinheisterkamp appointed as his temporary successor before Himmler decided on a more permanent replacement.

General Manstein congratulated the division in his 12 July Order of the Day: "I express my gratitude to the officers and men of this corps for their dedication; my recognition for your high achievements."[7] In private, however, Manstein held more ambivalent views on the military role of the Totenkopf Division—and of the Waffen-SS in general. He praised the division for its good march discipline and the way that it "always showed great dash in the assault and was steadfast in defense." But he was severely critical of what he saw as deficiencies in training and leadership:

> The division suffered excessive losses because its troops did not learn until they got into action what army units had mastered long ago. Their losses and lack of experience led them in turn to miss favorable opportunities, and this again caused unnecessary actions to be fought. I doubt if there is anything harder to learn than gauging the moment when a slackening of the enemy's resistance offers the attacker his decisive chance. The upshot of all this was that I repeatedly had to come to the division's assistance, without even then being able to prevent a sharp rise in casualties.[8]

It took several days for Totenkopf to prepare itself for further combat duties. This reorganization included the dissolution of the 2nd Infantry Regiment, its remaining personnel distributed among the other two infantry regiments. On 15 July Hoepner ordered Totenkopf to move forward to support Manstein's LVI Panzer Corps as it advanced toward Lake Ilmen.

As the Germans pushed deeper into Russia, the terrain became increasingly difficult for mechanized formations. Good roads were scarce, with trucks, artillery, and armored vehicles forced to struggle along unsurfaced roads and tracks. The sparsely populated countryside, a mix of swamp and forest, was crisscrossed by a multitude of rivers, streams, and lakes. These conditions played into the hands of the Soviet defenders, skilled in the arts of camouflage and close-quarters combat. They also provided an ideal sanctuary for the thousands of Soviet soldiers who had been cut off in the rapid German advance.

On 19 July Brigadeführer Georg Keppler arrived at divisional headquarters to replace Kleinheisterkamp (until Eicke was sufficiently recovered to return to the field). Chosen specifically by Himmler, Keppler came directly from the Reich Division now fighting its way through Belorussia (Belarus). As a former battalion commander in the "Deutschland" Regiment and CO of "Der Führer" during the invasion in the West, he had all the necessary experience to lead SS troops in battle.

On 31 July, to the dismay of Manstein and Totenkopf, the SS division was reallocated to join General von Wiktorin's XXVIII Army Corps. From the start, relations between the new army corps and Totenkopf were poor, the SS officers complaining of insults made to them by the corps staff. Keppler and Heinz Lammerding, Totenkopf's chief operational officer, also believed the division was being sacrificed to spare army formations.

In early August the SS Polizei Division, released from Army Group North's general reserve, arrived at the front. The former policemen received a warm welcome from the Red Army as they attempted to break through the Luga Line; the division suffered 2,000 casualties during the battle, including their new commander, Arthur Mülverstadt, who was killed by Soviet artillery fire on 10 August. From then on, the Polizei Division adopted a largely defensive role.

The growing strength of the Soviet defenses along the Luga and immediately in front of Leningrad had brought Army Group North's progress almost to a halt. A short while later, Hitler decided he would prefer to starve Leningrad into submission, ordering his divisions—with assistance from the Finnish Army—to cordon off the city.

The unhappy relationship between Wiktorin's corps and Totenkopf was brought to an end as a result of a surprise Soviet offensive. On 14 August, eight infantry divisions and a cavalry corps of the Soviet Thirty-Fourth Army drove into the line held by the German X Army Corps to the south of Lake Ilmen. Manstein was assigned the task of neutralizing this ominous threat to Army Group North's right flank, with Totenkopf transferred to his command.

Manstein ordered X Corps to hold its positions along the River Polist, as part of his plan to make the Red Army commander commit as many Soviet divisions to the frontline battle as possible and thereby reduce the number of formations held in reserve. While the fighting was ongoing, Manstein calmly marshaled his own forces for a devastating counterstrike against the Soviet's increasingly exposed left flank. Totenkopf and the 3rd Motorized Division would spearhead the attack.

Early on 19 August Manstein launched his assault, which drove into the surprised Soviet ranks. As darkness fell, Totenkopf was urged on by Manstein to seize the bridges over the Polist and prevent the enemy from escaping eastward to safety. The fighting continued without pause on the twentieth, allowing the Germans to encircle the now desperate Soviet troops. During the night, German artillery mercilessly pounded the Red Army positions in preparation for a final assault in the morning. The twenty-first of August was a glorious day in Totenkopf's history, the troops cutting through what remained of the Red Army positions, destroying anything that moved. The exhausted, demoralized Soviet soldiers were incapable of resistance, and those not killed by SS troops on surrender were sent to the rear as prisoners.[9]

The victory on the Polist was followed by an immediate German drive eastward, across a series of parallel rivers that ran southward from Lake Ilmen: the Redja, the Lovat, and the Pola. Despite its defeat, the Red Army high command was still able to commit sufficient numbers to make the German advance a slow and protracted business, especially as the onset of heavy rain transformed the already marshy ground into a quagmire.

The Red Army clung to its positions along the Pola, and it was only with an improvement in the weather on 7 September that the Germans were able to cross the river. Totenkopf pushed forward a few miles beyond the river to establish a line running around the settlement of Demyansk by 12 September, and here the advance halted.

This marked the high-water mark of Army Group North's invasion of the Soviet Union. As if to underscore this change of circumstances, Manstein was ordered to leave the LVI Corps and take command of Eleventh Army for the offensive into the Crimea. In the organizational changes that followed Manstein's departure, Totenkopf was assigned to the II Army Corps and ordered to construct field defenses along the Pola River line. As the divisional staff expected to resume offensive operations, no great attention was directed toward the task, some SS officers asserting that the Red Army was on the verge of collapse.[10]

On 19 September Eicke returned to take command of his division.[11] Although still suffering from his wounds—he walked with a limp and relied on a walking stick—he immediately set about galvanizing the division for action. Shocked at the poor physical state of his men, he dashed off his usual letters of complaint to remedy what he considered a dangerous situation. He wrote to Karl Wolff—Himmler's adjutant and SS liaison officer to the Führer—requesting that he persuade Hitler to have the division rested, and then to Hans Jüttner to demand that NCO replacements not be siphoned off into other parts of the SS, as had been the practice while he was convalescing. Eicke also reinstated regular ideological instructional sessions for the troops, something that had been allowed to lapse when Kleinheisterkamp and Keppler had led Totenkopf.

As Eicke was reimposing his authority, forward outposts began to report ominous signs of an impending Soviet offensive. On 22 September it was clear that Soviet reconnaissance units were probing German lines to discover weak points that might be exploited in any attack, which duly came on the twenty-fourth with a heavy aerial bombardment. The Luftwaffe was conspicuously absent from the battlefront, allowing the Red Air Force to attack the German lines at will. After this came the standard artillery barrage followed by swarms of advancing infantry. What was new, however, was the massed deployment of armor against the Totenkopf positions.

The main weight of the Soviet attack fell upon Kleinheisterkamp's 3rd Infantry Regiment, defending Lushno. Hopelessly outnumbered and outgunned, the Waffen-SS troops were slowly pushed out of the village, but then immediately counterattacked to regain possession. For the next three days Lushno would become the center of a desperate seesaw battle, neither side seemingly able to gain ascendancy over the other. On 25 September, SS troops holding the line to the north of Lushno were startled to see a herd of squealing pigs bearing down on them; they had been driven forward by their Soviet handlers in an attempt to clear a path through a recently laid German minefield. The porcine mine detectors failed in their mission, and the ensuing human attack also came to nothing.

The shortage of effective 5cm antitank guns was a recurring problem for the German defenders. As a short-term measure, Eicke encouraged the use of tank-killer squads, comprising up to a dozen men armed with mines, satchel charges, and grenades. In the constricted semiurban environment of Lushno, Soviet tanks were vulnerable to these squads—as long as they were sufficiently brave and enterprising.

In a typical encounter, a squad member would creep out from cover and clamber onto the rear deck of the enemy tank to place a high-explosive charge under the turret overhang. A grenade, with a short fuse, was normally used as a detonator, so the SS soldier had to make a hasty exit to avoid the blast. All the while, the remainder of the team would provide suppressive fire against any accompanying Soviet infantry. And if the tank was disabled they would shoot down surviving crewmen attempting to escape the vehicle. Hauptsturmführer Max Seela, from the combat pioneer battalion, became an expert tank killer; he and his team knocked out seven of the latest tanks in a single day.[12]

The focus of the Soviet attack briefly moved south to concentrate on Simon's 1st Infantry Regiment, but then returned to Lushno in a last attempt to destroy what remained of the 3rd Infantry Regiment. For the Totenkopf Division, this was the critical moment. The reconnaissance battalion—which was then acting as the divisional reserve—had been redeployed elsewhere. If the Red Army broke through the beleaguered infantry lines, there was nothing to block its progress. Eicke and Lammerding even began to prepare their headquarters staff for frontline combat. On 26–27 September the Red Army launched its final attempt to overwhelm the Totenkopf, but the fanatical ideological character of the division—where no Aryan could give way to a Slav—proved its worth. The line held.

Totenkopf casualties were inevitably heavy, nowhere more so than in the 3rd Regiment's II Battalion. By the end of 26 September every officer was dead, a figure that included 4 battalion commanders killed in quick succession. Overall, the battalion suffered 889 casualties between 24 and 29 September, leaving approximately 150 men to fight on, which they did, launching a final counterattack to retake the village. On 28 September the Red Army ceased offensive operations.

Perhaps the most outstanding single action of the battle was carried out by Sturmann Fritz Christen. His exploits were recounted by Toten-kopf officer Karl Ullrich:

> Christen, an artilleryman in the anti-tank battalion, was with his battery north of Lushno on 24 September in the middle of Russian armored attacks. After the entire company had fallen except for Christen, he remained alone by his gun and destroyed six tanks. The remaining tanks turned back. Cut off from the rest of his unit, he remained at his 5cm PAK [antitank gun] for two days without water or rations and knocked out an additional seven tanks. He was finally rescued from his desperate position by a counterattack on 27 September. The division commander [Eicke] awarded him the Iron Cross First Class and recommended him for the Knight's Cross, which he later received personally from the Führer. He was the first enlisted man of the division to receive that award.[13]

While the men of the Totenkopf Division lacked the finer tactical skills displayed in offensive operations by the best army panzer divisions and other elite Waffen-SS formations, such as Reich or Leibstandarte, they had repeatedly proved themselves in defensive fighting.

A final, minor, German offensive was launched on 16 October to assist Army Group Center's attack on Moscow. By now the Red Army had built solid defenses in depth along the line allotted to Totenkopf, and the underresourced attack came to a limping halt a few days later. From this point onward, Eicke's men went over to a permanent defensive, while at the same time conducting ruthless antipartisan sweeps in their rear areas. During November the SS troops dug trenches and constructed wooden, earth-covered bunkers. The division's engineers laid swathes of barbed wire in front of the main defensive line, along with 1,557 antitank and 490 antipersonnel mines.[14]

As the men prepared their defenses, the weather got steadily colder. The first recorded snow came on 10 October—a fall of eighteen inches— and by November the climate alternated between heavy rain and vicious cold snaps whose biting frosts brought nighttime temperatures to as low as −29 degrees Fahrenheit.

Totenkopf infantryman Paul Kretzler—who had spent two months recovering from battlefield wounds—returned to the division with the onset of winter: "We were stuck in the mud and I had a terrible time trying to find the unit I was assigned to, for the old hands had gone—killed, wounded or missing—and the replacements, although good lads, were not of the same caliber. Quite suddenly it all turned to ice and snow and this was far worse for we had no winter clothing at all. There was much suffering as we tried to improve our position and keep our vehicles in motion. Everything froze and we were short of lubricants."[15]

Hitler and the German high command had been so certain of a swift victory that suitable provision for winter warfare had been ignored, with disastrous consequences for the men forced to fight in such extreme conditions. Kretzler's comment on the poor quality of Totenkopf's replacements had already been taken up by Eicke, who complained at the lack of suitable training of these new arrivals. He also considered them physically and morally inferior when compared to his old soldiers, being particularly contemptuous of the Volksdeutsche recruits now starting to join the replacement pool. In total, the division received just under 5,000 reinforcements, insufficient to cover the nearly 9,000 men who had become casualties since the beginning of Barbarossa—nearly half the division's regulation strength.[16]

Not unreasonably, Eicke demanded that the division be withdrawn from the front to recover and rebuild. His superiors were understanding of the division's plight but issued no withdrawal orders to the exhausted SS units. It was pointed out that other army formations were also in a similar situation. During November and December the Totenkopf Division held its ground, the bitterly cold weather its prime enemy for the time being.

EVEN MORE EXTREME climatic conditions would be encountered by Kampfgruppe Nord in the far northern part of Finland, fighting as part of a combined German-Finnish army. Hitler, fearful that a Soviet attack from the port of Murmansk might endanger the strategically vital

Swedish iron-ore mines, decided to eliminate the threat by capturing Murmansk. The first stage of the operation was to cut the Soviet supply line to the isolated port. Kampfgruppe Nord was assigned to take part in this action.

When Obergruppenführer Demelhuber took command of Kampfgruppe Nord in May 1941, he was horrified at its unreadiness for combat. Almost all of its men were former concentration-camp guards or policemen, reinforced with some overage reservists. While on occupation duty in Norway, the units had been allowed to stagnate. Demelhuber immediately asked for a couple of months of intensive training to bring the men up to a suitable standard before any frontline action was considered. With invasion imminent, however, the request was glibly refused on the basis that the troops' fervent commitment to National Socialism would overcome any military shortcomings.

On 1 July 1941 a German-Finnish force, including Kampfgruppe Nord, advanced through the pine forests typical of the region and crossed the border into the Soviet Union, their objective to capture the fortified town of Salla. A heavy Luftwaffe bombardment helped to suppress the Red Army defenses, although it had the unfortunate side effect of setting the trees on fire, which hampered and confused the German advance and provided the Soviet defenses with a useful smoke screen.

On encountering the enemy, the now disorganized SS units were easily repulsed. A resumption of the German attack was set for 4 July but was preempted by a Soviet armored thrust in the early hours of the same day. The sudden appearance of Red Army tanks crashing through the undergrowth caused panic among the SS troops; some even committed the cardinal military sin of throwing away their weapons as they ran for their lives.

The solid defense of the Germans and Finns on either side of Kampfgruppe Nord prevented the Red Army from exploiting its success, and the gap in the German line was restored. Waffen-SS casualties amounted to 73 killed, 232 wounded, and 147 missing (most of these prisoners).[17] The theater commander, General von Falkenhorst, was so unsure of Kampfgruppe Nord that he temporarily broke up the formation and distributed its individual units among his German and Finnish troops.

Himmler was mortified by Kampfgruppe Nord's disgrace, not least by the knowledge that most of the missing had allowed themselves to be captured (he believed an SS man should die rather than surrender). Himmler suppressed all intelligence of the defeat, although he did take practical steps to improve the formation by sending more experienced reinforcements when it was upgraded to become SS Division Nord in September. Early in 1942 it was redesignated as a mountain division, and with the arrival of better-quality manpower and improved training the SS-Gebirgs (Mountain) Division Nord would play a more effective role in the northern war against the Soviet Union.

Chapter 13

ACROSS THE UKRAINE: ARMY GROUP SOUTH

I N THE SOUTHERN sector of the German invasion front—stretching from the near-impassable Pripet Marshes to the Black Sea—were the Axis troops of Field Marshal von Rundstedt's Army Group South. In addition to his regular German formations, Rundstedt commanded a substantial Romanian force of uncertain quality. The spearhead of the German attack was provided by Colonel General von Kleist's First Panzer Group. Kleist's initial objective was the capture of Kiev and then, in conjunction with the supporting infantry armies, the destruction of Soviet forces to the west of the River Dnieper. Leibstandarte SS "Adolf Hitler" and the Wiking Division would provide Kleist's panzers with additional mobile firepower.

General Mikhail Kirponos, the Red Army commander facing Army Group South, had disregarded Stalin's order to ignore any German "provocations," and during the night of 21–22 June he alerted his troops to be prepared for action. As a result, his command was better prepared than most to react to the invasion, and from the moment German troops crossed the border they faced stiff resistance. Throughout the first week of Barbarossa, Army Group South made steady if unspectacular progress, with none of the dramatic panzer advances and encirclement battles that characterized the initial efforts of the other two army groups.

Sepp Dietrich and his Leibstandarte had to wait until the end of June before they were summoned forward in support of General von Mackensen's III Motorized Corps. Once over the border into Ukraine, they immediately found themselves fending off a series of fierce, if not especially skilled, Soviet counterattacks. For a full two weeks Leibstandarte would hold a defensive line to protect the northern flank of Panzer Group Kleist. Only on 16 July, with the arrival of the infantry from Sixth Army, was Dietrich given the signal to follow the panzers in their drive toward Kiev.

On 25 June the units of Felix Steiner's Wiking Division were attached to General von Wietersheim's XIV Panzer Corps in its advance past Lemberg (L'viv) and Tarnopol. The death of the "Westland" commander, Standartenführer Wäckerle, on 2 July led to his replacement by the fifty-nine-year-old Standartenführer Artur Phleps. It was not only his relatively advanced age that made Phleps an unusual choice for a regimental commander of a Waffen-SS fighting unit. Phleps had been born in the Siebenbürgen, an ethnic German enclave in Romania, then a part of the Austro-Hungarian Empire. He served as a staff officer in the Austrian Army during World War I and after 1918 returned to his homeland and joined the Romanian Army, reaching the rank of lieutenant general before political intrigue forced his retirement in 1941.

A committed German nationalist and Nazi supporter, Phleps moved to Germany and as a member of the Volksdeutsche community asked Gottlob Berger to be allowed to join the Waffen-SS (under his mother's maiden name of Stolz). Berger readily agreed, and he was initially assigned to the Wiking Division as an unattached staff officer. A tall, austere individual—sporting a distinctive Hitler mustache—he was well known for his plain speaking. He also proved an able leader of "Westland," before a subsequent promotion gave him command of the Volksdeutsche Prinz Eugen Mountain Division in 1942.

The 1940 campaign in the West had further convinced Steiner that operational flexibility was essential for mechanized formations. Thus, for the invasion of Ukraine he utilized three Kampfgruppen based around reinforced infantry regiments: von Oberkamp's "Germania," Stolz's (or Phlep's) "Westland," and Scholz's "Nordland." The use of such battle groups had become standard practice in the German armed forces, but Steiner

also encouraged more ad hoc groupings of infantry, artillery, and supporting arms that could be formed and dissolved according to short-term
need. A typical example of this approach was the way in which Oberkamp
exploited his success in the crossing of the River Slutsch on 6–7 July by
immediately forming an improvised "fast battalion" of two motorcycle
companies, an antitank company, and infantry-gun and Flak platoons.[1]

DURING JULY, AS the hard-marching infantry of Army Group South
began to make progress in their drive into Ukraine, the possibility of
conducting an encirclement battle became apparent to Rundstedt and his
staff. In the German advance toward Kiev, the bulk of two Soviet armies
had become marooned around Uman, to the south of the Ukrainian
capital. While General Stülpnagel's Seventeenth Army, with some Axis
support from Romanian, Hungarian, and Slovak contingents, marched
to the south of Uman, Kleist's First Panzer Group circled the city from
the north, the two pincers meeting on 2 August. Attempts by the Red
Army to break out were contained by the Axis, and after a week of increasingly hopeless fighting Soviet troops began to surrender. Red Army
casualties were heavy: approximately 100,000 killed or wounded and a
similar number captured.

During the operation, Leibstandarte had been temporarily loaned to
General Kempf's XLVIII Corps, which had taken Novo Archangelsk the
day before the pocket was sealed. Kempf was full of praise for the contribution made by Dietrich's men: "Committed at the focus of the battle
for the seizure of the key enemy position at Archangelsk, Leibstandarte
SS 'Adolf Hitler,' with incomparable dash, took the city and the heights
to the south. In the spirit of the most devoted brotherhood of arms, they
intervened on their own initiative in the arduous struggle of the 16th
Infantry Division (motorized) on their left flank and routed the enemy,
destroying numerous tanks."[2]

While the Uman operation was still ongoing, the Wiking Division
was deployed to the north, defending the encirclement from Soviet relief
efforts and pushing east toward the River Dnieper. By the end of July

Steiner ordered the division to go over to an all-out offensive, calling upon the Luftwaffe to provide support on a mass scale. At this stage in the war, the German Air Force was in the ascendant, its Stukas breaking up enemy tank attacks or pounding defenses, seemingly at will. Once the dive-bombers had done their work, Wiking advanced, alongside an army panzer regiment. "The enemy fled in panic," wrote the Wiking divisional history. "Cavalry units trying to reach safety in flight rushed together from all directions. Horse-drawn batteries were shot up as they attempted to withdraw. On the way stood abandoned anti-tank guns and overturned vehicles, while dead horses were strewn about."[3]

An improvised Soviet defensive line around Taraschtscha on the River Ros was broken in a determined attack led by Stolz's "Westland" Kampfgruppe, the enemy bundled eastward with heavy losses. Wiking casualties were also severe, especially in "Westland," which suffered 92 officers and men killed and 360 wounded. The battle bonded the Dutch and Flemish volunteers with their German comrades, proof that given the right training and leadership, non-Germans could fight to the standard of an elite German infantry unit.

As Wiking's forward units advanced beyond Taraschtscha, so Einsatzgruppen EK5 moved in to exterminate the town's large Jewish population. Assisted by troops from Wiking's rear echelon, the men of EK5 began their work, killing 1,000 Jews in the action.[4] The relationship between Waffen-SS field units and SS death squads was always much closer than that maintained by postwar Waffen-SS apologists.

During August, Wiking—now part of III Panzer Corps—took the operational initiative, fighting alongside army tank units in scattering the now disorganized Soviet forces. Wiking marched southward along the western side of the Dnieper toward the river's great bend at Dnepropetrovsk. The good progress made by Rundstedt's forces was, however, hampered by Hitler's sudden order to dispatch the bulk of Kleist's First Panzer Group northward to join Guderian's panzers in the great encirclement maneuver to the east of Kiev. It would only be from mid-September onward that Kleist's panzers were able to return to Army Group South and the ongoing battle for the southern and eastern Ukraine.

LEIBSTANDARTE, WITH KEMPF's praise still ringing in its ears after the Uman battle, was ordered south to capture Kherson on the Black Sea. The SS division reached the coast and after a short but fierce battle with Soviet marine infantry captured the port on 19 August. The engagement provided the division's antitank artillery with some unusual targets, such as ships attempting to escape from the harbor to open sea.

According to an account written by an Erich Stahl (also known as Erich Kern), an Austrian journalist then serving with Leibstandarte, during the drive to Kherson men of his regiment discovered the bodies of German soldiers mutilated by the Red Army. As a consequence, according to Stahl, an order was given by Dietrich not to take prisoners for the next three days, with the end result that 4,000 Red Army soldiers were killed while surrendering.[5] Although there was no documentary or other evidence to support this assertion, it was taken as fact by a number of authorities and, in one case, subsequently confused with the discovery of 6 mutilated Leibstandarte corpses in Taganrog in March 1942.[6] This is not to say that Leibstandarte did not kill enemy prisoners during Operation Barbarossa, and in one instance, at least, its troops—along with those from Wiking—were used in the roundup of Jews for execution in the autumn of 1941.[7]

On 20 August Leibstandarte was given its first rest after seven weeks of almost continuous combat. Casualties had been relatively light, but the wear and tear on vehicles had been immense, with half the division's inventory either destroyed or temporarily out of action.[8] Leibstandarte was given a vital two weeks for rest and repairs—and the assimilation of 674 reinforcements—before assignment to General von Schobert's Eleventh Army, and crossing the Dnieper in readiness for the assault on the Crimean peninsula.

The Germans pushed on toward the Perekop Isthmus, the sole land route into the Crimea. The day before the assault was to be launched, Schobert was killed in an air crash (succeeded by Manstein a few days later). The attack still went ahead, led by the army's 73rd Infantry Division and Leibstandarte's reconnaissance battalion, commanded by Kurt Meyer. The Soviet defenses were well prepared and included an armored train, more than a match for the armored cars and 3.7cm antitank guns of Meyer's battalion. This first German attack was repulsed with ease.

Further assaults also came to nothing, forcing the newly arrived Manstein to initiate full-scale siege operations.

―――――――

On 23 August, advance elements of Mackensen's III Motorized Corps, along with Steiner's Wiking Division, reached Dnepropetrovsk. An important industrial center, Dnepropetrovsk was sited on both sides of the Dnieper at the point where the river made its abrupt right-angle turn to flow southwest into the Black Sea. "Germania" and "Nordland" opened the assault, followed by "Westland." Within three days the southern half of the city was in German hands and a small bridgehead established on the far side of the river. Soviet artillery was rushed forward to support the defenders and accurately pounded German positions, making it virtually impossible to get more men and supplies to the bridgehead on the north bank. Only at night could the passage of the thousand-yard-wide Dnieper be made with any safety. The German gunners, chronically short of ammunition, could do little in reply.

On the night of 31 August–1 September, Standartenführer Fritz von Scholz led his "Nordland" infantry along the rickety bridges spanning the Dnieper to the north bank. Once there, they reinforced their army colleagues from the 198th Infantry Division, in readiness for a determined Soviet counterattack. For the next week the German defenders faced a blizzard of Soviet fire, their entrenchments blown to pieces during the day and hastily rebuilt at night. The "Nordland" commander was singled out for his inspirational leadership, as described in the divisional history: "Night after night and morning after morning, Scholz walked or crawled through his positions, fighting beside his men and serving as an example."[9] From then on, his soldiers would know him as "Old Fritz," in deference to the Prussian soldier-king Frederick the Great.

While Scholz was helping hold the bridgehead perimeter, the remainder of the division crossed the river by bridge and boat. On the evening of 7 September Mackensen and Steiner believed they had the manpower to take the offensive. Wiking was chosen as the lead attack formation. The Germans had stockpiled enough ammunition for a sustained artillery bombardment, which began on the morning of the eighth. Soviet counterfire was heavier than expected, however, and the artillery duel continued throughout the morning.

Mackensen and Steiner were sufficiently worried at the strength of the enemy fire that the infantry attack was repeatedly postponed. At 1:00 P.M. a sympathetic Mackensen told Steiner that he would accept a cancellation of the planned operation: "I realize that the attack will be very difficult, Therefore I will not demand it of you. In spite of the great difficulties the bridgehead presents us, I would rather forgo its enlargement than sacrifice a division for it."[10] Before Steiner was forced to make this difficult decision, Soviet gunfire began to slacken, the artillery battle finally going in favor of the Germans. By 2:00 P.M. "Germania" and "Westland" were forcing their way through the streets of Dnepropetrovsk's northern suburbs. Over the next two days the Germans ejected the Red Army from the city, looking forward to an exploitation of their hard-won success in having successfully crossed the Dnieper.

As LEIBSTANDARTE AND other army formations were battering themselves against the Soviet lines guarding entry into the Crimea, the remainder of Eleventh Army continued its eastward march toward Rostov-on-Don. The advance was halted by a surprise counterattack by two Soviet armies, launched on 23 September, which opened up a gap between Romanian and German forces. The success of the Red Army attack forced Manstein to temporarily curtail the Crimean operation and redirect forces to protect the now wavering spearhead.

As one of the few mobile formations at Manstein's disposal, Leibstandarte was rushed eastward, across the empty, forbidding Nogai Steppe to the north of the Sea of Azov. One SS man wrote of the barren conditions they encountered: "There is very little water and what there is salty. Movement is visible for miles; clouds of choking, red-brown dust hangs over our moving columns and pinpoint our exact positions. Paradoxically the only signs of life are the dead tree trunks of telegraph poles. Without them it would be difficult to orientate oneself. Sometimes we find a melon field, but the unripe ones have unhappy effects."[11] The normally positive Kurt Meyer was also affected by the nature of the Nogai Steppe, feelings accentuated by the ever-increasing distance from the fatherland: "I felt the terrifying emptiness of the open spaces for the first time. The yawning emptiness of the steppe had a depressing effect on us. How were we to operate in the east?"[12]

The initial Soviet success in disrupting the German-Romanian advance encouraged the Red Army commanders to press on farther, a move that was to leave them dangerously overextended. While the German troops from the Crimea advanced directly to the rescue of their comrades between Multipool and Bryansk, General von Kleist's powerful panzer divisions (soon to renamed First Panzer Army) had driven southward along the eastern bank of the Dnieper. By the end of September they had cut through the lines of communication of the Soviet armies, and on 6 October they met up with units from the German Eleventh Army—which included Leibstandarte—at Berdyansk. Poor Soviet intelligence as to the whereabouts of Kleist's armored formations and the sheer speed of the German reaction transformed the situation from seeming defeat to an easily won victory.

By 10 October at least 65,000 Soviet troops had laid down their arms, leaving the way open for the continuation of the German march eastward.[13] The port of Taganrog—at the mouth of the River Mius—was captured by a Leibstandarte battalion commanded by Fritz Witt on 17 October. A little to the north, Wiking was engaged in the attack on Stalino (Donetsk), which fell on the twentieth. The seizure of these two towns provided a good jumping-off point for Army Group South's prime objective: Rostov-on-Don.

Any chance of a swift drive on Rostov was confounded by the arrival of heavy rains during mid-October, turning the land into a virtually impassable quagmire. The history of the Wiking Division provided a good account of the effects of the *rasputistsa*, the local name for the Soviet Union's "rainy season" that brought operations to halt, both in the fall and in the spring:

In these miserable days the vast and desolate countryside of the southern Ukraine between the Dnieper and the Donets revealed the full malice of its black earth. Every movement by wheeled or tracked vehicles became a laborious exercise in the muddy lanes; vehicles were ruined and fuel consumption skyrocketed. Any tank or gun that deviated from the muddy roads or tried to move into position off the road sank into the soft earth up to its axles. Vehicles that did so could often only be pulled out after strenuous efforts. The only possible means of advancing was to use the tough little steppe horses. The Russians hitched them to small carts and were able to slowly negotiate the black earth tracks of the Ukraine.[14]

The rain and the increasingly cold winds sweeping across the steppes were not the only problem faced by Rundstedt's Army Group South. As the Germans pressed farther east, so their supply chain lengthened, and with that came attendant shortages of food, ammunition, and, above all, fuel. The only efficient means of transporting fuel were by rail, but Kleist's fuel-hungry mechanized divisions were now far from the nearest German railheads, reliant on trucks to bring up essential supplies. Danish volunteer Hauptsturmführer Paul Engelhardt-Ranzow was a staff officer with Wiking, and his diary entry for 15 October noted that, much to Steiner's irritation, the division had been able to advance only a few miles:

> Enemy disintegrating and in retreat but we are unable to pursue. Our division needs 136 cubic meters of fuel operating serviceable vehicles on passable roads. Today in the mud, 350 cubic meters. But we already need 700 cubic meters just to bring fuel from Dnepropetrovsk since the trains can't come any further. So we sit here without fuel—motorized units, tanks, aircraft. The water is very bad. I put a glass of boiled water down in the evening and the next morning the bottom of the glass was covered with a 1 cm thick layer of oil.[15]

A lowering of morale and the onset of illnesses through exhaustion, poor diets, and uncertain hygiene reduced the fighting ability of the men. Even the toughest soldiers were not immune. Kurt Meyer was laid low by a bout of jaundice and dysentery that forced him to relinquish command of his reconnaissance battalion. As October gave way to November, the weather alternated between windswept rain and bitterly hard frosts.

Despite their problems, the German mechanized divisions struggled along as best they could. An improvement in the weather in late October and the arrival of (limited) fuel allowed elements of the Wiking Division to advance with a degree of their former swiftness. Among these was the antitank battalion, which had the bizarre experience of repelling a Soviet cavalry charge on 6 November 1941.

On the same day that this throwback to nineteenth-century warfare was being played out, "Nordland" encountered a cutting-edge example of the latest Soviet technology. A regimental antitank gun commander saw several Soviet tanks bearing down on his lines: "My four guns opened fire simultaneously and I could clearly see that the 3.7cm tracer rounds were on target. I was startled to see the tanks carry on and circle the infantry's dugouts. Round after round was fired by our guns with no discernible effect. The rounds simply bounced off the tanks and only a hit in the suspension or tracks achieved any results. In short, we had the first T-34s in front of us."[16]

The sudden arrival of the T-34 tank came as a shock, the Soviet tank superior to anything fielded by the German army at that time. In addition, Wiking and Leibstandarte soldiers found themselves enduring barrages from Katyusha rocket launchers. The Germans had been schooled in the idea that Russians were subhuman, and the surprise created by these new weapons was as unsettling as it was unwelcome. And as the Red Army gained in material strength and confidence, so the Germans in the Ukraine began to reach the end of their ability to conduct offensive operations. But Hitler was determined that Rostov would fall, and on 17 November Kleist's First Panzer Army twitched in one last spasm of offensive action.

On 13 November the alternating wet and cold weather finally gave way to permanent winter conditions. For the poorly equipped German soldiers in their summer uniforms, this meant yet more misery, with the onset of widespread cases of frostbite that included Sepp Dietrich, who suffered first- and second-degree frostbite on the toes of his right foot. One Leibstandarte soldier recalled how in this weather, "the wounded die quickly; the blood freezes as it leaves the body and a sort of shock sets in which kills. Light wounds that heal in three days in summer kill you in winter."[17]

For the mechanized formations, the lack of suitable cold-weather lubricants and antifreeze to protect the engines was a troublesome complication. During the coldest periods a tank crew would have to light a wood fire underneath their vehicle in the morning to generate sufficient heat to get the engine started. But once these difficulties were surmounted, the armored vehicles could, at least, roll forward into action over the hard ground.

General Mackensen's confidence in Leibstandarte was sufficient for him to choose it to lead the assault on Rostov, supported by the 14th Panzer Division. Dietrich's troops, reinforced with an army tank regiment, crossed the Tusloff River on 17 November, just fifteen miles north of Rostov. After a swift breakthrough phase, the Germans encountered heavy resistance as they fought their way into the northern suburbs of the city. On 20 November, SS troops reached the River Don, and in a daring action led by Obersturmführer Heinz Springer the main rail bridge over the river was captured intact. The following day Rostov was in German hands.

But as the Germans were fighting their way into Rostov, the Red Army was assembling powerful forces to mount a counterattack. North of Rostov, the German line came under severe pressure, and on the night of 21–22 November Wietersheim's XIV Corps conducted a fighting withdrawal to the Tusloff, with Wiking's "Westland" Regiment providing the rear guard. This retirement left Rostov as an increasingly vulnerable salient, and an anxious Kleist began to consider its evacuation. On 28 November, as Red Army infantry penetrated the outer districts of Rostov and Soviet armor pressed from the north, Rundstedt and Kleist ordered a general withdrawal behind the River Mius, some fifty miles to the west of Rostov.

Hitler was outraged when he discovered how far the Germans had retreated, the first such reverse his forces had suffered since the outbreak of war in 1939. Kleist was upbraided as a coward, while Rundstedt—ultimately responsible for ordering the retreat—was sacked and replaced by General von Reichenau, commander of Sixth Army and an enthusiastic Hitler supporter. Dietrich bravely came to Rundstedt's support and informed Reichenau that there had been no realistic possibility of holding Rostov and that retreat had been the only option. Dietrich asked Reichenau to pass on his views to the Führer. Dietrich also dispatched

Leibstandarte's combat strength returns to Hitler, which from an establishment figure of 290 officers and 9,704 men had fallen to 157 officers and 4,556 men, with just 15 percent of vehicles in a roadworthy condition.[18]

Hitler was sufficiently perturbed by the whole situation that on 2 December he flew out to Army Group South headquarters at Mariupol, where Dietrich once again defended his army superiors against Hitler's criticisms. Hitler, partially mollified, then returned to his headquarters, leaving Army Group South, with Leibstandarte and Wiking, to hold the line along the River Mius through the grim winter of 1941–1942.

Chapter 14

THE DRIVE ON MOSCOW:
ARMY GROUP CENTER

FIELD MARSHAL VON Bock's Army Group Center was assigned the most ambitious task in the German invasion plan, the destruction of the Soviet armies defending Moscow. Accordingly, it was provided with a greater offensive capability. Whereas the other two army groups were allocated a single panzer group, Bock's force had the advantage of Colonel General Hoth's Third Panzer Group and Colonel General Guderian's reinforced Second Panzer Group. Used in conjunction, the two panzer groups would win a series of brilliant encirclement battles in the initial stages of the campaign.

Hausser's SS Reich Division joined Guderian's panzers, as part of General von Vietinghoff's XLVI Panzer Corps. The other two formations in the corps comprised the reinforced Infantry Regiment "Grossdeutschland"— old rivals in the race to Belgrade—and the 10th Panzer Division, the latter forming a close bond with Reich during the advance to Moscow.

Fully exploiting Stalin's slow response to the German invasion, the two panzer groups easily broke through the Red Army's defenses. On 27 June advance units from the panzer groups met to the east of Minsk, trapping three Soviet armies in the process. Over the following days German infantry divisions broke up the encircled Soviet forces into two pockets, at Bialystok and west of Minsk, which they then proceeded to liquidate, the battle concluding on 10 July. Although a substantial number of Soviet troops managed to slip through the German cordon, out of a total force of 625,000 men just under 100,000 were killed and approximately a third of a million men taken prisoner.

This victory, and others along the front, produced an intoxicating elation among OKH, the German Army high command. Franz Halder, the army chief of staff, wrote on 3 July, "It may be said that the objective to shatter the bulk of the Russian Army this side of the Dvina and Dnieper has been accomplished. It is thus probably no overstatement to say that the Russian campaign has been won in the space of two weeks."[1] Hitler even began to talk of ceremonial parades and firework displays in Moscow.

FOR HAUSSER'S REICH Division, the invasion of the Soviet Union began slowly, its pioneers and artillerymen constructing bridges across the River Bug while the rest of the division waited impatiently for the order to move. On 26 June Reich joined the queues of vehicles crossing the Bug, its role to provide security to the southern flank of Guderian's Second Panzer Group as it pushed forward into Russia.

Skirting the northern side of the Pripet Marshes, Hausser's Reich Division faced a series of river crossings that included the Berezina and the upper reaches of the Dnieper. Speed was of the essence, and the division's vanguard consisted of reconnaissance and motorcycle troops along with a battalion from the "Deutschland" Regiment, with extra firepower provided by the StuG IIIs of the new assault-gun battery. Each assault gun was given its own name, taken from ships of the Imperial Navy and drawn in turn from famous Austro-German soldiers. The assault gun "Yorck" was the first into action and in a confused encounter on 30 June knocked out several Soviet tanks and antitank guns.

On 3 July Hausser was pleased with the performance of the division's "new" infantry regiment, SS Infantry Regiment 11, when it drove back Soviet forces in the forests bordering the main supply route. During the Balkans campaign the regiment had been kept back in reserve, and it was only now that the former concentration-camp guards from the

11th Totenkopf Standarte found themselves fighting an enemy with military training.

The next obstacle was the River Berezina, but this was crossed by the division on 4 July with minimal opposition. Guderian believed that the Soviet forces—still in disarray after the Bialystok-Minsk encirclement—were hoping to make a stand on the Dnieper and the Stalin Line defenses that lay behind the river. As they pushed forward to the Dnieper, the SS advance was encumbered in the wooded regions made swamp-like by heavy rain. Ordered to press on without delay, there was little the Reich soldiers could do when Red Army infantry fell back into the relative safety of the forests. This was a recurring problem for all German forces advancing into the Soviet heartland in the summer and autumn of 1941. One German soldier outlined the problem:

> The Russians again proved their mastery in forest fighting. With sure instinct they moved among the impenetrable undergrowth. Their positions, not on the forest's edge but deep inside, were superbly camouflaged. Their dugouts and foxholes were established with diabolical cunning, providing a field of fire only to the rear. From the front and from above they were invisible. The German infantrymen passed them unsuspecting, and were picked off from behind. The Russians were also very good at infiltrating into German positions. Moving singly, they communicated with each other in the dense forest by imitating the cries of animals, and after trickling through the German positions they rallied again and reformed as assault units.[2]

By 9 July Reich and the other formations of Vietinghoff's XLVI Panzer Corps closed on the Dnieper. Hoping to surprise the Soviet defenders, Vietinghoff insisted on elaborate deception measures and a covert advance. On 11 July Reich and the 10th Panzer Division prepared to assault the Soviet positions on the far side of the river, which at this point was roughly a hundred yards wide. To prepare the way, an aerial bombardment was launched against the Stalin Line. The divisional history recorded the attack carried out by "Der Führer": "To our great surprise, the devastating Stuka attacks made the enemy evacuate the heavily fortified positions on the eastern bank. Thus the regiment began crossing in the great heat at 1530 hours. Contrary to our expectations, it occurred without a fight or any complications."[3]

Oberführer Keppler was immensely relieved that he had gotten his men across the Dnieper and through the Stalin Line virtually without loss. As he was preparing to go over the river, he received a surprise order to immediately stand down as CO of "Der Führer" and take command of the Totenkopf Division following the incapacitation of Theodor Eicke. Having nurtured the regiment from its inception in Austria in 1938, Keppler had deep reservations regarding the "promotion," but in accordance with his orders he handed the regiment over to Sturmbannführer Otto Kumm of the III Battalion.

Another abrupt command change occurred two days later. The Red Air Force, having recovered from the disasters of the first week of combat, was beginning to fight back. On 13 July Soviet bombers struck the command post of the 11th SS Infantry Regiment, mortally wounding its commander, Obersturmbannführer Brandt, and killing or wounding almost all of his regimental staff. Brandt, with his doctorate in engineering and pioneering work with camouflage uniforms, had been a staunch pillar of SS-VT from the outset, becoming the first commander of the division's illustrious reconnaissance battalion and upgrading 11th Regiment in a remarkably short time.

AFTER BREACHING THE Stalin Line, the Reich Division was directed to seize the high ground to the east of the town of Yelnya. Whereas previously the division had acted to support the drive of the panzer divisions, it now became the spearhead of the German advance, engaged in the next great battle intended to trap three Soviet armies around Smolensk. As the most easterly point in the German encirclement maneuver, Yelnya would face the full force of Soviet attempts to break through to their comrades in the Smolensk pocket.

Driving forward with the 10th Panzer Division, Reich passed through Yelnya on 21 July. On the following morning Hausser personally briefed his commanders for the assault on the high ground to the east; while the meeting was in progress, they were subjected to a Soviet mortar barrage, two officers being wounded by shell splinters. Throughout the 22nd the "Deutschland" and "Der Führer" Regiments led the attack, gaining their objectives as evening fell. According to the divisional history, "The exceedingly difficult, costly fighting in the burning heat completely exhausted the men of the division. They received exemplary support from the assault guns, which reached the Russian positions without a single remaining round of ammunition."[4]

Ammunition shortages were now a chronic problem for the Germans, as was a shortage of fuel that temporarily grounded the tanks of the adjoining 10th Panzer Division. That this should be the case after just a month's fighting reflected the fundamental weaknesses of the whole logistical system and fatally undermining operational effectiveness. During the coming weeks the artillery commanders at the front were forced to husband their stocks of ammunition at all times.

The initial Soviet counterattack on 23 July pressed hard on the German defenders, while on the following day it threatened to overwhelm them. Unterscharführer Erich Rossner, commander of a 5cm (Pak) anti-tank gun, saw a column of eight Soviet tanks driving toward his position. According to the after-action report:

> He ordered fire to be held until the lead vehicle was within 50 meters. Rossner used the familiar tactic: kill the first vehicle, then the last and, finally, destroy the trapped remainder at leisure. The first Russian tank was hit and "killed," but the second was a flame-throwing vehicle which projected huge gouts of flame at the anti-tank gunners. The Russian crew then leapt from their machine and raced towards the gunners, who grabbed entrenching tools, pistols and grenades, doubling forward to meet the Russian charge. On that bright July morning a small knot of men, Germans and Russians, fought for their lives and when, at last, the Russian tankmen had been killed the SS gunners went back to their Pak and carried on firing until all the Russian tanks had been destroyed.[5]

Rossner later reckoned the entire action had lasted just five minutes; he was subsequently awarded the Knight's Cross.

The moment of crisis came in the late afternoon. The SS troops had successfully held their position, but an army unit, having run out of ammunition, gave way on their left flank, close to the village of Ushakova. This was the most bitterly contested section of the line, the village having changed hands several times since the fighting began. A gap now appeared in the German line; if the Soviets could push sufficient forces through the gap, then the whole German position would be outflanked. Almost all of Reich's reserves had already been committed to the battle, but at 5:00 P.M. Obersturmbannführer Ostendorff, the division's senior staff officer, deployed what forces he had been able to collect: the pioneer battalion; the assault guns "Seydlitz," "Ziethen," and "Derfflinger"; and four antitank guns. Personally leading the battle group, Ostendorff attacked the left side of Ushakova, the assault guns and antitank guns taking on enemy armor and guns while the pioneers fought their way through the village to eject the Soviet infantry and restore the line.

On 25 July the Red Army brought up more artillery and subjected the Yelnya position to massed bombardments that the SS troops had never before encountered. They dug furiously to improve their positions, all the while repulsing further Soviet attacks. By the twenty-seventh, the intensity of the enemy attacks began to diminish, and with the arrival of reinforcements and supplies of ammunition the front line stabilized, taking on the appearance of a World War I battlefield. On 9 August the first Reich units were taken out of the front line, the rest of the division joining them over the next ten days. Casualties for the period 22 July–8 August amounted to 1,663, relatively light given the intensity of the fighting.[6]

The Reich Division and the other formations holding the Yelnya position prevented Soviet attempts to release their comrades trapped in the Smolensk pocket. Approximately 300,000 Soviet troops were captured, but the battle had exhausted Army Group Center. On a wider level, it was now clear to OKH that the Red Army had not collapsed in this opening phase of Barbarossa. It had suffered terrible casualties, but its determination to fight remained undiminished. General Halder, once so confident that the war was nearly won, expressed his doubts as early as 11 August:

The whole situation makes it increasingly plain that we have underestimated the Russian Colossus. This applies to organizational and economic resources, as well as the communications system and, most of all, to the strictly military potential. At the outset of the war we reckoned with about 200 enemy divisions. Now we have already counted 360. These Divisions are not armed [or] equipped according to our standards, and their tactical leadership is often poor. But there they are, and if we smash a dozen of them, the Russians simply put up another dozen.[7]

Despite overoptimistic calls from Guderian and Hoth to push on toward Moscow, Army Group Center required time to reorganize. All the while, the Red Army counterattacked the line held by the Germans to the east of Smolensk, preventing any realistic prospect of an immediate advance toward the Soviet capital.

Throughout August, a fierce debate raged within the German high command regarding the primacy of German objectives. Most of the generals argued for a drive on Moscow, while Hitler favored the seizure of the industrial regions of the Donets basin in the eastern Ukraine, a first step in a drive to capture the oil fields bordering the Caucasus Mountains.

Hitler's focus on the Ukraine grew stronger after receiving intelligence that vast numbers of Soviet troops around Kiev had failed to retreat to relative safety to the east. They were ripe to be destroyed in another encirclement battle using the panzer groups of Guderian and Kleist (diverted from Army Group South). During the middle of August, Hitler's plan was put into effect.

The Reich Division was assigned to Guderian's southward drive, "Der Führer" taking the lead with the rest of the division following. On 7 September "Der Führer" reached Makoshin on the River Desna, defended by a Soviet force attempting to hold open a gap for their comrades to escape the rapidly closing German pincers. During the fight for the village, the SS troops were bombed by the Luftwaffe: "There were frightful casualties and many curses were shouted up at the Stukas."[8] Later in the day an intrepid SS patrol captured the bridge over the Desna, dismantling the explosive charges that were due to be blown and establishing a bridgehead on the far side. Over the next couple of days the bridgehead was strengthened, and on 9 September "Deutschland" broke out in a general exploitation of the battle that led to contact with German armor from Army Group South.

The Kiev encirclement was another military disaster for the Soviet Union, the Germans capturing more than 600,000 enemy soldiers. The Reich Division, meanwhile, was withdrawn from the front on 24 September for rest and a refit.

As the Germans pushed eastward into the Soviet Union, they created a vast area of occupied territory containing many of the enemies of the Nazi state: Soviet soldiers on the run and millions of Jews who were especially populous in the Baltic States, Belorussia, and the Ukraine. It was this behind-the-lines zone that came under Himmler's jurisdiction. As well as the police and Einsatzgruppen death squads, Himmler deployed his own army, the Command Staff of the Reichsführer-SS. Under the overall direction of Kurt Knoblauch, it would provide additional weight in the Nazi program of genocide.

Himmler's private army was deployed across the whole eastern theater. The 1st SS Infantry Brigade initially followed Army Group South into the Ukraine, operating on the southern borders of the Pripet Marshes in antipartisan operations. Toward the end of 1941, it was redeployed within Army Group Center's sector and briefly thrown into the front line during the Soviet winter offensive of 1941–1942 before returning to antipartisan duties. It would later become the cadre for the 18th SS Volunteer Panzergrenadier Division Horst Wessel.

The 2nd SS Infantry Brigade operated with Army Group North, and like the 1st SS Brigade it was also involved in rounding up and killing enemies of the Reich in antipartisan actions. During the winter of 1941–1942, it began to incorporate some of the Germanic Legions from northwest Europe, and in 1942 it began a close association with SS recruits from Latvia, eventually forming the cadre for the 19th Waffen Grenadier Division of the SS.

The Pripet Marshes had been bypassed by the German Army during Operation Barbarossa. The German high command left its pacification to the SS and second-line army units. Himmler seized his opportunity for military action and sent in Obersturmbannführer Hermann Fegelein's SS Cavalry Brigade to bring the area under German control and to liquidate its large Jewish population. Himmler believed the (largely) mounted Cavalry Brigade would be most effective in the boggy terrain of the area.

In this early phase of the war, there were few if any partisans in the Pripet Marshes, so the SS Cavalry Brigade concentrated its activities on the local Jews. On a direct order from Himmler, all Jewish men were to be shot, while "women and children were to be driven into the swamps and drowned." The two cavalry regiments of the brigade swept through the marshes, killing and destroying as they went, following Himmler's orders to the letter. One subsequent report on the atrocities read: "A farmer stated that when the women did not want to move on and held up their children to keep them from drowning, the soldiers ruthlessly machine gunned those wading in the waters." By the end of September the SS Cavalry Brigade was withdrawn from the Pripet Marshes, having killed as many as 23,700 people in its short but bloody reign of terror.[9]

On 29 September the brigade was dispatched to Toropets, roughly 120 miles north of Smolensk, operating on the northern flank of Army Group Center. It was here that Fegelein's cavalry had to contend with real partisans for the first time. Their pacification mission was not particularly effective, however. In a standard tactical set piece carried on throughout Eastern Europe and the Balkans, partisan groups attacked an enemy weak point and then melted away, leaving the inhabitants of the nearest town or village to face the wrath of the vengeful Germans. The SS cavalry units caught few partisans but killed many civilians.

As THE SS Cavalry Brigade was advancing toward Toropets, so Army Group Center prepared what it hoped would be the knockout blow of the war: the drive on Moscow, code-named Operation Typhoon. The offensive opened on 2 October, and in keeping with its name the Germans advanced at a whirlwind pace. Guderian's Second Panzer Army scored a major success at Bryansk, while the Third Panzer Army, cooperating with the redeployed Fourth Panzer Army, developed another encirclement battle around the town of Vyazma.

The Reich and 10th Panzer Division captured the town of Gshatsk (east of Vyazma), with SS troops riding into battle on the tanks of their army comrades, before penetrating the outer line of the Soviet Moscow Defense Position. During the attack, the Germans came under fire from massed batteries of Katyusha rockets, the experience described by one SS officer: "As I had not dug a slit trench I just flung myself behind a tree and watched the terrifyingly beautiful display of rocket shells. The memory of the smell of the high-explosive and of black, red and violet colors as the shells detonated and took on the shape of tulip heads will always remain in my mind."[10]

On 14 October, Paul Hausser came forward to inspect the advance made by "Der Führer," but on arrival at the regimental command post he was seriously wounded by Soviet tank fire. Hausser survived his wounds—losing an eye in the process—but this marked the end of his command of the Reich Division. When he returned to duty he was earmarked to lead the new SS Panzer Corps, command of the division passing to Wilhelm Bittrich, CO of the "Deutschland" Regiment.

The Vyazma encirclement yielded as many as 500,000 Soviet prisoners, and for a while it seemed that Moscow would fall to Hitler. The Red Army was badly shaken, but the Germans had also suffered heavy casualties, and with a growing shortage of fuel, ammunition, and serviceable vehicles, the advance faltered. The deteriorating weather was also a factor, as outlined in the "Der Führer" regimental history: "Each day the weather became less favorable: heavy snow showers mixed with rain; light frost during the night; temperatures above freezing during the day; the roads and terrain were transformed into clinging mud."[11]

On 22 October "Der Führer" pushed on through the mud to capture Borisovo before being forced to halt until the ground was sufficiently frozen to resume motorized operations. While at Borisovo, an eyewitness described how Reich troops rounded up the village leaders and heads of collective farms and had them shot on the basis that they were partisans.[12] It would seem that the frustrations produced by the slowing of the offensive were making themselves felt throughout the division.

As the troops of the division "eagerly awaited the winter, for the frost that would make the ground passable again," it underwent a basic reorganization.[13] Reinforcements had failed to keep up with casualties, and as a consequence the 11th Infantry Regiment was disbanded, its remaining soldiers distributed among "Deutschland" and "Der Führer."

By 7 November, with the weather becoming progressively colder and the terrain firmer, limited offensive operations resumed, the division preparing itself for the push to capture Moscow. The order came on the seventeenth, as temperatures were falling fast and the ground was rock hard. Supported by newly arrived Nebelwerfer rocket launchers and the last two serviceable assault guns, "Prinz Eugen" and "Yorck," the SS troops drove over the snow-covered fields to engage the enemy. Progress was good, although the Germans were disconcerted to find they were facing fresh, well-equipped units that had recently arrived from Siberia.

By 25 November Reich had fought its way to Istra, only twenty-five miles from the Soviet capital and a stronghold in Moscow's inner defensive ring. It was famous for its New Jerusalem Monastery, a complex of religious buildings complete with golden cupolas and towers, surrounded by a sixteen-foot wall now manned by Red Army troops. The SS infantry breached the walls and fought their way through the monastery buildings and into the town itself. The Soviets were forced to retreat when the twenty-eight remaining tanks of the 10th Panzer Division pushed around the town and threatened to encircle the defenders.

Once beyond Istra the Germans prepared for the final assault. Even with the reallocation of soldiers from the 11th Regiment, casualties were sufficiently heavy that companies were down to twenty-five or thirty men each. As with the rest of the German armed forces, the men of the Reich Division lacked suitable winter clothing to fend of temperatures that by the end of November were regularly dropping to minus 20 degrees Fahrenheit. But despite the cold and rising numbers of frostbite cases, the Germans in front of Moscow fought on with undiminished resolve.

On 29 November the offensive was resumed, and by 4 December the suburb of Lenino had been taken by Reich and the 10th Panzer Division, the latter now down to just seven tanks. On the same day, the Reich motorcycle battalion reached a terminus of the Moscow tram network, roughly twelve miles from the city center. The "Deutschland" regimental history reported: "In the bright winter weather one could make out the Kremlin towers. My God! How close we were to that historic objective."[14]

But this was as far as the Germans were to go. To the indignation of the SS soldiers, an order to retreat was issued on 6 December; all the pain and suffering they had endured over the past months seemed to be for nothing. Yet the German high command had no other option. The Red Army had launched its great winter offensive on 5 December, and the exhausted German troops on the front line around Moscow were in real danger of being overwhelmed. On Bittrich's instructions, the battered SS forces fell back to Istra, and when the full might of the Soviet offensive became apparent, the retreat continued to the more defensible Ruza Line, reached on 21 December. From this position the Reich Division would spend the winter fending off waves of Soviet attacks.

Chapter 15

HOLDING THE LINE: THE EASTERN FRONT, 1941–1942

B Y EARLY DECEMBER 1941 the German Army on the Eastern Front was exhausted, its forces stretched to the limit. Stalin's Red Army, by contrast, had built up substantial strategic reserves. Among these were divisions from Siberia, released from their eastern deployment after the intelligence discovery that Japan was about to attack the United States and not the Soviet Union, as originally feared. The Red Army launched its great winter offensive along the entire length of the Eastern Front, although the main weight of the attack fell on Army Group Center on 5 December.

Senior German field commanders issued orders for withdrawals to less exposed positions. The Führer had not been consulted, however, and when informed of the German retreat, he flew into one his increasingly violent rages, countermanding the withdrawal orders and insisting that his troops stand their ground whatever the cost. Hitler's fury was followed by retribution. Bock followed Rundstedt into retirement in a wave of sackings that included Guderian and two other army commanders. The commander in chief of the German Army, von Brauchitsch, had already been dismissed, his position absorbed by Hitler.

By the end of December, the Soviet offensive began to run out of steam, with a semblance of normality returning to the German front line. Hitler took full credit for this, increasing his already expansive self-belief

177

in his abilities as a general. As 1941 drew to a close, Hitler could boast that his forces had inflicted terrible casualties on the Soviet armed forces and captured vast swaths of territory. Yet, with hindsight, Barbarossa must be seen as a failure. Despite the massive material damage inflicted on the Soviet Union, Germany had suffered heavily too, more than 900,000 casualties sustained in the period from 22 June 1941 to 31 January 1942.[1]

The German plan for Barbarossa had called for the destruction of the Red Army to the west of the Dvina-Dnieper line in the first phase of the campaign. Franz Halder, the army chief of staff, had made this clear, noting on 17 March 1941: "We must score successes from the very start. There must be no reverses."[2] And while the Germans had achieved a series of stunning encirclement victories in western Russia and the Ukraine, the Red Army had not been destroyed, remaining an effective fighting force throughout 1941.

By failing to secure victory in the opening campaign, Germany was fated to lose the war. It could never match the economic and demographic might of the Soviet Union, and the Red Army's subsequent growth in size, confidence, and ability would coincide with the slow but inexorable decline of the Wehrmacht. And when Hitler declared war on the United States on 11 December 1941, his destruction was guaranteed.

The Führer's contempt for the higher echelons of the German Army was now in the open. It did not, however, extend to the Waffen-SS, whose performance during Barbarossa greatly impressed him. His earlier misgivings over Himmler's requests for the mass expansion of the Waffen-SS gave way to a new idea of inducting German youth into the organization. During 1942 discussions were initiated for the formation of two panzergrenadier divisions, to be raised from young men engaged in compulsory duty in Germany's labor service. In December of that year the two divisions were formally authorized, eventually to become 9th and 10th SS Panzer Divisions. Confirming Hitler's acceptance of Waffen-SS expansion was his decision to allow the development of an SS corps system during 1942.

On a personal level, Hitler was especially pleased with the performance of his Leibstandarte and its commander, Sepp Dietrich. In January 1942 Hitler invited him to fly to Berlin, where he personally awarded him the

Oak Leaves to his Knight's Cross. Lionized by the Nazi Party, Göring publicly applauded Dietrich during his own birthday celebrations, while Goebbels trilled that he made "one think of a Napoleonic general."[3] Hitler, for his part, described him as a "national institution."[4] A short while afterward Hitler secretly awarded Dietrich 100,000 Reichsmarks for "special services." Hitler gave all his leading commanders lavish secret gifts to tie them to the Nazi system, and Dietrich was no exception.[5]

Praise for the military performance of the Waffen-SS in the Soviet Union extended beyond Nazi Party circles. The endorsement of Leibstandarte by General Kempf during the Uman encirclement battle was joined by that of General von Mackensen. He wrote an unsolicited letter to Himmler expressing his admiration for the SS formation: "Herr Reichsführer, I can assure you that Leibstandarte enjoys an outstanding reputation not only with its superiors, but also among its Army comrades. Every division wishes it had Leibstandarte as its neighbor, as much during the attack as in defense. Its inner discipline, its cool daredevilry, its cheerful enterprise, its unshakeable firmness in a crisis, its exemplary toughness, its camaraderie (which deserves special praise)—all these are outstanding and cannot be surpassed."[6]

The Wiking Division was also held in high regard, not least from one of its opponents, subsequently captured by the Germans. Major General Pawel Artemenko informed his captors: "The Wiking's fighting power was characterized as fabulous. One battalion of these SS would easily smash the [Soviet] Army's best regiments. They breathed a sigh of relief when the SS was relieved [by other German formations]."[7] This was true of the Totenkopf Division, which, according to a German staff officer, was consistently ranked at the top of the Red Army's Capability Assessment Tables.[8]

These favorable assessments of the Waffen-SS came with a high price in casualties. By the beginning of December 1941, total Waffen-SS losses for the campaign had reached 38,000 killed, wounded, and missing, and at the end of the winter, even allowing for reinforcements, most frontline units were less than two-thirds of their regulation strength.

THE TROOPS SHIVERING at the front were particularly unfortunate that the winter of 1941–1942 was more severe than usual, with temperatures along the entire line dropping between minus 20 and minus 40 degrees Fahrenheit on a regular basis. In early February—in positions held by the Reich Division—the temperature apparently reached an extreme low of minus 65 degrees.[9]

Unlike their army comrades, the Waffen-SS at least enjoyed the advantage of purloined clothing supplied from the concentration-camp system. In December Leibstandarte received a shipment of winter clothes, gathered by the SS in the Polish General Government,[10] while in early January Totenkopf was provided with clothing drawn from SS warehouses in Latvia.[11] But these shipments were enough to equip only relatively small numbers of troops.

Early in 1942 official measures were made to rectify the clothing shortage, but for most soldiers the winter-issue clothing arrived when the worst was over. Hendrik Verton, a Dutch volunteer in the "Westland" Regiment, recalled that "at the end of January and beginning of February, the long-promised winter clothing arrived from home. It included fabulous fur hats, padded jackets, thermal boots and warm pullovers, as well as balaclavas knitted in haste and faith by the girls and women at home. But it all arrived too late."[12]

The easiest way to find suitable clothing was to improvise and take padded jackets, fur hats, and felt boots from the many Soviet corpses littering the battlefield. The Germans increasingly looked to Russian solutions to counter winter conditions. Sleighs drawn by the hardy *panje* pony were sometimes the only means to transport heavy goods, which included munitions and food as well as individuals. In one instance in early 1942, a panzer division had barely a serviceable vehicle in its inventory but instead relied on 2,000 *panje* ponies.[13] The ordinary soldier dragged "Finnish" sleds behind him in the snow. They resembled small boats and could carry weapons, ammunition, and personal effects with minimal physical effort.

The sudden drop in nighttime temperatures made the acquisition of shelter essential if troops were to survive until morning. This dictated a new daily tactical cycle, as Hendrik Verton recalled: "In the afternoon we no longer fought to advance but to find a warm place for the night."[14] The artillery of both sides made a point of firing on any potential shelters the enemy might use. For those left out in the open, the consequences were often catastrophic. During his march to rejoin the "Westland" Regiment, Verton and a comrade had become separated from the main column and were struggling to find their way through thick snow:

> To our relief we stumbled on a German bus. It lay slanted to one side of the road and the door was frozen, so that we could not open it. We scratched the frosty snow from the windows and looked inside. We saw German soldiers sitting in the seats, wrapped in blankets. All had their collars turned up to their ears, some sitting upright. Of the driver there was no sign. Had he sought help and returned? Was he lost in the snow? All had a somewhat strange yellow pallor and there was no sign of life. But any help that we could have given was no longer needed, for rigor mortis had set in. We slowly realized that all had died in their sleep.[15]

The two SS soldiers departed "the metal coffin on wheels, shaken to the core," although they were later picked up by a German *panje* column delivering artillery shells to the front.

The winter of 1941–1942 placed enormous strain on Germany's armed forces, and only the better units were able to endure these conditions and still function effectively. Erwin Bartmann of Leibstandarte certainly believed this was the case in his division: "In contrast to the Wehrmacht, most of our comrades were about the same age and our leaders, although often only ten years or so older than the men under their command, displayed excellent leadership abilities. This was a great advantage when things got difficult, we pulled together to overcome problems as best we could."[16]

Leibstandarte did, however, have an easier time than most other formations on the Eastern Front during the 1941–1942 winter. The main weight of the Soviet offensive lay well to the north. Dietrich's men faced only occasional local attacks to keep them on their toes, while taking part in the usual patrols and trench raids that characterized fighting from fixed positions.

As part of a general upgrading of the elite Waffen-SS formations from motorized to panzergrenadier divisions, Dietrich was informed that Leibstandarte would be receiving a new tank battalion to be crewed by volunteers recruited from the Hitler Youth. Leibstandarte's fifth battalion, based in Berlin for ceremonial duties, was now assigned a combat role and dispatched to the Eastern Front. During the late spring of 1942, as OKH prepared for a resumption of offensive operations, Hitler decided to withdraw Leibstandarte for a complete reorganization, and in July it entrained for France.

Steiner's Wiking Division, deployed a little farther north on the Mius Line, repulsed a number of minor enemy attacks in January and February. More serious was a Soviet breakthrough on 18 January on either side of Isjum, close to the key city of Kharkov. A Kampfgruppe based around "Germania's" I Battalion was dispatched northward to help contain the Soviet threat. It was joined by a battery of artillery and the newly arrived assault-gun battery. Under the command of Sturmbannführer August Dieckmann, the battle group was battered by repeated Soviet attacks. The StuG IIIs were destroyed by vastly superior tank forces, while the "Germania" battalion was virtually annihilated in a series of defensive actions that ended on 25 February. On its return to the Wiking Division in March 1942, what remained of the Kampfgruppe was rebuilt, with reinforcements arriving from Germany.

FARTHER NORTH, THE Reich Division improved its defenses around Ruza. "Where shovels and picks failed against the hard-frozen ground," wrote "Der Führer's" regimental history, "excavation was done with blasting cartridges and anti-tank mines. After three days of indescribably hard work, which was repeatedly interrupted by the need to repel enemy attacks, the regiment was ready to defend the Ruza position." The defenses were sufficient to deter further Red Army assaults, which by 24 December had petered out into long-range artillery bombardments. The regimental history described conditions for the troops: "So the regiment approached Christmas of 1941—frozen pea soup, frozen bread, boots and socks almost completely worn out, supply very much in question on account of a shortage of locomotives able to operate in cold weather, and huge snow drifts on all main and secondary roads. Nevertheless, at this point the regiment finally received some winter equipment: fur-lined parkas and pants, fur-lined boots and fur coats. Transport aircraft of the Luftwaffe (Ju 52s) dropped extra rations for Christmas, however most landed in enemy territory."[17]

In mid-January the Reich Division was withdrawn from Ruza to new positions around Rzhev, soon to be the focus for a renewal of the Soviet winter offensive. The SS soldiers were immediately thrown into a counterattack, and despite the fact that they had had almost no rest since the start of Operation Barbarossa, they fought with their customary tigerish determination. Morale had slumped when the division had been ordered to abort its attack on Moscow, but the resumption of active operations led to a resurgence in fighting spirit, with the "Deutschland" Regiment noting that there was "a fabulous feeling among the troops."[18]

The division was spread in a line, with "Der Führer"—just 650 active infantrymen under the command of Obersturmbannführer Otto Kumm—deployed close to the frozen River Volga by the village of Klepino. That the regiment was defending a key position was confirmed by regular inspection visits from the Ninth Army commander, Colonel General Model. At the end of January the Red Army launched its offensive, which would last for three weeks. Fortunately for the SS defenders, they would face not a concentrated assault but rather a succession of uncoordinated attacks that were repulsed with relative ease.

On 17 February Kumm was informed by Gruppenführer Kleinheisterkamp, who had succeeded Bittrich as Reich's commander, that his battered regiment was to be relieved the following day. Of Kumm's small force, 150 had been killed and most of the rest either wounded or incapacitated by frostbite. When Kumm reported back to divisional headquarters, General Model was present and asked for the strength of "Der Fuhrer." Kumm replied that his regiment was outside the HQ office, and when Model looked through the window he could see just thirty-five men standing on the parade ground.[19]

Meanwhile, the remainder of the Reich Division continued its defense of the Rzhev salient. There was little letup in the renewed Soviet attacks until the end of March. Some idea of the toughness of the ordinary soldier and the close officer-man relationship of the Waffen-SS can be gleaned in this account from Georg Schwinke during the battle for "Jackboot Wood" on 23 March:

> I was feeling terrible. My head buzzed like a bee-hive from where I had been buried when a heavy shell scored a direct hit on our dug-out. I had been slightly wounded in the head but had pulled the shrapnel fragment out of my skull. In addition, a bullet had wounded me slightly in the right leg during the day's attack. When I reached Company HQ my officer asked why I was limping. He tried to take off my jackboot but the leg was too swollen. He cut the boot off, and pus and blood poured out from a leg which was now colored dark-blue and black . . . frostbite. Frost had got into the wound on my leg, entering a wound so slight that normally a sticking plaster would have covered it.[20]

The remnants of the division remained in place until 1 June, when they received orders to withdraw from the front and return to Germany for a complete overhaul.

Deployed close to the Reich Division was Hermann Fegelein's SS Cavalry Brigade, engaged in antipartisan duties since the autumn of 1941. Before the Red Army's winter offensive Fegelein had been in a positive mood, especially after the arrival of reinforcements and supporting units, which included signals and medical companies and an antiaircraft battery. His optimism reached new heights in a report written in December 1941: "The Brigade with its current equipment and armament and in its actual strength has the value of 1–2 front-line divisions."[21]

When the Soviet armored thrust broke into the Cavalry Brigade's lines on 17 January, the SS troopers were swept aside. They lacked the experience, numbers, and firepower to have any hope of defending their positions. In an attempt to hold the village of Basry, the brigade rounded up Soviet prisoners from a nearby holding camp and sent them forward as human shields, all killed in the Soviet advance.[22]

In March 1942 Fegelein was withdrawn from the front to take up a new role as an inspector for mounted troops. The remainder of the brigade was left at the front as a battalion-size Kampfgruppe under a new commander, Sturmbannführer August Zehender. By 1 April the brigade's strength was down to 421 men, although plans were being made to reform and expand the formation into a full SS cavalry division for further service on the Eastern Front.

———————

THE SOVIET STORM fell upon Army Group North on 7 January 1942. The Totenkopf Division was spread across a relatively wide area, and as the Red Army offensive developed it was divided in two: one smaller element—including infantry, engineer, reconnaissance, and artillery units—was based at Staraya Russa, the rest of the division stationed farther east around Demyansk. The SS troops holding Staraya Russa took the brunt of the opening attack but defended the position so firmly that they pushed the Soviet advance farther east. They would cling to their positions throughout the entire offensive. Hauptsturmführer Max Seela— one of the heroes of the battle for Lushno back in September—was again an inspiration for the defenders.

While the Germans clung to Demyansk, the Red Army surged forward on either side of the position. By 12 January Demyansk was increasingly isolated, and Field Marshal von Leeb, Army Group North commander, asked OKH for permission to withdraw the troops to a safer and better-defendable position. Hitler refused any retreat whatsoever, and after some strained exchanges Leeb's resignation was accepted (replaced by Colonel General von Küchler). Leeb's departure on 17 January marked the demise of the last of the three army group commanders who had led the invasion of the Soviet Union in June 1941.

Küchler, however, lacked the reserves to help the defenders of Demyansk. On 20 January advance units from the two Soviet pincers met, and by 8 February the Soviet encirclement was complete. As well as most of Eicke's Totenkopf, the trapped forces included the bulk of five army divisions, totaling 95,000 troops with as many as 10,000 auxiliaries in addition. The Red Army had turned the tables on the Germans, who, for the first time, would be involved in a Kesselschlacht (cauldron battle).

Hitler ordered the men in the pocket to stand their ground, promising them resupply from the air while a relief force was assembled. The pocket contained two usable airfields, and with a short gap of between thirty and fifty miles separating the pocket from the main German lines, the Luftwaffe was able to conduct a fairly regular shuttle service to Demyansk. Supplies and reinforcements were flown in and the wounded taken out.

All the while, the Soviets maintained a tight grip around Demyansk. Much to Eicke's irritation, his force was divided in two, one group under the command of Max Simon, assigned to stiffen the line in the east of the pocket, while Eicke led the slightly larger group on the western side. As the days turned to weeks, the SS troops repulsed the Soviet attacks with a determination that earned them the respect of their army comrades.

Meanwhile, a relief force—based around a reinforced X Corps—was being assembled, though not ready for action until 21 March. After a promising start, the relief effort stalled in the face of determined Soviet resistance, and it was only on 14 April that it captured Ramusho, the half-way point to the Demyansk pocket. This was the signal for the defenders to mount their own attack to link up with X Corps.

As Eicke's units were closest to the relief force, they led the breakout. While the operation was in progress the spring thaw began, as described by Totenkopf engineer officer Karl Ullrich: "For all practical purposes there were no longer any roads. The streams were bursting their banks; the thaw had turned fields and meadows into mud and swamps. Wherever there was a small depression, a lake soon appeared. The dugouts and bunkers sank into the morass. No one had worn dry clothes for days."[23]

Offensive operations were now all the more difficult, the SS troops struggling through chest-high water and mud. Eicke drove his men onward with his customary vigor, yet the advance was pitifully slow, little more than a mile a day. On 21 April Totenkopf soldiers finally reached the swollen River Lovat, now more than a half-mile wide, with troops of the X Corps just visible on the far bank. On the following day supplies were ferried over the river, officially marking the end of the seventy-three-day siege.[24]

For Hitler, his order that the Germans hold Demyansk had been triumphantly vindicated, a success that would influence his later decision to defend Stalingrad, but, in this case, with disastrous consequences. Hitler oversaw a generous distribution of medals for the defenders, which included a then unprecedented eleven Knight's Crosses for Totenkopf. But while the siege was over, the fighting continued with little respite. The Red Army attempted to sever the land bridge that connected the former pocket to the main German lines; so tenuous was this link that German sources continued to refer to the salient as the Demyansk "pocket."

After the razing of the siege, Eicke made the first of several fruitless demands that his men be withdrawn from the front to recuperate. The division in early May had a strength of just 6,700 men, roughly a third of its regulation figure. And of these men, their physical and mental state was greatly reduced. Dr. Eckert, a medical officer in the division, concluded that as a result of food shortages, intense cold, and inadequate shelter, 30 percent of the battalion's soldiers were unfit for military service, while the remainder were desperately in need of rest. Without a hint of irony, he compared the physical state of the worst of his soldiers to the inmates he had come across as a concentration-camp doctor.[25]

The Totenkopf Division did at least receive some reinforcements, which included the Danish Legion (Freikorps Danmark), flown into Demyansk on 8 May 1942. On 22 May the Danes were committed to a local offensive alongside the Totenkopf reconnaissance battalion, a successful action that inflicted a sharp blow on the Soviet forces opposite them. The legion's commander, Christian von Schalburg, was killed on 2 June during a Soviet counterattack. His replacement, the German Hans von Lettow-Vorbeck (nephew of the German World War I hero), was killed a few days later in the battle for Bolshoi Dubowyzi, an action that cost the Danish battalion 346 casualties.[26]

With its third commander, Knud Børge Martinsen, the Danish Legion settled down to the positional warfare typical of the salient during the summer of 1942. Heavy rainfall through much of the period turned the scrub into swamp, the troops sloshing around in mud and water on a near-continuous basis, with the attendant miseries of dysentery, malaria, and swamp fever. Per Sørensen, a soldier in the 1st Company, wrote home with this complaint: "Unfortunately it has been raining for two days and nights in a row and most of the men fled their bunkers last night around one o'clock, because they feared drowning."[27]

Despite these wretched conditions, the Danes held their section of the line, earning a commendation from the German corps command in Demyansk, which noted that they had displayed "exemplary toughness and endurance."[28] But there was a price to be paid: from an original strength of 702 soldiers, the legion had been reduced to 219 officers and men by the end of July. It was then that the legion was withdrawn from Demyansk for rest and reorganization back in Denmark.[29]

Eicke was recalled to Germany in June, as his wounds had failed to heal while in the field. Eicke handed the division over to Max Simon, and while Eicke was reluctant to leave his men in such difficult conditions, he welcomed the chance to argue his case to his superiors on a personal level. Following meetings with both Hitler and Himmler, Eicke was assured that should conditions permit, the Totenkopf Division would be relieved in August and re-formed as a fully equipped panzergrenadier division, complete with a tank battalion. In July recruits were sent to the training grounds at Sennelager for the establishment of new infantry units, while officers assigned to the tank battalion began training at Buchenwald.

While Eicke waited impatiently for the withdrawal and reorganization to take place, the existing division was facing yet more Soviet attacks, preventing any summer transfer to Germany. Common sense called for a German withdrawal from the exposed salient—little more than a few ruined villages in a swamp—but Hitler's prestige was at stake and the defense continued.

Standartenführer Simon tried to maintain a grip over his troops, but declining morale led to increased instances of theft and self-inflicted wounds. The strain of command began to tell on Simon, too, evident in a series of increasingly despairing letters sent to Eicke. Shades of paranoia fell across Simon, who began to believe that the army was deliberately sacrificing his men for its own advantage. The only good news, Simon reported, was the covert removal of 170 key personnel from Demyansk, so that they could be sent to the re-forming Totenkopf in Germany (officers returning from leave or convalescence were redirected to the "new" division).[30]

Eicke demanded to be allowed to return to Demyansk, but Himmler refused and sent him on indefinite convalescent leave. With Eicke fuming on the sidelines, the remains of the Totenkopf Division fought on. In early September the Soviet assaults lost impetus, although the division's combat strength had been reduced to that of an infantry battalion.[31] With enemy pressure removed from the salient, Hitler finally agreed to Totenkopf's withdrawal, which began in mid-October 1942.

The salient was quietly abandoned in March 1943, rendering the Germans' heroic defense largely irrelevant. There was understandable bitterness among the Totenkopf survivors when they heard the news. One of them wrote, "The men of Demyansk considered the great sacrifice [was] made in vain. Words can't describe what the men in the Demyansk pocket suffered and experienced from winter 1941–42 on."[32]

The removal of Totenkopf was part of the transformation of the best Waffen-SS field formations into panzergrenadier and then fully fledged panzer divisions. Other Waffen-SS formations still remained at the front, however, among them the SS foreign legions and the Wiking Panzergrenadier Division, the latter earmarked for a lead role in Hitler's summer offensive of 1942.

Chapter 16

AT THE EDGE:
THE EASTERN FRONT, 1942–1943

For Germany's 1942 summer campaign Hitler focused his resources on a drive into the southern Soviet Union. The Wiking Division would help spearhead the advance toward the Caucasus Mountains, crossing the old geographic boundary from Europe into Asia. Elsewhere on the Eastern Front, Germany would remain on the defensive. In Army Group North's sector, the recently arrived SS national legions would face the full might of the Red Army.

The Flemish Legion (Legion Flandern) was the first of the SS national legions to see action, subordinated to the 2nd SS Infantry Brigade. It was organized as a reinforced motorized infantry battalion, with the standard three rifle companies and heavy-weapons company, plus an antitank company (with heavy mortars). Although dispatched eastward in November 1941, a shortage of vehicles and the necessity of acclimatizing to the bitter winter conditions meant the legion was initially held back behind the front, nominally engaged in antipartisan duties. The Soviet offensive in January 1942 transformed the situation, with all available forces—including the Flemish Legion—rushing forward to defend the Volkhov Line.[1]

Under the command of Sturmbannführer Michael Lippert, the Flemish troops fought alongside the Spanish Division, volunteers from Franco's Spain under German Army direction. The men of the Flemish

Legion had received only the most basic training, and while they fought with commendable tenacity their lack of combat experience brought censure from their German operations officer. A report of March 1942 criticized the battalion's uncertain leadership and poor coordination with other units. By June, however, lessons seemed to have been learned, and the battalion was praised for its combat skills. At this point, the Germans had gone over to the offensive, encircling the Soviet Second Shock Army. A breakout was attempted, but it failed miserably, and in early July the pocket was liquidated.

Some six months on the front line had greatly reduced the Flemish Legion; its original strength of just over a 1,000 had fallen to a combat deployment of 13 officers, 26 NCOs, and 288 men.[2] Lippert had been one of the casualties, replaced by Obersturmbannführer Konrad Schellong. A former soldier in the Totenkopf's "Oberbayern" Standarte, he would continue to lead Flemish troops throughout the war. Despite the heavy casualties sustained by the battalion, the men were given little opportunity for rest but instead were sent into line on the Leningrad front. Reinforcements arrived from Belgium to bring the unit back up to strength, and it remained in this static position through the winter of 1942–1943, helping repel a Soviet offensive south of Lake Ladoga in February. By early spring, the Flemish Legion was reduced to less than half strength, and with no prospect of immediate reinforcement it was transferred to the SS Polizei Division until withdrawal from the Eastern Front in April 1943.

The Danish Legion (Freikorps Danmark) had won its spurs fighting with the Totenkopf Division in the Demyansk salient. Withdrawn from Demyansk at the end of July 1942, the battalion returned to Copenhagen, receiving a generally hostile reception from the Danish people, who, in the main, considered the "Crusade against Bolshevism" as collaboration with a hostile power.

Transferred from Denmark in the fall of 1942, the Danish Legion was reorganized, and by October it could field approximately 1,100 officers and men. In November it returned to the Eastern Front, engaging in antipartisan sweeps with the 1st SS Infantry Brigade. In December the brigade took part in a failed attempt to rescue a German force trapped in the rail junction of Veliki-Luki. After that, the Danes within the 1st SS Brigade settled down in the trenches and outposts between Veliki-Luki and Newel. They departed the front on 24 March 1943, to be disbanded a couple of months later.

In the Norwegian Legion (Legion Norwegen), uncertain relations between the volunteers and their German commanders continued after reaching the front at Leningrad as part of the 2nd SS Infantry Brigade. To the Germans, the men from the fjords proved to be awkward individualists who failed to conform to military demands with the alacrity that was expected. Vidkun Quisling, Norway's fascist leader, also soured Norwegian-German relations. He repeatedly argued that Norwegian participation in the war against the Soviet Union should be rewarded by increasing levels of national independence. Apart from the fact that Hitler and Himmler instinctively opposed any form of national autonomy, the Norwegian contribution to the SS remained far too small for any consideration to be given to such a notion.

The five-company-strong Norwegian Legion was deployed on the Leningrad front in February–March 1942, subsequently becoming part of the 2nd SS Infantry Brigade. Jutte Olafsen, the former teacher suborned into the SS, was taken out on patrols into no-man's-land to prepare him for any subsequent action, but most of his time was spent in a quiet sector: "Our lives then took on a routine, for day after day we were either on watch or sleeping in the dug-outs, with very little sign of the enemy."[3]

The absence of enemy pressure could not last indefinitely, and a few weeks after their arrival at the front the Norwegians found themselves under fire. Olafsen's account of the Soviet assault revealed his own fears during the action, the high quality of the German NCOs organizing the defense, and the effectiveness of the machine guns and antitank guns providing fire support:

> I heard a whistle which meant the Russians were coming. I was as usual very frightened, I'm sure we all were. But we leapt out of our holes and into the firing trench as the German NCOs rushed along to get us organized. Our training had included this kind of thing and the NCOs told us to keep calm as the Russians would be stopped. Our anti-tank guns were blazing away from concealed positions and two of the enemy tanks went up in flames. The noise was tremendous, one great racket as we opened fire with all our weapons and we saw lots of Russians staggering

and falling about, but many more came on. Most of the execution was done by our machine guns.

Our NCOs were shouting at the Russians, partly to encourage us I believe, but still the remnants came on, and these were now firing with rifles and machine carbines, and you could hear the whistle and whine of the bullets. The remaining Russian tanks were knocked out but not before one of them reached our lines where its guns did a lot of damage. It was then attacked by our resolute NCOs and went up in flames. It happened in about five or ten minutes, and during that time the Russians had lost 12 tanks, all T-34s, and I don't know how many hundred men. I sat down in the trench and drank some water and the German NCOs went through the trench system making sure we were in good shape.[4]

The Norwegians remained on the Leningrad front throughout 1942 and into early 1943. A steady drain of casualties was not countered by sufficient numbers of replacements, and the battalion's combat effectiveness steadily declined. Added to this was a similar decline in the unit's motivation, with only 20 percent of the volunteers being prepared to extend their period of service.[5] And while a "ski company" of Norwegians was raised to serve with the SS Nord Division in northern Finland, the prospects for the Norwegian Legion as part of Army Group North were not promising. In March 1943 it was withdrawn to Germany.

The Netherlands Legion (Legion Niederlande) comprised a full three-battalion infantry regiment just under 3,000 men strong. Arriving at the front in January 1942, it took part in holding the assault by the Soviet Second Army and then eliminating it in the Volkhov pocket. General Seyffardt, the legion's commander, had remained in the Netherlands to supervise further recruitment but was assassinated by the Dutch resistance on 6 February. He was replaced briefly by Otto Reich—a former comrade of Dietrich's and one of the SS executioners during the Night of the Long Knives—and then by Obersturmbannführer Josef Fitzthum, who had briefly led the Flemish Legion. More sensitive to the needs of a non-German force, Fitzthum proved an effective and generally popular commander of the Netherlands Legion.

At the end of July the Netherlands Legion was redeployed farther north to the Leningrad sector, where it joined other national contingents as part of the 2nd SS Infantry Brigade. For most of the remainder of 1942 the Dutch troops were engaged in static positional fighting.

In January 1943 the Red Army launched an offensive to relieve the siege of Leningrad. The Dutch troops were heavily involved, their antitank guns prominent in the defense. Recently appointed as gun-crew leader, nineteen-year-old Geradus Mooyman proved a skilled tank hunter. Equipped with the latest 7.5cm Pak 40 antitank guns, the well-dug-in Dutch troops had little difficulty halting the repeated Soviet assaults.

On the first day of action Mooyman knocked out two T-34s, and by the close of the offensive in mid-February he had amassed a combined figure of twenty-three destroyed Soviet tanks. On 20 February 1943 Mooyman became the first foreigner to be awarded the Knight's Cross. An exultant Himmler whisked the teenage hero back to the Netherlands for an extended propaganda tour to increase the still modest number of Dutchmen coming forward for SS service. Himmler also had other ideas for the Netherlands Legion, which was taken out of the line in April 1943, the last of the SS legions to depart the Eastern Front.

Despite extended teething problems, the national legions under SS control had fought well on the Eastern Front, but they were too small to effectively operate on their own and so were combined with the two SS infantry brigades. The legions' German commanders also resented political interference from the various national politicians who had been part of the legion concept and maintained close ties with their soldiers.

As Gottlob Berger began a new recruitment drive in early 1943, Himmler decided to abandon the legion concept and instead develop a new Germanic division on similar lines to that of Wiking, which had proved such a success in the Ukraine. Although predominantly a formation of German Reich nationals and Volksdeutsche, Wiking's contingent of Germanic soldiers was seen as an example that might successfully be developed further if sufficient recruits could be found.

WHILE THE LEGIONS had played a minor and static role in the northern sectors of the Eastern Front, the Wiking Division would win further laurels in the drive to the Caucasus Mountains and then in the defensive fighting in the southern Ukraine during the winter of 1942–1943. The spring of 1942 was a relatively quiet time for Wiking, Steiner incorporating lessons learned from the Barbarossa fighting. Among these was an organizational change to "Westland," converting it into a "light regiment" of two five-company battalions, the fifth company acting as the heavy-weapons unit containing pioneer, infantry-gun, and "attack" platoons.

New arrivals included a battalion of Finnish infantry and an assault-gun battery, to replace the StuG IIIs lost in the February fighting south of Kharkov. And in June, with only a few weeks to spare before the opening of the new campaign, the division received its panzer battalion (Abteilung) under the command of Sturmbannführer Johannes Mühlenkamp. Hausser and Steiner had long campaigned for their divisions to have a tank capability, enabling them to act independently without help from other panzer units.

Mühlenkamp was an ideal panzer commander, combining an aggressive attacking impulse with sound tactical knowledge. An early member of the SS-VT, his prowess as a competition motorcycle rider led to command of "Germania's" motorcycle company. After recovering from wounds suffered during the advance on Moscow, Mühlenkamp was given command of one of the four panzer battalions being raised for the Waffen-SS (the other three being assigned to Leibstandarte, Das Reich, and Totenkopf).[6]

The SS tank crews were trained by the army at Wildflecken, beginning on captured French Hotchkiss tanks before graduating to German models. Mühlenkamp's battalion comprised just under sixty tanks divided into three companies. The 1st and 2nd Companies were equipped with the Panzer Mark III, whose new high-velocity 5cm L/60 gun gave improved battlefield performance (although still inferior to the Soviet T-34). The 3rd Company was equipped with the Panzer Mark IV, whose original low-velocity 7.5cm L/24 gun had been replaced by an L/43-armed model with a reasonable antiarmor capability (subsequently upgraded with an L/48 gun).

Hitler's 1942 summer offensive was intended to secure the Caucasus region and provide Germany with new sources of urgently needed fuel (and correspondingly deny them to the enemy). The attack would be directed toward the oil fields of Maikop, Grozny, and then Baku, the ultimate prize on the Caspian Sea. A subsidiary advance was directed toward Stalingrad to protect the left flank of the main drive. For the offensive—code-named "Fall Blau" (Case Blue)—Hitler had assembled approximately 1 million German and 300,000 Axis soldiers, supported by 1,900 tanks and 1,600 aircraft. This was an impressive force, which tore through the Soviet lines with almost contemptuous ease. Such was the success of the initial phase of the campaign, launched on 28 June 1942, that it turned Hitler's head toward the seizure of Stalingrad. But the attempt to capture Stalingrad would fatally divert air and ground forces from operations in the Caucasus.

On 18 July the Wiking Division readjusted its position slightly farther south along the River Mius Line near Taganrog. Its objective was the recapture of Rostov, the city on the Don that Leibstandarte had been forced to relinquish in November 1941. Steiner used an imaginative combination of combat pioneers, infantry, and armored vehicles to break through the concentric defensive lines that protected Rostov. Bombarded by artillery and massed waves of aircraft, a surprised Red Army offered little resistance so that on 24 July the city fell to the Germans. Among the wounded was the medical officer of the pioneer battalion, Obersturmführer Josef Mengele, who had previously been awarded the Iron Cross for rescuing two crewmen from a burning tank. Declared unfit for further frontline service, Mengele returned to his former interest in racial genetics, achieving lasting infamy at the Auschwitz concentration camp.

Once past Rostov, Wiking's orders were to cross the Kuban River and secure the Maikop oil fields situated in the foothills of the western Caucasus Mountains. The tanks, assault guns, artillery, and truck-borne infantry raised huge plumes of dust as they raced southward. The divisional history reported how its troops "drove through the masses of still retreating Russians who scattered before the panzers and disappeared in the fields of sunflowers." The changing landscape also seemed to reflect Germany's improved military fortunes:

> The villages were prettier than in the Ukraine, the roads better and coun-
> tryside was covered with golden corn and red tomato fields. In the village

gardens the trees were heavy with ripening fruit. Everything the heart desired was there: melons of a size never seen before, apples, pears and other delicious fruit which made the soldiers' mouths water. Every pause was used to gorge on the fruit and quench their thirst. It was very hot and dusty; so dusty that the only feature recognizable through the thick layer of dust on the faces of the young European volunteers were their eyes.[7]

The progress of the German land forces was facilitated by the close air support provided by Colonel General Wolfram von Richthofen's Luft-flotte Four. Richthofen—a cousin of the World War I fighter ace—was an intelligent, uncompromising airman who had pioneered air-ground cooperation. The Luftwaffe's contribution to the campaign was readily acknowledged by the Wiking officers: "Soon it became customary for the Luftwaffe commander, Major Diering, to land at dawn at the command post by Storch [light aircraft]. He would take part in the briefing and issue orders to his liaison officer accordingly. As the Panzerkampfgruppe deployed it would be accompanied by an air patrol of two ground-support aircraft. These would call up the remainder of the unit's aircraft, which were on alert at Rostov, when heavier air support became necessary."[8] This period marked the high point of German air-ground cooperation, soon to be undermined by a chronic shortage of aircraft and aircrew as Hitler's demands stretched the Luftwaffe beyond breaking point.

The physical barrier of the Kuban River was crossed in stages between 4 and 7 August. This opened the way for a direct advance on the oil fields around Maikop, occupied by German troops on the tenth. A team of oil specialists had been sent to restore the wells to production, but the retreating Soviet forces had destroyed the plant facilities so thoroughly that no oil was ever extracted.

As Wiking advanced south of Maikop, it entered the foothills of the Caucasus, whose narrow defiles and high passes impeded operations. The division was ordered to halt and await the arrival of German moun-tain infantry. Wiking's last offensive action in this region was fought on 14 August, when its Finnish battalion scattered the remnants of a Red Army cavalry division during the capture of Linejuaja.

For the rest of August and into September Wiking took part in an-tipartisan operations against Soviet forces hiding in the hills. During this period the army-organized Walloon Legion (Legion Wallonie) from southern Belgium briefly came under Wiking control. Among the legion's soldiers was Belgian journalist and nationalist politician Léon Degrelle, who was greatly impressed by the SS division. He would later use his influence to have the Belgian unit taken over by the Waffen-SS. When the German mountain troops arrived, they joined the Walloon Legion to drive through the mountains and capture the Black Sea port of Tuapse.

At one point—as the men of the Wiking Division awaited redeployment—they were entertained by a regimental orchestra, which set up its instruments a short distance from the front line. Sturmann Hepp, a Dutch soldier in "Germania," found the concert—which included uplifting works by Beethoven and Wagner—a deeply moving experience. It confirmed his belief in the moral, spiritual, and intellectual superiority of the New Order: "How characteristic for the humanity and culture we were defending that it was not some fiery dance music, some libidinally charged dance hall tune that was brought to the men at the fighting front. Instead it was the most sublime and challenging music that the occidental masters had created."[9]

ORDERS FROM OKH for Wiking's redeployment to the Chechen region of the East Caucasus were instigated on 16 September. The transfer took four days and saw the division assigned to Kleist's First Panzer Army, now bogged down in the Terek Valley around Mosdok.

When the chief of staff of the First Panzer Army explained the objectives to Steiner—a march on Grozny to be followed by a crossing of the Caucasus Mountains to strike Baku—the SS general was openly skeptical of the whole enterprise, especially given the Germans' limited resources and the lateness of the campaigning season.[10] The chief of staff agreed with Steiner's misgivings but emphasized that these were orders from OKH and were to be obeyed. This disjuncture between Hitler and his staff and the generals at the front would become ever greater, directly contributing to the failure of the campaign.

The Wiking Division was assigned to General Eugen Ott's LII Army Corps, whose drive from Mosdok had been stopped in its tracks. Ott's high-handed manner immediately caused friction with the bullish Steiner, and relations between the two commanders deteriorated as the campaign progressed.

Blocking any German advance to Grozny was the Malgobek ridge. A frontal attack had already been repulsed with heavy casualties. Steiner was ordered to launch a flanking maneuver along the valley of the River Kurp that ran behind the ridge. Wiking's first objective was the forti-fied town of Ssagopschin, several miles farther up the valley, which was crisscrossed with steep-sided gorges (*balkas*) and antitank ditches. Steiner expected close air support to help him rip open the Soviet defenses, but Richthofen flew in to LII Corps HQ to inform him that the Tuapse and Stalingrad operations had priority and all he could provide were a few obsolete bombers.

The troops moved into position on 26 September, ready for the assault on the following day. The plan of attack was for the infantry from "West-land" and "Nordland" to secure the higher ground running on both sides of the valley, while the tank battalion and assault-gun battery would ad-vance along the valley floor, reinforced by combat pioneers and infantry mounted on the armored vehicles. Fire support would be provided by the massed batteries of the Wiking artillery regiment and LII Corps.

To Steiner's dismay, the enemy defenses were harder to overcome than even he had anticipated. The well-supplied Soviet troops fought with the utmost resolve, while the German armored advance was slowed by minefields and Soviet tank-hunter teams who raced up to attack the panzers with bundled charges. On 28 September the Germans made bet-ter progress and were within reaching distance of Ssagopschin until a Soviet counterattack forced the SS infantry to temporarily retreat.

The Wiking troops not only faced concentrated artillery and machine-gun fire but were continually bombed and strafed by Soviet aircraft roam-ing over the battlefield at will. The infantrymen crouching under their fire noticed that many were from the United States, transported over-land through Iran to the Soviet Caucasus command. They also found themselves under attack from British-made Valentine tanks, an otherwise reliable and well-armored vehicle undermined by a woefully inadequate 2-pounder (40mm) main gun.

The Wiking armored vehicles managed to repel the Soviet counter-attacks but were unable to break through to Ssagopschin. All the while they were subject to a Soviet barrage from the heights on both sides of the valley. Sturmmann Neumann, a tank crewman in a Panzer Mark III, recalled coming under this heavy artillery fire:

> We were being engaged from all sides. The reports from an 18.2cm battery could be clearly distinguished. It was a damned tricky situation. The bastards were registering on us. The impacts came ever closer. Depending on where they landed we moved back and forth. The shells exploding right next to our tanks made an ear-deafening racket. In between, there was the whistling sounds of the anti-tank guns and the tank main guns. Dust and dirt penetrated the interiors of the tanks; shrapnel smacked with a clang against the steel walls of the tank. It was a terrible strain on the nerves, sitting there in the middle of artillery fire without being able to do anything, hearing the report of the guns and waiting for the impacts. There was no getting around the feeling of confinement in a tank.[11]

Neumann and his comrades were eventually able to escape their ordeal after withdrawing into a nearby tank ditch.

Despite the best efforts of the Wiking Division, there was no escaping the fact that the advance had been halted. Kleist and Ott pressured Steiner to capture Ssagopschin without delay.[12] Steiner also encouraged his men to press forward, but another attack on 30 September similarly failed to make headway. On 1 October Oberführer Fritz von Scholz, commander of "Nordland," insisted his troops could not advance farther and asked to be allowed to withdraw to a better position more than a mile to the rear. Ott expressly forbade any retreat, but Steiner, on discussing the situation with Scholz at the front, overruled the order and allowed the SS troops to retire. This proved a wise decision, enabling the now disordered SS units time and space to reorganize for further offensive action.

At dawn on 2 October the combined forces of the division advanced at speed, overrunning the Soviet positions and finally capturing Ssagopschin. Despite the success, criticism of Wiking continued, with First Panzer Army headquarters suggesting that its multinational nature caused problems of command and control. This accusation was vehemently refuted by the division, which pointed out that on 1 October 1942 foreign volunteers made up around 12 percent of the division's regulation strength and that combat had melded the various nationalities into a coherent whole.[13]

Ott, still furious that his orders had been disobeyed, instructed Steiner to capture the Malgobek ridge, now in an exposed position following the fall of Ssagopschin. The "Germania" Regiment was chosen to lead the attack. Steiner, on being told that again there would be no air support, lost his temper and shouted at Ott that "the attack could not be executed and that he would report the matter to Reichsführer-SS Himmler."[14] This threatened circumvention of the chain of command was clearly a breach of regulations, and Steiner was duly reprimanded by First Panzer Army Headquarters. But Steiner's foot-stamping did have one desired result: a flight of Stukas was promised for the attack.

"Germania" opened the assault on 5 October, supported by the rest of the Wiking Division from the south and by army units from the north. The SS troops secured a foothold on the ridge, which was cleared with comparative ease on the following day. The Red Army withdrew farther east to continue its defense of Grozny. Ott then insisted that the nearby Hill 701 be secured by Wiking and the army's 111th Division.

Both divisional commanders expressed reluctance to continue the offensive, which brought forth a sarcastic response from Ott: "If the authority or willingness to fight on the part of subordinate leaders is not sufficient, I request the esteemed division commanders to personally take the place of the regimental commanders and conduct it."[15] The first assault on the position was made on 15 October, and after a series of hard-fought seesaw battles Hill 701 was captured by the Finnish battalion on the sixteenth.

Steiner's reluctance to press forward had been informed by his first-hand knowledge of the growing weakness of the German forces in the area; any advance on Grozny without huge reinforcement was clearly impossible. In fact, the capture of Hill 701 marked the high-water mark of the German advance in the Caucasus; from this time onward, they would go over to the defensive.

Arguments between Waffen-SS field commanders and their army counterparts were extremely rare—normally confined to Theodor Eicke's splenetic outbursts—but the ongoing dispute between Steiner and First Panzer Army caused disquiet at OKH. On 20 October General Kurt Zeitzler—Halder's replacement as army chief of staff—flew out to the Caucasus to assess the situation. Steiner's reservations about his division's treatment were seemingly accepted by Zeitzler, who also tried to allay anxieties as to the overall strategic situation.

In early November Wiking was withdrawn from the Malgobek area and redeployed a few miles away in defense of German positions around Alagir. During this period of relative calm, Steiner was informed that the division would henceforth be designated as 5th SS Panzergrenadier Division Wiking, in line with a comprehensive numerical overhaul of all Waffen-SS formations. (Each unit in the division was prefixed by its formation number, except for the two panzergrenadier regiments, which were all numbered sequentially, with Leibstandarte's two regiments numbered 1st and 2nd, Das Reich's numbered 3rd and 4th, and so on, with Wiking's two regiments numbered 9th and 10th.)

Of rather more significance was the troubling news that a Soviet offensive had trapped the German Sixth Army in Stalingrad and was threatening to cut off Army Group A in the Caucasus. On 22 December Wiking was ordered to drive northward to help the Fourth Panzer Army's attempt to break through to Stalingrad. This was the first stage in a wider German retreat from the entire Caucasus region.

After a relatively swift train transport north, advance elements of the division detrained on 30 December at a snowbound Simovniki, headquarters of Fourth Panzer Army. But on arrival the SS troops found the town deserted, the headquarters recently departed. Steiner was informed that Wiking was not to take part in a rescue attempt toward Stalingrad—now abandoned—but act as a rear guard for a general retreat back to Rostov. "Westland," supported by a battalion from "Germania" and 5th Panzer Battalion, held Simovniki for seven days, buying vital time for the withdrawal, not only for the rest of the division but also for Kleist's First Panzer Army, hurrying back to a new defensive line behind the River Don.

The harsh winter weather gave Wiking's withdrawal a nightmarish quality. The tank drivers—inexperienced in these conditions—found travel across the icy *balkas* a constant challenge; on such steep gradients, the caterpillar tracks could not always find sufficient traction, so the tank slithered back to the bottom of the ditch, entailing a long-drawn-out rescue process with other tanks acting as towing vehicles. On one occasion, three Panzer IIIs had to be abandoned due to the ice-ridden conditions.[16]

All the while, the retreating German troops faced the possibility of attack by packs of roving T-34s. Red Army units harried the retreating Wiking rear guards, but they lacked sufficient numbers to bring them to battle. By the beginning of February, Wiking approached Rostov with the major part of the First Panzer Army safely across the Don. On 5 February the battered division passed through the city to take up new defensive positions around Stalino (Donetsk). Once in place, Wiking was ordered to surrender its "Nordland" regiment, which would become the core infantry unit in a new Waffen-SS formation, the 11th SS Volunteer Panzergrenadier Division Nordland, with Scholz as its commander. A battalion of Estonian troops was sent to join Wiking as partial recompense for the loss of "Nordland."

Hitler's 1942 summer offensive had ended in calamitous failure. The Wehrmacht was back in the same position it had occupied in July 1942, but now there were huge gaps in the German line across the Ukraine, which the mechanized divisions of the Red Army were intending to exploit.

Chapter 17

KHARKOV COUNTERSTROKE

DURING 1942 LEIBSTANDARTE, Reich, and Totenkopf had been transferred to France for conversion into panzergrenadier divisions. The choice of destination was a consequence of Hitler's belief that the Western Allies might attempt some form of cross-Channel invasion of northern France. The Waffen-SS formations were earmarked as a temporary quick-reaction force. The Anglo-Canadian attack against Dieppe on 19 August confirmed Hitler's suspicions, and while Leibstandarte was put on alert, the raid was easily contained by local Wehrmacht forces.

After a victory parade through Paris on 29 July, Leibstandarte was stationed between Falaise and Caen, the very area they would be defending against the Allies two years later. The degree of coincidence was heightened by the arrival of Reich close to St.-Lô in Normandy in October, where they too would be deployed against Allied forces in 1944. Georg Keppler resumed command of the division, having recovered from meningitis. The Totenkopf Division was dispatched to southwest France, with Theodor Eicke back in charge after his enforced convalescence.

Replacing the soldiers lost in Operation Barbarossa and the ensuing winter battles was a priority in the process of reconstruction. On Hitler's insistence, many of the former barriers limiting Waffen-SS recruitment of German Reich citizens were removed, so that in early August 1942 OKW allowed the Waffen-SS to triple the previously authorized number of men to be selected from the class of 1924. At the start of Operation Barbarossa (22 June 1941), the Waffen-SS possessed a frontline strength of just less than 100,000 men, with a further 60,000 in reserve or undergoing training. At the beginning of September 1942, the Waffen-SS could field nearly 142,000 frontline troops, with a little more than 45,000 in reserve or training; on 1 September 1943, it deployed 280,000 men in frontline units, with 70,000 in reserve or training.[1]

The Totenkopf Division was assigned 6,000 recruits from the class of 1924, who were joined by Totenkopf reservists in Poland and the remnants of SS Infantry Regiment No. 9 to ensure the division was at full regulation strength.[2] The other two divisions were also predominantly reinforced by young Reich Germans.

Hitler's regard for the Waffen-SS produced a lavish allotment of weapons and equipment. Panzergrenadier divisions were usually assigned a single tank battalion, but the Waffen-SS formations were upgraded during 1942 to include a two-battalion tank regiment, along the lines of a standard panzer division. Measures were taken to mount towed artillery—and antitank and antiaircraft guns—onto armored vehicles, although this remained an ongoing process during 1942–1943.

In line with the divisional change of status, the infantry were reassigned as a panzergrenadiers. This was followed by the introduction of armored half-track vehicles to transport the panzergrenadiers into battle. The SdKfz 251—a forerunner of the postwar APC (armored personnel carrier)—had a two-man crew and could carry an infantry squad of up to ten men within an armored, open-topped rear compartment, armed with a fixed machine gun. The half-track—able to negotiate terrain otherwise impassable to trucks—allowed the infantry to ride into battle with tanks and other armored vehicles. The SdKfz 251 was intended to provide a reasonable degree of protection from shell splinters and small-arms fire, although in field conditions the armor plate was found to be inadequate. The panzergrenadier crews made their own ad hoc improvements, fitting extra armored plates, sandbags, and even wooden beams to vulnerable areas.[3]

As well as transporting infantry, the SdKfz 251 could be modified in a variety of ways, to provide fire-support (antitank, antiaircraft, infantry gun, mortar, flamethrower), command-and-control, engineer, and medical vehicles. Unsurprisingly, these half-tracks were always in short supply;

just one battalion in any panzergrenadier regiment was so equipped, the remaining battalions still forced to rely on trucks.

During this period Waffen-SS field units began to receive the new MG42 machine gun, supplementing and then replacing the existing MG34. Cheaper to manufacture than the old MG34, the MG42 also possessed a fearsome rate of fire of up to 1,400 rounds per minute, its distinctive ripping sound earning it the title of "Hitler's saw" from Soviet soldiers. Although potentially wasteful of ammunition, the MG42 was a superb infantry weapon in the hands of experienced soldiers.

The upgraded Waffen-SS divisions were also supplied with the PzKpfw Mark VI (Tiger I) tank. The Panzer IIIs and IVs that equipped the German panzer units had been developed in the 1930s, and even with continuous upgrades they were inadequate for the conditions encountered on the Eastern Front. In the autumn of 1942 the Tiger entered service, a fifty-seven-ton heavy tank that gave the panzer divisions a decisive qualitative edge over their opponents until at least early 1944. Despite being overly complex to manufacture and too heavy for its engine and transmission, the Tiger was a fearsome weapon. It was armed with an 8.8cm main gun, which, with its advanced optical sights, could hit and destroy a T-34 at a range of 1,500 meters, while its 100-millimeter frontal armor was all but invulnerable to Soviet tank and antitank guns. Each division was assigned a heavy company of approximately fifteen to twenty Tigers, although Totenkopf would not receive its company until after the 1943 Kharkov campaign.[4]

SENIOR OFFICERS IN the Waffen-SS had wanted to use their forces in a semi-independent manner, free from the constraints of army supervision. The development of the Waffen-SS's own corps system during 1942 was a step in realizing this ambition, its first tangible expression coming with the formation of the SS Panzer Corps—comprising Leibstandarte, Das Reich, and Totenkopf—under Obergruppenführer Hausser. The intention was to use this powerful formation as a strategic reserve on the Eastern Front, capable of making decisive interventions where required.

Great things were expected of the corps: its troops were commanded by battle-hardened veterans, and every effort had been made in the supply of the latest weapons and equipment. Training was conducted in earnest, so that even as the strategic situation on the Eastern Front deteriorated during the final months of 1942, the SS panzer divisions continued with their instruction in armored warfare.

The only disturbance to the training program came with Hitler's decision to occupy Vichy France. The successful Anglo-American landings in North Africa in November 1942 made Hitler fearful of the loyalty of his French ally, especially the possibility that the remnants of the French Fleet based in Toulon might slip anchor and sail across the Mediterranean to join the Allied-sponsored Free French. To forestall such an eventuality, the Wehrmacht sent armored columns across the old demarcation line on 10 November. The occupation was unopposed so that the whole country was under direct German rule by 27 November. A number of motorized units from both Leibstandarte and Das Reich briefly took part in the operation, although they were unable to prevent the French Navy from scuttling its ships in Toulon's harbor.

Due to its closer proximity to France's Mediterranean coast, Eicke's Totenkopf Division played a more substantial role in the operation and stayed on through much of December as part of the occupying force. This change in deployment seriously undermined the division's already wobbling training schedule, so much so that Eicke pleaded with Himmler for extra time to complete the process. Himmler was convinced by Eicke's entreaties, so that when the order came to transfer to the Eastern Front he persuaded Hitler to give the division an extra month to complete essential training and the integration of its new weapons and equipment.[5]

Himmler had been remarkably sympathetic to Eicke's predicament in light of the situation on the Eastern Front. The Soviet Stalingrad offensive—Operation Uranus—had begun on 19 November 1942 and in a two-pronged thrust had routed the predominantly Romanian, Hungarian, and Italian troops holding the line on either side of Stalingrad. The city was encircled by Soviet forces on 24 November, beginning the siege that ended on 2 February 1943 with the surrender of what remained of the German Sixth Army.

Part of the Red Army was directly involved in the reduction of Stalingrad, but larger forces drove into the 300-mile gap left by the collapse of the Axis armies in the eastern Ukraine. As Soviet armor drove forward, there was a real possibility that the Germans in the southern Ukraine would be encircled and crushed against the Black Sea. Toward the end of December Leibstandarte and Das Reich were ordered to prepare for a return to the Eastern Front to help plug the gap.

Throughout January the troops feverishly made ready for military operations in the Soviet Union. Training exercises gave way to the conversion of vehicles and equipment for winter fighting, in marked contrast to the absence of winter preparation for the 1941–1942 campaign. Herbert Maeger, a panzergrenadier in Leibstandarte, recalled that "in the second week of January we received a new issue of winter clothing. This consisted of quilted fur-lined jackets with fur hood and reversible warm fur-lined trousers white on one side and of a brown-grey pattern on the other, fur boots and fur-lined gloves. White meant Russia, we could all see that."[6] Vehicles and heavy weapons received a coat of whitewash.

The transport of an armored division by rail was an enormous undertaking, with Leibstandarte employing 200 separate trains for the operation.[7] The first trains left France in mid-January, taking around ten days to reach the railheads in and around Kharkov. A few trains were, however, given special priority and took just five days to cross Hitler's empire, all other traffic held back in sidings to let them pass.

The situation encountered by the SS troops in the Ukraine was grim; as they unloaded their vehicles, they came under long-range Soviet artillery fire and witnessed the tattered remnants of the beaten Axis armies in full retreat. It was still winter, with temperatures regularly falling to minus 4 degrees Fahrenheit. A soldier from the 1st Panzergrenadier Regiment wrote, "The cold was so severe that the sausage given the men had to be cut with an ax and the bread had to be thawed over the soldering gun."[8]

A combination of armor, infantry, and reconnaissance units from Leibstandarte arrived in late January, along with "Der Führer" from the recently renamed Das Reich Division. They were immediately committed to battle, pushed out to defend positions on the far bank of the River Donets, a short distance east of Kharkov. The original conception of the SS

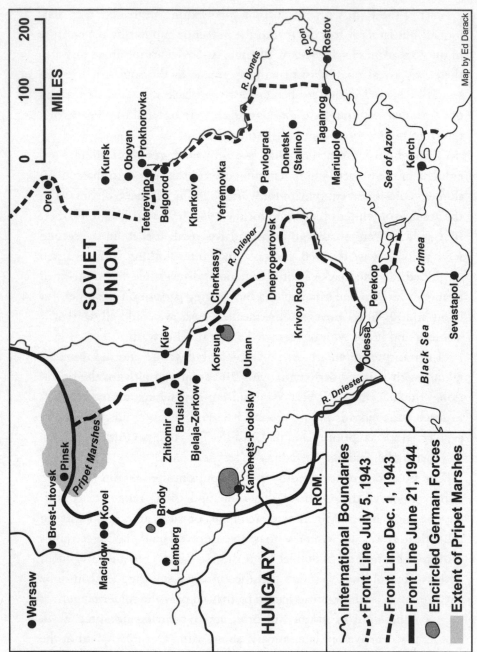

The Eastern Front in the South, 1943–1944

Map by Ed Darack

Panzer Corps acting as a unified force had to be temporarily abandoned, its units establishing a holding screen to keep the Red Army at bay and to allow German and other Axis units to fall back to safety.

The German 320th Infantry Division was slowly retreating back to the Donets, its progress hampered by an unusually large contingent of 1,500 wounded. Without outside assistance, it was quite probable that the wounded or even the entire division might be overwhelmed by the advancing Red Army. Aware of the division's plight, Hausser organized a rescue mission, a perfect task for one of the new half-track battalions; the wounded would be loaded into the armored vehicles and driven back to German lines.

The III Battalion of Leibstandarte's 2nd Panzergrenadier Regiment was chosen for the task, commanded by Sturmbannführer Jochen Peiper, an officer whose career would become synonymous with the division.[9] Born into a Prussian middle-class family in 1915, Peiper was a keen horseman and joined an SS cavalry Standarte in 1933. His self-confidence and matinee-idol looks were spotted by Himmler at the 1934 Nuremberg Rally; under the patronage of the Reichsführer-SS, he graduated from the SS officer training school at Bad Tölz and was posted to Leibstandarte in 1936. Two years later Peiper was transferred to Himmler's personal staff, accompanying him on his travels, whether to foreign capitals or concentration camps.

During the invasion of France in 1940, Peiper persuaded Himmler to let him return to active duty with Leibstandarte, winning the Iron Cross (2nd Class) for his spirited leadership in the assault on the Watten Heights on 24 May. At the close of hostilities Peiper returned to Himmler's staff and continued his administrative duties until the autumn of 1941. Both men held each other in high regard.

In October 1941 the now Hauptsturmführer Peiper was officially transferred to Leibstandarte to take over an infantry company of the 2nd Regiment's III Battalion, then involved in the fighting along the Black Sea coast toward Rostov. He proved himself an enterprising and forceful soldier, very much in Leibstandarte tradition, although some fellow officers considered him reckless with his men's lives.[10] During the summer of 1942, he was promoted to Sturmbannführer and given command of III Battalion. When the battalion was equipped with SdKfz 250/251 half-tracks, Peiper looked back to his equestrian roots as he attempted to create a modern, highly mobile heavy cavalry.

On 12 February 1943 Peiper led to his troops through enemy lines toward the Donets to rendezvous with the retreating 320th Division. When Peiper encountered the army formation struggling through the snow, he was immediately reminded of Napoleon's retreat from Moscow: "In front came those able to walk, then the wounded, with the seriously wounded at the rear. A parade of misery on sleighs and sleds. These were so full that some unfortunates were tied on and carried underneath the sleighs. Our doctors and medics had set up emergency facilities to receive them."[11]

Although aggrieved at the apparently dismissive attitude displayed to him by the division's commander, Lieutenant General Postel, Peiper successfully ferried the wounded to safety. On his own return to German lines, Peiper discovered that a small detachment from his battalion had been overrun in the village of Krasnaya Polyana. Rottenführer Otto Sierk described the incident: "In the village, the two petrol trucks were burnt and twenty-five Germans killed by partisans and Russian soldiers. As a revenge, Peiper ordered the burning down of the whole village and the shooting of its inhabitants."[12] The destruction of habitations harboring or suspected of harboring Soviet troops was commonplace on the Eastern Front, although Sturmbannführer Jakob Heinrich described Peiper as being "particularly eager to execute the order to burn villages."[13]

———————

THE GERMAN OUTPOSTS screening Kharkov were being pushed in by the advancing Red Army. Hausser also discerned that the main Soviet advance consisted of two thrusts to the north and south of the city. The drive to the south of Kharkov caused Hausser the most concern, as it threatened to capture Dnepropetrovsk, on the River Dnieper, separating his forces from those in the southern Ukraine.

On 11 February Hausser committed his available mobile troops to parry the Soviet advance. They consisted of mixed units from Leibstandarte and Das Reich, under Sepp Dietrich's direction. As well as two battalions from Das Reich's "Der Führer" Regiment and the division's motorcycle battalion, Dietrich called upon his own troops: Kurt Meyer's reconnaissance battalion and the Witt Regiment (a reinforced battalion from Fritz Witt's 1st Panzergrenadier Regiment). They would subsequently be joined by Leibstandarte's 1st Panzer Battalion, commanded by Max Wünsche. All in all, it was a formidable combination of units led by some of the most aggressive and dynamic officers in the Waffen-SS.

On 11 February the Kampfgruppe drove through a swirling snowstorm to capture Merefa and then advance farther south. Using speed and surprise to compensate for a lack of numbers, the Waffen-SS troops cut through the Soviet flank. Meyer's reconnaissance battalion swung round to capture Bereka, well behind enemy lines. The Soviets rallied, however, and Meyer found himself encircled by superior forces, with ammunition running low. "Der Führer's" II Battalion raced forward to the rescue, borrowing the half-tracks from the III Battalion to speed its progress. They were joined by Wünsche's panzers, which on 17 February scattered the Soviet troops surrounding Meyer. On the following day the Kampfgruppe was able to establish a defensive line that protected Kharkov from the south.

Before this action had concluded, the situation in Kharkov itself had become ominous, as the Red Army advanced to the city's outskirts and threatened to surround it from the north. Kharkov was one of the Soviet Union's major industrial centers—home of the T-34 tank—and a prestige target for both Hitler and Stalin. Hausser asked to withdraw, but Hitler insisted that there would be no retreat under any circumstances. This placed Hausser in an impossible position. Unconditional obedience to the Führer's orders was a foundation stone of the Waffen-SS, yet Hausser knew it would be madness to tie up the best part of two elite armored divisions in a static position when they should be free to carry out mobile operations. On 15 February, as Soviet forces closed in on the city, Hausser made his decision and withdrew from Kharkov to establish a new line to the west.

Although incurring the wrath of Hitler, Hausser's move was entirely in accord with the counteroffensive strategy being developed by Field Marshal Manstein, the commander of the newly formed Army Group

South. Manstein reasoned that the farther westward the Soviet spearheads advanced, the more overextended they would become and the more vulnerable to a German counterattack. But if the action was to be successful, Manstein would need to marshal all available mobile forces throughout the Ukraine, so as to fall upon the Red Army advance in a carefully orchestrated manner. Hitler, who wanted an immediate offensive to retake Kharkov, vehemently opposed this idea and even flew out to Manstein's headquarters to demand that his orders be carried out. On this occasion, however, Hitler listened to reason, as Manstein persuaded him to adopt his own flexible, mobile strategy, which would include the retaking of Kharkov, albeit at a later date.

On 19 February Manstein put his plan into action. In the southern Ukraine, Kleist's First Panzer Army (including the Wiking Division) advanced northward into the flanks of the massed Soviet tanks corps led by General Popov, while Hoth's Fourth Panzer Army (including the SS Panzer Corps) would utilize all the operational skills of a crack German panzer force to outmaneuver the Red Army to the south of Kharkov.

Manstein instructed Hausser to use Leibstandarte as a defensive shield. Das Reich would act as the maneuver force: driving due south to cut through and destroy the head of the main Soviet thrust (now close to Dnepropetrovsk), then briefly push eastward to rendezvous with the army's XLVIII Panzer Corps, before swinging north-northwest to hammer the main Soviet thrust against the anvil of Leibstandarte. Then, the combined SS formations would move northward to destroy the Soviet forces in and around Kharkov.

Das Reich experienced an unexpected change of command when Keppler was struck down with a brain hemorrhage on 10 February. He was replaced by Oberführer Herbert-Ernst Vahl, a former army officer then leading Das Reich's panzer regiment (he would relinquish command of the division after being seriously wounded on 18 March, indicative of the dangers faced by all Waffen-SS officers). Das Reich was to be joined by the Totenkopf Division, whose units began to arrive at the front in mid-February.

At this time, the cold weather began to alternate with brief periods of spring thaw that turned otherwise hard ground into a boggy morass. Vehicles—tracked and wheeled—that were not standing on asphalt roads would suddenly find themselves sinking up to their axles in mud. Theodor Eicke's Totenkopf armored units, perhaps overeager to reach their start line, were the first to fall foul of the spring *rasputitsa*, with most stuck fast on 18 February.[14] The following day, with the return of freezing conditions, the vehicles were winched out of the mud, ready for combat.

Night operations were commonplace on the Eastern Front, but they were made all the more difficult in winter weather with still inexperienced tank crews. Martin Steiger, a tank commander in the Totenkopf's I Panzer Battalion, described events on 21 February:

> It was a starlit, freezing night. The commanders stood rigidly in their hatches. The panzers began to slide on the slippery roads. Around midnight we reached Krasnograd, when a major mishap stalled the advance. Several panzers began to slide on the clear ice at a downhill spot near the exit from Krasnograd and crashed into each other. The panzers of Meierdress [commander of I Battalion] and his adjutant and the panzers of Reifkogel and Siebenkopf collided in a dip in the road and sustained considerable damage. They had to be towed away. It was light before we got going again.[15]

While the armored vehicles of Totenkopf were coming to terms with the Ukrainian steppe in winter, Das Reich was racing ahead. "Deutschland" and "Der Führer" leapfrogged each other in a sixty-mile two-day dash toward Novomoskovsk on the River Samara. Sturmbannführer Sylvester Stadler, commander of "Der Führer's" II Battalion, seized the bridges over the river on 21 February in a daring raid that enabled the rest of the division to drive on Pavlograd with minimal delay. In offensive operations where swiftness was essential, the division was divided into ad hoc Kampfgruppen. Three fast battle groups led the assault on Pavlograd, each comprising a company of infantry (from "Der Führer") mounted in half-tracks, with a panzer company and a battery of armored artillery.[16] The ease with which these changes were carried out was indicative of the tactical flexibility of German armored formations.

The speed of the German advance had caught the Soviets off guard, and short of fuel and ammunition they were unable to offer much resistance when Das Reich launched a surprise attack against Pavlograd on 22 February. Supported by waves of Stukas, the city fell with little resistance, Hausser going forward to congratulate his troops at the end of the day's fighting. Contact was now made with the army formations from Hoth's Fourth Panzer Army, thereby closing the gap in the German line. Das Reich then changed direction and drove northward to crush the scattered Red Army units, now caught in a trap south of Kharkov.

The Totenkopf Division moved alongside Das Reich, announcing its arrival by shelling nearby Das Reich units. There were no casualties in the incident, however, although Totenkopf was shortly to experience a unique loss of its own. On 26 February Eicke was flying over his forward positions in a Fieseler Storch reconnaissance aircraft when it was hit by Soviet small-arms fire. The aircraft crashed to the ground and was raked by further enemy fire; the bodies of Eicke and his crew were recovered the following day.

Eicke had created the Totenkopf Division in his own mold and seemingly against all odds had made it into a crack fighting force. If nothing else, Eicke proved that there was no reason that former concentration-camp guards should not make first-rate combat soldiers. Although his men were obviously dismayed at the loss of "Papa Eicke," the division was a well-run military formation that continued to function, regardless of individual casualties. Max Simon took command of Totenkopf as it renewed its advance on Kharkov.

———————

THE CONSTANT CHANGES of direction and relentless nature of the German armored attacks bemused the disoriented and increasingly demoralized Soviet forces. Advancing together, the tanks of Totenkopf and Das Reich sprinted over the snowbound steppe, casting aside the remnants of the Soviet First Guards Army before closing in on the Soviet Sixth Army, now threatened with total encirclement. The Soviet high command sent reinforcements to support their beleaguered comrades, but they too were caught in the encircling move that reached a crescendo in and around the village of Yefremovko on 3–4 March.

Leibstandarte had now been committed to the attack and was soon fighting alongside the other two SS divisions. Kurt Meyer's reconnaissance battalion was in the lead and for a time was briefly isolated in Yefremovko. Meyer, outraged that his men were fired upon by "armed civilians," ordered the village to be razed to the ground and its inhabitants shot.[17]

By early March the warm spells that caused the ground to turn to mud became more frequent, inevitably slowing the advance of the SS panzer units. The army's XLVIII Panzer Corps was directed to drive to the east of Kharkov and the SS Panzer Corps to advance to the west and then surround it from the north. Despite the meteorological problems, the SS troops faced little serious opposition, as what remained of Soviet opposition retreated into the city or attempted to flee eastward across the Donets. Herbert Maeger, of Leibstandarte, recalled the drive north: "Rolling forward over mainly flat terrain we found it strewn with Soviet army equipment relinquished in the typical sequence of a rapid flight. Next, we came upon a zone of abandoned weapons and ammunition containers of all kinds; one kilometer further on the field was littered with blankets and belts, and finally the fleeing hordes had literally left behind the last of all they had in their desperation to escape, for now we found only haversacks and greatcoats and last of all fur caps and lined boots."[18]

On 9 March the SS panzer divisions closed on Kharkov, with orders to drive around it from the west. What happened next remains a matter of controversy. The SS Panzer Corps claimed that on the ninth it received an order from Hoth's HQ at 12:15 P.M. to "take Kharkov in a coup de main."[19] On the next day Leibstandarte attacked the city from the northwest, while Das Reich supported the assault from the west. Totenkopf, meanwhile, provided cover by continuing to drive around the north of Kharkov toward the River Donets. In his postwar memoirs, Manstein criticized Hausser for being obsessed with the recapture of the city, with the implication that such an action could have been better carried out by infantry.[20] Hausser countered that his armored units needed to use the city center's superior roads in order to redeploy northward,[21] despite the fact that Totenkopf had already driven around the city on cross-country routes. There can be little doubt that Hausser was personally determined to regain the city he had previously lost.

The full weight of Leibstandarte smashed its way toward the city center. Some idea of the bitterness of the final battles can be seen in this letter from Sturmbannführer Heinz von Westernhagen, commander of the division's assault-gun battalion:

> What we left behind is appalling. If you were to come to Kharkov now, you would not recognize it. Hardly a house is left intact. Nobody is going to forget the street combat. Every single man deserves the Knight's Cross. In Kharkov itself we drove to within 30 meters of fortified houses and fired directly into them with our panzer artillery. From above, the [Soviet] brothers bedeviled us with satchel charges on our heads. And after the dust from bricks and explosives had settled, these dogs continued to fire. From a distance of 100 meters we fired artillery into them and in places killed them with Cossack sabers.[22]

The battle raged for nearly four days until the various SS columns converged on the city's central plaza, briefly renamed Leibstandarte Square. It was an epic moment in the division's history: the cameras captured Peiper's half-tracks driving into the square as Leibstandarte's leading officers—among them Dietrich, Witt, Wünsche, and Meyer—congratulated each other.

While Das Reich and Totenkopf secured the area around Kharkov, establishing a defensive screen along the River Donets, a Kampfgruppe under Peiper's command charged northward to capture Belgorod before the spring thaw brought a complete halt to offensive operations. As well as his battalion of half-tracks, Peiper could call upon two Leibstandarte Tiger tanks and a company of Panzer IVs commanded by Untersturmführer Rudolf von Ribbentrop (son of the German foreign minister).

As usual, Peiper drove his men with a wild enthusiasm, with several Panzer IVs knocked out in the hurry to get forward. But speed had its advantages. Just before the Kampfgruppe reached Belgorod, the Tigers were sent forward to lead the attack. Rottenführer Werner Wendt, a gunner in one of the Tigers, described the action on 17 March:

> As we burst into the next village the road curved slightly to the right. We couldn't believe our eyes; in position in front of us was an enemy 76.2mm anti-tank gun. It was obvious that our appearance had come as a surprise, for instead of being behind their gun, the Red Army men were

sitting on a bench in front of a nearby cottage flirting with several girls from the village. There was no need for us to fire. Without hesitating we drove over the gun at full speed; it [was] no threat to us now, having been reduced to scrap. As we continued down the road we were challenged by two T-34s which we destroyed easily. To the left of the road there was a vast expanse over which hundreds of Red Army troops were fleeing, driven by fear of being overrun by our rapid advance. Their coats flapped as they ran.[23]

Belgorod fell on 18 March, bringing a temporary end to the fighting. Any hopes Manstein held of pushing on to Kursk were dashed by the increasingly warm weather and the exhaustion of the German frontline units.

The Kharkov battle had been a signal German success: inflicting a painful blow on the Red Army, restoring a defensive line in the Ukraine when previously there had been an open space, and raising German morale after the disasters of Stalingrad. Manstein had provided a textbook lesson in how the German Army should use its armored forces, utilizing superior mobility to catch the enemy off guard and concentrating devastating firepower at the critical juncture. Hausser's SS Panzer Corps had played a key role in achieving Manstein's victory.

Hitler failed to comprehend the factors behind Manstein's strategy, but he understood the part played by the SS divisions, especially his beloved Leibstandarte and its commander, Sepp Dietrich. The Nazi propaganda machine went into overdrive to laud the SS heroes. Dietrich was awarded the swords to his Knight's Cross and prepared for command of a new SS Panzer Corps (Hausser, by contrast, was cold-shouldered by Hitler for disobeying his order to defend Kharkov to the last). Medals were handed out to the SS divisions with jubilant enthusiasm: Leibstandarte received fourteen Knight's Crosses, Das Reich ten, and Totenkopf five.[24] On the debit side, the SS Panzer Corps had suffered heavy casualties. Losses of killed, wounded, and missing totaled 365 officers and 11,154 NCOs and enlisted men.[25]

Following the victory at Kharkov, Hitler and OKH considered how best to continue the war on the Eastern Front. It centered on two, opposing, choices. The "backhand" strategy favored by Manstein called for a flexible, predominantly reactive approach, where the Wehrmacht was prepared to trade space to allow advancing Soviet forces to overextend themselves before carrying out devastating counterattacks—as had been the case at Kharkov. The other, "forehand," approach demanded a rigid defense combined with a proactive offensive outlook. This latter strategy was favored by Hitler and would form the basis for the attack on the Kursk salient during the summer of 1943.

Chapter 18

KURSK: CLASH OF ARMOR

Recalled to the Führer headquarters in April 1943, Dietrich was told by Hitler that he was to take command of I SS Panzer Corps. This would comprise Leibstandarte and a new division to be recruited from older members of the Hitler Youth (Hitlerjugend). On 10 February Hitler had agreed to the request by Reich youth leader Artur Axmann for a military formation primarily drawn from Hitler Youth volunteers born in 1926. Hitler had always shown a keen interest in the young—more ideologically malleable than their elders—and backed the idea, which would eventually turn into the 12th SS Panzer Division Hitlerjugend.

The training cadre for the new division was primarily drawn from officers and NCOs of Leibstandarte. Fritz Witt, of Leibstandarte's 1st Panzergrenadier Regiment, would become the Hitlerjugend commander, to be joined by Kurt Meyer and Max Wünsche, the latter taking over the new panzer regiment. Leibstandarte also lost a panzer battalion to the new division. As a consequence, it would go into battle at Kursk with just one battalion while a new unit was being raised in Germany, equipped with the latest Panther tanks.

Dietrich had been with Leibstandarte since its inception as Hitler's personal guard, and his departure would be keenly felt by the soldiers of the division. Staff officer Rudolf Lehmann knew him well: "He was no strategic genius, but a leader of the highest quality of soldiers and of men. His very rare and then very short speeches to his men did not contain any strokes of genius, but they were, as one realized, meant to come from his heart, and they went from heart to heart. This man had an extraordinary charisma."[1] Despite his promotion, Dietrich had little to command during 1943, Leibstandarte still operating under Hausser's direction while the Hitlerjugend remained a formation under construction.

Dietrich was succeeded by Theodor Wisch on 4 June 1943. He would lead Leibstandarte throughout the Kursk offensive and beyond, relinquishing command only when badly wounded in Normandy. Wisch—seen as a steady hand—had been a young officer in Leibstandarte's prestigious 1st Company before working his way up the career ladder to lead the 2nd Panzergrenadier Regiment. According to a subsequent Allied interrogation, he was "pleasant faced with a mild speaking voice and possessed with quite a sense of humor."[2]

There were changes in the other divisions, too. After the death of Eicke, command of the Totenkopf Division passed briefly to Max Simon and then to Hermann Priess, formerly the division's senior artillery officer. Eicke had formed a high opinion of Priess, praising his performance during the defense of Demyansk in 1942: "If it wasn't for Priess, none of us would still be here."[3] In Das Reich, the severely wounded Herbert-Ernst Vahl was succeeded by Walter Krüger, a former commander of the Polizei Division.

During the spring of 1943, Leibstandarte, Das Reich, and Totenkopf Divisions made good the losses they had incurred during the battle of Kharkov. Many of these replacements came from the Luftwaffe, whose bloated organization was being combed out by OKW for the personnel desperately needed by Germany's ground forces. Although considered good human material, the Luftwaffe servicemen were untrained in ground fighting and were consequently subjected to a crash course in infantry tactics.[4] While personnel losses were successfully made up, the three SS divisions were unable to achieve their regulation strength in armored vehicles. Apart from Leibstandarte's missing tank battalion, the armored vehicles for the Totenkopf Division were down by a third, while Das Reich adopted the unusual expedient of using a company of captured T-34s to augment its numbers.

FOLLOWING THE VICTORY at Kharkov, Hitler was determined to conduct a major offensive on the Eastern Front. He took up an idea originally suggested by Manstein for the elimination of the bulge in the Soviet front line that stretched around the city of Kursk. But Manstein's plan was for a swift attack by Army Group South—supported by Army Group Center—to be launched immediately once the ground was firm enough for armored operations. Hitler procrastinated, however, and repeatedly postponed the operation, justifying his vacillation on the need to build up Germany's panzer force to include the new Panther tank and Elefant tank destroyer. The delays caused Manstein to change his mind, and in concert with several of his fellow commanders—notably Model and Guderian—he tried to persuade Hitler to abandon the idea. In the discussions that continued through April and May, Zeitzler (OKH chief of staff) and von Kluge (Army Group Center) backed the offensive, and their arguments won the day.

The plan—codenamed Operation Citadel (Zitadelle)—comprised a simple pincer movement, with Model's Ninth Army attacking from the North and Hoth's Fourth Panzer Army driving toward Kursk from the South. Soviet intelligence was well aware of German intentions, however, and between April and the beginning of July the Red Army constructed a formidable series of defenses, many miles deep, which included fixed fortifications, minefields, artillery fire zones, and antitank strongpoints. Behind this the Red Army had gathered their strategic reserve, not only to thwart any German breakthrough but also to prepare a counteroffensive once the German attack had been held.

On 1 July 1943 Hitler finally ordered the offensive to go ahead, with the start date fixed for 5 July. The Wehrmacht had assembled a powerful force, concentrated on the northern and southern shoulders of the Kursk bulge, amounting to just under three-quarters of a million men, with nearly 2,400 tanks and assault guns, 7,500 guns and mortars, and 1,800 aircraft.[5] The larger of the two German forces was deployed in the South and consisted of three panzer corps (including Hausser's).

Air cover was provided by VIII Fliegerkorps, whose bombers, dive-bombers, and fighter aircraft would help the SS divisions break into the Soviet lines. For the first time, the Luftwaffe used its special tank-busting Stukas, armed with twin wing-mounted 3.7cm cannon whose armor-piercing shells proved devastating against the lightly armored engine decks of the Soviet tanks below.

Although the SS troops were grateful for the ground support provided them by the Luftwaffe, they also had to contend with a growing threat from the Red Air Force, making the divisional antiaircraft units all the more important. During the night the waiting German troops had to contend with the Polikarpov Po-2. The aircraft's distinctive engine sound gave it the name of the "flying sewing machine," and while its tiny bomb load caused few casualties, its nocturnal presence over German lines was a constant irritant. By day they faced the formidable Ilyushin Sturmovik ground-attack aircraft, whose armored underfuselage made it extremely hard to shoot down.

Werner Volker, an antiaircraft gunner in the Totenkopf Division, recalled in the days just before the offensive that "as soon as the first rays of sun touched the ground you heard the humming of the Ilyushins that came over to attack our infantry and artillery positions." Firing mixed clips of armor-piercing and explosive ammunition, Volkner and his 3.7cm gun crew took on the enemy aircraft: "Although it was the objective of the gunners to knock the enemy planes out of the sky, we were quite happy if we managed to divert their flight away from their targets, thereby protecting the infantry and artillery positions."[6]

As the soldiers waited for the order to advance, the weather became increasingly hot and sultry, with a threat of thunderstorms. When the rainstorms materialized, they were sufficiently heavy to make the going difficult for all vehicles, tracked as well as wheeled. Otherwise, the terrain was nearly ideal for armored warfare: open, rolling steppe, across which were scattered small wooden villages that could offer little resistance to the advancing panzers.

On the night of 4–5 July 1943 SS combat engineers crept into the Soviet front line, removing mines and dismantling defenses in preparation for the attack at dawn. The strike element of the German forces in the South comprised XLVIII Panzer Corps on the left (which included the Grossdeutschland Division and a brigade of the new Panther tanks), Hausser's II SS Panzer Corps in the center, and III Panzer Corps on the right. The three corps were deployed in line, forming the densest concentration of German armor yet seen on the battlefield. The SS contribution comprised 343 tanks and 195 self-propelled assault guns.[7]

The troops of the three SS division had received Hitler's order that this was to be a battle of supreme importance. On the morning of 5 July the SS Panzer Corps broke into the Soviet lines, with, at this point, Leibstandarte on the left, Das Reich in the center, and Totenkopf on the right.

Supported by an artillery barrage and dive-bomber attacks, the SS infantry crossed over no-man's-land into the first Soviet defensive line. Among the advancing infantry was Hans Huber, part of a flamethrower detachment in "Deutschland's" II Battalion. He recalled the fight for the village of Beresov:

> The enemy artillery had forced us to take cover. Soon we knew from the Very lights being fired that our No. 2 Platoon had gained a foothold in the village. Section commander Kiesel grew impatient. He ordered me to get the flamethrower ready and we worked our way forward into the trenches ahead of us. I fired a burst of flame as we approached every zig-zag in the trench and at every enemy strong point. It was a strange feeling to serve this destructive weapon and it was terrifying to see the flames eat their way forward and envelop the Russian defenders. Soon I was covered black from head to foot from the fuel oil and my face was burnt from the flames which bounced back off the trench walls. I could hardly see. The enemy could not fight against flamethrowers and so we made good progress taking many prisoners.[8]

Once the infantry and supporting arms had cleared a path, the panzers were committed to the battle. A Tiger crewman from Das Reich recalled the attack:

> Unnoticed, we had assembled at the bottom of the valley, the Tigers flanked by medium and light companies [Panzer IVs and IIIs]. Our field glasses searched the horizon, spying into the smoke of combat that covered the bunker heights like a veil of mourning. The engines howled. We loaded the guns and slowly the heavy panzers rolled onto the battleground.

After 200 meters the first enemy Pak fired. With a single shot we blew
it out of the ground. We rolled over the abandoned enemy trenches and
waved from our open hatches to our brave infantrymen. They were enjoying a short rest on the heights they had just stormed.[9]

The SS armor pushed forward in large armored wedge (Panzerkeil)
formations, designed to smash through the enemy lines. The emphasis
was not on subtle tactics but on raw battering power. The Tiger tank had
a key role here, able to destroy almost anything in its path yet remain
virtually invulnerable to T-34s and antitank guns except from the flanks
or rear (land mines were a different matter, knocking out many Tigers).
The fighting at Kursk was also an opportunity for the Tiger commanders
to demonstrate their growing skills; the tactical knowledge gained in the
battle for Kharkov was put to good use.

On the first day of action the commander of Leibstandarte's heavy
(Tiger) company, Hauptsturmführer Heinz Kling, and his gunner Sturmann Warmbrunn were responsible for knocking out four T-34s and
nineteen antitank guns, as well as destroying seven bunkers and ten fixed
flamethrowers. Even allowing for the fact that claims for knocked-out
tanks and other vehicles were exaggerated by all sides (similar to those
made by airmen for aircraft destroyed), the Waffen-SS wreaked carnage
among the Red Army's armored units. Untersturmführer Michael Wittmann, a Tiger commander who had gained armored experience in Leibstandarte's assault-gun battalion, claimed a score of eight tanks and seven
antitank guns on 5 July. Combining bravery with meticulous attention
to detail and a superb eye for the battlefield, Wittmann would become
Germany's most famous panzer commander.

In terms of individual exploits during the battle, arguably the most
extraordinary was that of Leibstandarte's Unterscharführer Franz Staudegger on 8 July. As the advance pushed on northward, Staudegger's Tiger
had been left behind in the village of Teterevino because of mechanical
problems, but as the vehicle was undergoing repairs he was told of an advance by fifty to sixty Soviet tanks against a position held by Das Reich's
"Deutschland" Regiment. Despite having only just assumed the role of
tank commander, the twenty-year-old Staudegger hurried the repairs and
immediately set off in pursuit of the Soviet force.

The lone Tiger sighted the enemy and in a series of short, deadly engagements—lasting two hours—knocked out seventeen T-34s. The Red Army advance faltered, and its tanks retreated to regroup. Fearlessly, Staudegger followed and resumed the attack. When he had run out of armor-piercing rounds, he continued to score hits using high-explosive shells. Only when all his ammunition was exhausted did Staudegger slowly return to his lines—and the cheers of the "Deutschland" infantry who had witnessed the battle. All told he had knocked out twenty-two Soviet tanks and brought the enemy advance to a standstill. He became the first soldier in the Tiger company to win the Knight's Cross.[10]

The Waffen-SS panzer divisions had made good progress during the opening phase of the offensive, breaking through two of the three belts of the Red Army's first defensive line. Although progress was not as swift as Hausser and Hoth had originally expected, it certainly alarmed the Soviet commanders, who began to order up their reserves. On 8 July the SS Panzer Corps paused, mainly to allow the other panzer corps to keep up with their advance; III Panzer Corps was particularly slow in coming up to protect the SS right flank.

On 9 July the SS troops weathered a storm of Soviet counterattacks, while at the same time continuing to push forward. The fighting was intense and relentless. A battle report from the 10th Company of Das Reich's "Der Führer" Regiment illustrated the bravery of its men. When the company commander was put out of action, Untersturmführer Krueger took over and despite being wounded on two occasions refused to give up the fight: "A rifle bullet struck his pocket and ignited an incendiary grenade he was carrying. Krueger tore off his trousers and underpants and continued to fight on dressed only in a jacket, shirt and with his lower limbs completely naked. He fought at the head of the company until the object was gained."[11]

From the ninth onward, Das Reich took on a more defensive position on the right flank of the panzer corps' advance, while Totenkopf was redeployed to the left flank, its direction of advance due north. At the end of a day of hard fighting Standartenführer Karl Ullrich's III Battalion (1st Panzergrenadier Regiment) had forced a crossing over the River Psel, the last natural obstacle before Oboyan and then the city of Kursk itself. But to Ullrich's dismay, his men were forced to hold position as they waited for the bridging equipment to be slowly brought forward to allow the heavy units to cross the river.

Meanwhile, the Leibstandarte Division—now in the corps' center—had slogged its way forward in a northeasterly direction with the intention of capturing Prokhorovka on 10 July. Heavy rain and stiffening Soviet resistance checked the advance, as they did on the following day. On 12 July Hausser mobilized his three divisions so that both Totenkopf and Das Reich were directed to support Leibstandarte's attack on Prokhorovka. On the Soviet side, the concern at the gains made by the SS panzers led to the deployment of their main strategic reserves, which included the powerful Fifth Guards Tank Army. On 12 July the Soviet tank force arrived at Prokhorovka just as the Germans were launching their assault. The result was a devastating collision of armor. Although the forces involved were considerably less than originally believed (Soviet sources vastly inflating German numbers), the battle for Prokhorovka was one of the great tank encounters of World War II.[12]

The SS troops were shocked by the force of the Soviet onslaught but recovered with remarkable swiftness. Johannes Bräuer, a driver in Jochen Peiper's half-track battalion, described the opening of the attack:

> I had been around since the beginning of the war in Soviet Russia, from Zhitomir to Rostov, but never had I experienced anything like the hell of Prokhorovka. It all happened with such a small space of time that one hardly knew what to make of it. In a flash we were wedged in by T-34s, firing in all directions, ramming each other because so many were exploding and burning. We had limpet mines but no Panzerfäuste [shoulder-fired rocket launchers], and T-34s kept coming over the ridge, racing down the slope through our readiness position and tumbling over and over in the anti-tank ditch.[13]

Many German witnesses to the battle remarked on the clumsy and often desperate tank handling of their opponents. This was a consequence of the brief and inadequate training given to Soviet tank crews and the absence of a proper radio communication system, compounded by their orders to close with the enemy as swiftly as possible to minimize the long-range superiority of German tank gunnery. But as the Red Army T-34s raced wildly toward German lines, they were destroyed en masse. Leibstandarte bore the brunt of the fighting against the Fifth Guards Tank Army, whose vastly superior numbers enabled them to eventually work their way around the SS positions and close with the Germans. But even here, they were no match for their quick-witted opponents. Rudolf von Ribbentrop—commander of Leibstandarte's 7th Panzer Company—described his unit's reaction to close combat with Soviet armor:

> As we waited to see if further enemy tanks were going to appear, I looked all around as was my habit. What I saw left me speechless. From beyond the shallow rise about 150 to 200 meters in front of me appeared fifteen, then thirty, then forty tanks. Finally, there were too many to count. The T-34s were rolling towards us at high speed, carrying mounted infantry. Soon the first shell was on the way and with the impact a T-34 began to burn. It was only fifty to seventy meters from us. The avalanche of enemy tanks rolled straight towards us: tank after tank!
>
> We had only one slim chance: we must remain constantly in motion. A stationary tank would be immediately recognized by the foe as an enemy and fired upon, because all the tanks were rolling at high speed across the terrain. At the repaired bridge over the anti-tank ditch our tanks and anti-tank guns fired at the onrushing enemy. I had managed to roll into cover behind a knocked-out T-34. From there we took part in the battle against the enemy tanks. Burning T-34s drove into and over one another. It was a total inferno of fire and smoke. The entire slope was soon littered with burning enemy tanks.[14]

The ferocious combat in very a confined area gave the battle for Prokhorovka its infernal quality, encouraging subsequent writers to develop the mythology of "the greatest tank battle in history." Soviet losses were certainly massive, possibly as many as 650 armored vehicles across the whole front; postbattle accounts record Hausser coming forward and using chalk marks to list the destroyed tanks (93) littering the battlefield in front of Leibstandarte's position. Recent research suggests that German losses were surprisingly light, perhaps as few as 70 tanks among all three divisions of the SS Panzer Corps.[15]

Yet despite the disparity in tank casualties, the fighting on 12 July had brought the German attack in the South to a halt. The three panzer corps had simply run out of steam, while continuing enemy resistance made significant further progress almost impossible. What reserves the Germans possessed were held back to cover the impending Red Army offensive due in the southern Ukraine. The situation in the north of the Kursk salient was woeful; not only had Model's advance been held, but Soviet counter-attacks were also forcing his troops back with worryingly high losses.

If the tactical and operational aspects of the battle were a cause of concern for the Wehrmacht, then the wider strategic picture was even worse. On 10 July the Allies had launched their offensive against Italy, with successful amphibious and airborne landings in Sicily by U.S. and British forces. Hitler decided he needed to buttress his wavering ally and chose the SS Panzer Corps for this task, despite the fact that it was hotly engaged in a full-scale battle hundreds of miles away from Italy.

On 12 July Hitler told his generals that he was going to call off the offensive. Manstein protested that his forces were close to a breakthrough and asked for a continuation. Hitler briefly wavered, but on the following day he confirmed his original decision and the Wehrmacht went over to the defensive. On 16 July the German formations began to withdraw to their start lines, and on the seventeenth the SS Panzer Corps was ordered to disengage from the front in preparation for a transfer to Italy.

Although Hitler was to bitterly criticize his subordinates for the failure to achieve victory at Kursk, the performance of the SS Panzer Corps in achieving the deepest penetration of any German formation earned his fulsome praise. The SS troops certainly enjoyed the advantages of good weapons and equipment, but their greatest strength was the quality of their leaders at all levels and the amazing esprit de corps of the men.

THE BATTLE OF Kursk was the first major German offensive that failed to achieve a breakthrough, a consequence of inadequate resources and unimaginative strategy. Whereas in the past the Wehrmacht had gained success through a policy of concentration of force at an enemy weak point while using the cover of surprise, at Kursk it was the opposite, with a concentration of force at an enemy strongpoint without the slightest element of surprise.

Kursk was not the turning point in the war that some have claimed, but instead served to confirm the already obvious material weaknesses of the Wehrmacht in the East. The one significant direct outcome of the battle was the passing of the strategic initiative to the Soviet Union. After the failure at Kursk, the Wehrmacht was forced on to the defensive, fighting a vast, continuous rearguard action that would end only with Germany's surrender in May 1945.

Hitler's order to send the SS Panzer Corps to Italy was contested by his army commanders, who correctly argued that it should remain on the Eastern Front. To a plea made by Field Marshal Kluge, Hitler replied, "It is a very difficult decision, but I have no choice. Down there, I can only accomplish something with elite formations that are politically close to Fascism. I must have units down there which come under a political banner."[16]

Hitler's concerns over the political reliability of his Italian ally proved well founded: on 25 July Mussolini was dismissed from office by the Italian Fascist Grand Council and placed under arrest, while secret negotiations were instigated with the Allies to end Italy's participation in the war. But Hitler was wrong to doubt the Wehrmacht; when the Italian government announced an armistice on 8 September, German Army and Luftwaffe units swiftly and ruthlessly took control of the country with minimal assistance from those under the "political banner."

Hitler's plans were anyway thwarted by the Soviet summer offensive. The first (subsidiary) blow came in the southern Ukraine against Isjum and along the River Mius position in mid-July. Totenkopf and Das Reich were immediately sent to shore up the wavering front line, to be joined by Wiking, which had previously been held in reserve. From 30 July to the end of August, the SS formations managed to slow the Soviet offensive. Meanwhile, only Leibstandarte was transferred to Italy, entraining from 27 July onward.

Having helped stabilize the line in the southern Ukraine, the SS divisions were rushed back to the Belgorod area in an attempt to hold the main Soviet offensive directed from the Kursk salient southwest toward the River Dnieper. The Waffen-SS divisions had now become the Wehrmacht's fire brigade, moved from one crisis sector to the next. In a reprise of the struggle around Kharkov earlier in the year, the SS units fought desperately to prevent the Red Army from crossing the Dnieper. Despite Hitler's order that Kharkov (once again) be held at all costs, the beleaguered German commander of the city, General Kempf, ordered a withdrawal on 22 August. Das Reich and Totenkopf—and the army's Grossdeutschland Division—helped supervise a retreat during September to the Dnieper Line, the barrier protecting German-held western Ukraine.

While the SS divisions were battling on the Eastern Front, Leibstandarte was assigned priority rail transport to Innsbruck in Austria, before crossing over the Alps into Italy. As it left the Ukraine the division had handed over its armored vehicles and other heavy weapons to Das Reich and Totenkopf, helping those divisions make good the losses suffered at Kharkov and Kursk. While in Italy, Leibstandarte was rearmed with heavy equipment that included a Panther-tank battalion and sufficient Tiger tanks to begin construction of a new Tiger-tank battalion that would operate at corps level to support both Leibstandarte and the new Hitlerjugend Division.

Leibstandarte was deployed across northern Italy to overawe the local population and, postarmistice, to supervise the surrender of the Italian Army and the handing over of its weapons. In the process, substantial amounts of Italian camouflage clothing were acquired, subsequently to provide uniforms for both Leibstandarte and the Hitlerjugend Divisions.

During its time in Italy Leibstandarte took part in antipartisan actions that included the destruction of the village of Boves and the massacre of its inhabitants by Jochen Peiper's battalion on 19 September. This and a few other similar incidents apart, Leibstandarte troops saw their deployment as something of a holiday. While stationed in Italy Peiper indulged himself in horse riding, sports cars, and taking flying lessons.

In October the division was dispatched to northeastern Italy on the border with Slovenia to engage in more serious antipartisan fighting. But even this was temporary, and on 27 October the division was ordered to return to the East.

As the SS troops were enjoying their Italian interlude, a former Leibstandarte soldier was taking part in a daring and highly successful mission: the rescue of Mussolini from captivity at the hands of the new pro-Allied Italian government. Although the operation was primarily organized by paratroopers from the Luftwaffe, it also included a small unit of SS special forces—at this time part of the 502nd SS Jäger Battalion—under the command of Otto Skorzeny, previously a civil engineer from Austria.

Standing six-foot-four, Skorzeny's formidable appearance was heightened by dueling scars gained as a student. Joining Leibstandarte in 1939, he later transferred to the Reich Division as an engineer officer. He took part in the invasion of the Soviet Union but was struck down by illness toward the end of 1941. While recovering he became interested in the idea of developing a commando-style unit capable of operating behind enemy lines. His proposal was taken up by higher echelons, and SS intelligence chief Walter Schellenberg tasked Skorzeny with developing a school to create paramilitary soldiers trained in espionage, sabotage, and partisan operations.

According to Skorzeny's memoirs, Hitler personally chose him for the rescue mission, which would involve the landing of six gliders on a mountainous ridge at the Gran Sasso ski resort, where Mussolini was being held. On 12 September a mixed Luftwaffe/SS force successfully disembarked at the resort and overcame the guards without a shot being fired. Skorzeny bundled Mussolini into an accompanying Fieseler Storch light aircraft and flew him back to Rome and then on to a meeting with Hitler in Berlin.[17] Skorzeny and the SS were quick to take the lion's share of the credit for the mission, an invaluable propaganda coup for Himmler in his battle for power within the Nazi hierarchy.

Part Three

A CALL TO ARMS

I did not volunteer for the Waffen SS, but was, as were thousands
of my year group, conscripted. I did not then know as a 17-year-
old that it was a criminal unit. I thought it was an elite unit.

—GÜNTER GRASS

Chapter 19

AN ARMY OF EUROPEANS

Himmler and his trusted lieutenant Gottlob Berger never wavered in their efforts to develop the Waffen-SS as a multinational military organization. The recruitment of ethnic German Volksdeutsche from across Europe had provided a ready pool of reinforcements for existing Waffen-SS formations, and from 1942 onward this program also furnished the manpower for a series of new SS divisions. And in what seemed a bizarre twist, the SS also began to consider recruitment in Eastern Europe and the Balkans from groups normally considered to be well outside the Nazi racial pale. All the while, Berger and his SS Main Office continued in their attempts to mobilize Germanic volunteers from northwestern Europe.

The invasion of the Soviet Union had provided the impetus for the raising of the Germanic national legions from racially acceptable Europeans, but the program had proved a limited success at best. In northwest Europe, the response to the Nazi "Crusade against Bolshevism" had always been muted; all of the nations involved—Norway, Denmark, Netherlands, Flemish Belgium—had fielded units that were too small to have any impact on the Eastern Front. That there was no long-term future for the Germanic national legions was apparent to Himmler by the middle of 1942, and with Berger's help he began to overhaul the whole system.

At the front, as a short-term solution, the national legions were progressively absorbed into the 1st and 2nd SS Infantry Brigades in early 1943. For the longer term, Himmler adopted Felix Steiner's proposal for the development of a Germanic army corps, comprising the battle-hardened Wiking Division and a new formation recruited from Germanic countries, to be called the Nordland Division.

The ongoing problem for Berger's recruitment office was to find sufficient numbers of acceptable volunteers, especially now that the first flush of enthusiasm for overthrowing Soviet communism was over. In the home countries—as the Nazi occupation became more oppressive—membership of the Waffen-SS was increasingly less attractive. One way around this was to recruit directly from the tens of thousands of Germanic men working in Germany. They were considered more amenable to extending their support at the military level, free from the inhibiting influences present at home where cooperation was more usually considered to be collaboration.

In April 1943 Albert Speer's Organization Todt permitted Berger to draft foreign workers in Germany directly into the Waffen-SS. The results were initially impressive, with 8,105 men coming forward by the middle of August, although this figure was diminished by the still fairly strict selection standards that saw only 3,154 men accepted for military service.[1] After this the numbers of volunteers tailed off, forcing recruiters once again to rely on Volksdeutsche and Reich Germans to fill Nordland's ranks. By the end of the year the division's ethnic breakdown consisted of 4,100 Reich Germans—who predominantly held senior ranks and technical posts—and 5,900 Volksdeutsche from Romania supplying the majority of the infantry. The actual Germanic element was around 20 percent of the total: 1,400 from Denmark, a little under 800 from Norway, 274 from the Netherlands, plus 38 Swedes and 24 Flemings.[2]

That the division contained substantial numbers of Volksdeutsche was taken into account in its full title. First-category formations—composed of Reich Germans and Germanics who were deemed fit to join the SS Order—were designated by their formation number, tactical specialty and name, as in 5th SS Panzer Division Wiking. Nordland, by contrast, was rated as a second-category formation and was designated by formation number, the adjective *Volunteer* (Freiwilligen), tactical specialty, and name: 11th SS Volunteer Panzergrenadier Division Nordland.

The experienced military core of the division was based around the "Nordland" Regiment, detached from Wiking in the spring of 1943.

Fritz von Scholz, the former "Nordland" commander, was assigned leadership of the new division. Troops from the Netherlands were soon detached to form their own brigade, leaving the division's two infantry regiments—"Norge" and "Danmark"—to reflect its title. The Nordland Division had the standard artillery regiment and support arms, which included a battalion of Panther tanks.

Despite Steiner's hopes, the Nordland Division was never deployed with Wiking but instead fought alongside the Dutch contingent—subsequently designated 4th SS Volunteer Panzergrenadier Brigade Nederland—commanded by another former Wiking officer, Jürgen Wagner. The Nederland Brigade deployed two infantry regiments, "General Seyffardt" (named after the Dutch legion's recently assassinated founder) and "de Ruyter" (after the admiral who had fought the English in the seventeenth century). The brigade had a reasonable initial strength of 5,426 men, although only 40 percent came from the Netherlands, the remainder being Reich Germans or Volksdeutsche.[3] It was intended that the Dutch brigade would form the nucleus for a full division.

The two formations were combined as the III (Germanic) SS Panzer Corps, a reduced army corps that possessed few armored vehicles, despite its designation. Although its military potential was limited, Himmler showed great interest in the formation in the hope that it would act as a model for compulsory military service in the Germanic countries after the war. In September 1943 the corps was sent to Croatia to complete its training, which included engagement in antipartisan warfare.

IN MAY 1943 the Flanders Legion was re-formed as SS Volunteer Assault Brigade Langemarck, the "Langemarck" part of its title referring to a 1914 battle fought by the Germans against the British in Flanders and apparently intended to signify Flemish-German ties of friendship. Approximately 600 men crossed over from the old legion, reinforced by new volunteers and others transferred from SS replacement depots. As well as a reinforced infantry battalion, the formation—fully motorized—contained powerful support arms in the shape of a mechanized antitank company, an assault-gun battalion equipped with StuG IIIs, and an antiaircraft company. With an overall strength of just over 2,000 men, the assault brigade was a far more effective combat formation than its infantry-based legion predecessor.

Langemarck's training took place at the former Austro-Hungarian Army base at Milowitz in Bohemia. Himmler and Berger again issued orders to the instructing staff to refrain from the insults that were second nature to them and to exercise the greatest "care and attention" to the welfare of the recruits.[4] It would seem that these strictures finally began to make themselves felt—at least among the Germanic units.

Former officers from the various national armies, or those men showing officer potential, were encouraged to complete officer training at the Waffen-SS Junkerschulen at Bad Tölz and Braunschweig. The aim was to make them fully bilingual and well prepared in SS tactical and political doctrine and to be able to work alongside German officers in the field. By the end of 1943 growing numbers of these officers were graduating from the cadet schools, ready to take up commands with troops of their own nationality. These measures certainly helped improve the fighting quality of the Germanics within the Waffen-SS, as would be demonstrated in the campaigns of 1944.

The formation of the Langemarck Brigade was followed by two other similar assault brigades, but both from unlikely backgrounds. The French-speaking Walloons of southern Belgium and the French had traditionally been categorized by the Nazis as Latin peoples, quite distinct from those North Europeans considered to share a similar racial heritage to Reich Germans. During the early 1940s, however, Himmler's race experts began to suggest that Germanic racial influence might extend in limited and specific areas to southern Belgium and parts of France.

This idea was readily adopted by those right-wing politicians in Wallonia and France who wanted closer involvement with the Nazi system. Among them was the Belgian Rexist agitator Léon Degrelle, who was serving in the army-organized Walloon Legion. He had repeatedly lobbied Hitler and Himmler to persuade them that the Walloons were a "lost German tribe," but to little effect. Degrelle was nothing if not persistent, and as a fluent and persuasive public speaker he eventually managed to convince Himmler to have the Walloon Legion assigned to the SS.

The army made no objections to the transfer, so that in May 1943 it became the SS Volunteer Assault Brigade Wallonien under the command of Sturmbannführer Lucien Lippert (Léon Degrelle, with only limited military experience, was assigned a vague role of military-political liaison officer). Organization was similar to that of the Langemarck Brigade: a reinforced, motorized infantry battalion, with light artillery, engineer, and antitank companies, plus an assault-gun company transferred from the SS Polizei Division. By November 1943 the brigade—some 1,850 men strong—was considered combat ready and sent eastward to support the Wiking Division in the Ukraine.[5]

France had already supplied a national legion for the German Army, the Légion des Volontaires Français, which had seen action on the Eastern Front. Himmler, however, refused to have anything to do with the LVF and instead ordered the creation of a completely new formation— SS Volunteer Brigade Frankreich—that insisted on more rigorous racial selection standards than had been the case with the army-raised unit.

Training of the 1,700-strong Frankreich Brigade began in the summer of 1943 at the Sennheim camp in Alsace, a seemingly thorough program that included the integration of French officers who had graduated from the Bad Tölz cadet school. The brigade was commanded by former French Foreign Legion officer Paul Marie Gamory-Dubourdeau and comprised two infantry battalions along with antiaircraft, artillery, and assault-gun units. In July 1944 the brigade was dispatched to the Eastern Front to fight alongside the SS Horst Wessel Division.[6]

Another unit to see the light of day was the British Free Corps, recruited from British fascists and sympathizers living in Germany when the war broke out. Initially called the Legion of St. George, its leaders attempted to persuade disaffected British prisoners of war to join them, but despite a recruiting campaign conducted during 1943 in several POW camps, it proved an abject failure. When the unit was officially established under Waffen-SS control on 1 January 1944, it had just fifteen members, and throughout its lifetime its numbers at any one time never exceeded fifty.[7]

DESPITE SOME POTENTIALLY promising developments in the attempt to integrate Germanics within the Waffen-SS, the resources necessary to drive Himmler's plans for expansion would have to come from the Volksdeutsche in the Balkans and Eastern Europe. Under the guidance of Gottlob Berger, a small number of Romanians had been covertly integrated into the Waffen-SS in June 1940. Although Romania was an ally of Nazi Germany, it remained a sovereign country, and Berger could not openly take its citizens without governmental permission. An easier process was to conscript Volksdeutsche resettled in Germany and from communities under direct German control, which included parts of the former Yugoslavia.

After the German conquest of Yugoslavia in April 1941, the country was broken up into constituent parts, with chunks of territory seized by German allies Italy, Hungary, and Bulgaria. Croatia, under its brutal fascist leader, Ante Pavelić, emerged as a Nazi puppet state, while Serbia came under German military administration.

Although Germany had won a stunning military victory in Yugoslavia, two Serb-based guerrilla movements soon emerged, the Royalist Chetniks and the communist Partisans under Josip Tito. To counter this insurgency, the ethnic Germans of the Banat—a region in northern Serbia between Belgrade and the Hungarian border—set up their own "self-defense" units. Berger wasted no time in co-opting them as the basis for a new Waffen-SS division.

The new formation would become 7th SS Volunteer Mountain Division Prinz Eugen, named after the renowned imperial Austrian general who had successfully fought the Turks in the region during the early eighteenth century (that the prince had been a close ally of the English Duke of Marlborough was glossed over). In January 1942 the newly promoted Brigadeführer Artur Phleps—formerly commander of Wiking's "Westland" Regiment—was assigned to lead the division. Phleps, whose background as an ethnic German born in Transylvania made him an appropriate choice, set about his task with enthusiasm. His attitude contrasted with that of most other (Reich-born) German officers, who considered a posting to the division as a form of punishment.[8]

Military-eligible Volksdeutsche from the Banat were urged in the strongest terms to sign up for the new division. They were subsequently joined by Volksdeutsche from Croatia, Hungary, and Romania, who considered service in a German-organized formation preferable to that of their home nation. Fred Umbrich, a Transylvanian Saxon, was one such volunteer who wrote that "any price was worth paying to avoid the Romanian Army. I shuddered as I recalled the kicks and curses I had witnessed at the area inspection more than a year earlier."[9]

Prinz Eugen was formed on 1 March 1942; thereafter, recruitment began in earnest. After a short flurry of interest, the numbers of volunteers dried up, with Himmler and Berger forced to introduce conscription in the region. In October 1942 the division was considered ready for operational deployment, and was 92 percent Volksdeutsche, the remaining percentage coming from Reich Germans occupying senior or technical positions.[10]

Berger then turned his attention to the Nazi puppet regimes of Croatia and Slovakia. As was becoming a defining pattern, the Volksdeutsche communities in both states seemed to lack the necessary commitment to the Nazi German cause to provide the numbers expected of them, forcing the SS Main Office to apply various degrees of coercion. The Croat and Slovak governments were sluggardly in cooperating with Berger's recruiting agents, but they were legally unable to stop the impressment of their ethnic Germans.

Hungary and Romania were next, and while agreements had to be negotiated, Himmler and Berger pressed hard to gain access to their Volksdeutsche communities. Himmler held the view that Volksdeutsche were not citizens of their "host" countries but Germans who happened to be living in these countries and, as such, were subject to conscription into the Waffen-SS.

Following the debacle at Stalingrad, the demand for manpower increased ever more, sufficiently so for the SS Main Office to override the wishes of the Hungarian and Romanian governments and impose conscription on ethnic Germans in both countries during 1943. Berger's measures seemed to work, so that by the end of year the Waffen-SS had inducted the following numbers of Volksdeutsche:[11]

Serbia	21,516
Croatia	17,538
Slovakia	5,390

Romania   54,000
Hungary   22,125

The obvious problem with Berger's emphasis on quantity was the consequent loss of quality. As his responsibilities essentially ended once the recruit had signed the SS enlistment papers, he had limited interest in what happened down the line. The training and deployment of this influx of manpower became the concern of Hans Jüttner of the SS Leadership Main Office, and he was understandably outraged at the poor physical and mental standard of the recruits he was receiving. On one occasion Jüttner complained to Berger about a batch sent from Hungary that included men with epilepsy and tuberculosis, pointing out that they had "not been seen by a doctor or SS officer. Because their physical disabilities are so obvious that a soldier could never declare these men fit for military service."[12]

Despite these criticisms, Berger's obsession with numbers remained unchecked. The once fixed racial lines were also becoming increasingly blurred, something not lost on bemused Waffen-SS veterans. One of these was Karl Hummelkeier, who had volunteered for the "Germania" Regiment in the 1930s. He recalled how the decline in standards "was one of amazement for us, after all the concepts of racial purity, the true Aryan race and how precious the SS were, the need to be kept pure, and all the rest of it. To see this huge variety of soldier material bearing the SS insignia was rather staggering."[13]

At a practical level, Untersturmführer Hans Werner Woltersdorf of Das Reich was exasperated at the low caliber of the Volksdeutsche he was expected to train at Montboyer in France during 1943. Among the recruits was Alfons, assigned as his orderly:

Alfons could neither read nor write, and there were others who hadn't learned more than to scrawl their names in capital letters. They came from Yugoslavia, Hungary, Romania or Poland—"adopted Germans." They had never learned to march or stand properly, in the scouts or other youth organization, and came to us from the sugar-beet field, the cow stall, or a herd of goats. Some had volunteered, others had not, but none of them had any idea of what was in store for them. In October 1939

An improvised armored vehicle of a Freikorps unit stands guard on a Berlin street during the attempted Kapp Putsch of 1920. The aggressive and nihilistic attitudes of the Freikorps were an important influence in the development of the fighting ethos held by the Waffen-SS. *(Bundesarchiv)*

Adolf Hitler takes the salute of an honor guard of the Leibstandarte in Berlin, 1938. The prewar Leibstandarte's close attention to parade-ground drill would earn it the derisory nickname "the asphalt soldiers" from other Waffen-SS units. *(Bundesarchiv)*

Heinrich Himmler, the SS leader whose ambition was for a Pan-Germanic Europe under SS control. *(Bundesarchiv)*

Paul Hausser, a former Army officer who laid the foundations for the Waffen-SS as an elite combat force. *(Bundesarchiv)*

Josef "Sepp" Dietrich, commander of the Leibstandarte and an embodiment of the fighting spirit of the Waffen-SS. *(Bundesarchiv)*

Theodor Eicke, main architect of the SS concentration-camp system and successful commander of the Totenkopf Division. *(Bundesarchiv)*

Felix Steiner, first commander of the Wiking Division and proponent of wider European involvement within the Waffen-SS. *(Bundesarchiv)*

Gottlob Berger, a close ally of Heinrich Himmler whose recruitment policies saw the expansion of the Waffen-SS into a multinational mass army. *(Bundesarchiv)*

Herbert Gille, the most highly decorated member of the Waffen-SS and commander of the IV SS Panzer Corps during the final battles in Hungary during 1945. *(Bundesarchiv)*

Wilhelm Bittrich, who served in the Leibstandarte and Das Reich divisions and commanded SS troops during the battle for Arnhem in September 1944. *(Bundesarchiv)*

Infantry of the Leibstandarte rest in a roadside ditch around Pabianice during the invasion of Poland, September 1939. *(Library of Congress)*

Accompanied by Jochen Peiper (far right), Himmler visits Waffen-SS troops in Metz after the German victory over France in 1940. Peiper acted as Himmler's adjutant before taking a field command in the Leibstandarte. *(Bundesarchiv)*

Armored cars of the Leibstandarte lead a motorized column through Bulgaria in preparation for the attack on Yugoslavia and Greece, April 1941. *(Bundesarchiv)*

In a show of gratitude for their battlefield exploits, Himmler rewarded the officers of the Reich Division with a guided tour of Mauthausen concentration camp in 1941. In this photograph, Hausser (in greatcoat) walks up the infamous "stairs of death," while behind him is Fritz Klingenberg—center, second row—hero of the capture of Belgrade. *(Bundesarchiv)*

Horse-drawn artillery of the Wehrmacht and armored cars of the Leibstandarte drive through a burning village in the Ukraine during the early stages of Operation Barbarossa, August 1941. *(Bundesarchiv)*

Officers of the motorized Totenkopf Division pause to assess the tactical situation, while acting as a spearhead in Army Group North's drive into the Soviet Union, September 1941. *(Bundesarchiv)*

Soldiers of the Wiking Division stand in front of their Marder II tank destroyer during the advance into the Caucasus, August–September 1942. *(Bundesarchiv)*

Leibstandarte officer Fritz Witt marches past his half-track armored personnel carrier as Kharkov is recaptured, 14 March 1943—the most outstanding solo victory of the Waffen-SS in the Soviet Union. *(Bundesarchiv)*

Troops of the Freikorps Danmark swear allegiance to the Nazi cause, following the establishment of the Danish Legion on 29 June 1941. By August 1941 over 1,000 men were under arms. *(Bundesarchiv)*

An awards ceremony for soldiers of the Legion Niederlande on the Eastern Front, February 1943. Among the countries of northwest Europe, the Netherlands supplied the largest contingent of volunteers for the Waffen-SS. *(Bundesarchiv)*

Belgian Rexist politician Léon Degrelle shakes hands with a decorated soldier from the SS Assault Brigade Wallonian, April 1944. The brigade had distinguished itself in fighting on the Eastern Front earlier in the year. *(Wikipedia)*

A French volunteer proclaims his enthusiasm for the Waffen-SS prior to transit from Paris to training camps in Germany, October 1943. *(Bundesarchiv)*

A recruitment poster for the Ukrainian 14th SS Waffen Grenadier Division of the SS, January 1943. An initial response of 80,000 volunteers was eventually winnowed down to provide sufficient men for an infantry division. *(Wikipedia)*

The German Army had originally been responsible for the raising of anticommunist Cossack cavalry in the southern Soviet Union, although in November 1944 these units were transferred to the Waffen-SS where they served in an antipartisan role in Yugoslavia. *(Bundesarchiv)*

Soldiers of the Muslim Handschar Division—recruited primarily from Croatian Bosnia—read an SS propaganda tract on Islam and Judaism. Their distinctive headgear comprised a red fez for ceremonial occasions and a gray fez for field conditions. *(Bundesarchiv)*

Troops of the SS Cavalry Brigade halt during an antipartisan sweep in the Soviet Union, September 1941. As the war developed the formation was increasingly recruited from Hungarian Volksdeutsche. *(Bundesarchiv)*

The fearsome sight of a Tiger I tank of Das Reich Division as it advances over the Soviet Steppe in June 1943 during the buildup to the battle of Kursk. (*Bundesarchiv*)

Wounded SS troops are transported on a half-track that is struggling through the mud in the wet conditions typical of the Eastern Front during spring and the fall. (*Bundesarchiv*)

The charismatic special forces leader Otto Skorzeny inspects men of the SS Parachute Battalion in Pomerania, February 1945. Skorzeny achieved fame for his part in the rescue of Mussolini in September 1943 and in the coup against the Hungarian government in October 1944. *(Bundesarchiv)*

An armored column and Waffen-SS infantry await orders during the advance through Hungary as part of the ill-fated Operation Spring Awakening, March 1944. *(Bundesarchiv)*

A Panzer Mark IV of the Hitlerjugend Division rolls through a Belgian village in a training exercise, early 1944. Half the tanks allotted to the division were Mark IVs while the remainder comprised the more powerful Mark V Panthers. *(Bundesarchiv)*

Senior officers of the Hitlerjugend in Normandy, June 1944. Max Wünsche (left) engages in an animated discussion with Kurt Meyer (right) while the divisional commander, Fritz Witt (center) looks on. *(Bundesarchiv)*

Armored vehicles of the 9th SS Panzer Division Hohenstaufen move up to crush the lightly held British defenses around Arnhem. The swift deployment of German armor was a key factor behind German success in the battle. *(Bundesarchiv)*

US soldiers surrender to Kampfgruppe Peiper at Stoumont, 19 December 1944. Given the massacre of US troops near Malmédy two days earlier, the concerned expression of the leading captive is well founded, although in this instance the US prisoners received good treatment. *(Bundesarchiv)*

Soldiers of the Hitlerjugend Division, captured by US forces during the Battle of Elsenborn Ridge, December 1944. The captives' youthful appearance reflects the desperation of Nazi Germany in the final stages of the war, when the very young and very old were thrown into battle in a futile attempt to hold the Allied advance into Germany. *(US Army)*

An American soldier surveys the aftermath of the Malmédy massacre, where men of the Leibstandarte, under the command of Jochen Peiper, shot and killed eighty-six recently surrendered US troops on 17 December 1944. Repeated battlefield atrocities committed by the Waffen-SS were a feature of the campaigns fought on both Western and Eastern Fronts. *(US Army)*

twenty per cent of my company of recruits might have consisted of college students, athletes, or at least well-trained scouts with a minimum of average intelligence, but in Montboyer I found a motley crew that made a mockery of any idea of "elite."[14]

The Volksdeutsche recruits—many with little interest in Germany or National Socialism—found military life especially hard, forced to undergo the rigorous training methods of the Waffen-SS while constantly ridiculed by their instructors and other Reich-born recruits. In the Nordland and Wiking Divisions they also found themselves scorned by Germanics, who resented their presence in otherwise select military formations. One former Danish farmer claimed the sound of Romanians eating was worse than a "bunch of old seasoned sows."[15]

For those Volksdeutsche who had genuinely volunteered for the Waffen-SS, the disparaging comments from those who were supposed to be their comrades was particularly hard to endure. After being insulted by a German officer at his training camp, Fred Umbrich wrote: "We all felt as if the *Reichsdeutsche* saw us as second-class soldiers who did not measure up to 'real' Germans. We all felt bitterly disappointed. We had thought we were joining a good cause; we had thought we were helping Germany and Romania in their fight with the Russians."[16]

THE WEHRMACHT'S VICTORIES during 1941–1942 brought a large swath of Muslims under German control in southern Russia and the Balkans. While the German Army recruited extensively from Muslims in southern Russia and the Caucasus region, the Balkans became the preserve of the Waffen-SS. Nazi racial experts had conveniently come to the conclusion that the Croats—and the Bosnian Muslims within Croatia— were not, in fact, South Slavs but were descended from Aryans and thus suitable candidates for inclusion within the wider Germanic community.

During the latter part of 1942, Himmler began to show interest in the idea of inducting Muslims into the Waffen-SS, claiming an affinity with what he considered the inherently martial nature of the Islamic religion. His interest was encouraged by the grand mufti of Jerusalem, an anti-Semitic, anti-British Islamic cleric who had sought refuge in Nazi Germany. Berger welcomed the formation of an entirely Muslim division within the SS, which he also saw as a useful propaganda tool: "Through the creation of the Croatian-Bosnian Division, it is our desire to reach out to Muslims all over the world, who number around 350 million people and are decisive in the struggle with the British Empire."[17]

Croatia—which had already lost many of its Volksdeutsche to the Waffen-SS—opposed the creation of a Muslim division recruited from its own subjects, but objections by the Croatian government were ignored by Himmler and Hitler, the latter also showing an interest in a Muslim military commitment. The division was ordered into being on 10 February 1943, with Artur Phleps assisting in its formation. The grand mufti arrived in Bosnia to coax the local Muslims to take up arms against the communist partisans, fraudulently promising them that the SS would act as a protector of Islam.

Several thousand men came forward, although the overall standard was very low, few having any prior military experience. Most were illiterate, and many suffered from diseases and other physical ailments that should have immediately barred them from military service. Others arrived at the recruiting centers in rags, with the promise of new uniforms a major incentive to sign up. Wilhelm Eberling, one of the German recruiting officers, wrote that "some of the men took their newly issued uniforms and sold them on the black market. They would then report in again the next day as if they were new."[18] The recruits had no interest in Himmler's empire-building program, but joined the division primarily to secure weapons to protect their own communities from the depredations of Serb partisans and Croat paramilitaries. The prospect of regular pay and the opportunity to loot the villages of ethnic opponents were further incentives to accept the SS offer.[19]

The Muslim division was a major departure for Himmler and Berger, the first time a formation had been raised for service in the Waffen-SS that had no Aryan or German connection. In contrast to the anti-Christian tone set in most of the rest of the SS, care was taken not to offend the religious sensibilities of the recruits, the grand mufti helping organize the supply of imams to act as military "chaplains." The uniforms issued to them were those of German mountain troops, but instead of caps the men were kitted out with fezzes, gray for field conditions and red for ceremonial occasions.

The new division was rated as a third-category formation and was designated accordingly: the term *Waffen* was followed by its tactical specialty and the phrase "of the SS" (*der SS*), then its name and, in brackets, its nationality. Thus, this division raised in Croatia became the 13th Waffen Mountain Division of the SS Handschar (Croatian). The name Handschar referred to the Bosnian scimitar, which was also used in the formation's collar insignia.

By the summer of 1943 a little less than 10,000 men had been selected from the volunteers, insufficient for a full-strength division. This shortfall led to the imposition of conscription, so that from 11 July onward the SS took two-thirds of those Muslims who would have otherwise been conscripted into the Croatian armed forces.

The German Reich and Volksdeutsche officers and NCOs engaged in organizing the division were fearful that if training took place in Bosnia, it would be too easy for unhappy recruits to simply slip away to their hometowns and villages. Rather than choose somewhere else in the region, the Handschar recruits were transported to an isolated camp in the French Pyrenees, a cause of disquiet among the men.

As yet, Handschar had no commander, but on 9 August Colonel Karl-Gustav Sauberzweig was appointed to lead the division. The expansion of the Waffen-SS during 1942–1943 was such that there were insufficient SS officers to fill senior and staff positions, forcing Himmler and Jüttner to arrange the transfer of officers from the army. Promoted to Oberführer, Sauberzweig had been severely wounded during World War I (losing an eye), had no knowledge of the Balkans, and spoke no Serbo-Croat. Despite these limitations, he was considered a good organizer, and he seemed to have won the affection of at least some of his subordinates, one imam recalling that "he was a fine man. He treated the young soldiers as if they were his own children."[20]

Further batches of recruits arrived during the summer so that by September, the division mustered 20,000 men, although this figure contained a number of Catholic Croats included to make up the numbers. Hidden among these reinforcements were partisan sympathizers, who helped further the sense of discontent felt by the recruits. They also brought news of the massacre of the Muslim Bosnian village of Kosutica, carried out during a counterinsurgency sweep by their supposed comrades in the Prinz Eugen Division. This brought matters to a head, with the secret pro-Tito supporters leading a mutiny on 17 September 1943. The revolt came to little, however, and was soon suppressed, but Himmler was sufficiently alarmed at the incident to have the division transferred to Germany to complete its training. In February 1944 the Handschar Division was judged to be combat ready and was dispatched to Croatia to take on Tito's partisans.

———————

STALIN'S BRUTAL TREATMENT of the Ukrainian people during the 1930s helped create a groundswell of support for the Germans as they drove into Ukraine in 1941. Berger had argued from the start that the Waffen-SS should exploit this support, but Himmler and Hitler rebuffed all Ukrainian offers, not only for racial reasons but also because this would provide an opportunity for the well-organized Ukrainian nationalist movement to press for independence. The Germans preferred to use Ukrainians in paramilitary antipartisan battalions or as forced labor. Despite the Nazis' vicious overlordship of the Ukraine, many Ukrainians still held hopes of accommodation with Germany in order to free themselves from the Soviet-Russian yoke. And post-Stalingrad, offers of military support became more acceptable to the Nazi hierarchy.

In April 1943 the order was given for the creation of a Ukrainian Waffen-SS division. Himmler overcame his scruples in accepting Slavs into the SS on the basis that the western Ukraine had formerly been the Austro-Hungarian province of Galicia and consequently had a German connection; his race experts claimed that roughly half of the people from the former province had a substantial amount of "Germanic blood."[21] This was reflected in the name of the new formation, which after several changes became the 14th Waffen Grenadier Division of the SS (Galician).

Recruiting centers were established across the western Ukraine, and the response to this call for arms proved remarkably effective, with some 80,000 men registering to join the division by November 1943. The motivations for joining were not pro-German but anti-Soviet. One anonymous volunteer described his reasons: "There were three choices, work in Germany, join the Division, or wait for the Russians and be conscripted into the Soviet Army to fight and die for the hated Stalin and his regime or be sent to Siberia."[22] The numbers seemed impressive but were progressively winnowed down to a far smaller figure: 53,000 were admitted to the Waffen-SS; 25,000 were considered fit for military service, and 13,245 of the volunteers went forward to undergo training.[23] Some dropped out during training, but others arrived to provide sufficient men for an infantry division.

The quality of the Ukrainian volunteers was generally considered to be good, and their training was taken seriously. But by the end of 1943 the whole Nazi empire was facing a universal and chronic shortage of almost every important war material, and this became apparent to the Ukrainian recruits who not only lacked suitable weapons and equipment but were often short of such basics as food and uniforms as well.

Although these shortages were eventually overcome, a more fundamental problem remained in the quality and attitude of the German officers and NCOs assigned to the division. As was the case with most of the other foreign SS formations, the instructing staff had little knowledge of the men they were expected to train, with language barriers a continual hindrance. This problem extended to the top with the appointment of Brigadeführer Fritz Freitag as commander. Freitag, promoted from 4th SS Polizei Division, was a difficult, inflexible character who showed little interest in his Ukrainian troops.

Wolf-Dietrich Heike—an army officer seconded to the division as its chief operational officer—got to know Freitag well and in a scrupulously honest assessment of his superior wrote that he "was driven by an almost pathological ambition to succeed, often manifested by excessive discipline towards his subordinates. He was suspicious of most people and made life unpleasant not only for his colleagues but also for himself. He was a theoretician who wanted to command a military unit from behind his desk."[24] These shortcomings would have serious consequences, initially in training but more so when in battle against the Red Army.

In February 1944 a number of Ukrainian units—about 2,000 strong and commanded by Sturmbannführer Friedrich Bayersdorff—were committed to antipartisan operations on the Polish-Ukrainian border.

Otherwise, training continued until June, by which time the division was considered operational but with a recommendation that it be assigned to a quiet sector of the front.

———————

STALIN'S ANNEXATION OF the Baltic States in 1939–1940 was followed by systematic repression as the Soviet Union sought to impose communist control over the former Russian-ruled territories. Thus, it was hardly surprising that in the summer of 1941, the advancing German troops should be greeted as liberators by the peoples of Lithuania, Latvia, and Estonia. Local elites within the Baltic States were keen to offer their services to the Germans in exchange for the return of their countries' independence. The Germans, once again, refused to countenance any idea of national self-determination, especially as Himmler had thoughts of annexing the states within his Greater German Reich.

Nazi Germany had a complex and often contradictory attitude toward the three nations. Lithuania—with its former association with Poland— was considered to be racially unsuitable for any close cooperation with the Reich. The Lithuanians, for their part, demonstrated little interest in cooperating with their German conquerors, in contrast to substantial numbers of Latvians and Estonians.

After initial reservations, Himmler decided that the peoples of Latvia and especially Estonia were racially acceptable for limited inclusion in the SS. As a consequence of Nazi determination to thwart any movement toward independence, military cooperation was initially limited to the formation of paramilitary police battalions who rounded up and killed Soviet sympathizers and aided the Germans in counterinsurgency warfare against Red Army partisans. In Latvia, the German arrival also occasioned an orgy of violence against the country's substantial Jewish population.

The failure to defeat the Soviet Union during 1941–1942 encouraged the Germans to look again at utilizing manpower from the Baltic States. In August 1942 the creation of the Waffen-SS-organized Estonian Legion was formally announced, a brigade-strength organization that first saw action late in 1943 in defensive fighting around Nevel. While the legion was undergoing training, a battalion was raised from the more promising volunteers and dispatched to the Ukraine to reinforce the Wiking Division after the loss of its "Nordland" Regiment. The formation of the Latvian Legion followed, also deployed near Nevel. The puppet regimes in both countries had hoped that this display of military support would encourage the Germans to adopt a more favorable attitude toward independence, but when this was not forthcoming cooperation slumped.

The Germans imposed conscription in Estonia and Latvia during 1943. The idea was to convert the Baltic legions into infantry divisions, albeit with limited supporting arms. The ominous westward advance of the Red Army in early 1944 became an incentive for many Estonians and Latvians to take up arms against the Red Army, Germany being considered the lesser of the two evils. As a result, the Germans were able to field a substantial force from Latvia and Estonia.[25]

The first of the Baltic divisions was formally created in May 1943: the 15th Waffen-Grenadier Division of the SS (Latvian No. 1), comprising three infantry regiments whose cadre was drawn primarily from the old Latvian Legion, with new recruits arriving through the introduction of conscription. The German officers sent to command the division were, in the main, former police officers of inferior quality; they repeatedly clashed with the junior, but more experienced, Latvian officers and NCOs.[26]

A second Latvian formation—the 19th Waffen-Grenadier Division of the SS (Latvian No. 2)—was formed in February 1944. The Latvian troops in this formation were better trained and possessed more military experience than their comrades in the 15th Division. The origins of the 19th Division lay in the old 2nd SS Infantry Brigade. Three Latvian Schuma (police) battalions had been integrated into the brigade in January–February 1943. Himmler was impressed by the conduct of the Latvians, and following the withdrawal of Germanic legion units from the brigade early in 1943, he decided to convert it into an all-Latvian force, incorporating three battalions from the Latvian Legion and redesignating it as the 2nd SS Latvian Brigade. The brigade took part in the defense of the Volkhov River sector on the Leningrad front, before its upgrading to the 19th Waffen-Grenadier Division.

The introduction of conscription in Estonia in March 1943 witnessed the expansion of the Estonian Legion, which in turn led to the establishment of the Estonian SS Volunteer Brigade in May 1943. A further general mobilization in February 1944 produced sufficient recruits to create the 20th Waffen-Grenadier Division of the SS (Estonian No. 1) under the command of Brigadeführer Franz Augsberger. A veteran SS officer from Das Reich and the Wiking Division, Augsberger had been sent to organize the formation of the Estonian Legion at the end of 1942, and he continued to lead the Estonians at the divisional level. His sense of empathy with his soldiers was appreciated, and his death in action on 19 March 1945 was greatly mourned. As with the other Baltic divisions, the Estonian Division was an infantry-heavy formation with limited fire support.[27]

HIMMLER'S DESIRE FOR an SS-dominated Pan-Germanic Europe and the need to find extra recruits for the Waffen-SS ran hand in hand for a long time. By mid-1944, however, the rapid expansion of the Waffen-SS—to include national and ethnic groups with little or no affinity to the ideas and prejudices of National Socialism—was beginning to undermine the project. Himmler had been wildly overoptimistic to expect men conscripted from the European periphery to even understand, let alone adopt, his vision; their viewpoints were understandably local in character, reflecting their own ethnic and national interests.

Gottlob Berger's mania for cannon fodder also compromised military effectiveness. The formations raised in northern and western Europe and the Baltic States demonstrated their battlefield utility, but the weaker formations from Eastern Europe and the Balkans acted as a drain on German officers and NCOs—and weapons and equipment—to the detriment of the German war effort as a whole. Yet such was the momentum of the SS enlistment system that in the last twelve months of the war, Berger would preside over a last frenzied bout of recruitment that defied all military logic.

Chapter 20

DEFENDING THE UKRAINE

THE SOVIET SUMMER offensive of 1943 pushed the Germans back across eastern Ukraine toward the River Dnieper. Manstein had managed to persuade Hitler to relinquish the industrial Donbass region and establish a new defensive line along the river. The retreat across the eastern Ukraine during August and September was relatively orderly thanks to the rearguard actions fought by the German panzer divisions that included Das Reich, Totenkopf, and Wiking. While Wiking organized the withdrawal across the Dnieper at Cherkassy, Totenkopf and Das Reich were responsible for shepherding the slow-moving infantry divisions over the river at Kremenchug.

To the dismay of the retreating Germans, the Dnieper Line turned out to be a construction on paper only, so the Red Army had little difficulty in establishing several bridgeheads over the river by early October. The SS divisions were then engaged in rushing from one danger spot to another to prevent Soviet breakouts. Totenkopf maintained a resolute defense of Krivoy Rog, a key communications and logistical center within the Dnieper bend. A Soviet armored column seemed on the point of capturing the city when on 27 October it was attacked in the flank by the hastily assembled XL Panzer Corps, led by Totenkopf. The Soviet force was caught by surprise and in the space of a few days thrown back toward the Dnieper. Thanks to this action, Krivoy Rog remained in German hands until a planned withdrawal was undertaken in February 1944.

Farther upstream, Wiking defended the area around Cherkassy, which its troops had driven through in triumph during the heady days of the Barbarossa summer. Although they had been unable to prevent the Red Army from establishing a bridgehead on the river's west bank, they contained any further enemy advances. In November the division was reinforced by the arrival of the well-equipped 5th SS Volunteer Assault Brigade Wallonien. The Belgian troops were immediately employed in a successful action against Soviet irregulars in the Irdyn marshes that bordered the Dnieper.

The main danger for the German defensive line came farther north around Kiev. At the beginning of November Soviet forces broke out of the twin bridgeheads established close to the Ukrainian capital. The Germans were forced to abandon the city, and as the Red Army advanced at speed to capture Zhitomir, the entire German position in Ukraine, from Kiev to the Black Sea, faced the possibility of encirclement. A proposed German attack in southern Ukraine was abandoned in order to stem the Soviet advance to the north. Das Reich and Leibstandarte, newly arrived from Italy, were dispatched to contain the rapidly expanding Soviet salient.

The Tiger company of Das Reich was among the first to arrive on the battlefield, its tanks unloaded at the rail junction of Bjelaja-Zerkow on the night of 6–7 November. Tank commander Ernst Streng recalled the confusion as the panzers detrained: "The whole city was about to leave. Evacuation trains were rolling out of the station; fires were flaring to burn mountains of files. The headquarters of all German departments were in the process of pulling out. The Russian tank spearheads were expected any hour. Panic and fear drove the people through the streets. Looting and destruction were everywhere."[1]

The Tigers advanced northward covered by the screen of the reconnaissance battalion. A couple of days later they were joined by units from the Leibstandarte Division, and together they helped stabilize the front. On 11 November Streng came across enemy forces around the village of Slawia:

We could hear the Russian tanks milling about. A short briefing by the adjutant followed. We moved out of the village, broke through the cover of bushes, and suddenly saw, among the smoke and haze, the black, massive belly of the first enemy tank at 200 meters. Quickly taking aim, we fired and a long lance of flame shot from the barrel. Immediately we saw the yellow-white fireball of the explosion. Smoke and fire mushroomed and obscured the picture of destruction. Two hundred meters east of Slawia we knocked out our second Russian tank that had broken through our lines. Around 8 p.m. the enemy shelling slowed down and then stopped altogether. The infantry of the Leibstandarte came out of their foxholes in the badly damaged positions. The men warmed up at the glowing exhausts and the engine at the rear of our panzer.[2]

The main German thrust against the Soviet positions would be made by General Balck's XLVIII Panzer Corps, temporarily expanded to seven divisions (mostly understrength, however). Among them were the army's 1st Panzer Division and Leibstandarte, who together would lead the assault. Their orders were to cut the Zhitomir-Kiev road and isolate the enemy in Zhitomir. The panzers roared forward on 13 November and caught the Red Army in disarray. On 17 November the road was crossed, and in the evening Zhitomir was captured. Balck then turned eastward to destroy the Soviet defenses around Brusilov.

Leibstandarte's attack on 20 November was halted, however. Balck's chief of staff, Major General Mellenthin, noted somewhat acidly, "The frontal attack of Leibstandarte on Brusilov failed; it was the first time in the war that this famous division had launched an attack and failed to gain its objective."[3] Flanking attacks by the other panzer divisions were more successful, and the town fell to the Germans, although Balck was angry that large numbers of Soviet troops had managed to escape his enveloping maneuver. After the capture of Brusilov, Soviet resistance stiffened, slowing the pace of the German advance. On 26 November a sudden rise in temperature—and attendant slush and mud—brought armored operations to a temporary halt.

German panzer forces had once again proved superior to those of the Red Army. Leibstandarte's Tiger tanks were to the fore with Michael Wittmann adding further laurels to his crown as a panzer ace. On the morning of the opening day of the offensive, Wittmann knocked out ten

T-34s and five Paks (antitank guns). By early January 1944 his combined total of destroyed tanks would rise to sixty-six. But for Wittmann and his fellow panzer commanders, the Red Army's deployment of Pak fronts—where lines of well-camouflaged antitank guns would lie in ambush—was a growing threat. Wittmann made clear that "every tank counts, but each Pak counts double."[4]

Leibstandarte's Tiger company dealt with the Pak fronts with a simple yet risky tactic of assembling a platoon of Tigers in a concealed position and then sending one tank forward to act as bait: as the enemy antitank guns opened fire, so their muzzle flashes revealed their positions to the waiting Tigers. Sturmmann Lau, a panzer crewman, described acting in one such mission: "We drove ahead in order to bring the Ivans out of their reserve and draw their antitank fire. We came under terrific fire. Later, while refueling, we counted a total of 28 hits on the Tiger. Some of them were smaller, of course, but there were also some big enough to easily put one's fist into. All of the hits were on the frontal armor."[5] If nothing else, Lau's account confirmed the durability of the Tiger's armor protection.

Early in December a renewed freeze allowed a resumption of hostilities. Balck's panzer corps once again threw itself forward in the attempt to drive the Soviets back to Kiev and across the Dnieper. Leibstandarte had now received its battalion of Mark V Panther tanks, and while the tank had still not fully solved its mechanical teething troubles, armor-piercing shells from its 7.5cm L/70 high-velocity gun could slice through T-34 armor with devastating ease.

After the death in action of Georg Schönberger, Leibstandarte's panzer regiment commander, his position was controversially filled by Jochen Peiper, formerly the commander of the 2nd Panzergrenadier Regiment's APC battalion. Some officers complained that Peiper was an infantryman who had no experience commanding tanks and that the increased tank casualties suffered by the regiment during this period came through his reckless attitude toward armored operations. Peiper even had a stand-up row with Obersturmbannführer Albert Fry of the 1st Panzergrenadier Regiment over his unit's tactical methods.[6]

In Peiper's defense, he made good use of combining the II Battalion (Mark IVs) with his former APC battalion, so that armor and infantry

fought together in the manner originally envisaged by tank-warfare dis-
ciples such as Heinz Guderian. Hauptsturmführer Gührs, a company
commander in the APC half-track battalion, wrote approvingly of his old
superior: "Peiper's transfer to the Panzer Regiment was not a problem for
us: in a way we remained 'his battalion.' Because the Panzer regiment had
not yet adapted itself to Peiper's often Hussar-like style of leadership, he
would happily place 'his battalion' ahead of the panzers. I remember him
saying then, 'Fetch up the Battalion, we'll show them!'"[7]

Peiper's armored units achieved some spectacular successes as the Germans drove into the Red Army defending Kiev. After making a twenty-
six-mile penetration of the Soviet front line, Peiper's roving force captured
the staffs of four enemy divisions and destroyed a hundred tanks and sev-
enty-six antitank guns. With a characteristic flourish, Peiper subsequently
wrote of his time in the Ukraine, "Where we were standing was Germany
and as far as my tank gun reached was my kingdom."[8]

Yet despite these victories, the German advance began to waver through
lack of resources, and on 21 December the offensive was brought to a close.
Waffen-SS casualties had been heavy, notably among Leibstandarte and
Das Reich, the latter division in almost constant frontline combat since
the battle of Kharkov earlier in the year. As a consequence, Das Reich
was withdrawn to France for refitting, although a strong Kampfgruppe
of around 3,000 men remained at the front, its numbers and equipment
drawn from all units so that it resembled a miniaturized division.[9]

THE REPULSE OF the Red Army advance from Kiev was a useful victory,
but Manstein and OKH feared the launch of a further and larger Soviet
offensive. On 24 December 1943 the storm broke, a skillfully orchestrated attack that ran along the entire Dnieper front. The German defenses could not hold, as Soviet armored columns punched holes in the
weaker sections of the line. As usual, Hitler's orders were to stand fast,
which had the consequence of leaving the better-defended sections of
the line as dangerously isolated salients. The German positions around
Cherkassy, which included Wiking and the Walloon Brigade, held firm.
By mid-January the Red Army began to encircle the German position;

on 28 January the Soviet pincers met, creating the first of several German pockets in the Ukraine.

Five German divisions and other corps troops totaling around 59,000 men were trapped in the Korsun-Cherkassy pocket (the actual area of the pocket was centered around Korsun, while Cherkassy, already in Soviet hands, lay several miles to the east).[10] Manstein had powerful armored units at his disposal and in early February prepared to come to the aid of the troops in the pocket. But he was overruled by Hitler, who, instead, ordered the rescue force to adopt an ambitious plan to counterencircle the Soviets besieging Korsun. This proved a failure, yet all the while the Red Army was squeezing the troops in the pocket ever tighter.

Hitler's plan was abandoned, and on 11 February III Panzer Corps was ordered to fight its way to the pocket. The rescue attempt was hampered by fuel shortages and the strength of Soviet resistance, as well as fluctuating changes in the weather where sudden warm spells turned the battlefield into glutinous mud. The spearhead of III Panzer Corps came to halt at the Gniloi Tikich River on 16 February, unable to proceed farther. To avoid annihilation, the encircled troops—under General Wilhelm Stemmermann—were ordered to fight their way out of the pocket as best they could.

The breakout meant the abandonment of most artillery and heavy equipment. As the only armored formation in the pocket, Wiking was assigned to lead the breakout, although its fighting vehicles were pitifully few in numbers. The SS Walloon Brigade would assist the rear guard. The pocket had been slowly moving westward over several days, so that on the evening of 16 February its lead units had closed to within five miles of III Panzer Corps on the Gniloi Tikich. A narrow corridor of sorts had been established to link up with the rescue force, but as the German troops struggled through the mud and snow on the seventeenth, the Red Army struck with a vengeance.

While the Wiking panzers fought to hold open the ever-narrowing corridor, the Walloons and German infantry brought up the rear. The Walloon commander, Sturmbannführer Lippert, had been killed by a sniper bullet on 13 February, the brigade briefly passing to Léon Degrelle before he was wounded and evacuated from the pocket by motor transport. Soviet artillery pounded the retreating Germans from both sides of the corridor, while marauding tanks and Cossack cavalry broke through the defenses to wreak havoc on those in their path. The large numbers of ill and wounded were an easy target. Fernand Kaisergruber, an exhausted and wounded infantryman in the Walloon Brigade, was temporarily resting in a shell hole when he encountered a Soviet tank zigzagging across the terrain little more than thirty yards away:

> What I then see freezes me with horror and suddenly brings me wide awake. It has chosen several bodies lying on the ground, perhaps still moving, as its target. It squashes them and pivots on them to be quite certain of achieving its goal. I see clearly the face of a man who was not dead and whose trunk disappears under the tank track. His face becomes all red, as if ready to explode, as if the blood was going to come out through his pores! When the tank pivots again, I see a sleeve torn from the uniform stuck between links of the track and turning with them, the arm in the sleeve, and the hand at the end! I see this arm make several complete rounds with the track, hitting the armor each time, just above the track. I do not move, holding my breath for fear of attracting the attention of these modern-day Huns! The tank moves on and I see two more, a bit farther off, venting their fury on the wounded, lying in the snow, disarmed, defenseless, left to their mercy.[11]

Despite the relentless nature of the attacks on the retreating German rear guard, large numbers of men reached the Gniloi Tikich, with sanctuary lying on the far bank. Pioneers from III Panzer Corps had laid temporary bridges over the river, but the rearguard troops seemed unaware of their existence and were forced to swim across the thirty-yard river, swollen with meltwater. Attempts were made to form a makeshift bridge, but the current was too fast, carrying away all attempts at a crossing. Under Soviet artillery fire, the troops attempted the crossing of the icy torrent, many of the nonswimmers and wounded swept away to their deaths. Kaisergruber was put on a horse and with another man hanging on to its tail managed to get across, their sodden uniforms freezing in the air as they made their way through the German outpost line.

Of the approximately 59,000 men originally trapped in the pocket, 19,000 were killed or taken prisoner and a further 11,000 wounded (although escaping the pocket)—a casualty rate of 50 percent.[12] Without the dedication of the breakout troops—and some initial complacency among the Soviet commanders—the German defeat would have been far worse. Both Wiking and Assault Brigade Wallonien suffered heavily, the latter with more than 1,200 casualties from its original 1,850-strong force. The Germans did their best to paint the escape in glowing colors, emphasizing the fortitude of the *Tcherkassykämpfer* during the battle. One victor of the breakout was Léon Degrelle, whose modest contribution was vastly magnified by German propaganda and, especially, himself.[13] He was awarded the Knight's Cross by Hitler and then sent on a publicity tour of Belgium to drum up recruits for the now heavily depleted Walloon Brigade.

DURING LATE FEBRUARY the Soviet offensive began to slow. Hitler and OKH considered it to be at an end in the belief that the Red Army was exhausted. This proved to be dangerous wish fulfillment, however, as in early March the offensive resumed with even greater intensity. Once again this was a broad-front operation stretching from the Pripet Marshes southward to the Black Sea. General Hans-Valentin Hube's First Panzer Army, deployed in the western Ukraine with its center around the town of Kamenets-Podolsky, was soon in danger. As Hube's forces held their ground in accordance with Hitler's orders, the effect was to produce a salient. As was the case at Cherkassy, Red Army commanders sensed the possibility of another cauldron battle, and units from both Soviet encircling formations met on 25 March.

On this occasion Hitler accepted the seriousness of the situation and instructed Manstein to allow Hube to fight his way out of the pocket. The obvious breakout route was due south across the River Dniester toward Romania, with the Red Army deploying a large blocking force in anticipation of such a move. Aware of this, Manstein ordered Hube to drive westward across more difficult terrain but with less enemy opposition. A powerful relief force was also assembled, led by a reconstituted II SS Panzer Corps under the command of Paul Hausser.

The II Panzer Corps comprised two completely new Waffen-SS formations: 9th and 10th SS Panzer Divisions. Their genesis dated back to December 1942 when Hitler agreed to the creation of three divisions to be raised from the youth of the German Reich. One of the divisions would come from the Hitler Youth itself—the 12th SS Panzer Division Hitlerjugend—while the other two would recruit directly from teenagers in the Reichsarbeitsdienst (RAD), the Reich labor service. As many of these recruits were minors, typically sixteen or seventeen at enlistment, they were below the permitted recruitment age and, officially at least, had to be volunteers who had been given parental permission to sign up.

Although the Waffen-SS still enjoyed enormous prestige in Germany, many parents were understandably reluctant to send their children to join an organization where heavy casualties were the norm. Gottlob Berger and his SS recruiters dealt with this problem by pressuring the boys into joining when away from their homes during labor service and then simply ignoring any subsequent parental protests. German writer Günter Grass, while performing his labor service, had volunteered to join the submarine arm of the Kriegsmarine but was forcefully persuaded to join the Waffen-SS. He was inducted into the 10th SS Panzer Division as a tank gunner in the summer of 1944, although he proved a reluctant warrior for the Führer.[14]

Berger was able to recruit 27,000 individuals, of whom 13,100 were volunteers. More recruits would be required to furnish two full-strength panzer divisions of just under 20,000 men each, and this shortfall was remedied, as usual, by drawing from the reservoir of Volksdeutsche. The officers and NCOs who would provide the divisional cadre were drawn from across the existing Waffen-SS divisions. Training began in February 1943, both divisions stationed in France in the expectation that at some point they might be used to thwart an Allied invasion. Originally designated as panzergrenadier divisions, they were upgraded as full panzer divisions during the latter part of 1943. In all, there would be seven SS panzer divisions—1st Leibstandarte, 2nd Das Reich, 3rd Totenkopf, 5th Wiking, 9th Frundsberg, 10th Hohenstaufen, and 12th Hitlerjugend—the military elite of the Waffen-SS.

The 9th SS Panzer Division received the name "Hohenstaufen" after the medieval German royal dynasty and was commanded by the veteran

Brigadeführer Wilhelm Bittrich. He had commanded Das Reich until wounded and on recovery was sent to lead the SS Cavalry Division engaged in antipartisan operations.

The title "Frundsberg"—from the sixteenth-century German Landsknecht Georg von Frundsberg—was assigned to the 10th SS Panzer Division, and in November 1943 it came under the command of Gruppenführer Karl von Treuenfeld. By early March 1944 both divisions were considered combat ready, and given the parlous military situation on the Eastern Front, rather than be stationed in France they entrained for the Ukraine from the twenty-fourth onward.[15]

Advance units of II SS Panzer Corps were committed to battle on 4 April. Meanwhile, the pocket containing the 200,000 men of the First Panzer Army steadily shuffled westward. Hube and his subordinate commanders did their utmost to ensure there was no panic, and good order was maintained in what the Germans called the "traveling pocket." The First Panzer Army included both Das Reich Kampfgruppe and Leibstandarte, the latter so reduced by 14 March that its 1,400 officers and men (plus a handful of tanks) were effectively downgraded to Kampfgruppe status.[16]

A further SS formation was also trapped in the pocket: 6th SS Volunteer Assault Brigade Langemarck. The brigade—drawing its recruits from Belgian Flanders—had been sent to reinforce Das Reich Kampfgruppe in December 1943. The soldiers of the brigade—just over 2,000 strong on arrival in Ukraine—had established themselves as reliable comrades alongside Das Reich since initial deployment in March 1944.

The escape from the Kamenets-Podolsky pocket took its toll on the troops, who were forced to fight defensive battles during the day before disengaging as darkness fell and then marching through the night only to resume battle the next morning. The history of Das Reich's "Der Führer" Regiment gave an indication of the conditions experienced by the ordinary soldier:

Casualties grew daily. The winter clothing of many men hung down in tatters and in many places the red stuffing of the insulated vests was visible. The state of the men's footwear deteriorated. The last haircuts and last shaves lay in the past. On the other hand they were still being relatively well supplied with ammunition and food. Increasingly the units replaced their lost vehicles with the brave and hardy *panje* ponies, and soon we were jokingly calling our panzer battle group the "*panje* battle group."[17]

Contact between Hausser's SS troops and the First Panzer Army was made on 6 April and the following day a corridor was established to allow the escape of the trapped Germans. Given the scale of the enterprise, the approximately 12,000 casualties suffered by the Germans were surprisingly light, considerably less than those of their opponent. Once out of the pocket the First Panzer Army took up new positions on the front line.

As had been the case at Korsun-Cherkassy, heavy equipment and weapons had been abandoned during the panzer army's breakout, losses the Germans could ill afford when set against superior Soviet rates of weapons production. The Red Army was also beginning to receive qualitative improvements in battlefield equipment from early 1944 onward, which included an upgraded T-34 with a more powerful 85mm gun, increasing numbers of SU-85 assault guns, and the first production models of the Josef Stalin heavy tank, complete with a formidable 122mm main armament.

By April 1944 the Soviet Union had liberated almost all of the Ukraine, and in May the Crimea was recaptured and the Germans pressed back to the Carpathian Mountains with both Romania and Hungary vulnerable to renewed Soviet attacks. During May, however, the Red Army called its offensive to the south to a halt as it shifted its strategic focus farther north.

The II SS Panzer Corps was redeployed in Poland as a strategic reserve. Totenkopf and Wiking were taken out of the line to refit but remained in the East, while Leibstandarte and Das Reich Kampfgruppe were withdrawn to Western Europe to rebuild and to prepare for the long-awaited Allied invasion of France. The Flemish Langemarck Brigade—with just 400 combat-ready troops—was transferred to Bohemia in late April, although following a rapid rebuilding program it was ready for action by the end of June with a strength of more than 1,700 men.[18]

SINCE THEIR LAST triumph at Kharkov in February–March 1943, the Waffen-SS divisions had experienced more than twelve months of military setbacks. No matter how much damage was inflicted on the Red Army at a tactical level, the elite German formations had been forced to retreat or be overwhelmed. While morale remained surprisingly high among the troops, senior commanders, with a greater knowledge of the overall military situation, began to guardedly mutter their doubts about the war's future. Sepp Dietrich went so far as to openly express his misgivings, and his complaint made in early 1943 that "we can no longer beat the Russians" eventually came to Himmler's ears.[19] Dietrich was let off with a mild rebuke, not least because Himmler was also concerned by Germany's deteriorating fortunes, which might well lead to the destruction of his grand project for an SS-led Germanic Europe.

Dietrich apart, Himmler was informed of the growing sense of disillusion within the Waffen-SS at higher levels, how the savage and relentless combat of the Eastern Front had drawn senior Waffen-SS officers to a closer association with their counterparts in the army. Veteran commanders, such as Steiner and Bittrich, did little to hide their disregard for the niceties of the SS order. Gottlob Berger reported back to his boss on the ribald comments of Wiking officers toward the Nazi Party and the Reichsführer-SS himself, while a Wehrmacht lieutenant briefly serving with Leibstandarte was shocked to hear open and repeated criticisms of Nazi officials from the division's officers.[20]

Himmler, however, realized that this was not the first step in treasonous insubordination but the almost inevitable outbursts of men under extreme pressure. Revealing considerable prescience, he had been aware of the dangers of the alienation of the "front fighters" even before the outbreak of war, noting that "sooner or later" the armed units of the SS "would at some point become a division of the Army which just happened to wear a black uniform."[21] Himmler nonetheless worked hard to keep the Waffen-SS loyal to his vision of a radical Nazi Germany and not allow it to backslide toward what he considered the old, reactionary attitudes of the German Army.

Berger demonstrated similar attitudes to those of his master. He was alarmed when he read a report in early 1944 celebrating changes in army attitudes that brought them closer to those held by the Waffen-SS. At first sight, it would appear natural that such a development would be welcomed by the SS, but as Berger explained, "If we continue in this fashion we will lose our leading position, just as our troops will lose it if the Wehrmacht succeeds in aligning its officer corps along the same lines we have chosen."[22]

Consequently, both Berger and Himmler were assiduous in trying to maintain the separateness of the Waffen-SS from the Wehrmacht. In their view, the special SS ideological indoctrination must not be allowed to slip despite wartime pressures. When Brigadeführer Peter Hansen, Das Reich's original artillery commander, suggested a reduction in ideological training at the Waffen-SS officer schools, he was severely reprimanded by Himmler.[23]

How successful Himmler was in maintaining the ideological distinctiveness of the Waffen-SS remains hard to assess. In the formations led by older officers such as Steiner and Bittrich, increasingly cynical at the prospect of ultimate victory, Himmler appears to have made little headway. In his history of the SS, Heinz Höhne wrote of "Himmler's suspicion that he was surrounded by ungrateful generals who already had a foot in the other camp—that of the Wehrmacht. One after another he saw his generals as apostates from the SS Order."[24]

Höhne exaggerated the situation, as many senior SS officers were fully in accord with the most extreme Nazi views, especially those of the younger generation—such as Kurt Meyer and Max Wünsche—who had entered the SS at an early age and were now assuming positions of responsibility. And for every disrespectful Steiner and Bittrich, there were plenty of older officers who were enthusiastic Nazis. Among these, Frundsberg commander Gruppenführer Treuenfeld (born in 1885) insisted that his young soldiers were to be inculcated with the Führer's messianic call for the "historic unity of all Germans." And in a directive issued to his troops on 3 December 1943, he made it clear that "every man should be trained to be a fanatical hater. It doesn't matter on which front our divisions engage in combat, the unyielding hate toward every opponent, Englishman, American, Jew or Bolshevik, must make every one of our men capable of the highest deeds."[25]

Officers like Treuenfeld would be influential in providing the inspiration for SS soldiers not to waver on the battlefield, even when the tide of war had so obviously turned against Germany. They repeatedly demanded "fanatical" resistance from their men regardless of the outcome. Meanwhile, the doubters and cynics within the Waffen-SS would also continue to fight on, partly in the hope of some sort of political settlement but also in the sober realization that as professional soldiers who had given their oath to Adolf Hitler they were bound to their master.

Chapter 21

BATTLE IN THE NORTH

LENINGRAD HAD BECOME a quiet sector on the Eastern Front after the German failure to capture the city in 1941. German and Soviet soldiers faced each other from fixed positions in conditions reminiscent of World War I, and when offensive action did take place it was limited in scope and easily contained. This was all to change on 14 January 1944 when the Soviet Union launched an offensive with overwhelming force, raising the siege of Leningrad and pushing the Germans back into the Baltic States.

As the Red Army broke out of the Leningrad lines and the nearby Oranienbaum pocket, the weakened German Army Group North was forced into an immediate retreat, relying on a few experienced armored formations to help stem the Soviet tide. Among these was Felix Steiner's III SS (Germanic) Panzer Corps, comprising the 11th SS Panzergrenadier Division Nordland and 4th SS Panzergrenadier Brigade Nederland.[1] A number of Wehrmacht formations had been subordinated to Steiner's command—including 9th and 10th Luftwaffe Field Divisions—but they were swept away in the Soviet advance.

Forced to rely on his own troops, Steiner was still able to inflict a number of sharp reverses on advancing Soviet armored columns. One such encounter took place at Gubanitzy on 26 January when Nordland's armored reconnaissance battalion—containing most of the division's contingent of Swedish volunteers—was assigned to defend the village. The antitank platoon in the battalion's 5th Company had already repelled an attack by a Soviet reconnaissance patrol, when a second, larger, assault was made. The action was described by platoon commander Alfred Weiss:

> Just behind the crown of a hill, a widely spread formation of heavy tanks thundered towards the village. As soon as the heavy tanks went over the crown of the hill's front slope, they were fired on by all four of our 7.5cm anti-tank guns. The distance was well within our range and every shot hit its target. The tank formation was immediately thrown into enormous confusion. When the command tank, made apparent by the profusion of antennas on its turret, was hit, the enemy was apparently reduced to panic. No one dared continue the advance. They drove back and forth, from right to left and back again. This tactic eventually caused them to ram into each other, and crash.[2]

After the company commander, Untersturmführer Langendorf, arrived at the scene, he mobilized all available forces to focus their fire on the helpless Soviet tanks; out of an estimated sixty enemy armored vehicles, the SS gunners claimed forty-five destroyed.

Rearguard actions of this sort helped the Germans withdraw with minimal losses to the Narva River, the border between the Soviet Union and Estonia. The newly established Narva Line stretched along the river from the Baltic Sea past the city of Narva to Lake Peipus, forming a strip of territory approximately thirty miles long that acted as a natural choke point, one that the Germans could defend against a numerically superior enemy without their flanks being turned. The German defensive force— Army Detachment "Narwa"—comprised III SS Panzer Corps and two infantry corps from the army, plus various support units. Steiner's corps was assigned the key defense of the city of Narva, complete with its medieval castle from the Teutonic Crusades that overlooked the Narva River and the Russian fort on the opposite bank.

The Red Army gave the Germans little rest and in early February managed to establish a number of small bridgeheads over the Narva. Throughout February and into March, Army Detachment "Narwa" fought to eliminate the bridgeheads and repel further attacks across the river. Steiner, wearing his trademark civilian coat and field cap with motorcycle goggles, was a familiar and reassuring sight to his SS troops.

On 20 February the III SS Panzer Corps was bolstered by the arrival of the Estonian 20th Waffen Grenadier Division of the SS. The division was thrown into battle without delay and on the twenty-ninth set about destroying the Soviet bridgehead at Siivertsi. The position was defended with minefields and machine-gun strongpoints, supported by artillery firing from the far bank of the river. The Estonians fought the Soviets with all the resolve of men defending their country against a hated oppressor.

The I Battalion of the Estonian 2nd Panzergrenadier Regiment had managed to cross the Soviet minefield but, in the process, had lost most of its officers, and with ammunition running low the attack was on the point of stalling. Unterscharführer Harald Nugiseks took control of the situation, using sledges to haul the necessary ammunition over the minefield to the soldiers on the front line. Then, well armed with hand grenades, Nugiseks and his Estonian troops broke into the Soviet trenches, setting in motion a wider attack that eliminated the bridgehead by 6 March. For his inspired leadership, Nugiseks was awarded the Knight's Cross.

Soviet artillery and aerial bombardments turned Narva into a pile of rubble, but nothing could dislodge the SS troops from their defenses. Brigadeführer von Scholz adopted a civilian bus as a mobile headquarters, enabling him to travel around his command to deploy reserves where needed and raise the troops' morale.[3] Operating as a mobile heavy-weapons team were the Panthers of Nordland's panzer battalion and the Tigers of the army's crack 502nd Heavy Tank Battalion. By the end of March the Germans had stabilized the line, the Red Army forced to regroup and lick its wounds.

III SS Panzer Corps listed more than 7,500 casualties, with the Nederland Brigade especially hard hit. On the credit side, a modest contribution of 1,336 soldiers from the broken 9th and 10th Luftwaffe Field Divisions were redistributed among the SS units.[4]

Army Detachment "Narwa" was able to relax during April and May, although in June increasing Soviet activity suggested the likelihood of renewed action. The German position was made more tenuous when several army divisions were withdrawn in June as a result of Soviet successes in Finland and Belorussia (Belarus). With this in mind, Steiner conferred with the overall "Narwa" commander, General Friessner, to organize a withdrawal to the more defensible Tannenberg Line, a few miles to the

west. As the Germans prepared for their withdrawal in July, the Flemish
and Walloon SS Assault Brigades each dispatched a battalion to reinforce
the German positions.

––––––––––

THE GREAT SOVIET summer offensive of 1944 in Belorussia led to the
total collapse of Army Group Center. As a consequence, German forces
to the north were forced to fall back or be surrounded. Among these
were the two Latvian SS divisions. The 15th Waffen Grenadier Division
of the SS had originally been deployed around Staraya Russa—scene of
fierce fighting by the Totenkopf Division during 1941–1942—but had
retreated to the Velikaya River during February 1944, where it joined
the newly formed 19th Waffen Grenadier Division of the SS. They were
then briefly combined as the VI Waffen Army Corps of the SS (Latvian)
under Karl Pfeffer-Wildenbruch, the former commander of 4th Polizei
Division. This corps was a paper organization only, without a proper staff
and the usual support units. The Latvian soldiers were certainly unaware
of their corps status as they slowly fell back toward their home country,
sustaining heavy casualties in the process.

Toward the end of the summer of 1944, the two battered and understrength divisions were briefly incorporated into Kampfgruppe Jeckeln
in defense of Latvia itself. The fighting was relentless, the Latvian troops
ground down by the advancing Red Army. The Latvians' did have occasional successes, however. Mintauts Blosfelds, a machine gunner from
the 15th Division, provided this account of repelling a Soviet infantry
attack:

> Although suffering heavy losses the Russians kept coming forward, but
> when the scattered groups of enemy soldiers were only about 80 yards
> away they came upon an invisible obstacle which stopped them in their
> tracks. There, in front of our trenches, sappers had cut down some young
> trees, leaving the short stumps hidden in the grass, and had attached
> lengths of barbed wire to them. As the Russians advanced across the belt
> of barbed wire, we were able to pick them off at ease. By now they were

in range of our hand grenades and very soon those Ivans who were still
alive began to panic. Very few of them reached the cover of the bushes
and many dead and wounded littered the ground in front of our trenches.
We were excited and jubilant, shouting to each other and continuing to
fire into the bushes. Any enemy wounded who were still moving in no-
man's-land were shot dead. The Company Commander walked along the
trench distributing cigarettes and congratulating the men.[5]

As the Latvians retreated, a reduced battalion from the Walloon Assault Brigade took up positions close to them around Dorpat, just south
of the Narva position. The Walloon deployment was little more than a
gesture, however, far too small to make any difference to the wider military situation.

As the Latvian and other Wehrmacht formations retreated, the situation of Army Detachment "Narwa" in Estonia grew ever more perilous.
On 25 July the troops were ordered back to the Tannenberg Line. The
Soviets, aware of the withdrawal, launched an immediate attack to catch
the Germans when they were most vulnerable. As a result, the retreat did
not go according to plan, and the Dutch "General Seyffardt" Regiment
was surrounded and all but annihilated on the twenty-sixth.

At the center of the Tannenberg Line were several small hills forming
a ridge that dominated the surrounding low-lying terrain. The Red Army
hoped to exploit the confusion caused by the withdrawal and threw all its
troops forward to capture the ridge. During the last days of July, III SS
Panzer Corps fought its most intense battle, to secure their new position
and repel the Soviets hard at their heels. At this point the newly arrived
battalion from the Flanders Brigade was committed to battle.

Holding a line on the key Orphanage Hill, the Flemish troops acted as
a rock against the Soviet tide. Among them was Remi Schrijnen, an antitank gun commander who had already established a reputation for coolness under fire. On 26 July he helped repel the Soviet tank advance, and a
few days later he found himself the sole survivor of his antitank company.
Although wounded, he continued to fire his gun single-handedly against
another assault, and in a David-versus-Goliath encounter he knocked out
at least eight Soviet tanks before he and his gun were put out of action by

a direct hit. Although severely wounded, Schrijnen survived to receive the Knight's Cross—one of twenty-seven such medals to be awarded during the Narva campaign.

For several days it seemed that the Tannenberg Line would fall to the Red Army. On 27 July Scholz was hit in the head by a shell splinter while supervising his division's defense of Orphanage Hill; the Austrian commander—known to his men as "Old Fritz"—died the following day. Crisis point was reached on the twenty-ninth, with the Germans thrown back to Tower Hill, the last line of defense. It was then that Steiner committed his final reserve, led by the seven remaining tanks from Nordland's panzer battalion.

The attack was sufficient to catch the advancing Soviet troops unawares, and their confusion was exploited by an ad hoc Kampfgruppe led by Estonian officer Hauptsturmführer Paul Maitla. The Estonians helped regain the key Grenadier Hill and bring the Red Army attack to a standstill. Maitla became another Knight's Cross winner. On 10 August the Red Army called a halt to its offensive operations.

The German defense along the Estonian border—lasting more than seven months—was one of the few success stories for German arms during 1944, much of the credit due to Steiner's sure handling of his III SS Panzer Corps. Events elsewhere, however, made the German position untenable. As a result of the destruction of Army Group Center in June–July, the Red Army advanced into Latvia with the intention of cutting off all German forces in Estonia. Farther north, Soviet pressure on Finland had led its government to sue for peace. On 4 September 1944 Finland agreed to a cease-fire with the Soviet Union, which opened Finnish waters to Soviet naval forces and gave them free access to the Baltic Sea.

On 14 September Army Detachment "Narwa" abandoned its positions and retreated through Estonia into Latvia, where it subsequently withdrew into the Courland Peninsula. A substantial force remained there until the end of the war, although other troops were evacuated by sea to Germany, including III SS Panzer Corps, shipped out in January 1945. They were joined by the remnants of the 15th Latvian Division and much of the Estonian Division. Some Estonians and Latvians returned to their homelands but others fought on, even though their hopes of national independence had been brutally dashed as, once more, the Soviet Union took control of the Baltic States.

———————

THE GERMANS HAD made a significant military contribution to Finland in its war against the Soviet Union, but little had come of it after the capture of a thin strip of Soviet territory in 1941. By 1944 some 200,000 German troops of the 20th Mountain Army were stationed in Finland, but, as was the case with the Leningrad front, it had become another military sideshow. The Waffen-SS contribution to this force came from 6th SS Mountain Division Nord, deployed as part of the XVIII Mountain Corps in central Finland. The Finnish-German armies lacked the strength and will to sever the supply link from the northern ports of Murmansk and Archangel to the rest of the Soviet Union. On the other hand, they were strong enough to repel the series of relatively minor Soviet assaults made along their front during 1942–1943.

For the men of the Nord Division, this was a war of patrols and trench raids, fought across a terrain dotted with a multitude of lakes and covered by thick birch forests. In winter the troops were snowbound in their trenches and shelters, daylight lasting just a few hours at most. With the advent of spring, the melting snows turned naturally marshy ground into an impassable quagmire; in the short summers, the relief of warmer weather and firmer ground was tempered by the clouds of mosquitoes that swarmed over the landscape.

Movement over this terrain was always difficult. During the winter skis and snowshoes were essential, while in summer the men had to fight their way through thick forests. Johann Voss, a machine gunner in the division's 11th Mountain Infantry Regiment, described a reconnaissance mission through virgin forest during the summer of 1944:

> It was considered impenetrable for any substantial force. The Jägers are said to be a quick-moving unit in difficult terrain; but this terrain beat all we had experienced. The woods were full of all sorts of obstacles; trunks lying all over the ground; underbrush, rocky barriers, water and

bogs, which, again and again, posed new problems for our progress. Except for the steady rumble of the artillery, the area was eerily still. The complete absence of darkness and the bizarre light of the sun lingering about the horizon for hours and hours added to the awe most of us felt as we penetrated this unknown wild.[6]

After their disgrace at the battle of Salla in July 1941, Waffen-SS troops in Finland were provided with reinforcements of a higher quality than the partially trained policemen and concentration-camp guards of the original Kampfgruppe Nord. The Nord Division improved sufficiently for the German Army leadership to consider it a combat-ready formation that could confidently take up its position on the front line.[7] Soviet attacks during the winter of 1943–1944 were repulsed, and the division did well in holding its section of the line against the major Red Army offensive of June 1944. But it was this offensive that forced the Finnish government to conclude its previously long-drawn-out peace negotiations with the Soviets.

Finland's cease-fire with the Soviet Union—confirmed by an armistice on 19 September—placed the German forces in Finland in an impossible position. The German high command briefly considered the idea of forming a redoubt in northern Finland but discarded it in favor of withdrawing to friendly territory in northern Norway. The transfer to Norway was made more difficult by the Finnish demand—in accordance with the terms of the Finnish-Soviet agreement—that all German troops must leave the country or lay down their arms by 15 September. The deadline was clearly impossible to fulfill, with conflict inevitable.

As 6th SS Mountain Division Nord vacated its frontline positions on 8 September, relations between Germans and Finns remained at a friendly level. In the village of Kuusamo, SS engineers helped bury the bells from the local church to prevent them from being stolen or destroyed by oncoming Soviet forces.[8] For their part, Finnish troops helped the Germans with transportation. The chief concern faced by the retreating Germans was shrugging off roving Soviet armored columns, but after a few days of skirmishing the Nord Division was clear of the Red Army.

A mountain infantry division like Nord had limited motor transport, most troops forced to proceed on foot, and with the Norwegian border nearly 450 miles away, the march would be an epic undertaking by any standards. During September the division made good progress without opposition, but in October Finnish attitudes toward the retreating Germans became increasingly hostile. The Soviet liaison officers who had entered Finland to supervise the armistice pressured the Finnish government to make good its agreement to disarm all Germans in their country. Finnish troops began to attack German columns, while the Germans adopted a rigorous scorched-earth policy to retard the progress of those coming after them.

The town of Rovaniemi was reached on 14 October, at which point the SS troops changed direction to march due north. They crossed the Arctic Circle, and with winter on its way the struggling troops had to endure freezing winds and falling temperatures. By the end of October the division's two infantry regiments were marching along separate roads that converged on Muonio, which from a Finnish perspective was the last point to trap the Germans before they could make their getaway into Norway. On 26 October Finnish units attacked the SS columns in strength, wiping out a supply train and killing one of the German regimental commanders. The Nord soldiers, desperate and angry, flung themselves at the Finns, who were thrown back into the woods. Muonio was held by Nord to allow all retreating Germans to begin the final leg of their march to the border undisturbed by any Finnish intervention.

Johann Voss recalled the sense of betrayal felt by his commander—called the "battalioner"—toward his former Finnish comrades in arms. A fellow soldier pointed out the village sign to Voss: "What I saw were several Finnish medals nailed to the sign, while above the word 'Muonio' the words 'Das war . . . ' ('That was . . . ') were crudely painted in black letters. Seeing my puzzled face he explained. It was the battalioner who had nailed up his Finnish decorations first, his officers following his example." The order was given to destroy the village. As he marched away, Voss paused: "Standing on a spot high above Muonio, we had a view of the village, which was on fire. When the flames would eventually go out, only the church and the town sign would be left of the village on the river."[9]

The division continued its northerly march without interference, finally crossing the border into Norway in the first week of November. But for the exhausted troops, their ordeal was far from over. There was no rail or motorized road transport, and the men had to march—mainly in the freezing dark—down the coastal roads of northern Norway before they reached the railhead at Mo i Rana on 10 December. There, at last, they could rest, having spent more than three months covering a total distance of just under 1,000 miles in the most arduous conditions. From Mo i Rana they traveled by rail and ship to refit in Denmark as Christmas approached. But they would have little time to rest. Their next assignment would be on the Western Front in a last-ditch attempt to repel the advancing U.S. Army.

Chapter 22

SHORING UP THE LINE

Operation Bagration—the Red Army's offensive in Belorussia—was launched on 22 June 1944 (the third anniversary of Barbarossa) and in a matter of weeks destroyed Army Group Center, the Germans suffering 400,000 casualties. The German disaster sucked in all available reserves, including Totenkopf and Wiking, to help fill the gap created by the Soviet breakthrough. In July the Red Army extended the scope of the offensive to include northern Ukraine, a blow directed at the German line in front of Lemberg (L'viv). As a consequence of the emergency in Belorussia, the defenders had few tanks and virtually no air cover. Holding the area around the Ukrainian town of Brody was the German XIII Army Corps, which had recently been joined by the Ukrainian 14th Waffen Grenadier Division of the SS.

In April 1944 the Ukrainian Division had a strength of 14,000 officers and men, slightly under the regulation figure for a 1944-pattern infantry division. It comprised three infantry regiments (Waffen Grenadier Regiments 29, 30, and 31), an artillery regiment, and some basic support services, although the latter contained just a single antitank company. Under the command of Brigadeführer Fritz Freitag, the bulk of the division (11,000 strong) was committed to positions just south of Brody.

On 13 July Soviet armored formations—supported by massed squadrons from the Red Air Force—drove into XIII Corps. The German line buckled on each side of Brody, and units from the Ukrainian 14th Division were deployed in a piecemeal fashion to reinforce the wavering army formations. On 15 July the 30th Waffen Grenadier Regiment was the first Ukrainian unit to be sent forward to aid the 349th Infantry Division, all the while coming under heavy artillery fire and repeated aerial attack.

On the following day a platoon commander described the chaotic scenes encountered by the 30th Regiment: "Towards morning it passed Sasiv and had to plough through German soldiers running away from the front. Some were without weapons, many shouting that the Russians were not far behind and that we should turn back, some were sitting and staring, some were even crying. This was a very demoralizing example, especially for our soldiers from the 'Galician Division' who had never seen real fighting and its cruelties."[1]

On arrival at the front the 30th Regiment was immediately thrown into action without any preliminary reconnaissance. Advancing in the open, the regiment was caught by a Soviet tank attack and badly mauled, with command and communications breaking down irrevocably. The other two infantry regiments were then committed to battle, having some success in holding the Soviet advance. An NCO on the staff of the 29th Regiment took up a position with his men and a heavy-weapons company to fend off an attack that was headed by a Soviet penal battalion, emboldened by extra vodka rations:

> From our concealed position we watched the Soviets attack, against all military training in tight formation stumbling and shouting obscenities. With cries of U-r-r-a! the drunken ranks of the Soviets were advancing one after the other not bothering to fall to the ground and take cover. We waited in silence until they got to within 100 meters of us and then opened fire from the flank with seven MG42s. They were taken completely by surprise and within minutes the remaining Soviets were fleeing in panic into the wood leaving some fifty corpses on the battlefield.[2]

This was an isolated success. The Red Army pushed onward, encircling 30,000 German and Ukrainian troops in the Brody pocket by 18 July. Attempts were made to relieve the pocket, but they were poorly handled, leaving the trapped soldiers to fend for themselves. Within the Ukrainian Division, Freitag and his staff found communications increasingly difficult, as Colonel Heicke, the chief operations officer, explained: "Telephone lines had been shredded so completely that only radios could be used. But the radio sets began to overload and would not function, so orders had to be transmitted by courier."[3]

As Soviet pressure increased, the strain on the inexperienced Ukrainian soldiers began to reach breaking point. This was acknowledged by Heicke: "Reports kept coming in from unit commanders saying they could no longer hold their positions. It became apparent that the Ukrainians were not psychologically prepared for such heavy fighting. More could not be expected of them, since many German units had panicked as well."[4]

On 19 July General Hauffe, the XIII Corps commander, made plans for a breakout on the following day and in the evening radioed Freitag for a situation report. To Heike's amazement—"I could hardly believe my ears"—Freitag calmly informed Hauffe that his troops were no longer under his control, and consequently he was resigning his command.[5] Instead of having Freitag arrested for gross dereliction of duty, Hauffe tamely accepted the resignation and placed him on the corps staff. Leadership of the Ukrainian Division temporarily passed to Major General Lindemann of the 361st Division.

The scheduled breakout attempt on 20 July was repelled. On the following day a renewed attempt saw the breakup of the division, although this did allow small groups of Ukrainians to flee through the still fluid Soviet lines. The pocket was eliminated on 22 July, with 2,807 Ukrainians managing to reach safety, joined by a further 800 survivors over the next few days.

After the battle, recriminations began in earnest with General Lange, commander of the broken 349th Division, blaming the conduct of the Ukrainian Division in the strongest terms. His condemnations were joined by those of Freitag himself—much to Heike's disgust.[6] Himmler, however, rejected the complaints out of hand, relying on other, seemingly more reliable, sources that suggested the division had fought as well as possible in the circumstances. Freitag pleaded to be allowed to return to the SS Polizei Division, but Himmler reinstated him as commander of the Ukrainian Division and, by way of encouragement, cynically handed him a Knight's Cross for his "leadership" at Brody.

Himmler was determined to rebuild the division, kick-starting the process with the dispatch of 1,000 German officers and NCOs. And the old idea that it was somehow not actually Ukrainian was abandoned (the official title of "Galician No. 1" was replaced by "Ukrainian No. 1"), and the troops were allowed to wear various Ukrainian national symbols. By 20 September 1944 it was on the way to reaching its authorized strength of 14,689 in all ranks, although weapons and heavy equipment remained in short supply.[7] Training was still ongoing when the reconstituted division was ordered to Slovakia, its next battleground.

———————

A FEW MILES north of Brody, 5th SS Panzer Division Wiking had already been in action in the defense of Kovel. The extensive refit and reinforcement of Wiking after its ordeal in the Cherkassy-Korsun pocket was far from complete when elements of the division were ordered back into combat. The German garrison in Kovel had come under increasing Soviet pressure, and on 12 March 1944 the new Wiking commander, Gruppenführer Herbert Gille, was ordered to support the position with all troops at his disposal. At this time, the separate components of the division were spread out across Europe, with the panzer regiment headquarters and one of the tank battalions undergoing training in France. Gille flew into Kovel, while infantry from the "Westland" and "Germania" Regiments—equipped only with small arms—managed to march into the city just before it was surrounded by the Red Army.

Gille reorganized Kovel's defenses, while awaiting the arrival of a suitably armed and equipped German relief force (a breakout was deemed impractical in light of the 2,000 German wounded held within the city). A scratch relief force had been assembled by 29 March, spearheaded by 8th Company of the Wiking's 5th Panzer Regiment. Commanded by Obersturmführer Karl Nicolussi-Leck—a former law student from South Tyrol—the company had sixteen new Panther tanks. Determined Soviet resistance and heavy snowfall brought the German advance to a halt, but despite orders to abort the relief mission Nicolussi-Leck and his seven remaining Panthers managed to fight their way through to Kovel on the evening of the thirtieth.[8] In early April other Wiking and army units attacked in force, and by 24 April they had destroyed what remained of the Soviet forces around Kovel.

For the Wiking Division, the Kovel action was just a foretaste of what was to come as the Soviet summer offensive gained momentum. Mühlenkamp's 5th Panzer Regiment fielded two powerful tank units: I Battalion was equipped with twenty-seven combat-ready Panzer Mark IVs and twenty combat-ready StuG IVs, while II Battalion had seventy-seven combat-ready Panzer Mark V Panthers.[9] Wiking had withdrawn from Kovel in early June to position a few miles to the west around Maciejow. The II Battalion spotted a vast Soviet tank force about to advance past their positions on 6 July. Obersturmführer Lichte described the German reaction:

> The panzer crews—the commanders in their turrets, the gunners at their sights, the loaders, drivers and radio operators—could not believe their eyes when they saw the dust-shrouded steel armada dive out of the horizon like a steamroller crushing everything in its path.
>
> The companies stood ready in their partially covered and well-camouflaged positions so that they were able to bring concentrated fire to bear with the assurance of getting a hit. Detached from them was Obersturmführer Olin who had driven into position with several Panthers. This daring Finnish officer, who had not returned home with his comrades from the Finnish Battalion, had the assignment to open fire first and draw the enemy's attention. Cold-bloodedly, Olin first allowed 10 enemy tanks to drive past and then knocked out the first and last, and eventually the rest. As expected, the Soviet tanks oriented themselves in the wrong direction and, strung out in a long formation, presented a full broadside to the German guns.
>
> "Open fire!" Soon after the first barrage nearly 50 Soviet tanks were destroyed. Everywhere were burning steel hulks and smoldering wreckage. One armor-piercing shell after another left the barrels of the Panther's guns. The duel lasted half an hour and ended in a battle in which 103 Soviet tanks were hit and destroyed.[10]

The battle continued for another three days: Mühlenkamp's panzers, supported by army units, knocked out nearly 300 enemy armored fighting vehicles, repulsing the entire Soviet attack. This was arguably Wiking's finest defensive action, but the panzer regiment had no time to rest on its laurels: on 13 July it was dispatched northward to join the rest of the division in Poland.

An attempt to defend Bialystok, on the Polish-Belorussian border, was abandoned, with the advance units from Wiking falling back in good order while awaiting the remainder of the division. Also dispatched to defend western Poland was the 3rd SS Panzer Division Totenkopf. It had been forced to abandon Grodno on 18 July, and like Wiking it con-ducted a series of rearguard actions intended to slow the advance of the Red Army as it drove toward Warsaw.

During the retreat, news reached SS soldiers of the attempted assas-sination of the Führer on 20 July by a group of army officers. They had hoped to kill Hitler by setting off a bomb in his headquarters at Rasten-burg in East Prussia and to then negotiate a peace with the Allies. Hitler was only slightly wounded by the blast, but the attempt sent shock waves throughout the entire Nazi system. It would seem that most soldiers found the whole business deeply repugnant. The reaction from Werner Volkner, a Flak gunner in Totenkopf, was fairly typical: "The men are full of rage, and their anger knows no bounds. How was it possible that such a criminal act could be perpetrated by officers of the Wehrmacht? It was like a stab in the back for the soldiers on the front line."[11] One im-mediate consequence of the failed coup was to enhance the prestige and importance of Himmler and the SS at the expense of the army, now very much in disgrace.

Shortly before the bomb exploded, Hitler had authorized the formation of IV SS Panzer Corps in Poland, an expedient combination of the Wiking and Totenkopf Divisions. Gille—promoted to Obergruppenführer—was appointed to command the new formation, with Mühlenkamp taking over Wiking. The IV SS Panzer Corps was assigned a crucial role in the defense of Warsaw, and during August it received reinforcements that included the 19th Panzer and 73rd Infantry Divisions, in addition to a Hungarian cavalry division and some SS corps troops that included a heavy-artillery battalion.

As the Red Army advanced on Warsaw, the Polish Resistance—in the form of the Polish Home Army—launched an audacious bid on 1 August to take control of the city. Substantial areas of central Warsaw were captured by the Poles in the opening phases of the uprising, but in the end German might prevailed, and in an exceptionally brutal operation the revolt was completely suppressed by 2 October.

The Warsaw Uprising has become one of the more controversial episodes of World War II. Stalin totally refused to help the Polish Home Army—ideological opponents of Soviet communism—and he was condemned in the West for not ordering his troop to drive into the city. Yet the Red Army, despite being exhausted by several months of hard campaigning, continued to batter the German defensive lines around Warsaw right up until the end of October.

The Germans divided the defense of Warsaw against the Red Army into three linked battles. In the First Defensive Battle (18–30 August), Gille's panzer corps, deployed to the northeast of Warsaw, fought several successful delaying actions. One exception was the skirmish at Slanzany when the bridge over the River Bug held by Wiking's I Panzer Battalion was destroyed by Soviet artillery fire on 26 August. In the ensuing confusion the battalion commander was killed, and twelve panzers had to be abandoned on the river's far bank.[12]

During the Second Defensive Battle (31 August–9 October) the Red Army methodically ground down the German defenses. After the collapse of the 73rd Infantry Division, they captured the Warsaw suburb of Praga on the east bank of the Vistula on 14 September. At this point they halted the direct attack on the capital, leaving the Polish Home Army to its fate. But there was no slackening to the north of Warsaw, as the Soviets drove against the positions held by Wiking and Totenkopf.

As the SS frontline troops defended their positions, they could look back and see the clouds of smoke over the city center. Fritz Messerle, commander of the SS heavy-artillery battalion, recalled that "fires raged day and night, explosions flashed and a dull rumble was heard in the distance. Clearly visible through field glasses were Stukas frequently flying combat missions against the city." On 18 September Messerle was alerted that an Allied airborne attack was under way:

A formation of American B-17s could be seen coming from the west. The 8.8cm Flak opened fire, and individual B-17s fell to the ground in

flames. Then the giant formation opened its bomb-bay doors. The sky
was sown with parachutes in a matter of seconds. Those must have been
the paratroopers. Damned! This could get hot! The main objective of the
drop was behind the positions to the right. Then relief! It was apparent
through field glasses that there weren't any human beings hanging from
the chutes; instead were rather respectable supply canisters, of which several dropped in the immediate vicinity and were gleefully chased down.[13]

Few of the canisters reached the Home Army, and for several weeks the
Germans were the grateful beneficiaries of American chocolates and cigarettes, as well as small arms and ammunition. In the Wiking Division
there was a vogue for carrying Colt automatic pistols.[14]

During the first week in October the IV SS Panzer Corps was squeezed
into a V-shaped piece of land between the confluence of the Narew and
Vistula Rivers, immediately to the north of Warsaw. Known as the "wet
triangle," this forested and marshy ground would be the setting for the
Third Defensive Battle for Warsaw (10–30 October). Aware that his position would be the objective of a Soviet attack on 9–10 October, Gille
lobbied his superiors for reinforcements, but these were refused. As the
former senior gunner in the SS-VT, he assembled all the artillery resources
at his disposal to lay down orchestrated disruptive fire on the Soviet assembly areas during the forty-eight hours before the proposed offensive.

Gille's fire plan seemed to have worked, with reports coming in that
the enemy attack was repeatedly postponed, and when it went ahead on
10 October the SS units were well prepared. On 12 October "Westland's"
III Battalion, holding a forward position in the German line, was completely overwhelmed by the Soviet attack and annihilated. The sacrifice
helped slow the Soviet advance, subsequently blocked by Totenkopf. On
the fifteenth, Alfred Titschkus, an NCO in Totenkopf's reconnaissance
battalion, demonstrated the bloody-minded attitude of his division:

Titschkus repulsed repeated Russian attacks in close combat with his small
group of men. Alone, he fought off the enemy who had briefly penetrated
his sector with his submachine gun and hand grenades, although he had
already been wounded several times by grenade shrapnel. Even after the

Russians penetrated his squad's sector again and killed five of his six men
in their hole, he didn't abandon his position. He fought on alone at close
quarters against the overwhelming enemy forces. After the immediate and
successful friendly counterattack, one could count the 25 enemy soldiers
that Titschkus had killed in front of and behind his position.[15]

In the intense and confused fighting of this engagement, victory
or defeat hung in the balance for several days. Totenkopf's Werner
Volkner—just as his antiaircraft position was on the verge of being overwhelmed—saw the arrival of the most bizarre reinforcements: "I couldn't
believe my eyes. There were chaps in partial German uniform, some of
them had top hats and bowler hats instead of steel helmets and one or
two of them were in top hats and tails. It looked if these chaps were going
to a carnival instead of going into action. Later we were told it was a unit
of men from a penal battalion."[16] As in the Red Army, the Wehrmacht
made extensive use of penal units for military transgressors, victory or
death their only option. Whatever the success of this unit, the Soviet
attacks were held, so that by the end of October the fighting around
Warsaw died into insignificance—and would remain so for the remainder
of 1944.

Chapter 23

PARTISAN WARS: THE EASTERN FRONT

THAT GERMANY MUST dominate central and eastern Europe was central to Hitler's worldview, and even before the invasion of Poland in 1939 the SS had drawn up plans to impose its authority over its subject peoples. Himmler and the Wehrmacht high command had agreed that while the army would control the frontline areas, the SS would be responsible for security in territories to the rear. In Poland armed SS police battalions operated with Einsatzgruppen killing squads and the Totenkopfstandarten. Once the Soviet Union had been invaded, Himmler sent in his private army—the SS Cavalry Brigade and 1st and 2nd SS Infantry Brigades—to support the repression of the civilian population. A prominent figure in these actions was Erich von dem Bach-Zelewski, a senior SS police officer who coordinated police, Waffen-SS, and army units—plus local nationalist auxiliaries—in the occupied territories.

The concept of counterinsurgency or antipartisan warfare developed by Hitler and Himmler differed from the usual understanding of the term. In this, the occupying power acted in a reactive manner, taking military action against armed insurrection and using the police to punish lesser forms of dissent, all to ensure a compliant subject population. The Nazi model, by contrast, was proactive, systematically seeking out those who they deemed enemies of the state.

Central to Nazi propaganda was the association of Jews with partisans, analogous to the other myth of Jews being synonymous with communists. One of its maxims stated: "Where the partisan is, the Jew is, and where the Jew is, the partisan is."[1] When interrogated by the Allies after the war, Bach-Zelewski admitted to this conflation: "The fight against the partisans was used as an excuse to carry out other measures, such as the extermination of the Jews and gypsies, the systematic reduction of the Slavic peoples."[2]

Once an area was conquered by the Wehrmacht, the SS would take immediate measures to find and hunt down their enemies. On a practical level, these measures placed enormous demands on the SS counterinsurgency units, a task they were unable to fulfill on their own. To prevent a breakdown in these actions, all sections of the German armed forces and their allies could be called upon to engage in antipartisan operations when demanded.

After the war, Wehrmacht commanders assiduously denied involvement in actions against the civilian population, placing the blame elsewhere. Senior officers from the Waffen-SS, in their turn, followed the line that the atrocities inherent in antipartisan operations were the work of other elements of the SS. Their repeated denials were clearly nonsense. In addition to his Waffen-SS cavalry and infantry brigades, Himmler created numerous other Waffen-SS formations—such as the Prinz Eugen and Handschar Divisions—specifically for antipartisan operations.

And while the crack field divisions of the Waffen-SS were normally engaged in conventional military operations, they too, on occasion, were deployed in support of antipartisan actions. During the invasion of the Soviet Union in 1941, Leibstandarte and the Wiking Division were involved in the rounding up and killing of Jews in the Ukraine;[3] in 1943 the Nordland Division was engaged in counterinsurgency operations in Croatia;[4] and during the 1944 Warsaw Uprising units from both Wiking and Totenkopf worked with other SS troops in antipartisan sweeps that led to the destruction of Polish villages and the killing of civilians.[5]

The Wehrmacht possessed a well-developed body of theory and practice for countering insurgency, derived from the German Army's experiences as an occupying power in the Franco-Prussian War and World War I and from its colonial campaigns in Africa. Central to German thinking was the idea of *Schrecklichkeit* (frightfulness), involving severe reprisals for civil disobedience, including the taking and shooting of hostages and the destruction of villages and even whole towns. During its march through Belgium in 1914, the German Army had taken this a step further by enacting "reprisals" before the "provocations" had a chance to take place. This, it was believed, would cow the civilian population into submission and free as many soldiers as possible from occupation duties to service at the front.

Hitler was fully in accord with this approach to managing enemy civilians, as he made clear in his war directive of 23 July 1941:

> The troops available for securing the conquered Eastern territories will, in view of the size of area, be sufficient for their duties only if the occupying power meets resistance, not by legal punishment of the guilty, but by striking such terror into the population that it loses all will to resist. The commanders concerned are to be held responsible, together with the troops at their disposal, for quiet conditions in their areas. They will contrive to maintain order, not by requesting reinforcements, but by employing suitably draconian methods.[6]

In the Nazi lexicon of counterinsurgency, the word for antipartisan warfare (*Partisanenbekämpfung*) was officially replaced by antibandit warfare (*Bandenbekämpfung*). This was, in part, to downplay any positive military associations with the term *partisan* and to emphasize the criminal element of the word *bandit* as a gangster or outcast. But more than this, *Bandenbekämpfung* was co-opted by the Nazis as an ideological tool, to justify the killings, the mass deportations of civilians from the East as forced labor in the Reich, and the asset stripping of agricultural, industrial, and financial resources. Those civilians who opposed Nazi Germany were designated as bandits, beyond the protection of any law.[7]

In the initial stages of Operation Barbarossa, antipartisan activities consisted, in the main, of killing Jews and rounding up Soviet soldiers cut off from their units by the speed of the German advance. During 1942 this began to change, with attempts by local people to organize resistance. They, in turn, were backed by the Soviet government, which, after initial indifference, began to see the merits of guerrilla warfare. Although still relatively low-key, the partisan activity was sufficient for Hitler to issue

Directive 46—"Instructions for Intensified Action Against Banditry in the East"—on 18 August 1942.[8]

The directive underlined the importance of antipartisan warfare to all German civil and military organizations and to regulate and codify how this war should be fought. The directive confirmed the role of higher SS and police leaders (Höhere SS und Polizeiführer), who acted as Himmler's deputies in the occupied regions, coordinating the various SS agencies (including the Waffen-SS) in security matters.

Erich von dem Bach-Zelewski, a higher SS and police leader for Belorussia (Belarus), had demonstrated his efficiency in the killing of Jews in Latvia as well as Belorussia. Following the issue of Directive 46, he was made inspector of Bandenbekämpfung, to better organize antipartisan operations in the East. Success in this post led to his promotion on 19 June 1943 to chief of Bandenbekämpfung, with responsibilities for operations throughout the Reich. Philip W. Blood, a historian of German counterinsurgency, summed up the contradictory nature of its senior officer: "Bach-Zelewski was an intelligent man, a Junker, a political opportunist, and a self-confessed serial killer . . . and as a Great War soldier, he was awarded medals associated with heroism and courageous deeds. He was an exponent of modern warfare, security actions, resettlement programs, and mass killing. In addition, he held a close personal relationship with many senior officers in the German Army high command; they trusted him."[9]

THE TACTICS OF armed insurrection in World War II differed little from guerrilla actions in other wars. If the insurgents were to have any chance of success, they required wide expanses of rugged terrain—impassable to road-bound regular forces—within which they could operate, a civilian population that either supported or at least tolerated their actions, and some level of military and economic assistance from the outside. Western Europe, for example, lacked suitable terrain, forcing resistance movements to adopt more circumscribed tactics such as sabotage, assassination, and intelligence gathering. On the rare occasions when insurgents tried to take on the Germans in open confrontation—as happened with the French Resistance at Vercors in 1944—they were destroyed.

On the Eastern Front, the vast Pripet Marshes were ideal for partisan operations, while the dense forests of southern Poland and Belorussia also provided necessary sanctuary for insurgent groups. The mountains of Greece and Yugoslavia performed a similar function in the Balkans, as, at a later date, did the Apennines in Italy. Partisan strategy at a military level was to concentrate on hit-and-run attacks against enemy weak points and to avoid large-scale combat, while, by contrast, the Germans sought to bring the partisans to battle where their superior military resources would give them a decisive advantage

The German conduct of antipartisan operations was influenced by *Kleinkrieg* (*Little Wars*), a 1935 study into the subject by counterinsurgency expert and Abwehr officer Arthur Ehrhardt. During the war he transferred to the Waffen-SS and worked in the Reichsführer's headquarters, analyzing antipartisan operations.[10] Ehrhardt argued for a more subtle approach than was usual in the German armed forces, which included a "hearts-and-minds" element within a wider counterinsurgency doctrine. This, of course, ran counter to Nazi philosophy on the treatment of its non-Aryan subjects, where it was a case of all "stick" and no "carrot." Inevitably, the Nazi view prevailed, with a consequent alienation of most people under its rule.

On a tactical level the Germans worked hard to assimilate the lessons of counterinsurgency. They emphasized a need for flexibility in the field, as an "adherence to rigid principle has to be avoided, since the [partisan] bands quickly react and take the necessary counter-measures."[11] At Bad Tölz a course on antipartisan warfare was organized for Waffen-SS officer cadets.

In active operations against partisans, a linked three-tier system was adopted.[12] Hunter patrols (Jagdkommandos) consisted of companies or platoons used in small-scale actions, such as intelligence gathering or pursuing insurgents on the run. At the next (battalion) level, attack-pursuit operations, hopefully based on good intelligence, were intended to catch partisan leaders by surprise and destroy their strongholds with superior firepower. At the highest level were encirclement operations that might involve a multitude of units and formations, their function to act as a steadily constricting ring around the partisans until they had nowhere to hide.

To CARRY OUT these operations on the Eastern Front, the Waffen-SS supplied specialist antipartisan formations. Himmler was sufficiently impressed by the SS Cavalry Brigade to have it upgraded to divisional status in June 1942, when it became 8th SS Cavalry Division. It was subsequently given the title of "Florian Geyer," after the German knight who led his "Black Company" during the German Peasants' War (1524–1525). The division now had three cavalry regiments, each equipped with machine-gun and mortar units. Fire support was provided by an artillery regiment and mechanized antiaircraft, antitank, and assault-gun detachments, along with engineer, intelligence, and medical units.[13] At the end of 1943 the division was expanded to include a fourth cavalry regiment, which gave it a strength of around 13,000 officers and men.

The additional manpower needed for the SS Cavalry Division came from Hungarian Volksdeutsche, on the basis that Hungary's famous light-cavalry tradition would still have meaning in the 1940s. This was of little interest to the division's training staff, however. Few of their new recruits had a grasp of German, a problem amplified by an absence of the semimilitary background that was standard for young Reich Germans entering the armed services. This made the training process all the more difficult and inevitably led to strained relations between staff and recruits. Once again, Himmler and senior officers of the division had to repeatedly remind the instructors not to insult the men, especially refraining from calling them "gypsies"—a grave racial slur in Nazi Germany. Such was the problem that a list of acceptable "disciplinary insults" had to be issued; it included descriptions such as "dirty pig," a "sad sack of shit," and even a "limp dick" (Schlappschwanz).[14]

Himmler assigned command of the new division to the highly experienced Das Reich officer Brigadeführer Wilhelm Bittrich. Himmler and Bittrich had a difficult relationship that would not improve as the war went on, and this appointment to a second-level Waffen-SS formation could be seen as a slap in the face for Bittrich. But for the division itself, securing the services of a highly experienced battlefield commander was an obvious plus. Bittrich would continue to lead the SS cavalry formation in antipartisan operations until February 1943, when he was released to take over the new 9th SS Panzer Division. He would be replaced by SS police officer

Fritz Freitag (before his assignment to the SS Ukrainian Division) and then by Hermann Fegelein, commander of the original SS Cavalry Brigade.

From the summer of 1942 onward, Himmler and Bach-Zelewski worked to improve the coordination of the disparate antipartisan units under their control. Among these was the Sonderkommando Dirlewanger. Previously based in Poland, Oskar Dirlewanger's antipartisan unit had earned a reputation for corruption, disorder, and depravity sufficient even to shock the SS authorities, who preferred a more orderly approach to the ongoing destruction of the Polish state. Complaints made to Himmler led to the redeployment of Dirlewanger's thugs into the badlands of Belorussia, where they could operate with virtual impunity.

The SS Cavalry operated alongside the 320th Infantry Division with some success, the staff of the army formation commenting favorably on the "passion" of the SS troopers as they went about their pacification duties. Indeed, such was the SS cavalrymen's enthusiasm for the chase that in December 1942, they were censured by their own officers for not providing enough prisoners for interrogation. During the winter months of 1942–1943, the pace of operations slowed, although growing confidence among partisan units began to make itself felt with unfortunate consequences for the Germans. In one instance, in January 1943, an SS patrol was ambushed by a superior partisan force, with just six men escaping to safety. The survivors reported how their badly wounded comrades had shot themselves rather than be captured.[15]

Once the campaigning season had begun in earnest in the late spring of 1943, the SS Cavalry Division became increasingly stretched. As well as operating over its old battlegrounds in Belorussia and the Pripet Marshes, the division was also committed to support Army Group South in the Ukraine. The days of simply rounding up and killing civilians were over; the division faced well-armed partisans whose strength was increasing. The Soviet insurgency campaign of the summer of 1943—to destroy German infrastructure, especially bridges and railway lines—was bearing fruit, with OKH complaining of its inability to move supplies and reserves where they were needed.

The way in which the main war on the Eastern Front was turning against Germany was replicated in counterinsurgency operations. And as the Red Army drove westward, so German antipartisan units increasingly found themselves being used in conventional operations. In January 1944 the SS Cavalry Division was withdrawn from the Eastern Front for a thorough overhaul in Croatia, although its 17th Cavalry Regiment remained in place until April, supporting the Wiking Division in the defense of Kovel. The two SS infantry brigades had already lost their main antipartisan function through their divisional upgrading in early 1944.

———————

THE FOCUS OF antipartisan warfare on the Eastern Front moved toward central Europe, especially Poland and Slovakia. In April 1943 the Jews in the Warsaw Ghetto had risen up against their persecutors, who were finalizing plans for the final transfer of Warsaw's Jewish population, around 60,000 strong, to the death camps. Jewish leaders in the Ghetto knew their uprising would have no chance of success but reasoned that it was better to die fighting than submit to the gas chambers.

The uprising began on 19 April, catching the Germans unawares. A scratch force of just over 2,000 men under Brigadeführer Jürgen Stroop was assembled to deal with the unrest. Stroop, a veteran of the Totenkopf Division, relied on a mix of units from the Wehrmacht, the German and Polish police, and the Waffen-SS, the latter providing the bulk of the military muscle in the form of two training and replacement battalions, one from Totenkopf and the other from the SS Cavalry Division.[16]

The Jewish insurgents were armed only with rifles, pistols, and hand grenades but managed to fight on until 16 May, when, with the destruction of the city's main synagogue, Stroop declared the uprising over. He calculated that 56,065 Jews had either been killed or captured, with around 5,000 unaccounted for, although, in his words, they were "destroyed by being blown up or by perishing in the flames." Stroop had nothing but praise for his troops: "The longer the resistance lasted, the tougher the men of the Waffen-SS, Police, and Wehrmacht became; they fulfilled their duty indefatigably in faithful comradeship and stood together as models and examples of soldiers."[17]

A second, far larger, revolt took place in Warsaw in the following year. On 1 August 1944 resistance fighters of the Polish Home Army attacked key German-occupied buildings within the city. Once again, the Germans were caught by surprise, and within twenty-four hours much of central Warsaw was in Polish hands. An outraged Hitler gave Himmler responsibility for the suppression of the uprising, to be carried out with the utmost brutality.

Himmler passed direct control of the operation to Bach-Zelewski with instructions that all Poles—including women and children—were to be killed. Bach-Zelewski followed orders with his usual enthusiasm. A key role was assigned to Oskar Dirlewanger's unit—upgraded as the SS "Dirlewanger" Brigade—which had been forced back into Poland from Belorussia as a result of recent Soviet advances. Bach-Zelewski was able to call on a ragtag collection of other antipartisan units that had been raised in the Soviet Union by the German Army but had now been handed over to the SS. The most notorious of these was the Kaminski Brigade, led by Bronislav Kaminsky, whose gang of anti-Bolshevik Russians grandly called themselves the Russian Army of Liberation.

Warsaw was subjected to mass bombing from the Luftwaffe and heavy shelling from the army, while the Dirlewanger and Kaminski Brigades (along with a unit of Azerbaijanis) ran riot through the city, murdering and raping with impunity. The brutality of their actions set a new low in Nazi antipartisan operations. Civilians were herded into factories, which were then set on fire, while hospital patients were killed in their beds. According to one account of the operation, "The Dirlewanger Brigade burned prisoners alive with gasoline, impaled babies on bayonets and stuck them out of windows."[18]

During the opening five days of the German operation, approximately 40,000 Poles were massacred.[19] Despite the ferocity of the German assault, the Polish Home Army continued to fight, above and below ground. The Germans brought in heavy artillery to pound the Polish positions and used flamethrowers and high explosives to break down resistance house by house. An exasperated Bach-Zelewski was forced to admit that "the Poles fought like heroes."[20]

On 1 October Polish commander General Bór-Komorowski concluded that without outside help, his forces could no longer continue the struggle. He suggested a negotiated surrender to the Germans, who, exhausted by their efforts, were prepared to accept. As a result, most of the insurgents of the Home Army were recognized as combatants and instead of being shot out of hand were sent into captivity as officially recognized POWs.

Warsaw's remaining inhabitants were expelled from the city, and Himmler—with vengeance in his heart—set about destroying the remains of the city center. The final toll of casualties amounted to 15,000 insurgents killed, along with at least 200,000 civilians. Total German casualties amounted to 17,000.[21] For their efforts in the suppression of the Warsaw Uprising, Dirlewanger and Bach-Zelewski were both awarded the Knight's Cross. The drunken, volatile Kaminsky was considered a liability, however. He was shot on Bach-Zelewski's orders, his death attributed to Polish "bandits."

———————

WHILE THE FIGHTING in Warsaw was at its height, elements of the Slovak Army, supported by nationalists, social democrats, and communists, rebelled against the Nazi puppet government of Jozef Tiso. The revolt began on 29 August 1944, but on this occasion the Germans had some forewarning of the conspiracy and were swift and decisive in taking appropriate countermeasures. Gottlob Berger achieved his long-held ambition of leading troops in the field when Himmler gave him command of the military units to be used in the suppression (although he was subsequently replaced by the more experienced SS police general Hermann Höfle). The Waffen-SS reinforced the German Army with units from the Ukrainian 14th SS Division and the 18th SS Division Horst Wessel, followed by the SS Dirlewanger Brigade.

The Slovak insurgents had assembled a strong force, rising to 60,000 men, but they were poorly organized and received little or no help from the Allies. Consequently, the Germans were able to overwhelm Slovak resistance with relative ease. Terror was effectively used as a weapon to subdue the population, as this account of the uprising explained:

> The brutality began almost immediately as the German troops, aided
> by the Tiso government's loyal Hlinka Guard, plundered livestock and

equipment for their own needs and torched scores of Slovak communities. The fear of the local populations was palpable. This fear limited assistance to the [insurgent] Slovak army as ordinary citizens learned the Germans were murdering entire families and burning down the homes of anyone caught sympathizing with the rebels. Following their brutal suppression of the Warsaw Uprising, the infamous SS Sturmbrigade Dirlewanger arrived to assist with the suppression, using notorious "mediaeval methods" against the Slovaks.[22]

The uprising was declared over on 28 October, although guerrilla warfare continued into early 1945, as remnants of the Slovak resistance retreated into the mountains. While other Waffen-SS formations were withdrawn from Slovakia in October, the Ukrainian Division remained in place to root out the last Slovak rebels. Before this could be achieved, however, the Red Army began to break through the barrier of the Carpathian Mountains and enter Slovakia. The Ukrainians were only partially involved in this phase of the fighting, as on 21 January 1945 the entire division was transferred to Slovenia. According to senior staff officer Wolf-Dietrich Heike, the division's experience in Slovakia was extremely useful: "It armed itself there, capturing the necessary weapons from the partisans; it kept peace and order in its perimeter; it gained anti-partisan experience and attained a high degree of physical fitness thanks to the constant marching and action in mountainous terrain. It also gained experience in action against the Red Army. The Division left Slovakia as an operational military unit ready for battle."[23]

By early 1945, partisan operations against the Germans on the Eastern Front had come to an end for the simple reason that Germany had lost control of most of its conquered territories. The counterinsurgency units of the Waffen-SS, which had earned such an infamous reputation in the East, were now thrown into the desperate battle to defend the German Reich from the Red Army.

Chapter 24

PARTISAN WARS: THE BALKANS

U NDER THE LEADERSHIP of Josip Broz "Tito," the communists partisans of Yugoslavia would become the chief hindrance to German
domination of the Balkan region. Other insurgent movements emerged
in Greece and later in Italy, but it was against Tito's partisans that the
Germans were forced to devote their main military effort. Within Yugoslavia, Germany deployed troops from the Wehrmacht, Waffen-SS, and
the Croatian armed forces, plus a formation of Cossacks transferred from
southern Russia. In theory, at least, Germany also had the support of
Italy, with several of Mussolini's infantry divisions stationed along Yugoslavia's Dalmatian coast.

With a few exceptions, notably the German Army's crack 1st Mountain Division, the quality of the Axis troops engaged in the region was
below average. A strong Luftwaffe presence—until the end of 1943—
was a partial compensation for these shortcomings, with German ground
commanders able to call upon a variety of aircraft for support in antipartisan operations. They included the Fieseler Storch for aerial reconnaissance, the Ju-52 for the swift transport of men and supplies to the
battle zone, and the Ju-87 Stuka for ground-attack sorties.

The 7th SS Volunteer Mountain Division Prinz Eugen was the largest
and longest serving of the Waffen-SS formations operating in Yugoslavia. As a mountain infantry division, it was organized around its two
infantry regiments, each with four "overstrength" battalions. The mountain battalion had the standard three infantry (Jäger) companies and one

machine-gun company but, in addition, received a heavy company (with engineer, antitank, infantry-gun, and mortar platoons) and a specialist patrol company, responsible for reconnaissance and flank security. Initially, armament was distinctly second-rate and included Yugoslav rifles, Austrian and Czech machine guns, and French and Czech artillery, with obsolete French tanks for the panzer company.[1] Over the course of time, they would be replaced by superior German weapons.

Throughout the spring and summer of 1942, Gruppenführer Artur Phleps attempted to train his division to an acceptable standard. In October 1942 Phleps considered Prinz Eugen ready to take part in a combined arms exercise under combat conditions. The operation consisted of an advance against a Chetnik band led by Major Keserović in mountainous terrain near Kriva Reka. In what was an inconclusive action, the troops of Prinz Eugen proved themselves under fire, although were unable to catch the enemy.

The harsh, mountainous topography of Yugoslavia—its limestone rock carved through with deep gullies—made off-road travel painfully slow. Such terrain inevitably favored defenders who knew the country well and were unencumbered by heavy equipment. For the men of Prinz Eugen, it meant a great deal of hard marching. According to Romanian Volksdeutsche infantrymen Fred Umbrich, "We often covered 20, 30, 40 or 50 kilometers within 24 hours—and this over rock and bush, carrying our food, weapons and ammunition."[2]

During the winter of 1942–1943, the Axis high command in Yugoslavia made plans for an ambitious encirclement action intended to destroy the partisans as a military force. Operation White would involve 90,000 Axis troops (with a further 60,000 in support), dispersed over a wide area in readiness to ensnare Tito's main force (roughly 45,000 strong) centered around Bihac. The Axis force included not only Germans, Italians, and Croatians but also units of Chetniks who had decided that Tito's communists were their major threat. Great effort had been invested in the operation, which began at the end of January 1943 and continued into March.[3]

The Germans pushed the partisans back with ease and managed to kill substantial numbers when enemy units were trapped in combat. But this happened only rarely, as Tito and his commanders were becoming veterans in guerrilla warfare and knew when to disengage from open confrontation with better-armed opponents. The encircling Axis forces were supposed to provide an ever-constricting steel ring around the partisans to prevent any breakout, but the poorly trained and motivated Italian and Chetnik forces had little interest in the operation and allowed the vast bulk of the partisans to slip away unharmed. The Germans claimed a total of around 5,000 partisans killed, wounded, or captured, but even this modest figure was almost certainly an overestimate.[4]

Operation White was followed by Operation Black during May and June, a more limited action that netted another haul of enemy dead but still failed to eradicate the partisan threat. These operations revealed to the Germans the enormous difficulties of fighting a well-disciplined and highly motivated guerrilla force operating in terrain of its own choosing— as well as the depressing fact that they could expect little help from their erstwhile allies. The Germans had no Plan B to deal with Tito's partisans, so throughout 1943 and most of 1944, they would launch similar operations in a fruitless attempt to capture their elusive enemy.

The fighting in the Balkans was arguably the most vicious that took place in any theater of war in Europe. The bitter ethnic differences that lay below the surface in prewar Yugoslavia reemerged after the German invasion of April 1941, made immeasurably worse by the presence of the foreign invaders. In October 1941, General Franz Böhme, the German plenipotentiary general in Serbia, set the tone with this directive: "In the future, for every fallen German soldier, 100, and for every wounded soldier, 50 prisoners or hostages are to be shot."[5]

Murder, rape, and torture became commonplace during military actions. This account from a letter written by a Danish soldier from the Nordland Division—briefly deployed in Croatia in 1943—provided lurid details of common atrocities:

Every day we fight the partisans, and we burn their houses down over their heads, and we take everything away from them from clothing to cows and horses. Yesterday we burned four towns the size of F (700 inhabitants). One day 20 of my pals were captured. And when we found

them, their noses and ears were gone and their eyes had been cut out and
were tied behind their necks . . . but that town was also punished, I tell
you; every female had their breasts cut off and we were allowed to take
aim at them until they all lay dead on the fields and in the streets, and the
men were put up against a wall and shot.[6]

The scale of the killings began to worry the German military administration. Edmund von Glaise-Horstenau, the German plenipotentiary in
Croatia, wrote, "The SS acted as if they were in enemy territory, led by
the bad example of their commanders. Robbing and looting were widespread. No action was taken against any offender. The example of the SS
and Cossacks also had its influence on the regular Wehrmacht troops,
who wondered why they could not have the same privileges."[7]

Such was the mania for atrocity and counteratrocity that Axis forces
even massacred those ostensibly on their own side. In July 1943 the Prinz
Eugen Division discovered a dead SS soldier in the village of Kosticuta
and without hesitation assembled the remaining inhabitants in the village
square and gunned them down, killing forty old men, women, and children. Among the dead were close relatives of soldiers in the SS Handschar
Division then training in France—one of the factors behind its mutiny in
September. Himmler briefly admonished Phleps for this action, but this
did not prevent the Prinz Eugen commander from continuing his ram-
page along the Dalmatian coast that led to a further 3,000 civilian deaths
during the summer of 1943.[8]

Himmler held Phleps in high regard and nominated him to lead a
new SS corps being formed in 1943. Designated as the V SS Mountain
Corps, it would comprise the Prinz Eugen Division and a floating number of German Army and Croatian formations and, eventually, the SS
Handschar Division. Phleps's replacement was the commander of Prinz
Eugen's 13th Infantry Regiment, Karl von Oberkamp, a Waffen-SS staff
officer who had also briefly led the "Germania" Regiment. Having served
in both the elite Reich and Wiking Divisions, Oberkamp seemed a suitable choice to lead Prinz Eugen, but he was to prove a weak commander,
vacillating in moments of crisis.

On 8 September 1943 Prinz Eugen's antipartisan campaign was transformed by the shock announcement that Italy had signed an armistice

with the Allies. The German high command ordered that all Italian troops in Yugoslavia must be immediately disarmed and placed under their control. The Italians themselves were also in a state of shock, their officers unsure what their response should be. Some units accepted the German terms, while others refused, prepared to fight their former ally if necessary. On an individual level, many Italians soldiers walked away from their regiments in the hope of returning to Italy as soon as possible; some continued to support the fascist cause, while a few crossed over to join the partisans.

The Prinz Eugen Division was dispatched to the Adriatic coast to supervise the disarmament and soon found itself fighting both Italians and partisans. A German war correspondent described the febrile atmosphere of the time as the division marched toward the Croatian port of Split: "Thousands of Bolshevik partisans, deserters and [pro-Allied Italian] Badoglio units had assembled around Split during the chaotic days right after the collapse of Italian authority. The latest news called for the establishment of a Bolshevik republic in Split. Reconnaissance aircraft provided air photographs of fires in the major Dalmatian cities. Fleeing Italian soldiers reported uprisings, disarmament, murder and drunken fraternization between Badoglio soldiers, British agents and partisan leaders. We were marching against chaos."[9]

As the SS division closed on Split, some units became isolated and were surrounded by partisan and antifascist Italians. Initial relief efforts came to nothing, and in the ensuing confusion Oberkamp ordered a general withdrawal on 17 September. Although the cutoff units were eventually rescued, Prinz Eugen had suffered a reverse. The divisional history made this muted yet telling criticism: "The failure influenced the mood of the division and considerably damaged the prestige of the divisional commander."[10] The attack on Split was renewed a few days later by Prinz Eugen and an army division, the city falling to the Germans on the twenty-sixth. More than 9,000 Italians were captured in the operation.

By November 1943—with the threat of anti-German Italian intervention over—the Prinz Eugen Division returned to its antipartisan war, advancing toward Mostar. The strain of campaigning was beginning to tell on the division, the commander of II Battalion of the 14th Regiment noting in his diary that his unit was "completely exhausted and shredded."

On 26 November, as Prinz Eugen prepared for a new operation, Oberkamp suddenly asked for leave. The divisional history recorded that he
"was no longer physically or emotionally able to take any more. He was
granted leave."[11] An apparently recovered Oberkamp subsequently returned to the division, but he had lost the confidence of his officers and
left for good on 11 January 1944. His permanent replacement was the
able Otto Kumm, a former commander of the "Der Führer" Regiment,
then acting as a staff officer in the V SS Mountain Corps.

The fighting during the winter of 1943–1944 further exposed weaknesses within the division. During Operation Waldrausch in January,
the 13th Regiment's I Battalion broke and ran from the battlefield. The
divisional history was forced to admit, "It was no longer the division of
the summer of 1943."[12] Phleps agreed to Kumm's request to take it out
of the line for a period of extensive retraining with a special emphasis on
improving morale. By April Kumm felt sufficiently confident to return
Prinz Eugen to offensive operations.

In February 1944 units of the 13th Waffen Mountain Division of
the SS Handschar began to arrive in Yugoslavia. After a preliminary
toughening-up operation in the Syrmia region—complete with a massacre
of local Serb civilians—the division was ordered to cross the Sava River
into Bosnia on 15 March. The Handschar commander, Brigadeführer
Karl-Gustav Sauberzweig, exhorted his men to action with a rather bizarre
open letter that concluded, "Before long, each of you shall be standing in
the place that you call home, as a soldier and a gentleman; standing firm as
a defender of the idea of saving the culture of Europe—the idea of Adolf
Hitler." As the troops forded the river, each man was handed a photograph
of Hitler and informed that this was a "personal gift" from the Führer.[13]
What the ordinary Handschar soldiers made of this, one can only guess.

Once across the Sava, the Handschar units drove away the partisans to
establish a defensive zone in preparation for Operation Easter Egg (Os-
terei) in April, intended to gain access to local coal mines vital for the
German war effort. The operation went well, sufficiently so for an excited

Himmler to withdraw an infantry battalion to form the nucleus of another Muslim formation, the predominantly Albanian 21st Waffen Mountain Division of the SS Skanderbeg. Later in the month, Handschar was included in the German spring offensive, Operation Maypole (Maibaum), where it fought alongside Prinz Eugen for the first time. Although the operation failed in its intended mission to encircle and destroy a partisan force, it, at least, disrupted their activities and was considered a success by the Germans.

The Handschar Division then adopted a largely defensive role, with a small group of soldiers being detached from the division in June to provide a cadre for another Croatian Muslim formation, the 23rd Waffen Mountain Division of the SS Kama. As with the Albanian Skanderbeg Division, Kama was a division in name only and was dissolved in October without making a military contribution to the war in the Balkans.

DESPITE THEIR BEST efforts in two years of hard fighting, the Germans had failed to defeat Tito's partisans, and the prospect of victory was as elusive as ever. The Germans' exploitation of race and ethnicity had served them well in previous antipartisan operations, but they had been trumped by Tito, who refused to play their game. While Tito's core support was Serbian, his appeal was always based on broad multiethnic and class-based lines. As a result, he was able to draw upon an array of diverse support denied his opponents, and his vision of a communist "better world" was more attractive to the people of Yugoslavia than anything proposed by Nazi Germany.

As the Germans were ideologically unable to change their political strategy, in Yugoslavia they looked to the skies for a tactical solution. Germany had pioneered airborne operations, but Hitler had been shocked at the heavy casualties suffered by his paratroopers and glider-borne infantry during the seizure of Crete in 1941. As a result, airborne operations had been put on hold. Himmler, however, held no such reservations and had encouraged the development of his own, albeit modest, paratroop force for special operations.

The 500th SS Parachute Battalion was formed in October 1943, its manpower drawn on a fifty-fifty basis between volunteers from existing Waffen-SS formations and from Waffen-SS disciplinary units. Training by the Luftwaffe began in Yugoslavia and then in Hungary, the battalion considered combat ready by early 1944. In previous operations against the partisans, Tito and his staff had always had time to slip away from the advancing German columns. The appropriately named Operation Knight's Move (Rösselsprung) was an attempt to catch Tito unawares through a combined parachute and glider assault directly onto his headquarters.

German intelligence was aware that Tito had set up a semipermanent base in the Unac Valley around the town of Drvar. He had been joined there by British, U.S., and Soviet military missions, who were providing the partisans with increasing levels of material support. A force of between 12,000 and 15,000 partisans was stationed in the valley and hills around Drvar. The Germans believed Tito to be staying in Drvar itself, although he was in fact hiding out in nearby caves, partly a result of British intelligence advice that some form of German action was in prospect. The German plan was for the airborne troops to kill or capture Tito and then await the arrival of a combined German and Croatian force, including Prinz Eugen, driving overland toward Drvar.

The operation began on the morning of 25 May with a heavy Luftwaffe air strike on Drvar and the surrounding area.[14] The airborne force—commanded by Hauptsturmführer Kurt Rybka—landed immediately after the aerial bombardment: 314 soldiers by parachute and 340 by glider (with a second wave of 220 paratroopers due around midday). Good weather and the skill of the Luftwaffe ensured a concentrated landing, and after a short, intense fight the SS paratroopers captured Drvar. Valuable documents were captured, but there seemed no sign of Tito. Initially, it was thought he might be among the many dead strewn around the town, but the inability to make a positive identification suggested he was elsewhere. This was confirmed by one partisan group mounting a determined defense of a cave in the nearby hills, while elsewhere they had swiftly fallen back from the initial German attack.

As the SS paras advanced toward the cave, they came under heavy fire from the partisans. Although the Germans received reinforcements and extra supplies from the second-wave parachute drop, they were now outnumbered and facing the full wrath of the partisans, converging on Drvar in growing numbers. Meanwhile, the German overland relief force was held up by partisan resistance along the mountainous roads leading to the battle site.

By late afternoon the paratroopers were sustaining increasing numbers of casualties, including Rybka, who was badly wounded and evacuated in a Fieseler Storch. With the battle turning in the partisans' favor, the paratroopers retreated to a central position on high ground around the local cemetery. There they would wait for rescue by the German ground forces.

While it was still daylight the beleaguered paratroopers were provided with fire support from the Luftwaffe, but as darkness fell they were on their own. The partisans redoubled their efforts to break into the German defenses established along the cemetery walls. A German war correspondent described one of their attacks: "Around 2200 [hours] the song and dance starts again. The Bolsheviks shoot at the cemetery with phosphorous rounds. Mortars take over and place the cemetery under fire, putting us into one situation after another. Holding onto tombstones, behind the wall, and behind the graves, the men press behind these for dear life. Despite the seemingly hopeless situation, there is a lot of fire discipline."[15]

The paratroopers fended off repeated attacks during the night. As dawn broke the Luftwaffe returned to overfly the area, the partisans withdrawing from their exposed positions by the cemetery. Later in the morning the paratroopers heard the distinctive ripping sound of MG42s in the distance, heralding the arrival of the German relief force that included Prinz Eugen's reconnaissance battalion. By midday the whole area was under German control, including the cave used as Tito's headquarters.

Tito had escaped from the cave as the paratroopers began their landings, whisked away to safety by a pilot from the Soviet mission who flew him to British-occupied Italy. The men of Prinz Eugen's 13th Regiment discovered a U.S. jeep and Tito's marshal's uniform hanging over a chair. Among other booty was a rucksack belonging to Randolph Churchill, the British prime minister's son, who was a member of the British military mission (but not in the area at the time). After destroying the partisan headquarters, the Germans withdrew in the face of mounting Allied air attacks.

Although the Germans had inflicted casualties on the partisans, the mission had obviously failed in its prime mission of eliminating Tito, primarily as a result of inadequate intelligence that failed to locate the exact position of their target. The German paratroopers had fought with great tenacity and had paid a heavy price. In twenty-four hours of fighting, the original force of 874 men had suffered 624 casualties.[16] What was left of the battalion was withdrawn from the battle zone for rest and rebuilding, while Prinz Eugen continued in its Sisyphean task of hunting the partisans.

For much of the war, Yugoslavia had been a "closed arena," with the Axis forces solely engaged in their war against the partisans. This began to change in mid-1944 with the Anglo-American advance through Italy, exposing Yugoslavia's coast to Allied intervention. But it was the Soviet invasion of Romania in late August 1944 that transformed the strategic situation. What was left of the Romanian Army collapsed, and on 23 August—following a coup—the country suddenly changed sides and allied itself to the Soviet Union. Bulgaria followed suit on 8 September. The German position in the Balkans was on the verge of disaster. Their forces in Greece were in danger of being cut off, as the Red Army drove through Romania unopposed, in preparation for a direct assault on Hungary and German-held Yugoslavia.

For the Romanian Volksdeutsche, who formed a large proportion of Prinz Eugen's rank and file, the news that their towns and settlements had been overrun by the Red Army was deeply unsettling and did little for morale, although Oberführer Kumm and his officers ensured the division's continuing viability as a military force. This was in contrast to the Handschar Division, which was already beginning to collapse in the summer of 1944; desertions rose from 200 in April–June to 2,000 in the first three weeks of September. In October preparations were made to disarm the division, although a few thousand Muslim soldiers chose to join a Kampfgruppe sent north to defend Hungary.[17]

IN 1943 4TH SS Polizei Division had been withdrawn from the Eastern Front to be reorganized as a panzergrenadier division. It was then sent to

Greece to act as part of the occupation force. Most of Greece had come under Italian control, but following the Italian surrender in September 1943 there was an immediate demand for German troops to disarm the Italians and maintain order throughout the country.

The resistance movements in Greece never operated on the same scale as those in Yugoslavia. Much of the military action in Greece directed against the Germans—as opposed to conflict between rival resistance organizations—was sponsored and organized by British special forces and by teams from the American Office of Strategic Services. For every act of resistance, the Germans would enact reprisals. John Mulgan, a New Zealander engaged in British Special Operations Executive activities, witnessed a typical German reprisal action around Kastania in October 1943: "They burned several villages in that area, all those that could be reached easily and without too much trouble, carrying petrol and incendiary grenades. They were very smart, SS troops for the most part and quite young, and very efficient, not only in fighting—for which they had no immediate call—but also in reprisals and incendiarism. During the next month of November and into December it seemed to me that villages were burning all over Greece."[18]

The Polizei Division's time in Greece was distinguished by its atrocities, two of which were acknowledged as such by the German military authorities and consequently gained a wider notoriety. On 5 May 1944 soldiers of 7th Panzergrenadier Regiment entered the town of Klissoura, following a nearby ambush by partisans that had led to the deaths of two SS men. The villagers were rounded up and 215 were shot, including 128 women and 50 children under the age of ten.[19] Little more than a month later, a company of soldiers from the same regiment, under the command of Hauptsturmführer Lauterbach, ran amok in the Distomo area on 10 June. Apart from looting and rapes, 296 civilians were killed before the soldiers moved on.[20] In September 1944 the Germans began their retreat northward into Macedonia and Yugoslavia, the SS troops once more leaving behind a string of burning villages as part of their legacy of occupation.[21]

THE MILITARY SITUATION in Italy after the Italian surrender in September 1943 was especially perplexing for the Germans. They faced a conventional war with the Western Allies in southern Italy, while at the same time operating alongside fascist Italians in a counterinsurgency war against Italian partisans, amid a population that resented their presence and longed for the war to be over. These contradictions were faced by the 16th SS Panzergrenadier Division Reichsführer-SS, simultaneously fighting the Allies in the long retreat up the Italian peninsula while engaging Italian partisans and enacting reprisals on the civilian population.

The origins of the division dated back to 1941 and the formation of the Escort (Begleit) Battalion of the Reichsführer-SS, Himmler's personal lifeguard. The battalion was upgraded to an assault brigade in 1943, the expansion taking place in Corsica, where it was involved in fighting against Italian troops in the immediate aftermath of the Italian surrender. The brigade was evacuated from the island in October, to be upgraded as a full panzergrenadier division. Initially, the division was spread between Livorno in Italy and Ljubljana in Slovenia, its recruits drawn from existing Waffen-SS units and Romanian and Hungarian Volksdeutsche. Max Simon, the former Totenkopf commander, was sent to lead the new division.

The Allied landings at Anzio on 22 January 1944 called for an immediate response from all German units in the vicinity. Although it was still undergoing training, a Kampfgruppe from the Reichsführer-SS Division was dispatched from Livorno to confront the seaborne invaders. The Germans were able to contain the Allied beachhead around Anzio for several months, and the Reichsführer Kampfgruppe took part in what became a grim attritional struggle, until transferred back to its parent division in April. By this time the Reichsführer-SS Division had been sent to Hungary in support of Operation Margaretha, the German occupation of the country that had taken place in March to prevent it from breaking away from the Axis and negotiating a separate peace with the Soviet Union.

The division returned to Italy at the end of May and took up positions opposite the U.S. Fifth Army. During heavy fighting on 17 June the forward headquarters of the Reichsführer-SS was overrun by troops from the U.S. 34th Division, although elsewhere the SS troops were able to hold their positions. In early August the division was pulled out of the line for rest and refitting. From then on it was primarily engaged in antipartisan warfare, countering the growing strength of the Italian partisans.

Obersturmbannführer Walter Reder, commander of the Reichsführer-SS reconnaissance battalion, was tasked with destroying the troublesome communist Red Star Brigade, operating in the Apennine Mountains south of Bologna. Reder was a Waffen-SS soldier to the core, a former Totenkopf officer who had fought on the Eastern Front from Barbarossa onward. Wounded on numerous occasions, he lost an arm during the fight for Kharkov in March 1943, for which he was awarded the Knight's Cross.

Reder despised the Italians and set about destroying the partisan threat with a vengeance. Civilian massacres inevitably followed, at Sant'Anna di Stazzema on 12 August and then at San Terenzo Monti on the nineteenth. The operation culminated in a major action against the Red Star Brigade around Monte Sole, beginning on 29 September.

The Germans surrounded the partisan position and in a well-executed five-day operation, they closed the net, killing partisans and civilians alike. The final action took place around the scattered commune of Marzabotto, the terrified villagers hoping for sanctuary in the local churches but killed without mercy. Initial reports from the locality claimed a death toll of 1,835 people, although later estimates suggested a lower figure of around 770; Reder totted up a figure of 728 "bandits" killed in his after-action report.[22] Nonetheless, the operation was a military success for Reder's men, with partisan activities in the area greatly reduced thereafter. During the fall of 1944 the Reichsführer-SS Division withdrew into reserve, in preparation for a transfer to Hungary in January 1945.

IN ITS COUNTERINSURGENCY warfare strategies, Germany experienced mixed fortunes. Himmler was well prepared for antipartisan operations, although he failed to anticipate the growing power of Soviet-organized insurgency on the Eastern Front and, especially, the effectiveness of Tito's partisans in Yugoslavia. The partisans tied down large numbers of Axis formations—including those from the Waffen-SS—which could have been better employed in conventional operations against the Allies. Nonetheless, Himmler's troops had a number of successes, not only against such obviously soft targets as Jewish civilian communities but also against more serious military opponents, as was the case in the suppressions of the 1944 uprisings in Warsaw and Slovakia.

In counterinsurgency warfare, Himmler had the advantage of being able to call upon powerful forces from the Waffen-SS and Wehrmacht when required. He also had the advantage of not being bound by the ethical factors that typically constrained other nations' actions. Indeed, the use of terror to intimidate opponents was a deliberate Nazi policy and was often highly successful. Yet, despite the intensity and violence of antipartisan operations, they would have only limited influence on the overall course of the war, which, in the end, would be decided by the conventional clash of arms on the battlefield.

Part Four

WAR IN THE WEST

Make peace you Fools!

—FIELD MARSHAL VON RUNDSTEDT,
ON BEING ASKED BY OKW FOR HIS
RESPONSE TO THE NORMANDY LANDINGS

Chapter 25

BATTLE FOR THE BEACHHEAD

B Y THE SPRING of 1944 the German high command was aware that an invasion of France was imminent. The more perceptive officers also knew that the Allied amphibious landings must be defeated on the beaches without delay; if they failed in this, then the campaign would almost certainly be lost. Substantial German forces had already been deployed in the West and would subsequently include five Waffen-SS panzer divisions. But what was not clear to the Wehrmacht was exactly where or when the invasion would take place.

The 12th SS Panzer Division Hitlerjugend and the army's 21st Panzer Division were deployed close to what would become the actual invasion site in Normandy. On the night of 5–6 June, increased aerial activity along the coast suggested to Brigadeführer Fritz Witt, the Hitlerjugend's commander, that this might be the beginning of the assault. Witt, with a reputation for a cool head in a crisis, calmly woke his chief of staff at 1:30 A.M. and instructed him to prepare the division for action.

Witt's hunch was confirmed when reports began to filter in that enemy paratroopers had landed along the coast north of the city of Caen. Yet there was no official reaction to news of the invasion, largely a consequence of the cumbersome, overlapping command structure established by Hitler in France. Field Marshal Rundstedt was nominally in charge of all forces in France and Belgium but was repeatedly overruled by Hitler and OKW. Command of Army Group B—responsible for northern France—was assigned to Field Marshal Rommel, while the vital armored formations were part of a separate panzer group under General Geyr von Schweppenburg. There was little agreement between the various senior commanders of how best to repel any Allied invasion. Overall, the German reaction to the D-Day landings was sluggish and poorly coordinated.

Only at first light on the sixth was Witt's division ordered to move toward Caen. Formed in June 1943, the Hitlerjugend Division had been organized and trained by officers and NCOs from Leibstandarte SS "Adolf Hitler," and together the two formations—along with a heavy artillery battery and a battalion of Tiger tanks—made up Sepp Dietrich's I SS Panzer Corps. As a leader of men in battle, Dietrich had few equals, but his military ability at a higher level was dismissed by army and Waffen-SS colleagues alike. The complexities of leading an army corps seemed beyond him, but the German system of command, dating back to the Franco-Prussian War, had taken this into account: every senior commander was given a highly trained staff officer, with the knowledge and authority to actively direct operations where necessary. In Dietrich's case his "coequal" was former army colonel Fritz Kraemer. They worked well together, Dietrich providing the public face and heart of the team, Kraemer the behind-the-scenes brains.

The Hitlerjugend Division drew its rank and file from members of the Hitler Youth born in 1926.[1] Some of the recruits had been "persuaded" to join, but the majority had come forward of their own free will, the thrill of being part of a military elite a sufficient inducement to sign up for the division. Observers were impressed by their enthusiasm. They included Fritz Kraemer: "Again and again it was gratifying and surprising to see the zeal and ardor with which these young men endeavored to attain the skill of soldiers."[2]

Military instruction began as the recruits arrived at the division's main training ground at Beverloo in Belgium. The emphasis at Beverloo was on improving physical fitness (many recruits were considered undernourished) and providing realistic battlefield training. The instructing staff from Leibstandarte, with recent frontline experience, were of the highest quality, and the transformation of the recruits from boys into soldiers went smoothly. Witt, who was well known for his acts of kindness to the men under his command, insisted that the instructing staff adopt a fatherly approach to training. When satisfied with the progress of the recruits' transformation from boys into "young men who know the military craft," he had their candy ration replaced by tobacco and alcohol.[3]

There was no lack of recruits. In fact, by May 1944 the division was sufficiently overstrength for 2,000 NCOs and enlisted men to be transferred to Leibstandarte when it began refitting in Flanders after its ordeal in the Ukraine. The only Hitlerjugend manpower shortages were evidenced in a demand for specialist and technical officers. They were supplied by the transfer of fifty Wehrmacht officers, who kept their uniforms and ranks but otherwise were an integral part of the SS division. The most serious problem facing the division was a shortage of vehicles, fuel, and ammunition, although by the spring of 1944 these material shortcomings were slowly being rectified.

The senior officers of the new division were hardened Leibstandarte veterans. The 25th Panzergrenadier Regiment was commanded by the inspirational Standartenführer Kurt Meyer. Obersturmbannführer Wilhelm Mohnke was assigned to lead the 26th Regiment. He had been severely wounded during the invasion of Yugoslavia in 1941, effectively losing the use of a foot, and the continuing pain he suffered seemed to have exacerbated his already difficult, tempestuous personality. The Hitlerjugend's 12th SS Panzer Regiment—comprising a battalion of Mark IVs and a battalion of Panther Mark Vs—was commanded by Obersturmbannführer Max Wünsche. Fair-haired, blue-eyed, and a former leader of the Führer's personal bodyguard, Wünsche was a pinup boy for Goebbels's propagandists. An enthusiastic Nazi, he was also a first-rate tank commander.

As the Allied invasion got under way on 6 June, Leibstandarte was still in the process of completing its refitting and was not available for immediate commitment to action. As a result, Dietrich was summoned from his Brussels HQ by Field Marshal Rundstedt to lead a new, if temporary, corps command, comprising Hitlerjugend, 21st Panzer Division, and the powerful Panzer Lehr Division.

IN THE DAYS preceding the invasion, Witt had prepared the best routes for his troops to get to potential landing sites close by Caen, but his plans were stymied by orders to travel through the notorious bottleneck at Lisieux. The division's advance almost immediately slowed to a crawl. In an attempt to remedy the situation, Witt dispatched a Kampfgruppe commanded by Meyer to race ahead of the division. In addition to the three motorized battalions of his panzergrenadier regiment, Meyer's force included tank and artillery units, plus the heavily armed reconnaissance battalion, commanded by the tough, thuggish Sturmbannführer Gerd Bremer.

Witt ordered Kampfgruppe Meyer to take up position alongside the 21st Panzer Division, now battling Anglo-Canadian troops marching inland from the beaches. The poorly routed advance through Lisieux and attacks by Allied fighter-bombers delayed Meyer, who arrived in Caen only at nightfall, with the remainder of his Kampfgruppe rolling in during the early hours of 7 June. Meyer tracked down the commander of the 21st Panzer Division, Lieutenant General Feuchtinger, who recalled the SS officer's belief in a swift victory: "I explained the situation to Meyer and warned him of the strength of the enemy. Meyer studied the map, turned to me with a confidant air and said, 'Little fish! We'll throw them back into the sea in the morning.'"[4]

As he was leaving his meeting with Feuchtinger, Meyer received a telephone call from Witt, ordering him to secure Caen and the nearby airfield at Carpiquet. He was also instructed to liaise closely with the 21st Panzer Division to ensure a coordinated attack by both formations at midday on the seventh. By this time, it was believed, the remainder of the Hitlerjugend Division would be close at hand.

In the event, the various units of the Hitlerjugend were slow in arriving, forcing Meyer to maintain a defensive posture with the troops under his direct command, the attack postponed to the late afternoon. He established his headquarters in the Ardenne Abbey, a couple of miles northwest of Caen, its towers providing a clear northward view of the open landscape to the coast. Meyer was joined by his old comrade Max Wünsche.

Meyer surveyed the battlefield through his binoculars, and at around 2:00 P.M. on the seventh he spotted Canadian tanks advancing between the villages of Buron and Authie—directly across the front of his carefully hidden troops. He telephoned his frontline officers to hold their fire. At the last moment, as the tanks were virtually over his men, he gave the order to attack: "There was a report of guns and muzzle flashes. The lead enemy tank was ablaze, and I watched the crew bailing out. More tanks were torn to pieces with loud explosions. Canadian infantry tried to reach Authie and continue the battle there, but it was in vain. The enemy had been struck deep in his flank at that point. We took Franqueville and Authie through energetic offensive action. St Contest and Buron had to follow. The enemy forces seemed to be totally surprised."[5] Meyer raced out of the abbey and leaped on his motorcycle to personally direct the operation at close quarters. The Hitlerjugend had sprung an almost perfect ambush, yet as the SS troops advanced, they came under heavy fire from concealed anti-tank guns. German panzers were repeatedly hit, and casualties mounted.

Meyer urged his troops forward at every opportunity, but the Canadians held firm. To his dismay, Meyer was informed that the commander of II Battalion, Sturmbannführer Scappini, had been killed, decapitated by a Canadian tank shell. Making matters worse was the failure of 21st Panzer Division to attack on the right, while the remainder of the Hitlerjugend Division had still not arrived to protect Meyer's exposed left flank. With light fading, the attack was called off, Meyer reluctantly admitting that the enemy were by no means "little fish."

This small opening action would set the pattern for the fighting throughout the Normandy campaign. The tactical advantage lay with the defense—whether German or Allied—and unless the attackers could mobilize a massive material advantage, offensive action would invariably falter in the face of well-organized resistance.

Despite his frustration in not being able to exploit his initial success, Meyer was profoundly relieved that his young panzergrenadiers had passed the test of battle. Apart from some wavering at one of the critical moments in the day's fighting, the resilience of the Hitlerjugend infantry had exceeded expectations. Meyer went on to record, "I was struck dumb by the positive attitude and spirit of the soldiers. We, the old soldiers, had been deeply concerned by the events of the day. The artillery fire and the enemy air attacks had affected all of us. Not so the young soldiers. For them it was a baptism of fire they had expected. They knew that many hard days and weeks of hard fighting lay ahead of them. Their attitude deserved respect."[6]

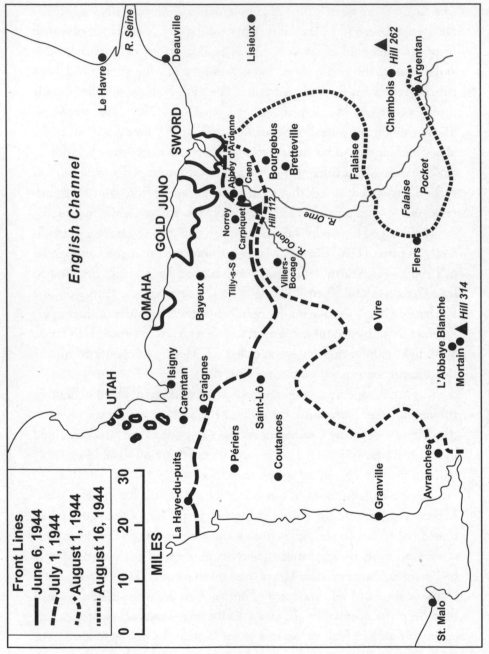

The Battle for Normandy, 1944

That first day of fighting on 7 June had certainly been fierce, sufficiently so for some Hitlerjugend soldiers to kill Canadian and British prisoners under their control. During this opening phase of the campaign, at least 156 Canadian captives were known to have been executed.[7] All sides were guilty of killing surrendered opponents, for reasons that ranged from bloodlust and revenge to simple expediency, but the Hitlerjugend gained a special infamy during the Normandy battles. The former Leibstandarte officers and senior NCOs had encouraged their recruits to display the utmost ferocity in combat at all times, and many of their teenage soldiers—full of vengeful thoughts after Allied bombing raids on their homeland—lived up to the expectations of their veteran mentors.[8]

One Hitlerjugend panzergrenadier privately admitted to the killing of Allied prisoners of war (PW) to an army soldier, shortly after they both had become prisoners:

> If people here know what we have done to their PWs we shouldn't live much longer either. [The PW] was interrogated a bit. If he said anything that was all right; if he didn't say anything, that was all right too. They would let him go, and then fire fifty rounds with the MG when he was ten paces away, and that would be the end of him. Our CO always used to say: "What am I to do with the swine? We haven't got enough to eat for ourselves."[9]

THE TACTICAL SKILLS of the Hitlerjugend in defense were of a high order. This was especially true of armor and infantry, where German superiority over the Allies was most marked. In terms of artillery, the Allies held the edge, any advantage conferred on the Germans by their massed Nebelwerfer batteries more than countered by superior command and control on the Anglo-Canadian side. And in this initial phase of the campaign, the Allies could rely upon the guns of warships stationed in the English Channel.

The most potent naval artillery support was provided by monitors and battleships, among them HMS *Rodney*, capable of firing a salvo of nine

16-inch shells—each containing nearly a ton of high explosive—to a distance of twenty miles. Meyer railed against the "damned naval gunfire," with "the heavy shells roaring above our heads like express trains."[10] But even worse for the Germans was the Allies' tactical trump card: aerial supremacy over the field of battle.

On D-Day, the Allied air forces had flown more than 12,000 sorties, the Germans just 319. From then on, the Luftwaffe was effectively absent over the skies of Normandy, thereby allowing the Allies to land men and vehicles on the beaches and advance inland without hindrance from the air. The Germans, by contrast, could barely move in daylight without being attacked by U.S. and British fighter-bombers that included the rocket-firing Typhoons of the RAF, known as "meatflies," or Jabos (Jagdbombers). Vehicles were particularly vulnerable to aerial attack, with rocket warheads able to penetrate the deck armor of even the well-protected Tiger heavy tank. Untersturmführer Herbert Walther, a Hitlerjugend panzergrenadier officer with long experience on the Eastern Front, complained bitterly:

> The Jabos were everywhere; you just couldn't escape them. We had to camouflage our vehicles with tree branches and leaves, so we looked like a moving forest. And if we travelled by day we had to be carefully spaced out, with at least a 100 meters between the vehicles, and with a man in each truck or APC acting as an aircraft spotter. When one of the Jabos saw us and turned into an attack dive, we had to stop and throw ourselves into a ditch. When they had gone we would push the destroyed trucks off the road and then carry on. We all asked ourselves, "Where is the Luftwaffe?"—but they never came.[11]

The failure of the powerful mobile elements of the German Army to close swiftly with the Allies around the beachheads would prove decisive. But this was due not only to air supremacy but also to the second great advantage enjoyed by the Allies: superior strategic intelligence. The Allies had confused the Germans as to the site of the invasion, and even after the Normandy landings many in OKW believed this to be merely a feint attack prior to the main invasion farther east along the coast around the

Pas-de-Calais. Accordingly, several panzer formations were initially held back from the fighting. They included the refitting Leibstandarte Division, ordered to remain in Belgium for ten vital days.

By the evening of 8 June the three panzer divisions of Dietrich's corps were slowly and painfully moving into position to open their assault, but their preparations were disrupted by the Allies' own advance. Whereas on the Eastern Front, German infantry would provide a screen for the panzer divisions to attack at a time and place of their choosing, in Normandy infantry reinforcements were still to arrive, forcing the panzers to act as both screen and reserve. As a result, the armored divisions were committed to the forward defense, launching local counterattacks to keep the Allies at bay, a process that deprived them of the tactical initiative and steadily drained their fighting strength.

Aggressive offensive action was the cornerstone of Waffen-SS military philosophy, but in this phase of the campaign it was overplayed by the Hitlerjugend commanders. Witt and Meyer—presumably worried at the wilting effects of a passive defense on their young troops—threw everything at the advancing Allies. Having secured the Caen and Carpiquet airfield, Meyer ordered repeated assaults against the enemy to the west of the city. The Canadian official history noted that the "attacks were pressed with courage and determination but with no particular tactical skill."[12] According to the Hitlerjugend's chief operations officer, the launching of successive raids against the Red Army on the Eastern Front claimed ground and undermined enemy morale.[13] This did not prove to be the case in Normandy.

A combined infantry-armor assault against Bretteville on 8 June promised much, but after a desperate house-to-house struggle the SS troops were ultimately repulsed. Of more concern, however, was the position taken by the Canadians in the village of Norrey, now a salient projecting two miles south of Bretteville. As a preliminary to the proposed general offensive to drive the Allies into the sea, Meyer ordered a night attack on 8–9 June to remove this obstacle.

During the opening stages of the battle, the Hitlerjugend Division had been forced to rely on the Panzer IVs from II Battalion, but the arrival of I Battalion's more powerful Mark V Panthers was eagerly welcomed by

Meyer. Max Wünsche led the panzers in the assault on Norrey, but the Canadians were well prepared, firing magnesium flares into the night sky to reveal the charging German vehicles to their antitank guns. The Germans broke into the village, but after a close-fought struggle they were beaten back by the Canadian Regina Rifles. Wünsche, hit in the head by a shell splinter, was driven back to Caen to have the wound dressed.

The determination to eliminate the Norrey salient led Meyer to order an unsupported tank assault on the afternoon of the ninth. Whether the presence of Wünsche would have been sufficient to deter Mayer's rash action cannot be known, but during the afternoon twelve Panther tanks of 3rd Company were ordered to drive on Norrey at full speed. The open countryside immediately to the west of Caen was excellent tank country, but it also provided perfect fields of fire to the Allied antitank guns and dug-in tanks that now defended the village. As the Panthers tore across the fields, they came under intense fire.

Unterscharführer Alois Morawetz, a commander in the platoon's far-right Panther, described his part in the action:

> After a muffled bang and a swaying as if the track had been ripped off, the vehicle came to a stop. It was quiet inside the vehicle. I thought we had driven over a mine. When I looked to the left to check the situation, I happened to see the turret being torn off the panzer driving on the left flank. At the same moment, after another minor explosion, my vehicle began to burn. The machine-gun ammunition caught on fire and there was a crackling noise like dry wood burning.[14]

Following a frenzied struggle with a jammed hatch, a badly burned Morawetz managed to bail out of the tank, where he joined other dazed and wounded survivors struggling back to German lines while under enemy mortar and small-arms fire. Seven Panthers had been knocked out, the remaining five in full retreat. Wünsche, on his return from the dressing station, saw the burning tanks. He later wrote, "I could have cried for rage and sorrow."[15]

The German fixation with Norrey continued. In the early hours of 10 June an assault was made by the Hitlerjugend's pioneer battalion, the only remaining reserve unit in the division. Preliminary German radio transmissions had alerted the Canadians to the attack. As soon as the pioneers began to advance, they were hit by heavy and accurate artillery and mortar fire. The attack failed, forcing the pioneers to go to ground as dawn broke.

The battalion's medical officer, Dr. Friedrich Zistler, personally carried wounded men away to safety in full view of the Canadians, who chivalrously refrained from firing on him. Zistler remembered coming across the body of his best friend, Oberleutnant Otto Toll, the 1st Company commander: "I can still see Otto lying before me. He had tried to make a tourniquet using the ribbon of his Knight's Cross and a flashlight to stop the bleeding from an artery."[16]

The fighting lessened on the tenth, representing the end of what the Germans called the First Battle of Caen. But the pause was short-lived: on 11 June the British launched Operation Perch—the Second Battle of Caen—that would comprise a two-pronged assault on both sides of the city.

The British offensive to the east of Caen—spearheaded by the 51st Highland Division—was contained with little difficulty. Of greater danger was the major British attack to the west of Caen, against the Hitlerjugend and Panzer Lehr Divisions. The hardest fighting was centered around Tilly-sur-Seulles, defended by Panzer Lehr; despite the Anglo-Canadians' best efforts, their advance was held.

The Allied attacks did, however, lock Panzer Lehr in place, preventing close liaison with the adjoining 376th Infantry Division, which faced the U.S. 1st Division. As the Americans advanced, the German infantry division fell back, distancing itself from Panzer Lehr. The British spotted the emerging gap, and General Dempsey, commander of the British Second Army, ordered his 7th Armoured Division to seize the opportunity and advance on the village of Villers-Bocage and the nearby Hill 213 that dominated the area. If the British could gain Hill 213, then the whole German position around Caen would be outflanked.

The British 22nd Armoured Brigade led the advance on 12 June, meeting virtually no opposition. The following morning, the brigade continued in a leisurely manner to Villers-Bocage itself, where it halted for a tea break. For whatever reason, the brigade's commander had not covered his advance with a reconnaissance screen and had no knowledge of the presence or otherwise of the enemy.

The only German forces in the area on the morning of 13 June were two companies of the 101st SS Heavy Tank Battalion, part of I SS Panzer Corps. The battalion's Panzer VI Tiger tanks had experienced a wretched march to the battlefield. The destruction of much of the railway system in northern France had forced them to detrain too early, with the resulting road march causing repeated breakdowns. Near-constant air attacks had also slowed progress, with each tank forced to travel several hundred yards apart. The Tiger companies had hoped to rest and refit on the thirteenth but would be flung straight into battle.

The five Tiger tanks of Obersturmführer Michael Wittmann's 2nd Company were closest to Villers-Bocage. Wittmann—who had already destroyed 117 Soviet armored vehicles on the Eastern Front—was unaware of the British advance and was surprised to see a long column of enemy armored vehicles parked on the road outside Villers-Bocage. Despite the odds stacked against him, he immediately saw this as an opportunity for swift, direct action. Climbing into the nearest serviceable Tiger, Wittmann roared toward the stationary British force, which comprised a mix of Cromwell and Sherman tanks with Bren Carriers.

The Tiger's first shot from its 8.8cm gun knocked out the lead Cromwell. Firing on the move and at close range, Wittmann then drove parallel to the British line, destroying the enemy vehicles one by one. The British were stunned, and the few shells fired in return that managed to hit the Tiger merely bounced off its heavy armor. One British officer recalled seeing Wittmann's tank drive past him: "Its commander waved his cap and laughed."[17] With the British column reduced to chaos, Wittmann drove into the village, where he destroyed several more British vehicles, but in the process his tank was brought to a halt by an antitank round that smashed one of its drive sprockets.

Having accounted for an extraordinary figure of twenty-five destroyed enemy vehicles, Wittmann and his crew promptly bailed out of their Tiger and made their way cross-country to the nearby headquarters of the Panzer Lehr Division. From there, a tank column was dispatched to support the two SS Tiger companies now heavily engaged in the fighting around Villers-Bocage.

The British had recovered from the shock of Wittmann's initial assault and managed to hold the German attacks. Lacking necessary infantry support, the German tanks were unable to capture the village. The British, for their part, had failed to send reinforcements to Villers-Bocage and tamely withdrew their forces on the fourteenth. It was a humiliating defeat that severely damaged the morale of 7th Armoured Division. By contrast, Wittmann's audacious solo effort represented the best in the buccaneering spirit of the Waffen-SS.

While the 101st SS Heavy Tank Battalion was fighting for Villers-Bocage, the Hitlerjugend, now firmly on the defensive, repulsed a series of Anglo-Canadian attacks along its front, with Mohnke's 26th Panzergrenadier Regiment bearing the brunt of the assaults. Mohnke lacked the charismatic touch so evident in the leadership of Witt, Meyer, and Wünsche. Never invited into the golden inner circle of old Leibstandarte officers, he was at least accepted as a conscientious soldier, capable of withstanding the hammer blows raining down on his panzergrenadiers defending Caen.

The Allies' chronic failure to integrate armor with infantry in offensive operations was cleverly exploited by Mohnke's soldiers. Typically, the Anglo-Canadian tanks would advance at speed, leaving their infantry well behind. The frontline panzergrenadiers of the Hitlerjugend—maintaining strict fire discipline—would let the enemy tanks roll past them, and then, from their camouflaged positions, deliver a devastating surprise barrage against the advancing Allied infantry, who now lacked armored support. Meanwhile, the Allied tanks were ambushed in the German second line by antitank guns and infantry liberally supplied with Panzerfaust antitank launchers.

Such tactics called for coolness and courage. Herbert Walther described how his young soldiers "were now veterans after just a few days fighting. They had a bright look in their eyes, eager to fight. They had been forged in battle and were determined to defend the Fatherland."[18]

Despite the heavy casualties inflicted on the Allies, the strain on the German front line was relentless. On 13 June Witt asked I SS Panzer

Corps headquarters for permission to withdraw to less exposed positions. Permission was denied, Dietrich and Kraemer fearful that in these conditions, any retreat might occasion a rout.

On the following day, a salvo of shells from HMS *Rodney* crashed around the headquarters of the Hitlerjugend Division, a shell splinter fatally wounding Witt in the head as he shepherded his staff to safety. Fritz Witt had been one of the originals in the prewar Leibstandarte, and his loss was keenly felt. On hearing the news, Dietrich muttered, "That's one of the best gone. He was far too good a soldier to stay alive long."[19] Witt's achievement lay in fashioning the teenage boys of the Hitlerjugend into a first-rate fighting force. His chief of staff wrote, "He was a rock in the sea, admired by his young soldiers and trusted by all."[20]

As the senior ranking officer, Kurt Meyer was given command of the Hitlerjugend and at thirty-three years and six months became the youngest divisional general in both the Wehrmacht and the Waffen-SS. Having assessed the situation, he requested the withdrawal first proposed by Witt, which this time was accepted.

Over the next few days the division held position in readiness for the arrival of reinforcements. On 17 June the bulk of Leibstandarte had been loaded onto trains in Belgium for the journey to Normandy. Hausser's II SS Panzer Corps (9th and 10th SS Panzer Divisions) had been dispatched from the Eastern Front, due to arrive on 25 June. The 17th SS Panzergrenadier Division was already locked in battle with the U.S. First Army, while units of Das Reich were expected to reach the front from the middle of June onward.

A violent storm in the English Channel that broke on 19 June came to the Germans' aid. Lasting for three days, it greatly reduced supplies to the Allied armies. As a consequence, the pressure on the German front line briefly relaxed, allowing the young soldiers of the Hitlerjugend a temporary respite. It also gave time for the Germans to organize a large-scale counteroffensive, their last opportunity to defeat the Allies in Normandy.

Chapter 26

UNEQUAL STRUGGLE

A CENTRAL PART of the Allied strategy for the Normandy landings was to create an aerial interdiction zone around the still vulnerable beachhead. Although the Allies could not prevent the Germans from reaching the beachhead, such was their aerial supremacy that they could seriously slow the progress of German formations and harry them so comprehensively that when they at last arrived at the battle zone, they were in a poor condition to fight. The 12th SS Panzer Division Hitlerjugend had been the first to suffer at the hands of the Allied air forces, but it was, at least, close to the invasion site on 6 June. The other Waffen-SS divisions would have farther to travel and so endure the full fury of the Allied aerial attack.

The 17th SS Panzergrenadier Division was stationed south of the River Loire in western France, and on 7 June it was instructed to advance northward to engage American forces pushing out of the Utah beachhead. A staff officer from the division recalled that "everyone was in a good and eager mood to see action again—happy that the pre-invasion spell of uncertainty and waiting was snapped at last." The officer's optimism was not to last, however, when the division came under attack from the air. The bombardment devastated the German columns: "The length of the road was strewn with splintered anti-tank guns (the pride of our division), flaming motors and charred implements of war. The march was called off and all the vehicles that were left were hidden in the dense bushes or in barns. No one dared show himself out in the open anymore.

Now the men started looking at each other. This was different from what we thought it would be like. It had been our first experience with our new foe—the Americans."[1] From then on the SS troops were forced to advance during the hours of darkness only, remaining well hidden during the day. The division would soon find itself embroiled in the close fighting of the classic bocage country, a network of small fields enclosed by high hedges growing on thick, earthen banks that made offensive operations especially difficult.

The 17th SS Panzergrenadier Division had been formed in central France during the fall of 1943, drawing its leadership cadre from replacement and reserve units, with the bulk of its manpower made up of Romanian Volksdeutsche conscripts with some French volunteers. The division was accorded the title of "Götz von Berlichingen," after a redoubtable sixteenth-century German knight who replaced an arm lost in battle with a steel prosthetic gauntlet (which became the divisional emblem). The division's commander, Brigadeführer Werner Ostendorff, was a former "Der Führer" officer and protégé of Paul Hausser. Ostendorff, a stern disciplinarian, had been chosen by Hausser to act as his senior staff officer in the Reich Division and then in the original SS Panzer Corps. During the early stages of Operation Barbarossa, Ostendorff had also proved a dynamic frontline soldier, in one instance personally leading a counterattack against superior Soviet forces during the Smolensk encirclement battles of September 1941.

The 17th SS Panzergrenadier Division did not benefit from the generous allotment of resources of the SS panzer divisions, lacking a tank battalion and being generally short of the vehicles usually assigned to a mechanized division. It was, however, equipped with a potent Panzerjäger (antitank) battalion, equipped with forty-two assault guns.

Advance elements of the division first encountered U.S. ground troops on 10 June, with the remaining units arriving on the battlefield over the next seven days. As in most encounter battles, there was confusion as the 17th SS Panzergrenadier Division took up its position alongside army units and those from a Luftwaffe Parachute Division, now acting as ground troops.

An attempt by the Waffen-SS to recapture Carentan on 13 June ended in ignominious failure, the German attack repulsed with ease by U.S.

armored units. Feeling let down by the troops on his flanks, an aggrieved Ostendorff turned on Lieutenant Colonel von der Heydte, the aristocratic commander of 6th Parachute Regiment, and in a furious row he threatened to have the Luftwaffe officer court-martialed for his earlier withdrawal from Carentan. Nothing came of the threats, however, as the whole German line fell back to better positions farther inland. On 16 June Ostendorff was seriously wounded during the retreat and did not return to the division until October, when the battle for Normandy had long been decided. In the interim, Ostendorff was replaced by Otto Baum, a tough, no-nonsense officer who had fought with distinction in the Totenkopf Division.

A notable absentee in these initial engagements was one of the premier formations in the German armed forces: the 2nd SS Panzer Division Das Reich. After the grueling series of attritional battles fought on the Eastern Front during 1943, the battered division was withdrawn to southern France in early 1944, subsequently joined by the remnants of Das Reich Kampfgruppe in April. Stationed around Montauban, near Toulouse in southwest France, the division began a rebuilding program. This had been done many times in the past, not only to replace casualties but also to replace the many officers and units transferred from the division to provide building blocks for other formations. Leibstandarte had suffered a similar dilution of its prewar core, and by 1944 the strains on the system were finally beginning to tell in both divisions.

The commander of Das Reich, Brigadeführer Heinz Lammerding, had joined the SS as part of Theodor Eicke's concentration-camp inspectorate. He had then risen up the ranks in the Totenkopf Division before transferring to act as chief of staff of Erich von dem Bach-Zelewski's antipartisan forces fighting on the Eastern Front. Lammerding was given command of Das Reich in January 1944, although as an outsider his appointment was not particularly welcomed by his fellow officers, who considered him too close to his mentor, Heinrich Himmler. One officer dismissed him accordingly: "As an engineer and smaller unit commander he was fully capable but was not skilled as a divisional leader."[2]

Lammerding's first task was to integrate the new recruits into the division and train them up to a battleworthy standard. Otto Weidinger, an officer in "Der Führer," bemoaned the poor caliber of men arriving from the

replacement depots, totaling fourteen different nationalities with a prepon-
derance of Balkan Volksdeutsche and conscripts from the Alsace. "There
could be no more talk of the cream of the crop," Weidinger wrote. "The
lowering of the quality of personnel replacements was also reflected in a
rise in military and criminal offences, as a result of which the division court
was forced to impose harsh sentences."[3] Desertion was a growing problem,
especially among the French-speaking Alsatian recruits, many of whom
were encouraged to flee their posts by members of the French Resistance.

Adding to the division's problems was a shortage of weapons, vehicles, fuel, and ammunition, admittedly commonplace within all German
units by 1944. During the spring of 1944, strenuous efforts were made to
rectify these shortfalls, but when the order was given to advance to Normandy, some units were not yet operational and were left behind until
deemed sufficiently well equipped. Despite these limitations, Das Reich
remained a powerful fighting force, able to field just over 200 armored
fighting vehicles and 15,000 men.

While the division was engaged in training its new recruits, the activities of the French Resistance increased in intensity, designed to stretch the
German armed forces in France prior to the Allied invasion. The division
then found itself engaged in antipartisan sweeps across the French countryside, where brutal reprisals for enemy action were the norm. When the
invasion began on 6 June, the resistance raised the tempo of its operations
still further, so much so that the division was initially ordered to come to
the assistance of isolated army units under attack from the Resistance in
the Limoges area to the north of Montauban.[4]

As the long vehicle columns of the SS panzer division advanced northward, they too came under attack. When they reached Tulle they discovered that the German garrison there had been overwhelmed by Resistance
fighters, who had shot nine members of the Sicherheitsdienst (SD), the
SS secret intelligence service. Waffen-SS reprisals were swift and deadly:
in a roundup of the town's civilian population, 117 people were killed
on 9 June—99 of them hanged from the town's lampposts—while a
further 149 were deported to Dachau. On the same day, Sturmbannführer Helmut Kämpfe, commander of "Der Führer's" III Battalion,
was abducted by the Resistance (later killed). The fury of the SS soldiers

at news of his capture culminated in the destruction of the village of Oradour-sur-Glane and the massacre of 642 civilians on 10 June.[5]

Even by the standards of the Waffen-SS, these atrocities were noteworthy, and as they occurred in Western Europe they received wider publicity and condemnation than would have been the case on the Eastern Front. But they were far from unusual in this period of heightened tension. As well as killing British and Canadian prisoners, the Hitlerjugend Division had shot eighty-six French civilians in the town of Ascq on 2 April 1944 as a reprisal measure for the derailment of a train carrying troops from Belgium into France. For its part, the 17th SS Panzergrenadier Division had gunned down wounded U.S. paratroopers and French civilians in revenge for the heavy casualties it suffered during the fight for Graignes between 10 and 13 June.[6]

Once the men of Das Reich had finished with their reprisals in the Limoges area, they continued their northward trek, well laden with loot plundered from the local population. They faced little activity from the Resistance, but progress remained slow, especially when the armored columns crossed the Loire and came within the Allied interdiction zone. The division arrived at the front in a piecemeal fashion to the west of St.-Lô from 17 June onward, with those units that had been left behind at Montauban not arriving until 7 July. The combined actions of the French Resistance and the Allied air forces had helped prevent Das Reich from playing a role on the battlefield when it was most needed.

The division was initially deployed on the far left of the German line around La Haye–du-Puits, where it fought alongside the army's 353rd Division, beating back repeated American assaults. Growing American pressure forced Das Reich to fall back to Périers on 10 July. There it managed to stabilize the line, operating beside the 17th SS Panzergrenadier Division and a mix of army and paratroop units until the decisive U.S. Army offensive of Operation Cobra on 25 July. A Das Reich Kampfgruppe—based around "Der Führer" and its new commander, Sturmbannführer Otto Weidinger—had already been dispatched eastward on 26 June to help repel a renewed British offensive around Caen.

THE OTHER LEADING Waffen-SS division—Leibstandarte SS "Adolf Hitler"—had also been delayed in its move to Normandy. In part this was a consequence of OKW's fear that the main Allied offensive might be launched in the Pas-de-Calais area and because the division was still completing its refitting process. On 13 June Hitler gave instructions for Leibstandarte to be released from its holding position in Belgium, although the transfer to the battle zone was painfully slow. By 20–21 June the division entrained in and around Ghent for the transit to Paris, where elements remained for several days, sufficient for some sightseeing, as Hans Quassowski recalled: "We moved into parkland by Versailles and took the opportunity to inspect the chateau. The Hall of Mirrors and especially Congress Hall impressed us greatly."[7]

In response to Dietrich's repeated calls for reinforcement, a Kampfgruppe based around two battalions of Obersturmbannführer Albert Frey's 1st Panzergrenadier Regiment was sent on ahead, reaching the front alongside the Hitlerjugend on the night of 27–28 June. The remainder of Leibstandarte reached its assembly area in the Forest of Cinglais between 2 and 6 July, where it acted as a strategic reserve in readiness to take over from Hitlerjugend on 12 July. Whatever the problems caused by Allied bombing of the rail network and the fighter-bomber attacks nearer the combat zone, the tardy progress of Leibstandarte must also be seen as a symptom of the malaise running throughout the German command system in the West.

Hausser's II SS Panzer Corps—9th SS Panzer Division Hohenstaufen and 10th SS Panzer Division Frundsberg—was forced to detrain in eastern France, its armored units facing a long haul to Normandy, with the inevitable catalog of mechanical breakdowns attendant on long cross-country drives. By 23 June the two divisions were in place at their assembly area close to Falaise, to be joined by the recently formed 102nd Heavy Tank Battalion, with a strength of forty-five Tiger tanks. The II SS Panzer Corps was to be used as a powerful, highly mobile strike force that instead of merely buttressing the German front line would smash through the Allied defenses and drive toward Bayeux and the coast, thereby splitting the Allied beachhead in two.

While the SS and army reinforcements were moving to the front line, the Hitlerjugend Division was continuing its defense around Caen. On 25

June the British struck against Mohnke's 26th Panzergrenadier Regiment, III Battalion fighting a desperate battle to hold on to Fontenay-le-Pesnel. But this was only a prelude to the main British offensive—Operation Epsom—launched on the twenty-sixth (the German Third Battle of Caen). This was the biggest British assault so far in the Normandy campaign and was intended to drive a wedge into the German lines to the west of Caen, sufficiently deep that the whole German position would be outflanked.

Standartenführer Kurt Meyer, the Hitlerjugend commander, was told to hang on as best he could against what were clearly superior forces and await the arrival of reinforcements. Throughout 26 June Meyer raced along the front, encouraging his young panzergrenadiers, who were taking on the enemy armor at close range with Panzerfausts and hand-applied shaped charges. The Germans were encouraged by the bad weather—rain and low cloud cover—which grounded the dreaded fighter-bombers, but they were shocked at the intensity of the Allied artillery barrage, which old veterans compared to the heaviest Trommelfeuer (drumfire) bombardments of World War I.

The fighting surged around the villages of Rauray and Cheux, vital strongpoints in the German defenses, with Hitlerjugend tank units also thrown into the fray. By the late afternoon it seemed that the line would rupture. Hitlerjugend's divisional headquarters at Verson came under threat, forcing staff officer Obersturmführer Bernhard Meitzel to organize a scratch force to repel the attackers. In a brisk engagement, Meitzel's cooks and bottle washers knocked out two British tanks within 225 yards of the headquarters.

In his diary Meitzel recorded how he had accompanied Meyer to one of the more intense firefights. There the reconnaissance troops of Meyer's old 25th Panzergrenadier Regiment "were squashed by British tanks and the accompanying infantry. We could not even help with artillery fire since we were out of ammunition. The divisional commander knew every one of these 17- to 18-year-old soldiers who were fighting their last battle in front of us now. When I looked at the Standartenführer, I saw tears in his eyes."[8]

The arrival of a few Tiger tanks stopped any further British advance in this sector. The British had made a dent in the German line, but the Hitlerjugend—at a cost of 730 casualties—had prevented any

breakthrough. Chester Wilmot, doyen of Normandy-campaign historians, paid tribute to the youthful defenders: "The troops of the 12th SS
fought with a tenacity and ferocity seldom equaled and never excelled
during the whole campaign."[9]

Initially, the Germans believed they had halted the British offensive,
and on the twenty-seventh Dietrich launched an armored counterattack
to recapture Cheux, while Hausser's II SS Panzer Corps moved up to its
assembly area for the drive on Bayeux. This optimism proved misplaced,
with the German tank assault ripped apart by heavy and accurate artillery
fire, followed by the resumption of the British offensive. On the morning
of the twenty-eighth, the British crossed the Odon River and advanced
on Hill 112, the summit of a ridge that dominated both the Odon and
the Orne River valleys and overlooked Caen. The steady British progress
caused consternation within the German command. Meyer pleaded with
Dietrich for reinforcement, who in turn demanded help from Rommel to
stem the enemy advance.

The arrival of Frey's Leibstandarte Kampfgruppe was welcomed by
Meyer but was far too small to affect the overall outcome. A more fundamental move was required, which came early on 28 June with the postponement of Hausser's offensive toward Bayeux, to be replaced by a local
counterattack against the western half of the bulge created by the British
advance. It was hoped this would be just a temporary measure, but the
redeployment of Hausser's panzer corps to frontline tactical action represented the end of any meaningful strategic initiative on the German side.

Hausser, seemingly unaware of the desperate predicament of the defending troops, protested that he had insufficient time to prepare for the
attack: "I wanted to wait another two days, but Hitler insisted that it be
launched on the 29th."[10] Fritz Kraemer, the hard-pressed chief of staff
of Dietrich's I SS Panzer Corps, unsurprisingly took the opposite view,
arguing that the attack was made far too late and should have gone in on
the twenty-seventh.[11]

Compounding German difficulties were a series of forced command
changes, initiated by the death of the Seventh Army commander General
Dollman on 28 June. As Rundstedt and Rommel were fruitlessly trying
to persuade Hitler to sanction a strategic withdrawal east of the Seine, an

overwhelmed Dollman, fearing court-martial for the loss of Cherbourg to the Americans, shot himself. Hausser was subsequently given command of Seventh Army—the first Waffen-SS officer to lead an army—while Wilhelm Bittrich, from the Hohenstaufen Division, took over the II SS Panzer Corps. Hausser briefly remained with his old corps to help supervise the coming counteroffensive.

A day prior to the opening of the main German attack, Kampfgruppe Weidinger had launched an assault on the western side of the bulge, but its two panzergrenadier battalions and support troops soon found themselves in close combat with advancing British troops and unable to make any progress. The makeshift nature of the Waffen-SS counterattacks was noted in a British intelligence report: "This seems to indicate that the enemy is not acting in accordance with a prepared plan, but is sending parts of the units into action when they arrive, 'a little bit here, a little bit there.' This does not show the vigor we had expected from these troops."[12]

On the other, eastern, side of the bulge, Meyer had instructed Kampf-gruppe Frey to drive forward on the twenty-eighth, to take pressure off the main Hitlerjugend defensive line and, hopefully, to link up with Weidinger's troops. Frey was unhappy with the idea of attacking without artillery support and made this clear to Meyer, who waved away his objections with a promise of assistance from the guns of the Hitlerjugend. In Frey's account, Leibstandarte did not receive the necessary support; Allied artillery and machine-gun fire brought the advance to standstill.[13]

For the main assault on 29 June, the Germans deployed almost all their Panzer assets to crush the British salient. The main thrust would be supplied by 9th and 10th SS Panzer Divisions of II SS Panzer Corps, supported by Weidinger's Kampfgruppe and the Tiger tanks of the 102nd Heavy Battalion. Meanwhile, Wünsche's Hitlerjugend panzers, Frey's Leibstandarte Kampfgruppe, the 101st Heavy Battalion, and elements of the 21st Panzer Division would drive forward from the south and east. On the Eastern Front such a concentration of force would have almost certainly guaranteed victory at the tactical level at least, but in Normandy the *Materialschlacht* feared by many German commanders had arrived with a vengeance: through overarching command of the air, Allied superiority in firepower was allowed to trump German skill in maneuver.

338 WAR IN THE WEST

Allied commanders were notified of the proposed German assault—
not least from aerial observation of the long columns of armor advancing toward the battle zone—and had temporarily called off their own
(Epsom) offensive to dig in and repel the coming attack. Hausser, as with
all generals new to conditions in Normandy, was yet to comprehend
the paralyzing nature of the Allied war machine. And, unfortunately for
Hausser, the twenty-ninth presaged a day of fine weather.

The assault by II Panzer Corps had been scheduled for 6:00 A.M., but
as dawn broke Allied fighter-bombers were already having a feast picking
off German panzers as they left cover to open the attack. Worse was to
come, when Allied artillery—guided by ever-circling spotter aircraft—
came into play. Such was the power of the naval and ground artillery fire
directed at the German advance that its victims assumed (incorrectly)
that they were also under an RAF aerial carpet-bombing attack.[14] The
II SS Panzer Corps' offensive was stillborn.

It was only during the midafternoon that Waffen-SS panzergrenadiers
and supporting armor were able to advance with any degree of cohesion
against the Allied lines. As ever, the tactical skill and bravery of the SS
soldiers were sufficient to force back their opponents wherever a weakness was discovered, but these were relatively few. In the tight hedgerows
of the bocage countryside, the defenders invariably had the advantage.
Elsewhere, the German Army and SS assaults were similarly unsuccessful.
The British Army in Normandy has been much criticized for its caution
in attack, but no such accusation could be leveled at its resolve in defense. When the Germans made inroads into the British lines, they were
typically expelled in brutal close-quarters combat. Weidinger's Kampfgruppe suffered heavy losses in the attack for limited gains. On 2 July the
battered Das Reich troops returned to their parent division, now heavily
engaged with the Americans.

In their initial advance during Operation Epsom, the British had
crossed the Odon and reached the slopes of Hill 112, and over the following days this modest summit would become a focal point for the battle
west of Caen. The Germans were determined to drive the British from
the hill and attacked with Wünsche's panzers and massed artillery that
included fifty six-barreled Nebelwerfer launchers. A British officer on the
isolated position described the bombardment, which seemed to come

from all sides: "A howling and a wailing grew until it filled the sky, rising in pitch as it approached, and ending in a series of shattering explosions all around us. Then more squeals, the same horrible wail, and another batch of 36 bombs exploded astride us, so that the pressure came first from one side, then from the other, then from both at once."[15]

On 30 June the Germans took Hill 112 after several more bombardments. Hitlerjugend panzer commander Willi Kandler observed the successful push on the summit from the turret of his tank: "Early in the morning, rockets from our launchers, trailing veils of smoke, howled into the English positions in the small square wood. These launchers decided the success of the attack during the morning. This was our fourth attack on Hill 112, and it was crowned by the capture of the square wood and hill. As we drove up, we saw numerous destroyed vehicles, among them knocked out Sherman tanks."[16]

The British had already decided to withdraw from Hill 112 and adopt defensive positions along the whole line. Any expectation of an Allied breakthrough to Caen was abandoned, for which the Waffen-SS formations in Normandy could take the major credit. But, at the same time, the German offensive had also failed. Another German attack on 1 July also came to nothing and confirmed to Hausser that any further progress was impossible, with both I and II SS Panzer Corps forced to hold their ground. On a tactical level Operation Epsom/Third Battle of Caen was something a of a draw, but at an operational level the Germans had been forced to deploy their strategic reserves on the front line and were now at a decided disadvantage. They lacked fresh armored formations to throw into the battle. The Allies knew this and continued to grind down the German defenders.

The gloomy prognoses made by senior German generals for the future of the campaign became too much for Hitler, and on 3 July he replaced Rundstedt as commander in chief in the West with Field Marshal Hans von Kluge. Geyr von Schweppenburg, the Panzer Group West commander and Rundstedt supporter, gave way to General Heinrich Eberbach. The equally despondent Rommel was spared the cull, on the basis that public knowledge of his removal might lower morale.

IN EARLY JULY the British moved the focus of engagement back toward Caen and its Hitlerjugend defenders. On 4 July Canadian forces struck against the Carpiquet airfield, just west of the city. Vastly outnumbered and outgunned, the men of Bernhard Krause's I/26th Panzergrenadier Regiment held out with remarkable tenacity, but in the end they had to give way.

The British felt they had to further increase their material advantage for the assault on Caen itself, so on 7 July a fleet of RAF heavy bombers turned the northern outskirts of the city into rubble (contributing to a combined figure of 1,150 civilian deaths in Caen).[17] Meyer's troops largely avoided the bombs, however, and when the British and Canadians advanced, they were met by well-organized German resistance amid the ruins of the city. But the weight of the Allied assault eventually pressed the German troops back toward the city center and withdrawal across the Orne, so that on 10 July Meyer held a broken line in Caen's southern suburbs.

From Meyer's own highly wrought account of the battle for Caen, it seemed that his division had almost been wiped out. In light of the intense and sustained fighting conducted by the Hitlerjugend, casualties were heavy but not excessive—approximately 5,000 up to 14 July—an indication of the good tactical discipline inculcated in the troops to dig in under fire.[18] But Meyer was right in his claim that his soldiers were worn out and must be relieved. Dietrich agreed with his subordinate, and between 9 and 12 June Leibstandarte took over most of the line held by the Hitlerjugend. Leibstandarte panzergrenadier Werner Josupiet and his comrades recalled helping troops from their sister division: "In a cave up on the slope we installed seven men from the Division HJ. They were suffering from total exhaustion. The rumor was that they were the only survivors from an entire battalion. I will never forget how they looked. Their cheeks were hollow, their faces gray, their uniforms caked with lime."[19]

During this brief interlude Meyer reorganized the Hitlerjugend Division, dividing it into three flexible Kampfgruppen, each named after their commanders: Hans Waldmüller, Bernhard Krause, and Erich Olboeter. A further (armored) Hitlerjugend battle group, led by Max Wünsche, was still engaged in supporting II SS Panzer Corps to the west of Caen.

Since the start of the invasion, Rommel had repeatedly visited his subordinate commanders to gauge the military situation firsthand. During his meetings with Dietrich, it was rumored that he was considering an attempt to make a separate peace with the Western Allies. On 17 July he visited the I SS Panzer Corps headquarters to further sound out the Waffen-SS response to any such a proposal. Kurt Meyer also attended the meeting, and he recalled Rommel declaiming, "Something has to happen! The war in the West has to be ended!"[20] It would seem that Dietrich was in broad agreement: shaking Rommel's hand, he said, "You're the boss, Herr Feldmarschall. I obey only you—whatever you're planning."[21]

Any possible further developments were brought to a sudden halt on that afternoon, when, after leaving the meeting, Rommel's car was shot up by a British Typhoon. Although Rommel survived the attack, his severe wounds forced him into a long convalescence in Germany. Three days later the failed assassination attempt on Hitler took place. Rommel was implicated in the plot, and rather than face a public trial and punishment of his family and staff, he accepted Hitler's offer to commit suicide. The brutal Gestapo clampdown that followed the 20 July bomb plot stopped any further rumblings of discontent. Dietrich escaped any investigation, and while he was disillusioned with Hitler, it seems unlikely that he could ever have brought himself to actively oppose him.

Despite the failure of the SS to protect Hitler against the assassination attempt, Himmler was a major beneficiary of the plot, given increased powers that included command of the Reserve or Replacement Army. As well as filling top posts in the Replacement Army with his own men, Himmler also used this vast reservoir of manpower—up to 2 million strong—to funnel recruits away from the Wehrmacht and into the Waffen-SS.

———————

THE BRITISH CONTINUED to apply pressure on the German line and on 18 July launched Goodwood, the operation British commander General Montgomery hoped would finally crack the German defenses and provide him with a breakthrough into open country. But Montgomery once again underestimated the amazing tenacity of the German defenders, especially those of the Waffen-SS. Despite massive preliminary aerial and artillery bombardments, the offensive soon bogged down, in part through British ineptitude and overcaution but also from the fire of the tanks and guns of Leibstandarte holding the Bourguebus ridge, just south of Caen. Farther to the west, the 10th SS Panzer Division Frundsberg had valiantly held Hill 112 until the British advance through Caen rendered its defense untenable.

Although senior Allied commanders were disappointed at the slow progress made by the British and Canadian forces in the struggle for Caen, the battle did at least absorb the bulk of Germany's panzer divisions. To the west, the U.S. Army faced lesser opposition. The German Army formations deployed there were of mixed quality, while the elite Luftwaffe paratroop units lacked the heavy support weapons of the panzer divisions. The Waffen-SS contribution comprised just the 17th SS Panzergrenadier Division Götz von Berlichingen—of only average quality—and the elite 2nd SS Panzer Division Das Reich.

In Normandy Das Reich was broken up into several Kampfgruppen, fighting alongside 17th SS Panzergrenadier Division and units from the Wehrmacht. From 10 July the SS units adopted an extended defensive position around Périers, which they held for fifteen days. Under the command of Obersturmbannführer Christian Tychsen, the well-dug-in tanks of Das Reich's panzer regiment took a heavy toll of U.S. armor. Panther tank commander Ernst Barkmann, the best known of the division's panzer aces, won the Knight's Cross for his intrepid actions against American tanks and antitank guns.

Unknown to the SS troops, however, Périers was a quiet sector; the main weight of the American breakout from the Normandy beachhead was to be made a little to the east, around St.-Lô. On 25 July General Bradley's First Army unleashed Operation Cobra. Under mass aerial and ground bombardment, the overstretched German line wavered and then broke. There were no German reserves to plug the gap, enabling the Americans to drive forward at speed and reach Avranches on 31 July.

This was the key action in the Normandy campaign, allowing General Patton's newly constituted Third Army to exploit the breakthrough. For the first time in the campaign, the Allies began to capture significant numbers of prisoners: 20,000 Germans were taken during the first six days of Cobra, with sixty-six tanks destroyed and fifty-six more abandoned in the retreat.[22] The British supported their American ally by launching their own offensive—Operation Bluecoat—which locked in place several German formations, including the two divisions of Bittrich's II SS Panzer Corps.

The American breakthrough at St.-Lô forced Das Reich and 17th SS Panzergrenadier Division to immediately retreat to avoid encirclement. The advance by the U.S. VIII Corps briefly produced panic among some units of 17th SS Panzergrenadier Division, who broke and ran to the rear.[23] Within Das Reich, the confusion of the retreat had been exacerbated by the loss of Lammerding, severely wounded on 24 July, and his temporary replacement by Tychsen. As an officer renowned for his reckless bravery, Tychsen did not last long, killed while driving in his Kübelwagen on 28 July. Command of the division then passed to Otto Baum, transferred from control of 17th SS Panzergrenadier Division—only days after taking up the post to replace the wounded Ostendorff!

As the two SS divisions fell back, individual Kampfgruppen were surrounded by U.S. forces on a number of occasions, but using their battlefield experience they managed to avoid capture and take up a new defensive line on 5 August, just to the east of Mortain, recently captured by the U.S. Army. Both SS formations had suffered heavily, especially the 17th SS Panzergrenadier Division, which was formally downgraded as a Kampfgruppe.

The gap forged by the U.S. Army around Avranches allowed Patton's mobile forces to drive westward into Brittany and, more significantly, advance eastward into the heart of France and threaten the entire German position in Normandy. The German commanders in the West, including Dietrich, pleaded for a strategic withdrawal in Normandy to at least east of the Seine and, if necessary, back toward the Westwall on the Franco-German border.

Hitler—ever the armchair strategist—looked at his maps and saw the potential vulnerability of the Avranches corridor. On 2 August he had ordered Kluge to redeploy his panzer divisions for a counterattack against

Mortain, followed by an advance to the coast at Avranches to cut off the American breakthrough at its root. Hitler seemed blithely unaware that his worn-down panzer formations were divisions in name only and that a transfer from Caen westward toward Mortain was exposing them to the real possibility of encirclement by the Allies. Despite his generals' protests, Hitler was adamant that his plan be carried out, and Kluge instructed Hausser to immediately prepare his Seventh Army for the offensive.

Chapter 27

COLLAPSE AND RECOVERY

T HE NEWLY PROMOTED Oberstgruppenführer Paul Hausser pulled together the separate elements of his Seventh Army to carry out the offensive demanded by Hitler, made more palatable with the promise of eight panzer divisions and 1,000 aircraft. The problem with this assurance was the unavoidable truth that most of the panzer formations were now fully committed to battle, with disengagement virtually impossible. As for aerial support, the Luftwaffe managed to cobble together a force of 300 fighter aircraft based at airfields around Paris. On the morning of the offensive, however, the fighters were destroyed or driven off by the Allied air forces. Not a single German aircraft appeared over the battlefield.

Against the initial German objective of Mortain, Hausser could draw upon the army's 2nd and 116th Panzer Divisions, plus the 2nd SS Panzer Division Das Reich and the 17th SS Panzergrenadier Kampfgruppe. Of the other panzer divisions, deployed against the British, only Leibstandarte could be spared to support the offensive, and its constituent units were dispatched in a piecemeal fashion, some arriving so late that they took no part in the fighting.

Hausser's plan called for the main attack to be made to the north of Mortain by the two army panzer divisions, their breakthrough to be exploited by Leibstandarte as it arrived. The assault on Mortain was as-signed to Das Reich and the 17th SS Panzergrenadier Kampfgruppe. A battle group based on the "Der Führer" Regiment would attack to the north of the town, while a second, more powerful battle group based on

"Deutschland" (with the panzer regiment and reconnaissance battalion) would attack from the south. The 17th SS Kampfgruppe was deployed between the two Das Reich regiments and would assault Hill 314. Situated just in front of Mortain, Hill 314 was defended by a battalion of infantry from the U.S. 30th Infantry Division.

Hitler had wanted a steady buildup of forces in front of Mortain, but Kluge, increasingly fearful of Patton's drive around his southern flank, argued that the assault must open on the night of 6–7 August, a request Hitler reluctantly accepted. It was hoped that a night attack would enable the Germans to break into the American lines before daylight and the arrival of Allied fighter-bombers.

The offensive immediately got off to a poor start. Sudden and bitter arguments between the senior officers of the army panzer formations were an unwelcome development for Hausser, as was the absence of an assignment of tanks for the 2nd Panzer Division. The progress of Leibstandarte units—especially the panzer regiment—seemed to lack urgency. Fritz Kraemer, the I SS Panzer Corps chief of staff, put this down to the absence of their commander, Jochen Peiper, sent back to Germany for health reasons (due either to heart problems or to the aftereffects of air-bombardment concussion).[1] General Eberbach, commander of the recently formed Fifth Panzer Army in Normandy, was normally an enthusiastic supporter of the Waffen-SS, but on hearing of Leibstandarte's progress, he remarked that the division "was worse than ever before."[2]

During the early hours of 7 August, Das Reich's "Der Führer" Regiment—led by the APCs of III Battalion—drove toward American lines to the north of Mortain, but almost immediately found its route blocked by armored vehicles from Leibstandarte that were beginning to arrive on the battlefield. As Leibstandarte had priority, "Der Führer" lost vital time and began to close on the enemy defenses only after dawn had broken. The troops of the U.S. 30th Infantry Division had been forewarned of the German attack and put up sufficiently stout resistance that the SS advance ground to a halt around L'Abbaye Blanche, only a few miles beyond the start line.

The early-morning mist provided the attackers with some cover from the air, but by midday it had cleared, giving the U.S. Air Force and

RAF free rein over the battlefield. The APCs and the assault guns that had spearheaded the advance by "Der Führer" came under intense fire. Columns of black smoke from knocked-out vehicles along the road to L'Abbaye Blanche marked the collapse of the attack, the SS troops forced to dig in to hold what little ground they had gained.

To the south of Mortain, "Deutschland" dispensed with any preliminary bombardment and at 2:30 A.M. launched a silent attack using just infantry without the noise of any motorized vehicles to alert the defenders. The Americans were caught unawares, and the SS units made good progress, capturing Mortain. Supported by the reconnaissance battalion, "Deutschland" gained the high ground to the west of the town by midmorning. But by then the U.S. 30th Infantry Division had recovered and prevented any further German advance, the halt confirmed by the arrival of Allied aircraft over the battlefield.

The German capture of Mortain had isolated the American defenders of Hill 314, but they repeatedly fended off the attacks made on their position by the 17th SS Kampfgruppe. To the north, the advance of the two army panzer divisions and parts of Leibstandarte had also been halted, so by the end of the day the entire German operation had been brought to a standstill.

Despite the obvious failure at Mortain, Hitler was determined to maintain the offensive, blaming his generals for a too hasty and inadequately prepared attack. He then ordered a further buildup of forces with the 10th SS Panzer Division withdrawn from its positions around Vire to support a further attack to the south of Mortain. By the time it had arrived at its new position, the Germans were battling against increasingly powerful American forces and were only just holding on to their positions. On 11 August the threat posed by Patton's Third Army—now driving east toward Alençon—was finally accepted by Hitler. In the evening he gave orders for a (temporary) withdrawal of the divisions around Mortain to check the American advance. The whole offensive had proved a costly failure for the Germans, who now faced the real threat of both Seventh Army and Fifth Panzer Army being trapped within what would be known as the Falaise pocket.

WHILE THE GERMANS were battering themselves against the American positions around Mortain, Dietrich and Kraemer at I SS Panzer Corps headquarters were attempting to fashion a new defensive line with army units that had replaced Leibstandarte. They were heartened by the arrival of desperately needed armored reinforcement on 7 August: seventy-two tanks with adequate supplies of fuel. But as soon as the vehicles arrived in the SS panzer corps sector, Kraemer was firmly instructed by Kluge that they were to be sent westward to support the Mortain offensive. A downcast Kraemer lamented: "The effect of this order was similar to a cold shower bath. It was evident even to a child that it would be two or three days before the tanks could arrive and that many of these would be incapacitated, even without considering enemy air attacks. It was certain the tanks would arrive there too late, whereas north of Falaise they could prevent an enemy breakthrough—a danger with which corps had reckoned from the very start."[3]

The growing shortage of armored vehicles was one of I SS Panzer Corps' most pressing problems; the loss of tanks, assault guns, and artillery pieces was undermining its combat effectiveness. On the plus side, the Germans had an excellent record of recovering and repairing broken-down or damaged vehicles, and the SS workshops hidden in the Forest of Cinglais worked without respite to turn around otherwise unserviceable vehicles in a matter or three or four days. Dietrich was so impressed by their endeavors that he took time to visit the workshops and award Iron Crosses to the mechanics.[4]

On 8 August Montgomery launched Operation Totalize, a drive due south from Caen to capture Falaise. He had assembled a powerful combination of British, Canadian, and newly arrived Polish troops, supported by two waves of heavy-bomber aircraft. The Allied advance made some early gains, especially against the second-grade German Army formations. At one point Kurt Meyer had to personally rally a group of fleeing soldiers from an infantry unit. But as had happened so often before, there was confusion on the Allied side between the separate arms and a general failure to press any advantage. The situation was made worse in the afternoon when a second bomber wave accidentally attacked Canadian and Polish forward troops. This gave Meyer and his stretched Hitlerjugend an opportunity to mount a successful counterattack that halted the Allies.

During the German counterattack, Meyer was joined by Wünsche's armored Kampfgruppe and the Tiger tanks of the 101st Heavy Battalion. Wittmann led five of his Tigers across open ground at full speed toward the Allied positions. It was then that the panzer ace's luck ran out, his patrol ambushed from the flank by a squadron of Shermans of the Northamptonshire Yeomanry. One of the British tanks was a Firefly variant whose high-velocity 17-pounder main gun was capable of cutting through the Tiger's armor. In a short, fierce engagement, the concealed Shermans destroyed three Tigers, including Wittmann's, with the other two German tanks destroyed shortly afterward.[5] After Wittmann's tank was hit, the ammunition and fuel exploded with sufficient force to blast the turret several yards away from the burning hull. Thus ended the meteoric career of Michael Wittmann, the talisman of the Waffen-SS panzer arm who was credited with destroying 138 tanks and 132 antitank guns.

The Allies continued the offensive on the following day but again failed to make headway, the Germans now able to draw upon the recent arrival of the Luftwaffe's massed 8.8cm Flak batteries to good effect. On 10 August the offensive petered out, but this was only a temporary pause before a continuation on the fourteenth (Operation Tractable). The combined British-Canadian-Polish force drove the Germans back into Falaise, the scene of a fierce battle that saw the town reduced to rubble. The grenadiers of the Hitlerjugend Division held what was left of Falaise with their customary zeal, the sacrificial defense of the École Supérior earning the praise of their Canadian opponents.

By 17 August Falaise was finally in Allied hands, but the Hitlerjugend continued its resistance along new positions to the south, its fighting spirit seemingly undiminished. During a counterattack by the division's armored antitank battalion on 18 August, the unit's wounded commander, Sturmbannführer Jacob Hanreich, was captured. A British officer described his new prisoner: "His extreme arrogance and offensive attitude almost led to his sudden death a few times. However, he was duly transported to a prison camp without suffering further damage."[6]

The fight put up by the Hitlerjugend Division and the two SS Tiger tank battalions, along with 21st Panzer Division, was vital in allowing the formations originally committed to the Mortain counteroffensive to withdraw from the trap being sprung by the Allies. On 15 August, U.S.

troops began to close on Argentan, leaving only a few miles between them and the British pushing southward from Falaise.

Hausser and Eberbach—only too aware of the gravity of the situation—dispatched mobile units to hold open the gap between Falaise and Argentan. Among these was a rejigged II SS Panzer Corps, now comprising 9th SS Panzer Division Hohenstaufen and 2nd SS Panzer Division Das Reich (with the remains of the 17th SS Panzergrenadier Kampfgruppe). The two divisions disengaged from the front on 12 August and through a series of night marches passed to the far side of the Falaise gap by the sixteenth, ready to assist the slower-moving formations in making their escape. The 10th SS Panzer Division Frundsberg and 1st SS Panzer Division Leibstandarte separately made their withdrawals along the southern flank of the pocket, Leibstandarte engaging with the Americans in a series of inconclusive skirmishes.

On 17 August Kluge was sacked by Hitler and recalled to Berlin; in the Führer's paranoid mind was the possibility that the German field marshal was privately negotiating with the Allies. Kluge, innocent of any collusion with the enemy, had, however, been slightly involved with the resistance movement against Hitler, and, fearful of what might come next, he committed suicide while flying back to Germany. He was succeeded by Field Marshal Walter Model, who had become a Hitler favorite for his resolute refusal to give ground to the enemy. Model, however, was quick to see the hopelessness of the situation, and he confirmed Kluge's original order for a general retreat. Guiding Model's decision was knowledge of the successful Allied invasion of southern France on 15 August, which made the adoption of any future defensive line within France all but impossible.

The Hitlerjugend continued its fighting withdrawal in the face of a combined Canadian-Polish advance. On this occasion, the Canadians failed to pursue the Germans with any real vigor. The Poles showed more spirit and on 18–19 August captured the tactically important Hill 262 that overlooked the German evacuation route. Attempts by the Germans—including the Hohenstaufen Division—to retake the hill were repulsed, although the Poles suffered heavy casualties in its defense. On the evening of 19 August units of U.S. and Free French troops met their Polish counterparts, but the encirclement was far from secure; determined attacks could still break through the Allied ring.

As the Falaise pocket was squeezed on all sides, the German escape routes became increasingly congested, easy prey for the Allied fighter-bombers that attacked without mercy. They were joined by batteries of artillery, who barely needed to aim to hit a target. In the face of this unrelenting bombardment, order began to break down among some infantry units, leaving the men of the panzer and paratroop divisions to set an example. Retreating SS soldiers were disgusted to see growing numbers of soldiers throwing away their weapons and sitting down to await capture.

Frundsberg and Leibstandarte fought their way through the Allied screen, although in the process Leibstandarte's commander, Theodor Wisch, was badly wounded and captured by the Allies on 20 August. Another casualty was the Seventh Army commander, Paul Hausser. While marching with his troops, he was hit in the head by shell splinters; after some basic first aid, he was successfully driven out of the pocket to a field hospital. Senior Waffen-SS officers did their best to rally all troops around them, although Meyer refused to have anything to do with any soldier without his rifle. Meyer and a mixed group of soldiers slipped out of the pocket on the twentieth, but his old comrade Max Wünsche was less fortunate: wounded in the leg, he hid to avoid capture but was apprehended by an Allied patrol on 24 August.

In the early hours of the twentieth, II SS Panzer Corps was ordered to open a gap in the Allied encircling ring. Due to fuel shortages, Hohenstaufen's attack failed, but the two regimental Kampfgruppen of Das Reich (subsequently joined by Hohenstaufen's reconnaissance battalion) were more effective. The two understrength battalions of "Der Führer"—each with six tanks in support—broke through the Allied line. During the assault, Hauptsturmführer Werner, leading III Battalion, observed a group of Sherman tanks from the Polish 1st Armored Division broadside on and firing into the pocket, oblivious to the arrival of the SS APCs. Werner brought up a nearby Panther tank, which then knocked out at least five of the Shermans to open an escape route for the streams of Germans still marching eastward.[7]

The "Deutschland" Kampfgruppe also managed to pierce the Allied defenses to allow more Germans to break out of the Allied trap. By the afternoon of 21 August, only a few stragglers were emerging from the pocket, allowing the soldiers of Das Reich to withdraw and join the general German retreat toward the River Seine.

The battle for Normandy—once longed for by Hitler as a chance to destroy the Allied armies on European soil—had turned out to be a disaster for the Wehrmacht. Not only had the Western Allies gained a foothold on continental Europe, but they were in the processing of liberating all of France as well.

German casualties in Normandy were heavy—approximately 240,000 men killed and wounded and 200,000 taken prisoner—but in the confusion of the escape from Falaise, they appeared even higher. A report sent to Army Group B on 22 August listing panzer-division casualties gave the impression of especially grievous Waffen-SS losses, with, for example, Hitlerjugend down to 300 men.[8] This was not the case, however. According to the meticulous records kept by the Hitlerjugend's chief operational officer, the division suffered around 8,000 casualties from the start of the invasion to 22 August, leaving in place a force (albeit scattered) of around 12,500 men.[9] Leibstandarte, according to its divisional history, sustained around 5,000 casualties in Normandy.[10] Casualties figures for the Hohenstaufen and Frundsberg Divisions were not tabulated, but in the immediate aftermath of the Falaise battle they could each muster around 6,000 soldiers.[11]

The SS divisions' greatest losses came in armored fighting vehicles and artillery, most lost in the Falaise pocket. As an example, the Hohenstaufen and Frundsberg Divisions came out of the pocket with no tanks at all, each reliant on the half dozen or so panzers undergoing repair in workshops outside the pocket.

As the Germans retreated eastward, the River Seine became a difficult obstacle, with so many of its bridges already destroyed by Allied aircraft. But a series of rearguard battles successfully held up the Allied pursuit, while combat engineers repaired damaged bridges and operated ad hoc ferries to get the German ground forces over the river. The Waffen-SS formations passed over the Seine around Rouen. Many of the few vehicles they still possessed were abandoned in the crossings that went on until the end of August.

The Waffen-SS continued its withdrawal through northern France and Belgium, fighting occasional skirmishes to keep the Allies at bay. The 9th and 10th SS Panzer Divisions of II SS Panzer Corps were directed into the Netherlands to reform and refit, arriving at bases around Arnhem on 7 September. The other divisions retired through Belgium to safety behind the Westwall in Germany.

During their retreat the Germans were repeatedly ambushed by groups from the French and, especially, the Belgian Resistance. The Hitlerjugend Kampfgruppe led by Erich Olboeter was attacked on 1 September. Olboeter had both legs blown off by a mine and died shortly afterward. The leader of Kampfgruppe Waldmüller, Hans Waldmüller, was killed a short while later. Kurt Meyer was captured by the Belgian Resistance on 7 September and after narrowly escaping execution was handed over to the British. It was an ignominious end to the career of one of the legendary figures of the Waffen-SS; he would subsequently be charged by the Canadians for war crimes committed in Normandy.

The Waffen-SS panzer divisions that fought in the Normandy campaign experienced mixed fortunes. They had been designed for aggressive offensive action, but success in this role had been denied them by superior Allied firepower. This did not stop them from trying, and they suffered heavy casualties for little gain. Forced onto the defensive, the Waffen-SS qualities of tenacity against all odds came to the fore. Time and again they repulsed Allied attacks, despite being outnumbered and outgunned on most occasions. They were unable to prevent the Allied advance from the beachheads in Normandy, but they certainly impeded its progress, and, later in the campaign, helped thousands of German soldiers escape from the Falaise pocket. The ferocity of the fighting in Normandy was at times comparable to that of the Eastern Front. Of the six SS divisional commanders who entered the battle, five were either killed or incapacitated by their wounds; only Heinz Harmel of the Frundsberg Division escaped unscathed.

By EARLY SEPTEMBER 1944 the Allied offensive had lost momentum, as lengthening supply lines from Normandy produced logistical shortages for the matériel-hungry Allied armies. Meanwhile, the Wehrmacht had largely recovered from its disasters in the West, establishing a new defensive position on the Westwall along the German border. The Allied drive came to a standstill, despite repeated and costly American efforts to break through in the Hürtgen Forest.

As a means of resolving the impasse, Montgomery proposed an imaginative but risk-laden plan to outflank the German defenses with a mass airborne assault into the Netherlands. The airborne troops were to seize the many river crossings in the area, culminating in the capture of the strategically important bridge over the Rhine at Arnhem. At the same time, a ground offensive would be launched on a narrow front to drive northward into the Netherlands and link up with the airborne units.

The U.S. 101st Airborne Division would occupy the area around Eindhoven, while, deeper into the Netherlands, the U.S. 82nd Airborne Division would secure Nijmegen and the bridge over the River Waal. Farthest north, the British 1st Airborne Division would land to the west of Arnhem and then secure the Rhine bridge. The British would be reinforced shortly afterward by the Polish 1st Independent Parachute Brigade. Once in place, the airborne forces would await the arrival of the British XXX Corps. Montgomery's plan was eventually accepted by Eisenhower, the launch of Operation Market Garden set for 17 September.

The Netherlands had become a vast assembly area for German troops ejected from France and Belgium. They included units from the army, Waffen-SS, paratroops, regular Luftwaffe, and even the German Navy. As well as the two reforming divisions of Bittrich's II SS Panzer Corps, there were other Waffen-SS units based around Arnhem: Hauptsturmführer Krafft's Depot and Reserve Battalion, troops from an SS NCO training school under Standartenführer Lippert, and a third-rate "Watch" battalion primarily made up of Dutch National Socialists.

Based just to the north of Arnhem, 9th SS Panzer Division Hohenstaufen and 10th SS Panzer Division Frundsberg were still very much understrength. Each division could field a maximum of 6,000–7,000 men, and while there had been an arrival of light vehicles, there were few tanks,

assault guns, and artillery.[12] On 10 September, OKW ordered Hohenstaufen to return to Germany for refitting, with Frundsberg to remain
in the Netherlands. Hohenstaufen was also instructed to hand over its
heavy weapons and equipment to Frundsberg, although this order was
only partially carried out.

The Allied landings on 17 September went with hardly a hitch, all
three divisions landing the vast majority of their soldiers within the designated zones. The Germans were taken unawares as the armada of nearly
1,500 C-47 transport aircraft and more than 3,000 towed gliders (plus es-
corts) flew over their heads. Field Marshal Model—commander of Army
Group B—was at lunch at the Hotel Tafelberg in Arnhem when the
Allies struck, fighter-bombers shooting up the hotel. Model left immediately to rendezvous with Bittrich at II SS Panzer Corps headquarters.

Despite the surprise of the Allied airborne landings, the German response was swift and efficient at all levels. Krafft's battalion was taking
part in a training exercise close to the British drop zone and promptly
engaged the gliders as they landed. Krafft correctly surmised that Arnhem was the British target and blocked one of the main routes into the
town. By the evening, a larger mixed SS and army force under Sturmbannführer Spindler, Hohenstaufen's artillery commander, had arrived
to reinforce Krafft. Despite these measures, they were unable to stop
Lieutenant-Colonel John Frost's 2nd Parachute Battalion from slipping
through the German screen and securing the north side of the road bridge
over the Rhine.

At II SS Panzer Corps headquarters, Model and Bittrich prepared
their countermeasures. In the first instance it was decided that the Hohenstaufen Division—under Obersturmbannführer Walter Harzer, who
had replaced the wounded Stadler—would be responsible for containing
the British, while Harmel's Frundsberg Division was ordered to cross
the Rhine and advance south to deal with the American threat at Nijmegen. Unfortunately for Harmel, Frost's seizure of the Arnhem bridge
prevented his SS soldiers, most of whom were on the north side of the
river, from crossing over the bridge toward Nijmegen. Harmel was consequently forced to use a nearby ferry, which only slowly fed his troops
into the battle.

Just before Frost's arrival at the bridge, Hohenstaufen's reconnaissance battalion had crossed it on its way toward Nijmegen. On the following day the Germans attempted to return over the bridge, now defended by British paratroopers. The SS battalion was led by Viktor Graebner, a typically thrusting reconnaissance commander who had just been awarded the Knight's Cross. Aware of the British presence, he decided to force the position. In a cavalry charge of armored personnel carriers and armored cars, the SS troops roared over the bridge, only to be met by a hail of fire that stopped them in their tracks, with Graebner killed in the attempt.

On 18 September a second wave of British airborne troops successfully landed in the British drop zone, and on the following day a concerted effort was made to link up with Frost's battalion. The Germans were also being steadily reinforced, and Spindler's blocking troops repulsed all British attempts to reach the bridge.

Bittrich simultaneously pressed his forces to eliminate the British position at Arnhem. Artillery, tanks, and assault guns provided fire support, before the panzergrenadiers were sent in to wrest control of what remained. SS soldier Alfred Ringsdorf recalled the intensity of the action: "This was a harder battle than any I had fought in Russia. It was constant, close-range, hand-to-hand fighting. The English were everywhere. The streets for the most part were narrow, sometimes not more than 15 feet wide, and we fired on each other from only yards away. We fought to gain inches, cleaning out one room after the other. It was absolute hell!"[13]

By 20 September the situation of the 2nd Parachute Battalion was critical: the Germans were literally blasting their defenses to pieces, while ammunition, food, and water were running out and casualties rising. During the afternoon the Germans allowed British wounded to be evacuated; in the evening the SS troops closed in, and by the early hours of the twenty-first all resistance had ceased. Once the bridge was back in German hands, reinforcements could swiftly cross the Rhine to support the defenders of the bridge over the River Waal, just north of Nijmegen. The tide of battle was now turning in the Germans' favor, with reinforcements reaching the front in growing numbers. And for once the Allies did not enjoy air supremacy, enabling German ground forces to move in daylight with relative impunity.

To the south of Nijmegen the U.S. 82nd Airborne Division had been drawn into the battle to secure the nearby Groesbeek Heights, unable to make progress in capturing the key Waal bridge until 19 September, following the arrival of armored units from the British XXX Corps. Kampfgruppe Euling—a battalion-strength unit under Hauptsturmführer Euling—maintained a resolute defense of the southern side of the bridge.

On the twentieth an intrepid group of U.S. paratroopers launched their own amphibious assault over the Waal using recently arrived collapsible boats. Despite coming under intense fire and suffering heavy casualties, the Americans managed to establish a bridgehead on the north bank of the river. At the same time, the tanks of XXX Corps beat back the German defenders and crossed the still intact road crossing. Harmel had been forbidden by Model from blowing the bridge, the German field marshal insisting that it be kept open for a possible counterattack. Once over the river, the British failed to exploit their advantage, tamely waiting for further reinforcement.

Meanwhile, the Germans north of the Rhine began to put the squeeze on the British paratroopers, now reduced to a pocket based around Oosterbeek. Lippert's NCO training unit joined army forces under General Tettau, pushing in the British perimeter from the west, while the Hohenstaufen attacked from the north and east. To the south, the British just about managed to keep open their access to the Rhine. The paratroopers inflicted heavy casualties on the Germans, forcing them to moderate the scale of their repeated infantry attacks. But with time on their side, the Germans could rely on their superior firepower to grind down the enemy.

Despite the ferocity of the fighting, the Arnhem battle became known for the chivalry displayed by both sides, allowing the evacuation of the wounded to receive medical attention in relative safety. Rottenführer Wolfgang Dombrowski described his surprise at the development: "What were we to do with our wounded? A red cross flag was produced and casualties approached, step by step. To our astonishment fire ceased immediately. Stretcher bearers picked up the wounded, moved off, and the shooting started again. We couldn't understand this as we were used to conditions on the Eastern Front. These paras were supposed to be hard men—we knew they were!—and yet we were allowed to pick up the wounded. The other side was then given the opportunity to do the same."[14]

On 21 September the 1st Independent Polish Brigade was dropped on a landing zone just south of the Rhine, suffering heavy losses from the now well-prepared Germans. Due to bad weather, the drop had been made two days late, and these otherwise valuable reinforcements could do little to change the outcome. On the following day, ground troops from XXX Corps linked up with the Poles, although attempts to reach the British paratroopers on the Rhine's north bank were largely thwarted.

On 24 September, as the perimeter around Oosterbeek began to shrink farther, the British admitted defeat and made the decision to withdraw across the Rhine. During the night of 25–26 September, the British managed to evacuate most of their troops, leaving just 300 men to be captured as dawn broke. The Anglo-Polish forces fell back to Nijmegen, a position they held over the winter of 1944–1945. The Allied hope of breaking into Germany's industrial heartland of the Ruhr via the Netherlands had been dashed.

Alongside indifferent Allied planning, the prime reason for the Germans' success lay in their ability to mobilize forces of all kinds at a moment's notice and throw them straight into battle. And key to this mobilization was the presence of II SS Panzer Corps, whose commanders directed their troops and those of the Wehrmacht with great skill. By an unfortunate coincidence for the Allies, the Hohenstaufen and Frundsberg Divisions had undergone their training in France, with emphasis given to repelling a potential airborne invasion. That training was put to good use at Arnhem. The close of Market Garden marked the end of significant Allied offensive action in the West for the remainder of 1944.

Chapter 28

FINAL GAMBLE IN THE WEST

THE INABILITY OF the Western Allies to break through into Germany during the fall of 1944 gave Hitler a chance to reorganize and rebuild his battered armies. Rather than husbanding his resources to conduct a dynamic defense to slow Allied advances on both the Eastern and the Western Fronts, he gambled upon an offensive in the West. This would consist of an armored assault through the Ardennes region in southern Belgium, scene of his great triumph in 1940.

While Hitler was preparing his offensive, Himmler and his chief recruiting officer, Gottlob Berger, considered how best to use a surprise windfall of new recruits. The loss of France and Belgium to the Allies had the paradoxical effect of briefly increasing the numbers of men available for service in the Waffen-SS. Collaborators from these countries, fearful of retribution, fled with their families for safety in Germany. Even in the Netherlands, still predominantly under German control, 30,000 members of the Dutch Nazi Party and dependents crossed the border to escape the coming wrath of their fellow countrymen.[1] Once in Germany, the collaborationist refugees were totally dependent on the goodwill of their host, and those of military age were conducted toward the Waffen-SS, ostensibly to take part in the coming reconquest of the territories recently lost in the West.[2]

The French contribution to the Nazi war effort had comprised the army-organized Légion des Volontaires Français and the SS Frankreich Brigade.[3] The Allied liberation of France led to the flight of Vichy

359

paramilitary groups to Germany—including 2,500 men from the Milice—along with various individuals who decided to throw in their lot with the Nazis. Hitler's virulent anticommunism and anti-Semitism had appealed to many on the French Far Right, among them journalist Christien de la Mazière. As the Allies closed on Paris, the aristocratic, idealistic Mazière refused to change sides or go underground. He instead asked to join the new French SS formation being organized by Himmler, which would become the 33rd Waffen Grenadier Division of the SS Charlemagne.

In marked contrast to the experience of most SS recruits, Mazière drove his own car into Germany—complete with some sightseeing on the way—arriving at the training camp for the French at Wildflecken in October 1944. After swearing allegiance to Adolf Hitler, he was inducted into the Waffen-SS. Mazière described his feelings at that moment: "These men fascinated me and I wanted to be assimilated into their ranks. I saw them as a race apart. They struck me as strong, courageous, and ruthless beings, without weakness, who would never become corrupt."[4] Even at this late stage of the war, the Waffen-SS still had the power to attract individuals into its military brotherhood.

Mazière found that his new formation was divided between the old members of the LVF, who saw themselves as representatives of France, even if fighting for Germany, and survivors from the Frankreich Brigade, who had more fully adopted the outlook and attitudes of the Waffen-SS. The men of Joseph Darnand's Milice contingent had hoped to operate as a semi-independent unit, but to their disgruntlement they found themselves distributed throughout the formation.

Nominally commanded by Colonel Edgar Puard from the LVF, actual control of the Charlemagne Division was taken by Brigadeführer Gustav Krukenberg. A Francophile German officer, Krukenberg did his best to combine the disparate elements of the division into a cohesive whole, albeit with only partial success. By early 1945 it could muster around 8,000 men, organized in two infantry regiments with a battalion each of artillery and antitank guns, plus some support units. Darnand lobbied for the division to be deployed in the West, but in February it was ordered to the Eastern Front to prop up the wavering German defenses in Pomerania.

With Belgium under Allied control by mid-September, the still committed Flemish and Walloon collaborators decamped across the border to Germany. The veteran Flemish SS assault brigade was upgraded to become the 27th SS Volunteer Grenadier Division Langemarck on 12 September 1944. Under the leadership of Standartenführer Thomas Müller, it was based around the old assault brigade, the formation drawing its extra recruits from the refugees from Flanders of military age. Workers from German industry and those acting as auxiliaries in the Wehrmacht were also redirected into the formation, which according to Flemish sources reached a total of 15,000 men. In theory this was sufficient to form a full-strength division, but shortages of weapons and equipment and lack of sufficient training reduced its battleworthy element to 5,000–6,000 men, divided into two infantry battle groups with antitank and antiaircraft support.[5]

On 18 September Himmler redesignated the 1,800-strong SS Assault Brigade Wallonien as the 28th SS Volunteer Grenadier Division Wallonien. Sufficient recruits of acceptable quality proved hard to find, however, so that even with the induction of some Frenchmen and Spaniards, the total figure comprised little more than 4,000 soldiers, organized on similar lines to its fellow Belgian formation. Command had originally been given to German SS officers, but in January 1945 Léon Degrelle achieved his ambition of undisputed command of the Walloon troops, with the rank of Standartenführer. It had been planned that the two Belgian SS divisions would follow the German offensive in the Ardennes and take control of the reconquered parts of Belgium. The failure of the offensive brought this proposal to an abrupt halt, and both formations continued their training until dispatch to the Eastern Front in early 1945.

The last of these new Western European formations was the 34th Volunteer Grenadier Division Landstorm Nederland, based around Dutch SS paramilitary units formed in March 1943 for antiresistance actions and to maintain public order in the event of an Allied invasion (some of its units fought against the British at Arnhem). The division was activated on 10 February 1945 under the command of Oberführer Martin Kohlroser, a veteran Leibstandarte officer who had first achieved notoriety during the Night of the Long Knives in 1934. By combing Dutch right-wing organizations—and through the offer of decent rations during the "hunger winter" of 1944–1945—a force of some 8,000 men was assembled. Not much was expected of the division, however, and it remained in the Netherlands as a garrison force for the remainder of the war.

———————

HITLER'S PROPOSED 1944 offensive through the Ardennes was a modified rerun of the victorious assault that had defeated France in 1940. The 1944 plan differed from the original in that instead of a drive west to the English Channel, the Germans would turn due north to capture Brussels and the vital port of Antwerp, thereby dividing the U.S. and British armies (Hitler still held to the notion that a military success over the Western Allies would force them to the negotiating table, separate from the Soviet Union). On the American side of the line, the hilly, densely wooded Ardennes was considered a quiet sector: not only was it lightly manned, but the troops deployed there were either refitting after sustained periods of combat or greenhorn units acclimatizing themselves to frontline conditions.

Despite its chronic manpower problems, the Wehrmacht assembled a substantial force for the coming offensive. The German Fifteenth Army—the most northerly of the German formations—would remain on the defensive but if the opportunity arose was to launch a limited assault to support the main attack. Directly to the south was Sepp Dietrich's newly formed Sixth Panzer Army, which contained two Waffen-SS panzer corps and, on Hitler's express orders, was to be the main strike force in the drive on Antwerp. Supporting Dietrich were General Manteuffel's Fifth Panzer Army (spearheaded by three panzer divisions) and General Brandenberger's Seventh Army, the latter an all-infantry formation of just four divisions acting as the southern flank guard to the main assault.

Under the overall command of Field Marshal Model, the Germans assembled around 250,000 men with 1,900 guns and 900 armored fighting vehicles. Germany was also scoured for all available aircraft, personnel, and aviation fuel, enabling the Luftwaffe to gather 1,500 pilots and aircraft to support the offensive.[6] Yet, despite these efforts, the Allies could muster four times as many aircraft, with better-trained pilots and seemingly unlimited supplies of fuel and ammunition.

Within the Sixth Panzer Army, I SS Panzer Corps (now led by former Totenkopf commander Hermann Priess) comprised Leibstandarte and Hitlerjugend Divisions, while Wilhelm Bittrich's II SS Panzer Corps had been reordered to include the Hohenstaufen and Das Reich Divisions (Frundsberg was held back in army reserve). Following their battering on the invasion front, the SS panzer divisions had undergone yet another period of rapid rebuilding, Gottlob Berger's SS Main Office working tirelessly to find replacement manpower.

The Hitlerjugend Division continued to draw upon the Hitler Youth for recruits, but the new teenagers lacked the fervor of the original volunteers, while the more experienced soldiers were still recovering from their mauling in Normandy. Hans Postenberg, who joined in June 1944, explained the situation:

> After my training I was sent to the 12th SS Hitlerjugend, which had retreated back across France and was a mere shadow of its former self. Most of the lads had been killed or wounded in Normandy and those that survived were very shaken and in no further state for further combat without a good rest and of course further reinforcements. We were sent to a rest area where a lot more lads waited, but the Hitler Youth Division never got back its old strength again.[7]

Even if the there were doubts as to the quality of the four Waffen-SS and three army panzer divisions leading the attack, a far greater weakness lay with the infantry who would follow the armored formations. Apart from two paratroop divisions—now of only average quality—the German infantry component was supplied by the newly designated Volksgrenadier divisions. These were based around a cadre of experienced officers and NCOs but in the main consisted of overage or underage recruits, along with those previously considered medically unfit for military service. Unsurprisingly, they would prove incapable of conducting the aggressive offensive action necessary to link up with the panzer divisions.

As support for the opening stage of the offensive, a nighttime parachute drop behind Allied lines was prepared, as was the deployment of an undercover SS commando unit—Panzerbrigade 150—led by Otto Skorzeny. In Panzerbrigade 150, English-speaking German soldiers were selected from the SS and Wehrmacht, fitted out with American and British uniforms, and provided with captured Allied vehicles. Their role was to slip through the American defenses and cause confusion and disruption by misdirecting traffic, issuing false orders, and changing signposts, as well as capturing key bridges over the River Meuse, the first objective in the German offensive.

By mid-December the SS divisions had managed to secure levels of manpower that were only a little below establishment strength. The numbers of tanks allotted to the armored divisions was reasonable, although there was a shortage of other vehicles, so that, for example, a battalion in each of Das Reich's two panzergrenadier regiments relied on bicycles for transport. Ammunition was also limited, but the overriding factor that compromised the Germans' chance of success was an acute shortage of fuel. The armored units were issued with just a few days' supply at best and were instructed to secure gasoline and oil from captured American stocks.

Under Hitler's direct order, the offensive was to start only when bad weather was forecast, so that low cloud cover would minimize the effect of Anglo-American air superiority. But a meteorological forecast could be reliable for only a few days, and if the weather improved, then the German armored formations would be at the mercy of Allied fighter-bombers. To minimize this danger, German field commanders were ordered to advance with the utmost speed, so that Antwerp would be in German hands in a matter of days. A further intangible was the Wehrmacht's arrogant belief that the Americans facing the assault would break with ease.

As a result of the Wehrmacht's strict security measures and some reprehensible complacency within the Allied high command, the German attack on 16 December achieved total surprise.[8] The winter of 1944–1945 was especially severe: the Ardennes was snowbound, and during mid-December fog and low clouds kept Allied aircraft on their runways. And, as in 1940, the Allies did not expect an armored attack through the tank-unfriendly Ardennes.

But those advantages enjoyed by the Germans also worked against them. The difficult terrain forced armored vehicles to advance along the country roads that wound their way through the region; any obstacle brought German columns to an immediate standstill, with traffic jams stretching back for miles. Temperatures that were rising and dipping around freezing—occasionally far below—not only caused hardship for the troops but also led to vehicles being constantly stuck in snow and mud. And whereas in May 1940 the Mark IIIs and IVs of the German panzer divisions weighed no more than twenty-five tons, in 1944 the offensive was spearheaded by the seventy-five-ton King Tiger (Tiger II). A formidable tank developed for the Eastern Front, it was too large and too heavy for the narrow roads and weak bridges encountered in the Ardennes.

At the end of a short, sustained artillery bombardment, the infantry of Dietrich's Sixth Panzer Army were sent ahead to clear the way for the advance of the SS armor, Priess's I SS Panzer Corps taking the lead with Hitlerjugend on the right and Leibstandarte on the left. Bittrich's II Panzer Corps also moved forward, ready to exploit any success by the forward units.

The vastly outnumbered American front line was unable to hold the initial attack, and as the Germans emerged out of the early-morning mist, units were overrun or broke and ran. There was enormous confusion within the U.S. command, especially at higher levels, so that a coordinated response was slow in coming. But at key points, individual units of the U.S. Army held firm and blunted the German advance. Nowhere was this more important than on the Elsenborn ridge, where the Americans refused to give way in an attack launched by the Hitlerjugend and two Volksgrenadier divisions.

The Hitlerjugend made some initial gains, although casualties among officers were high. Obersturmbannführer Richard Schulze explained: "Since the men were largely without combat experience, only the deployment of the officers on the front lines could help. In the first hours all the company chiefs were lost, either killed or wounded. Oberscharführers [sergeants] took over the companies. The continuation of the attack, swinging further south, then led to success."[9] But this was only short-lived, as an accurate U.S. artillery bombardment forced the Germans to go to ground, with some panzergrenadiers, including Hans Postenberg, taking refuge in recently captured U.S. dugouts:

> The barrage lasted a long time, but then our NCOs took us out of the comfortable dugouts and we advanced again. The respite had allowed the Amis [Americans] to get more organized and although our tanks had

advanced we had lost contact with them, as a result some of them were
ambushed and lost. Others were stranded for lack of fuel, so all in all the
grand offensive was not going too well. The American artillery was very
active all this time and hindered us, but it was really the nature of the
country which caused us problems as the tanks were confined to one road
of advance, and this alone hindered us too as we were supposed to protect
them from infantry attack.[10]

The German failure to gain the Elsenborn ridge had a crucial knock-on
effect, squeezing the main advance by Sixth Panzer Army into increasingly confined terrain, with attendant traffic confusion.

Leibstandarte was divided into battle groups, spearheaded by Kampfgruppe Peiper. This was a mixed armor and mechanized-infantry force
of around 3,000 men and 100 Mark IV and V (Panther) tanks, plus the
King Tigers of the 501st SS Heavy Tank Battalion and part of Skorzeny's
Panzerbrigade 150.[11] As he led his troops forward, Peiper also briefly corralled a battalion of parachute infantry into his Kampfgruppe.

Peiper's hopes of a swift advance were immediately stymied by the
inability of the Volksgrenadier infantry ahead of him to break into the
enemy lines on the morning of 16 December. Most of the day was spent
held in traffic, and it was only on the seventeenth that Peiper managed
to fight his way through the U.S. frontline defenses. As Leibstandarte
troops drove forward, they discovered a U.S. fuel dump at Büllingen and
refueled their vehicles with 50,000 gallons of gasoline. They continued
their advance westward, urged on by an increasingly frantic Peiper, determined to achieve his goal of crossing the Meuse with minimal delay.

As they churned through mud and snow, Peiper's frustrated and increasingly angry troops shot groups of surrendered Americans, culminating in the killing of eighty-six prisoners at the Baugnez crossroads on
the seventeenth. Better known as the Malmédy Massacre, news of the
atrocity quickly reached the U.S. high command, producing a dramatic
hardening of attitudes within the American armed forces.[12] Waffen-SS
rage had also extended to Belgian civilians caught up in the drive, with
men, women, and children shot in revenge for the attacks on their own
troops by Belgian partisans during the withdrawal from Normandy in
September 1944.[13]

On 18 December Peiper's tanks reached Stavelot but were held there by the crack U.S. 30th Infantry Division (victors of the battle for Mortain in August). Further attempts to circumvent American positions at Stoumont and Trois Ponts also came to nothing, especially after the arrival of the U.S. 82nd Airborne Division. Peiper's Kampfgruppe had been the only Leibstandarte unit to make any headway through the Ardennes, and by 20 December it was cut off from the rest of division. Radio communication with Standartenführer Mohnke at divisional HQ was patchy at best; on the twenty-third, with fuel and ammunition running out, Peiper was ordered to break out and return to German lines.

By now the Kampfgruppe was reduced to around 770 effectives, plus the badly wounded and a number of U.S. prisoners, whom Peiper treated with the greatest care. Abandoning their vehicles and heavy weapons (plus the badly wounded and prisoners), Peiper led his remaining troops on foot through enemy lines to successfully reach Leibstandarte positions around Stavelot on the morning of 25 December. Peiper's action was indicative of his fighting spirit, but it also signaled the end of I SS Panzer Corps' hopes of achieving a breakthrough. Further German setbacks included the disastrous failure of the Luftwaffe paratroop drop and the inability of Skorzeny's unit to cause any meaningful confusion behind enemy lines.

The II SS Panzer Corps—Hohenstaufen (to the right) and Das Reich (to the left)—had slowly moved forward to the south of I SS Panzer Corps. The southward squeeze on the Hitlerjugend and Leibstandarte impacted on II SS Panzer Corps, forcing it into Fifth Panzer Army's routes of advance, with the usual traffic confusion and shortened tempers among the opposing staff officers.

A tactical breakthrough by Das Reich on 20 December was brought to an immediate halt by lack of fuel on the following day. Apart from the overall fuel shortage, poor roads also prevented the movement of fuel tankers to forward units when most needed. Despite this, the divisions of II SS Panzer Corps made reasonable progress, pushing slightly farther ahead than their comrades in I SS Panzer Corps. But once again, difficult terrain slowed the advance, as confirmed in the history of II SS Panzer Corps: "The serpentine lines of vehicles jammed up behind any delays in the valleys. Thus it came about that almost always it was only

the spearheads of the divisions that were in contact with the enemy."[14]
In these tactical situations, American resistance could hold off superior
numbers, as occurred at the U.S. strongpoints of St. Vith and Bastogne.

On 23 December Das Reich captured the crossroads at Baraque de
Fraiture, knocking out fifteen U.S. tanks in the process. Exploiting this
success, the SS pressed on to the line stretching between Vaux Chavanne–
Freineux. But there the German advance was halted by the arrival of
U.S. reinforcements; throughout the Christmas period (24–26 December) Hohenstaufen and Das Reich fought vainly to break through the
enemy line.

A standoff between the two opponents followed, with devastating
U.S. artillery bombardments amid several tank actions. The Americans'
material advantage became painfully evident to the SS troops, now increasingly short of ammunition. The village of Freineux was fiercely contested, with the panzergrenadiers of "Deutschland" fighting off superior
numbers of U.S. tanks and infantry. During one action, Untersturmführer Heller eventually decided that he must retire and with three other
grenadiers set up a defensive screen to allow his men to get back to their
lines. A German account described the resultant fight and, despite the
Malmédy atrocities, the generosity of Heller's captors: "The house was hit
by a shell. Heller was rendered unconscious for a time by falling debris.
When he came to, he found himself under burning timber. Men from an
American scouting team who showed up soon after pulled him out with
great difficulty, some of them suffering burns themselves, and moved him
to a dressing station. The dead men of the SS 'Deutschland' were also
removed by the Americans."[15]

MANTEUFFEL'S FIFTH PANZER Army had pushed forward farther than
Dietrich's SS force, taking advantage of more level terrain for its three
panzer divisions to advance toward the Meuse. As a result, Model began
to redirect the Waffen-SS to support the army offensive, beginning with
units from the Hitlerjugend Division that had been brought to a halt on
the Elsenborn ridge. On 26 December troops from Leibstandarte were

similarly redeployed. Fifth Panzer Army's main problem was the continuing resistance of well-supplied American troops at the key road junction of Bastogne. The original American garrison had been reinforced by the 101st Airborne Division, and although surrounded, its commander contemptuously rejected German demands to surrender.

On 30 December units from both divisions of II SS Panzer Corps were transferred south to help their SS and army comrades eliminate Bastogne. The redeployment was too late, however, as the Allies began to draw upon their substantial reserves to squeeze the German "Bulge." Patton's Third Army advanced from the south and broke through German lines on the twenty-sixth to establish a corridor to Bastogne. A slight but continuing improvement in the weather from 23 December onward permitted increasing numbers of Allied aircraft to take to the air, strafing German forward units and interdicting their resupply from the rear.

The new year confirmed the turn of the tide in the Allies' favor. A battalion commander in the Hohenstaufen Division described the difficult conditions he faced in a letter of 5 January:

> Through unfavorable circumstances (inadequate training of the men and very serious shortages of supplies, in particular clothing and shoes) I have very high casualties; mostly due to artillery and, whenever the weather clears, from Jabos. Yesterday I received 200 replacements, unfortunately almost all men from the Ukraine, some of whom neither speak nor understand German. Everything is lacking; here a man really has to prove himself. I have already experienced what it means to attack without any heavy weapons, since the Pak, IG [infantry guns] and artillery could not be brought forward due to a lack of prime movers, or had to be left stuck in frozen ground as practice-targets for the enemy and the Jabos.[16]

By 8 January 1945 the German Fifth and Sixth Panzer Armies were in full retreat, closely harried by the advancing Americans. It was a difficult withdrawal for the Germans, repeatedly forced to abandon precious vehicles through fuel shortages, but it was conducted in good order so that from the seventeenth onward they were able to retire behind the relative safety of the Westwall. The Germans had inflicted substantial casualties on the U.S. Army—especially in destroyed armored vehicles—but their own losses had been heavy and now were almost impossible to replace. The minimum German casualty figures were listed as 67,675, with 23,451 coming from the Waffen-SS Sixth Panzer Army.[17] The SS panzer divisions would need time, reinforcements, new weapons, and fuel to return to a sound combat footing, but all of these were now in desperately short supply.

TOWARD THE END of December Hitler decided to extend the range of his offensive with a subsidiary assault farther south on the Western Front. As well as being an attempt to recapture Strasbourg and Alsace, the offensive—code-named Nordwind—was also intended to prevent the movement of U.S. reserves to the Ardennes sector. The troops assembled for Nordwind came from Army Group G and, to a lesser degree, from Army Group Upper Rhine, now under the command of Heinrich Himmler. Ever since the failed assassination plot of July 1944, Hitler had allowed Himmler to take over areas formerly under exclusive Wehrmacht control, which at the end of 1944 included leadership of an army group, albeit stationed in a quiet sector.

The offensive opened on 31 December 1944 with an attack by Gruppenführer Max Simon's XIII SS Corps, which despite its title contained just a single Waffen-SS formation—17th SS Panzergrenadier Division—with the remaining two divisions supplied by the army. Simon's attack was made against a well-defended section of the U.S. line and was easily contained. A little farther to the east the main German drive was more successful, breaking through the American front line.

Among the attacking German formations was 6th SS Mountain Division Nord, only recently recovered from its fighting retreat through Finland. The men had been away from Germany in a military backwater for more than two years. They were surprised to be reequipped with MG42 machine guns and Panzerfaust antitank launchers, and they were shocked to see the devastation of their homeland wrought by Allied bombers as they traveled along the Rhine Valley.

Nord had never been envisaged as an elite SS division, but its extended deployment in Finland had provided it with sound combat experience. And the weather conditions encountered in the winter of 1944–1945 were nothing new to the SS troops, in contrast to their opponents. As a result, Nord made useful inroads into the American front line.

On 16 January Nord's 11th Gebirgsjäger Regiment managed to surround a substantial part of the U.S. 157th Regiment. The Americans fought on, but on 20 January, with no hope of relief, they surrendered to the SS troops, who, impressed by the Americans' bravery, invited them to share their rations. Johann Voss, a soldier in the 11th Regiment, a short distance from the action, commented, "Rumor had it that all the [U.S.] men were handed a box of Schoka-Kola each, a fine gesture by our commander, although I heard some grumbling that there weren't any boxes left for us."[18]

After this success, the SS troops pushed forward, but the arrival of U.S. reinforcements and increasingly heavy, well-directed artillery fire brought the German offensive to a halt. By 25 January Nord had lost around half of its infantry to a combination of U.S. fire, illness, and frostbite. While unable to advance farther, Nord continued to hold position against repeated attacks, a performance that won praise from their American opponents. A battalion commander in the 157th Infantry later wrote, "They were the best men we ever ran into, extremely aggressive, and impossible to capture. There was no driving them out, for they fought till they were killed."[19]

Heinz Harmel's 10th SS Panzer Division Frundsberg—held in reserve during the Ardennes offensive—was redirected to support Nordwind. After a hazardous march to the battle zone, it was ready for action early on 16 January. While it was still dark a combined tank-panzergrenadier force broke through the American defenses at Drusenheim. On the seventeenth American resistance hardened, although it was on this day that Frundsberg's panzer regiment achieved one of its greatest individual successes. Obersturmführer Erwin Bachmann was an adjutant to the panzer regiment's CO, and while admitting that he "had never been a really aggressive officer . . . more the staff type," he asked to go forward to take over the 3rd Company, which had just lost its commander in the battle for the town of Herrlisheim.[20] Bachmann jumped into the sidecar of a motorcycle combination and drove into the town, which apart from the odd crackle of rifle fire seemed ominously quiet.

Advancing cautiously on foot, Bachmann saw a number of enemy Sherman tanks, one of which he knocked out with a Panzerfaust he was carrying. On the way into Herrlisheim he had passed two Panther tanks, which, on their own initiative, had followed him. Bachmann then set his trap, sending the Panthers along different streets to knock out the lead and rear vehicles of what turned out to be a substantial armored column. Both Panthers succeeded in their mission, leaving the remaining Shermans unable to move. At this point, the American commander, believing he was heavily outnumbered, came forward to surrender.

Along with sixty U.S. prisoners came twenty previously captured Germans. Seizing the moment, Bachmann ordered the drivers of the twelve undamaged Shermans back into their tanks, and with each guarded by a rearmed German soldier they were ordered back to German lines (where the tanks were incorporated into the panzer regiment). Bachmann then led the two Panthers through Herrlisheim and knocked out several more U.S. tanks on the edge of town.[21]

This daring action could not, however, disguise the fact that the German offensive was petering out. On 19 January, with SS casualties mounting for little gain, Harmel was given permission to halt his division's assault. The SS units were then redeployed to capture the nearby strongpoint of Hagenau on the twenty-fourth. But with the momentum firmly on the Americans' side, the attack was held, this failure signaling the abandonment of Operation Nordwind. The Germans began a fighting retreat back to their original lines. Frundsberg was then detached and sent eastward with several other SS formations in an attempt to hold the Soviet offensive in Pomerania.

While the Germans had achieved a number of minor tactical successes during Nordwind, the operation was another defeat for Hitler, adding to the larger failure to overcome the Americans in the Ardennes. The Waffen-SS had not emerged from the Battle of the Bulge with flying colors, and senior German Army officers were quick to blame the Sixth Panzer Army's contribution to the offensive, focusing on poor staff work at all levels.[22] While there may have been some truth in these criticisms, any such failings were only a minor factor in the German reverse. The whole plan—where victory was predicated on continuing bad weather and the acquisition of mass fuel stocks from the Allies—had little chance of success from the outset. And when combined with the exceptional bravery of small groups of American defenders in key positions, a German defeat was inevitable.

Hitler still kept faith with Dietrich and the Waffen-SS, with Sixth Panzer Army ordered to prepare for new offensive operations. Dietrich did not reciprocate these feelings, however, and in a conversation with armaments minister Albert Speer on the night of 30–31 December, he complained bitterly of the demands made on his overstretched forces and said that it "was impossible to convince Hitler that these [Americans] were tough opponents, soldiers as good as our own men." Speer concluded that, "in his own plain fashion, he too had parted ways psychologically with Hitler."[23]

Himmler, who had played little part in the Nordwind operation, was instructed on 15 January to prepare for a new role, command of Army Group Vistula. This formation was tasked with the defense of Pomerania against the Red Army's Vistula-Oder offensive. Himmler's lack of military experience made him totally unsuited to this vital and difficult task, but Hitler overruled all objections from OKH in the belief that his trusted lieutenant would somehow produce better results than those of his generals.

Part Five

FIGHT TO THE LAST

"Enjoy the war while you can, because the peace will be terrible."

—GERMAN SOLDIERS' QUIP

Chapter 29

DISASTER IN HUNGARY

HUNGARY HAD PROVED a useful ally to Nazi Germany, and under the leadership of Admiral Miklós Horthy it had sent many of its soldiers to fight on the Eastern Front. But heavy casualties had produced a tide of war weariness within the country. By early 1944 Horthy was looking for ways to disengage Hungary from its alliance with Germany, but in March Hitler forestalled any potential move by sending in German troops to occupy the country. This did not stop Horthy from continuing secret negotiations with the Soviet Union, and on 15 October—with the Red Army breaking through the Carpathian Mountains—he declared an armistice.

German intelligence had monitored these negotiations and covertly sent military detachments to Budapest with orders to replace the Hungarian government if necessary. Under SS commando leader Otto Skorzeny—a Hitler favorite after his rescue of Mussolini—this force included the rebuilt Waffen-SS parachute battalion and units from the army's Brandenburg special forces, now assigned to the SS. Skorzeny could also draw upon any German troops in Budapest, which included a panzer battalion equipped with the latest highly imposing King Tiger tanks.

On hearing news of the armistice, the Germans sprang into action. Horthy's son was kidnapped and flown out to Germany as a hostage, while Skorzeny seized the Budapest Citadel and other government buildings. After Horthy was confronted by the Germans, he was made to repudiate the armistice and appoint a new pro-German government led by the extreme nationalist Arrow-Cross Party. Horthy resigned and was imprisoned in Germany. The coup had been a great success for Germany: casualties on both sides had been minimal, and Hungary continued to fight as part of the Axis alliance.

One other favorable consequence of the takeover for the SS was the opening up of recruitment to include all ethnic Germans in Hungary, many of whom had formerly been inducted into the Hungarian armed forces. During 1944 Berger's recruitment officers assiduously tracked down anyone with the vaguest Volksdeutsche connections, so that by the end of the war around 120,000 Hungarian Volksdeutsche had served in the Waffen-SS—by far the largest single national group of non-Reich Germans.[1] This influx of recruits helped fill in gaps within existing Waffen-SS formations and also enabled the raising of new units.

The 8th SS Cavalry Division Florian Geyer, with its large Hungarian contingent, had been transferred from the Pripet Marshes to Hungary during 1944. Once there, it supplied one of its cavalry regiments to form the nucleus of a new division, the 22nd SS Volunteer Cavalry Division Maria Theresia (its honor title provided by the redoubtable eighteenth-century Austrian empress). The division was formed on 1 May 1944 and was declared combat ready in August, despite training being incomplete and heavy weapons in short supply.

The recruiters from the SS Main Office now extended their search to include Magyar or ethnic Hungarians and in an arrangement with the new Arrow-Cross government took men from the Hungarian Army (Honved) as well as new Hungarian recruits. According to the agreement, these SS organized and trained divisions would form the basis for a new fascist Hungarian Army. Four divisions had been planned, but only two were commissioned: 25th Waffen Grenadier Division of the SS Hunyadi (Hungarian No. 1) and 26th Waffen Grenadier Division of the SS Hungaria (Hungarian No. 2). Once the men had been assembled, they were sent to Germany at the end of 1944 to begin training, a move that ironically prevented them from taking any further part in the battle to defend their homeland from the Red Army.

THE COLLAPSE OF Romania and Bulgaria in August–September 1944 was immediately followed by their change of sides to join the Soviet Union. This transformation of the strategic situation in the Balkans caught the Germans off guard. Not only were Hungary and Yugoslavia vulnerable to direct assault by the Red Army, but German forces in Greece and the Aegean also faced the strong possibility of being cut off by a Soviet drive into Yugoslavia. German units in Yugoslavia were ordered to hold open all escape routes from Greece, to allow the retreating Germans a safe passage to the north. The German high command made plans for new defensive positions that would keep the Red Army at bay. Hitler was also determined to defend Hungary at all costs, as it contained most of the Reich's still functioning oil wells.

The 7th SS Volunteer Mountain Division Prinz Eugen was immediately diverted from antipartisan operations to help defend Yugoslavia from an October advance by Soviet and Bulgarian armies, the latter co-opted by the Soviet Union to join their "antifascist crusade." For the men of Prinz Eugen, this dramatic change from acting as hunters against Tito's partisans to being the underdogs in a battle against superior conventional forces was bewildering in the extreme. They would come under heavy artillery fire and massed armor attacks for the first time. To prepare them for this onslaught, the soldiers were issued with Panzerfausts and given a rapid course in antitank tactics.

The Prinz Eugen Division, under the command of Oberführer Otto Kumm, was ordered to defend the line around Nish (Niz) from a combined Soviet-Bulgarian advance. While Prinz Eugen held its positions, units on both flanks fell back, leaving the SS division isolated. Kumm then ordered a retreat, a fifty-mile march over steep mountains and through dense forests. At times it seemed that the division might fall apart, but by the end of October the various units re-formed to take up new positions at the Kraljevo bridgehead. It was here that Prinz Eugen fought off further Soviet and Bulgarian attacks to allow free passage for the German troops marching back from Greece. The retreating columns totaled 350,000 men and 10,000 vehicles, some of which passed by the SS defenders who, at one point, observed the bizarre sight of "a submarine anti-aircraft gun transported on a wagon drawn by oxen."[2]

That the Germans were able to escape the Soviet trap owed much to the efforts of a small number of German formations, including Prinz Eugen. This was arguably their finest hour in a war otherwise characterized by atrocity and counteratrocity. Toward the end of November, the SS division—reduced to a strength of just under 3,500 men and with almost no heavy weapons—withdrew from the Kraljevo bridgehead to begin a slow, fighting retreat through Yugoslavia.

In the aftermath of the Romanian collapse, Waffen-SS recruiters conducted a final trawl through the Batschka region between Serbia and Hungary, rooting out the last eligible Volksdeutsche to form the 31st SS Volunteer Division. German officers and NCOs from the disbanded Kama Division provided the training cadre for the new formation, which was formally established in September 1944. The poorly trained and underequipped division—led by former SS cavalry commander Brigadeführer Gustav Lombard—was ordered north into Hungary in November, where it suffered heavy casualties before withdrawal to Germany.

In October 1944 the Red Army crossed into Hungary, with the aim of cutting off the capital from the rest of the country. Soviet forces began to march on Budapest in early November, although, in the face of stiff German and Hungarian resistance, it was not until 26 December that the city was encircled. The headquarters of the IX SS Mountain Corps had been moved north from Yugoslavia, and under the leadership of Karl Pfeffer-Wildenbruch it was assigned responsibility for the defense of Budapest. Pfeffer-Wildenbruch—the original commander of the SS Polizei Division—had been given four understrength army and Waffen-SS formations that included the SS cavalry divisions Florian Geyer and Maria Theresia. With paramilitary and other Wehrmacht units, the German garrison totaled around 41,000 men. They were joined by 38,100 soldiers from the Hungarian Army who remained loyal to the German cause.[3]

Hitler, true to form, declared Budapest a fortress city, and forbidding any breakout attempt he insisted it must be held to the last man. He did, however, sanction a relief attempt, which was to be spearheaded by

Obergruppenführer Herbert Gille's IV SS Panzer Corps, comprising the veteran Totenkopf and Wiking Divisions. Gille's troops were, however, deployed in the defense of Warsaw, more than 400 miles distant from Budapest. The corps' removal would, of course, seriously weaken the German defenses in central Poland, especially now that a Soviet offensive was imminent.

The order for the transfer was issued late on 24 December, and by using priority rail transport the advance units of the corps began to arrive at their assembly points as early as 1 January, with the remainder following over the next few days. The Waffen-SS troops were joined by two infantry and two panzer divisions and a battalion of King Tiger tanks from the army, plus other corps units. As ever, in the conditions typical of the latter stages of the war, the German units were chronically short of fuel and ammunition and were understrength in armored vehicles.

The relief attempts were code-named Konrad, and Konrad I got under way as soon as the first SS soldiers arrived to support Hungarian units already in place. The plan had been hurried, however, with little attention paid to preliminary reconnaissance, thereby failing to realize that the hilly, wooded terrain made progress by armor against a well-dug-in enemy extremely difficult. The corps did at least inflict heavy losses on the enemy during Konrad I, claiming 79 tanks, 160 artillery pieces, and 107 antitank guns destroyed.[4]

On 8 January the offensive was abandoned and the German units redeployed on a better line of attack from Esztergom. Two days later Konrad II was launched against an unsuspecting Red Army. The Soviet forward defenses were breached on 11 January, and on the following day they could see the towers and spires of Budapest no more than thirteen miles away. Both Totenkopf and Wiking sensed victory, but at 8:00 P.M. on the twelfth an order was issued from army group headquarters that the assault was to be called off. The forward units were shocked by the order, but despite repeated requests from Gille to continue the advance, the attack came to a halt and the troops were withdrawn.

While the relief attempts were ongoing, the Red Army squeezed the ring tight around Budapest. The garrison and civil population of around 800,000 people were increasingly short of food and subject to sustained, heavy artillery bombardments. During January Soviet forces pressed toward Pest—on the eastern bank of the Danube—forcing the defenders back toward the hilly Buda on the western bank. On 18 January Pfeffer-Wildenbruch's forces established a new defensive line around the Citadel area of Buda, having destroyed the remaining bridges over the Danube.

Also on 18 January, Konrad III was initiated, an assault on Budapest from the south, once more led by Gille's IV SS Panzer Corps. In wretched conditions of alternating snow and driving rain, the SS troops drove into the Soviet lines. With Wiking in the lead, the Germans forged ahead, reaching the Danube on the twentieth. A few days later the other spearhead divisions—the army's 3rd Panzer and Totenkopf—arrived alongside Wiking, in preparation for the push north to relieve Budapest.

On 24 January the Germans opened their assault. Once again Totenkopf and Wiking made good ground, despite being forced to regularly halt and fend off attacks against their unsupported flanks. By the twenty-eighth, German units had managed to fight their way to within touching distance of Budapest, no more than ten miles from the Soviet encircling ring. For the men trapped inside the city, the German relief column's advance was enthusiastically monitored, as this account makes clear: "The news of General Gille seeped through to the last foxhole. At any minute he must open the pocket. His name was mentioned everywhere, everywhere he was the anchor of our morale. For hours everyone forgot the terrible privation, resigned themselves to the sickening conditions in the cellars. Our rescue was getting nearer!"[5]

The final push onto Budapest was planned for 29 January. The Wiking soldiers were told that they faced no more than a battered cavalry division, but they suddenly found themselves under attack from a freshly arrived Soviet armored corps, complete with 180 tanks. The Wiking Division was nearly overwhelmed, and only prompt action by the predominantly Norwegian "Norge" Battalion prevented disaster. The battalion's commander, Sturmbannführer Vogt, personally knocked out six enemy tanks with Panzerfausts. The strength of the Soviet attack halted the German advance, and on 1 February a fighting retreat was instigated, the SS panzer corps falling back to its start line. When news of the German defeat reached the defenders, that they had been abandoned to their fate, morale understandably plummeted.

By early February the Red Army was closing in on the Budapest garrison, now clinging on to just two square kilometers around Castle Hill and the Citadel. Running out of ammunition, with his men suffering from starvation and disease, Pfeffer-Wildenbruch decided on his own initiative to attempt a mass breakout through Soviet lines on the evening of 11 February. The combined German-Hungarian garrison had been reduced to around 32,000 men (excluding seriously wounded), and it would seem most took part in the breakout.[6] Complicating matters were the thousands of civilians also desperate to escape the city. The sheer size of the attempt initially overwhelmed the Soviets, but shells from their guns tore into the retreating masses, causing heavy casualties. Over the next few days the vast majority of escapers were either killed or rounded up by the Red Army. The two SS cavalry divisions, along with Wehrmacht units, were destroyed in the attempt. Only 624 German soldiers reached safety, around 170 of those from the Waffen-SS.[7]

Hitler, meanwhile, was absorbed in the planning for the new offensive in Hungary, intended to recapture the oil fields southwest of the Plattensee (Lake Balaton). Dietrich's reequipped Sixth Panzer Army (only officially designated as an SS Army in April 1945) had been transferred from the Western Front to its assembly area in Hungary in early February. The German high command had made elaborate attempts to disguise the move of the panzer army, ordering the removal of SS troops' special cuff titles and renaming all formations and units with innocuous-sounding designations, so that, for example, Das Reich was disguised as Training Group North. Dietrich's force comprised Priess's I SS Panzer Corps (Leibstandarte and the Hitlerjugend) and Bittrich's II SS Panzer Corps (Das Reich and Hohenstaufen), plus two mounted divisions of the army's I Cavalry Corps.

Before the main offensive could get under way, orders were issued for the elimination of a Soviet bridgehead over the River Gran to the north of Budapest. The I SS Panzer Corps was diverted to take part in this action on 13 February. In Leibstandarte, Mohnke—wounded in an air raid—was replaced as divisional commander by Otto Kumm, transferred from long service in the Prinz Eugen Division. Kumm ordered the advance to be led by a Kampfgruppe of mechanized infantry in APCs and panzers—including sixteen King Tigers—under Jochen Peiper.

On the evening of 17 February the Kampfgruppe broke through several lines (fronts) of antitank guns, one of its actions described by Rottenführer Reinhold Kyriss from the 1st Panzer Regiment's 7th Company:

> Peiper had five King Tigers drive onto the hill, what a sight! They sat on the crest as on a serving tray and were immediately fired on by Soviet anti-tank guns. One could clearly see the armor-piercing shells bouncing off the fronts of the Tigers. What a shock it must have been to the Ivans, especially since the Tigers for their part now began picking off the enemy anti-tank guns one after the other. The anti-tank fire lessened, and Peiper immediately gave the order: "Panzers forward!" When the battle group drove over the rise en masse there began a fireworks display in the truest sense of the word. Driving at top speed, the tanks and armored troop carriers fired everything they had, and the light trails left by the shells could be seen even better in the failing light; it was an imposing scene. This armored attack, mounted like a cavalry charge, left the Reds only one choice, run away. After overrunning the anti-tank front we halted to regroup.[8]

Although Soviet resistance increased in succeeding days, the tempo of the SS armored attack was too much for the Soviet defenders. By February the Gran bridgehead was destroyed, although at a cost of 3,000 SS casualties. I SS Panzer Corps was then transferred back to the start line for the main German offensive, code-named Operation Spring Awakening (Frülingserwachen).

Sixth Panzer Army—supported by the Army's III Panzer Corps—would advance from the northeastern side of Lake Balaton toward the Danube. Dietrich's troops would be supported by subsidiary thrusts from the largely infantry Second Panzer Army on the southwestern side of Lake Balaton and by a mix of formations from Army Group E (including the remnants of the Handschar Division) in southern Hungary. Together they would attempt to encircle the Soviet armies in central Hungary.

The plan was imaginative but vastly overambitious for the resources available to the Germans, who were outnumbered and outgunned by the Red Army. Moreover, despite the elaborate German efforts to camouflage

their intentions, Soviet military intelligence had identified the movement
of German armored formations to Hungary, and the Red Army was ready
for the impending assault. Multilayered defenses were constructed to en-
tangle the German assault, while a powerful force was already in place to
mount what would become a devastating Soviet counteroffensive.

As the Waffen-SS formations arrived at their assembly areas in western
Hungary, they were still receiving reinforcements from Germany. Hans
Woltersdorf, an officer in Das Reich's "Der Führer" Regiment, com-
plained about the quality of the new arrivals:

> One could hardly have called them "fresh." Most of them could have
> been my father. They showed me their hernias, their gout, and the photos
> of their grown up children. Some radical hero had combed the remotest
> places to find this bunch—an elite that was designed to inspire fear in
> us rather than in the Russians. When I surveyed the battered ranks of
> my company I was still unwilling to admit that we had lost the war, but
> the subliminal feeling rose up in me that we couldn't possibly win it. At
> this point I did not want to think about the alternatives there could have
> been, because we had two or at most three weeks in which to whip this
> crew into an elite brigade for the Eastern Front.[9]

Despite the uncertain quality of the newly arrived rank and file, overall
numbers in the SS divisions were impressive for this late stage of the
war: in II SS Panzer Corps, Das Reich deployed a total of 19,542 men
and Hohenstaufen 17,299 (although not all could be committed to the
offensive). But, as ever, there were shortages of fuel, ammunition, and the
armored fighting vehicles themselves. One of the better-equipped formations was Brigadeführer Sylvester Stadler's Hohenstaufen, which fielded
ninety panzers, a decent number when compared to other divisions but
still half the regulation allotment.[10]

Hitler was determined that the offensive should begin without delay,
and the formations of Sixth Panzer Army were rushed to their start lines,
with no time for reconnaissance of the attack routes, essential for success
in armored operations. The weather also conspired against an armored
offensive, with temperatures often rising above freezing during the day,

turning the Hungarian plain into an almost impenetrable marshland for heavy vehicles. The date of the offensive was set for 6 March at 4:00 A.M. As a result of the poor weather, many SS units had difficulty in reaching their jumping-off points in time. The divisional and corps commanders pleaded to have a twenty-four-hour postponement, but Hitler was insistent that the attack must go ahead as originally scheduled.

The panzergrenadiers of Bittrich's II SS Panzer Corps had an especially hard time in reaching their start line. As a result, the guns of the corps fired their opening bombardment on the morning of the sixth as ordered but without any attacking infantry, who only began to arrive later in the day. All element of surprise was lost when the bombardment was repeated the following morning, the panzergrenadiers advancing against alert and prepared Soviet defenses. Not surprisingly, the progress of Bittrichs's corps was minimal. As the attack began Das Reich's commander, Gruppenführer Werner Ostendorff, was mortally wounded, just one of many senior officers to be killed in the offensive; he would be replaced by Rudolf Lehmann, from the staff of I SS Panzer Corps.

The assault by the army's III Panzer Corps and Priess's I SS Panzer Corps on 6 March was more successful. On the following day SS troops broke through the second line of the Soviet defense system and then pushed on over relatively open countryside. Much of the fighting took place at night, the panzers following each other by the glow of their exhausts. Hauptsturmführer Hans Siegel described an assault by a mixed Kampfgruppe from Hitlerjugend, just after midnight on 8 March: "During the deployment of the unit into a wide wedge formation, our own artillery shelled the detected blocking position, mostly dug-in anti-tank guns. The concentrated force of fire and movement, added to which was the din of motors and the rattle of the tracked vehicles firing tracers in front of them, all that happening during total darkness, discouraged probably even the most hardened Red Army man. We overran the anti-tank barrier and the fortified positions without loss."[11] Leibstandarte and Hitlerjugend pushed forward twenty miles beyond their start line to capture Simontornya on 12 March. It was here that they were stopped by the Red Army.

The poor start made by II SS Panzer Corps was to continue, especially when Soviet reinforcements were sent to their sector. On 8 March Stadler reported on the difficult circumstances faced by his division: "A massed panzer attack is simply impossible. The entire landscape has turned to softened mud in which everything sinks."[12] He sent his panzer regiment commander forward to assess the situation, but after two of his tanks sank into the mud up to their turrets, a cross-country attack was abandoned. Instead, the Hohenstaufen vehicles were confined to surfaced roads—vulnerable to Soviet artillery fire—leaving the panzergrenadiers to cross open terrain with reduced fire support.

For the best-trained infantry this would be a difficult proposition, but for Hans Woltersdorf's aged conscripts in Das Reich, it was a battle too far: "In the uncertain light of dawn I led a charge and, as the noise of ammunition from friend and foe alike rendered communication impossible, I had to show my men how to do it. Jump up, forward march, move eastwards. When I jumped up and ran 15 meters they ran only ten, and when I remained under cover for ten seconds they remained for fifteen, and when I beckoned them forward they waved back in a friendly gesture." As Woltersdorf tried to inspire his reluctant panzergrenadiers, he was hit in the leg by Soviet machine-gun fire. Initially, his men thought he had been killed and halted in respectful silence, but when he shouted to them to continue the attack, they descended on him: "It seemed as if I was leading a company of medics, because one medic after another came to drag me back to the rear. In the process a real stampede ensued. Shouting curses and abuses I ordered them to press forward."[13] Woltersdorf (who subsequently lost the leg) was carried back to an aid station, his attack stalled.

———

BY 14–15 MARCH the German offensive was floundering. The I SS Panzer Corps had taken the Soviet defensive position at Simontornya but could go no farther. Elsewhere, the Second Panzer Army's attack had been repulsed, as had the northward drive by parts of Army Group E, which was also having to fend off a resurgent partisan army under Marshal Tito. The Soviet high command now decided that the time was right for their major spring offensive, designed to conquer Hungary and drive the Germans back across the Reich's borders into Austria. On 16 March an intense artillery bombardment heralded mass attacks by Soviet armor that tore into the Axis lines. The wavering loyalties of the Hungarian Army were put to the test; many formations simply laid down their arms, some even going over to the Soviet side.

The bulge in the Soviet lines created by Sixth Panzer Army's offensive now made it vulnerable to Soviet counterattacks, which came from all sides. The II SS Panzer Corps was particularly hard hit, and efforts were made to redirect the other SS panzer corps to come to its aid, but it was all too late. For a while Dietrich's forces were surrounded, and it was with some difficulty that they managed to fight their way back to their start line.

The Soviet offensive had always been more than a counter to the German attack, however, and a powerful thrust was made against the section of the German front line held by the Totenkopf and Wiking Divisions of Gille's IV SS Panzer Corps. It was vital that they hold their positions to allow the withdrawal of Dietrich's army and the other German forces retreating through Hungary. The Red Army—adopting the blitzkrieg tactics pioneered by their enemy—encouraged armored units to surge forward and leave strongpoints to be dealt with by follow-up troops. German defensive positions were regularly bypassed and isolated.

Holding a line between Lake Velencersee and the Vértes Mountains, both Totenkopf and Wiking were soon surrounded. Defending the village of Söred, the Germans—desperately short of ammunition—faced the might of a Soviet attack. Hans Geissendorf, an officer in Totenkopf's assault-gun (Sturmgeschütz) battalion, described the horrors of the fighting and the inevitable retreat:

The Russians opened up their attack on Söred at 1600 hours on 19 March 1945 from all sides. The Russians came in massed groups supported by super-heavy tanks. Resistance on our side was mostly through entrenching tools and knives; our ammunition was gone. I can still recall clearly how the Russians stood in the open next to their foxholes and called on us to surrender before the attack. They were about 50 meters away.

The Danes of SS Panzergrenadier Regiment "Danmark" [a rebuilt I Battalion, detached from Nordland and loaned to Wiking] fought heroically. I was with our Sturmgeschütz at the outskirts of the town with an infantry squad. In the midst of this inferno, a messenger came and yelled out that it was over and we should attempt to escape towards the west. When we moved to the designated assembly area we saw how all the other Sturmgeschütz had become bogged down in the swampy fields west of Söred and could go no further. Shortly thereafter, the same thing happened to us. I blew up our [assault] gun with a Panzerfaust. We ran for our lives between Russians, Germans and the artillery rounds always exploding just in front of us. I saw several of our officers from both our division and SS Panzergrenadier Regiment "Danmark" shoot themselves because they could go no further.[14]

The bulk of the Wiking Division and other army units were virtually surrounded in the nearby town of Stuhlweissenburg; just one road to safety was still open, forming part of a narrow corridor a couple of miles wide. Oberführer Karl Ullrich—Wiking's commander since October 1944—had been ordered to hold firm at all costs. As with many other senior SS officers, Ullrich was increasingly disenchanted with the higher direction of the war and decided to ignore the directive in favor of saving the men trapped in Stuhlweissenburg. He ordered a breakout for dawn on 22 March, his troops divided into two columns that began to battle their way through the ever-narrowing corridor.

The fighting grew in intensity, and it seemed that the German columns might be destroyed until the timely intervention of Stadler's Hohenstaufen Division. Stadler was aware of the predicament of the escaping soldiers and ignored a withdrawal order from his superior officer in the Cavalry Corps to keep the corridor open. He later wrote, "The 9th SS Panzer Division fought bitterly against a superior enemy, well aware of its responsibility to the threatened divisions that were still encircled in the Stuhlweissenburg pocket. The 9th Panzer Regiment destroyed 108 tanks on 22 and 23 March. What a great effort in such chaos!"[15] Thanks to Hohenstaufen's actions, Wiking and the other army units were able to escape the Soviet trap, although most of their heavy weapons and vehicles were lost in the process. During the last week of March all those German forces that had escaped the Soviet offensive fell back toward Austria.

Hitler was dismayed at the performance of his special guard. On 23 March he had ranted to his staff at his evening situation conference, "I now demand one thing: that Leibstandarte, moreover the entire Sixth

Panzer Army be sent the last man available anywhere. I mean immediately! Sepp Dietrich must be informed instantly. Immediately!"[16] But
he was too late: Sixth Panzer Army was in full retreat, regardless of his
orders. When Hitler discovered that the Waffen-SS had abandoned the
Spring Awakening offensive, he felt personally betrayed. On 27 March a
signal was sent to Sixth Panzer Army headquarters: "The Führer believes
that the troops have not fought as the situation demanded and orders that
the SS divisions Adolf Hitler, Das Reich, Totenkopf and Hohenstaufen
be stripped of their armbands."[17] Himmler was ordered to issue a reprimand to Dietrich in person, while all further promotions, due on Hitler's
birthday (20 April), were canceled.

For soldiers who had given everything to obey the Führer's orders in
nearly six years of combat, and had lost so many comrades in the process,
this was a cutting insult. A staff officer at Sixth Panzer Army headquarters handed the message to Sepp Dietrich: "Then he read—turned away
slowly, bent over the table, resting on it with both hands in such a way
that I could not see his face. He was deeply shocked and moved and it
took him a long time to rally again. Then, after a long interval, still bent
over the table, he said in an unusually quiet, almost fragile voice, which
reflected deepest disappointment and bitterness: 'This is the thanks for
everything.'"[18] Dietrich instructed that the message was to be forwarded
to the divisional commanders but go no further. Despite this, news of the
order spread through the SS units, but by now the troops were fighting
not for Hitler but for their comrades and themselves. And, of course,
most cuff bands had already been removed prior to the offensive.

Having fallen back to positions in Austria, the Germans were given
no respite as the Red Army drove toward its next objective, Vienna. The
loss of Hungary was a grievous blow to Hitler, but by now Nazi Germany
was entering its terminal phase. The main Soviet push against Germany
toward the Oder was gaining momentum, while in the West Anglo-
American armies had crossed the Rhine. It was only a matter of time
before the total defeat of Germany, although its leader was determined to
fight on, regardless of the destruction raging around him.

Chapter 30

THE WAFFEN-SS DESTROYED

Throughout his career as Reichsführer-SS, Heinrich Himmler had repeatedly made fulsome declarations of his loyalty to the Führer. Himmler both admired and feared Hitler, but from 1943 onward his own developing ambitions began to run counter to those of his master. Himmler had hoped at some point to succeed Hitler as leader of Nazi Germany, but the downturn in German military fortunes caused him understandable concern: Would he have anything left to inherit when the time came?

Following the successful Allied landings in Normandy, several leading Nazi politicians privately suggested the possibility of seeking a negotiated peace with either the Soviet Union or the Western Allies, but Hitler refused to consider any such proposal. Himmler then decided to take matters into his own hands, and at the end of August 1944 he secretly sent a message—via the Spanish government—to Winston Churchill, making soundings for peace talks. The British prime minister summarily destroyed the note.[1] In early 1945 Himmler resumed his covert attempts to secure terms with the Western Allies, primarily through Count Folke Bernadotte, head of the Swedish Red Cross. Himmler's entreaties were rebuffed once again, as the Allies kept to their joint agreement demanding Germany's unconditional surrender in all theaters of war.

While Himmler was attempting to secure a negotiated peace, he also ordered the creation of one last round of Waffen-SS divisions in February 1945. They consisted of an upgrading of existing regiments and brigades or the amalgamation of smaller units into slightly larger aggregations (see Appendix A). None of these formations had the manpower or heavy weapons required of a division, and with the exception of the Western European formations, they served no military or political purpose.

Himmler's military vocation was also running into trouble. His appointment by Hitler to command Army Group Vistula on 25 January 1945 proved a disaster. He arrived at the front in his special train, which lacked experienced staff officers and a suitable telephone and radio communication system to issue orders to his army group. Himmler was out of his depth, soon to collapse under the strain of command. From 18 February onward, he was "under doctor's orders" and seemed barely capable of coherent thought. Guderian insisted that he be replaced, a call initially rejected by Hitler. But after the failure of the counteroffensive in Pomerania, Hitler finally turned on his trusted lieutenant, blaming him for the defeat and relieving him of his command on 20 March. By this time Himmler had sought refuge in a sanatorium in Germany. From then on, the relationship between the two men cooled, with Himmler ever more anxious to find some form of accommodation with the Allies.

———————

IF HIMMLER WAS troubled by the loss of his cherished ambition to control a Germanic Europe, the people of Germany had more pressing concerns as defeat and enemy occupation stared them in the face. Although still cowed by the Gestapo, few in the civilian population now had much enthusiasm for the Nazi cause. Native Berliner and Leibstandarte soldier Erwin Bartmann discovered this changing atmosphere as he left his parents' house in readiness to defend the city against the advancing Red Army in January 1945. He encountered a crowd who, when they saw his uniform, shouted insults and even threw stones at him. Bartmann conceded, "Bearing the name 'Adolf Hitler' on the cuff band of my tunic, they saw me as the personification of everything they detested. The days when people would go out of their way to curry favor with any member of Leibstandarte had come to a bitter end."[2]

The threat posed by the Soviet drive on Berlin forced the German armed forces to throw everything against the advancing Red Army. As a result, a Leibstandarte soldier like Bartmann found himself sent to an ad hoc formation—Regiment Falke—on the River Oder rather than dispatched to Hungary to rejoin his division. On 16 January the Red Army had broken through German defenses on the River Vistula in Poland, driving west with the German capital its goal. Such was the determination of Stalin's generals to reach Berlin that little attention was given to German positions in the Baltic coastal region of Pomerania, directly to the north of the main Soviet advance.

Hitler and his military planners decided to attack the exposed Soviet right flank from Pomerania, the offensive code-named Operation Sonnenwende (Solstice). Overall command had been assigned to Himmler— as chief of Army Group Vistula—but through Guderian's intervention, the capable General Walther Wenck took operational control. The attack would be spearheaded by Obergruppenführer Felix Steiner's Eleventh Army, a mixed army and Waffen-SS force better known as the Eleventh SS Panzer Army.

The SS part of Steiner's force included the 10th SS Panzer Division Frundsberg, 11th SS Panzergrenadier Division Nordland, and 4th SS Polizei Panzergrenadier Division (transferred from Greece), plus the recently upgraded formations from Western Europe: 23rd SS Volunteer Panzergrenadier Division Nederland, 27th SS Volunteer Grenadier Division Langemarck, and 28th SS Volunteer Grenadier Division Wallonien. A formidable force on paper, in reality the SS units were understrength and short of fuel and ammunition. Such was the desperation to find sufficient infantry that a group of German soldiers leaving a cinema performance were "press-ganged" into the Nederland Division, only a day before the offensive was to be launched.[3]

After a preliminary attack made by Nordland on 15 February, the main German assault took place the following day. The Soviets fell back, and over the next two days the Germans made reasonable headway. The besieged outpost of Arnswalde was reached and its garrison and refugees escorted to safety. As the Soviet armies advanced into Germany, so hundreds of thousands of civilians fled to escape their vengeance. The German armed forces did their best to shepherd them westward, with the long columns of refugees clogging the roads making movement of all kinds difficult.

394

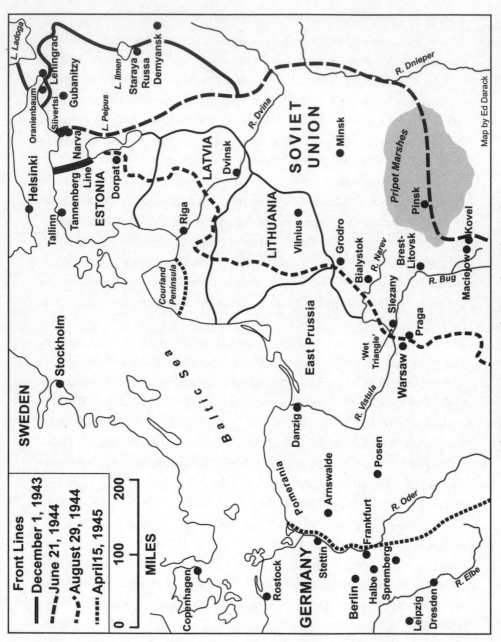

The Eastern Front in the North, 1943–1945

Map by Ed Darack

Front Lines
— December 1, 1943
– – – June 21, 1944
•–•–• August 29, 1944
•••••• April 15, 1945

MILES

0   100   200

SWEDEN

Stockholm

Copenhagen

Rostock

GERMANY

Berlin
Halbe
Spremberg
Leipzig
Dresden

Stettin
Arnswalde
Frankfurt

Pomerania

Danzig

Posen

R. Oder

R. Elbe

Baltic Sea

Courland Peninsula

Helsinki

L. Ladoga

Oranienbaum
Silvertsi
Leningrad
Gubanitzy

Tallinn
Narva
Tannenberg Line
Dorpat

L. Peipus

ESTONIA

Riga

LATVIA

Dvinsk

Staraya
Russa
Demyansk
L. Ilmen

R. Dvina

R. Dnieper

SOVIET UNION

Minsk

Pripet Marshes

Pinsk

LITHUANIA

Vilnius

Grodro
Bialystok

R. Narev

Brest-Litovsk

R. Bug

Maciejow
Kovel

Slezany

Praga

Warsaw

'Wet Triangle'

R. Vistula

East Prussia

On 18 February the arrival of Soviet reinforcements brought the armored drive to a halt, the offensive formally abandoned that evening to avoid more fruitless casualties in an attritional battle that would always favor the enemy. Operation Sonnenwende had failed to overcome the Soviet defenses, but it had bought time for Hitler. The Red Army high command now felt it necessary to redirect forces to eliminate the German positions in eastern Pomerania, delaying the proposed attack on Berlin.

On 24 February Brigadeführer Heinz Harmel's Frundsberg Division was sent south to defend Frankfurt on the River Oder, but almost immediately was ordered back to Pomerania in light of the Red Army's new assault. Arriving in early March, Frundsberg joined the other Waffen-SS formations in a series of delaying actions as they fell back to the River Oder, where a bridgehead was established at Altdamm. On 19 March Soviet pressure forced its abandonment, the Germans retreating to new positions around Stettin on the western side of the river.

Frundsberg was briefly held in army reserve before dispatch to Silesia when the Red Army launched its final offensive of the war on 16 April. This was a broad-front operation that smashed into the Oder-Neisse Line and broke through the German defenses in several places. The German Ninth Army was trapped in the Halbe pocket to the south of Berlin. Among the encircled formations were the V SS Mountain Corps, containing several low-grade Waffen-SS units, and Obergruppenführer Kleinheisterkamp's XI SS Panzer Corps, which, despite its designation, was primarily an infantry formation, its troops coming from the army. Of greater military significance were the King Tiger tanks of the 502nd SS Heavy Panzer Battalion, now attached to Ninth Army.

Farther south still was the Spremberg pocket, which contained Frundsberg and two battered army divisions. Only a few miles wide, the pocket came under intense Soviet bombardment, which included the Katyusha rocket launchers German soldiers called "Stalin's organ," after their pipe-like appearance and demented wailing sound when fired. Günter Grass, the trainee tank gunner in Frundsberg, had just arrived at the front and was walking through a grove of birch trees that contained some trucks, armored personnel carriers, and two Jagdpanthers. There he came under fire for the first time:

Two or three rocket launchers blanket the grove. They are ruthlessly thorough, mowing down whatever cover the young trees might promise. There is no place to hide, or is there? For a simple gunner, at least. I see myself doing as I was taught: crawling under one of the Jagdpanthers. We are protected by the tracks on either side. The organ goes on playing for what is most likely a three-minute eternity—scared to death, I piss my pants—and then silence. I crawled out from under the Jagdpanther. Still wobbly on my feet, I was assaulted by images. The birches looked as if they had been broken over somebody's knee. There were bodies everywhere, one next to another and one on top of the other, dead, still alive, writhing, impaled by branches, peppered with shell splinters. Many were in acrobatic contortions. Body parts were strewn around.[4]

Despite Grass's harrowing personal account, Harmel and his fellow divisional commanders had managed to construct a reasonable defensive perimeter, although their chief consideration was planning a breakout to the west. To their dismay, however, two orders arrived in quick succession, one from Field-Marshal Schörner, the commander of Army Group Center, and the other from Hitler himself. Addressed to Harmel, they both demanded he lead an attack due north to take the advancing Soviet forces in the flank. Harmel realized that this would entail their almost total destruction, but to disobey a direct Führer Order was a crime punishable by death and the imprisonment of the culprit's family in a concentration camp. On 20 April Harmel, after discussion with his army colleagues, took the decision to risk Hitler's punishment by refusing the order. He then gave the order to evacuate the pocket and escape westward.

By 26 April the remnants of the Frundsberg Division had managed to reach the relative safety of an assembly area near Dresden. Harmel was flown to Schörner's headquarters and summarily relieved of his command before transfer to the officer reserve. Given the nature of his crime, the punishment was relatively lenient: he was redirected to lead a collection of SS officer cadets and replacement units to keep open escape routes from northern Yugoslavia into Austria, before surrendering to the British on 8 May.[5]

The new commander of the Frundsberg Division, Obersturmbannführer Roestel, attempted to hold the new position to the west of Dresden, which by early May was surrounded by the Red Army. On 5 May Frundsberg began a second breakout, to reach U.S. Army lines on the far side of the River Elbe (surrender to the Western Allies rather than the Red Army had become a priority for the Waffen-SS). Obersturmführer Bachmann led what remained of the panzer regiment—including the last Sherman tanks captured during Operation Nordwind—to cut a path through enemy-held territory. As the division fought its way westward, it came under constant attack, eventually disintegrating into small groups and individuals, many killed or captured by the Red Army. The survivors reached the Elbe between 10 and 12 May.

General Busse's Ninth Army, in the Halbe pocket, also faced destruction, as superior Soviet forces began to squeeze the perimeter. On 23 April Hitler was persuaded to allow Ninth Army to break out of the pocket on the basis that it could link up with General Wenck's Twelfth Army and together drive forward to relieve Berlin, now under siege. Busse and Wenck had no intention of rescuing the Führer in Berlin, however, both having agreed to create a corridor south of the capital for Ninth Army to escape the pocket, before both armies marched toward the Elbe. Around 80,000 troops took part in the operation, joined by thousands of civilians from the Halbe area fleeing the Red Army.[6]

An initial breakout attempt on the night of 25–26 April achieved little, and it was only on the twenty-eighth that the main German force was able to fight its way past Halbe. With the remaining King Tigers of the 502nd SS Panzer Battalion in the lead, the Germans struggled through the sprawling forests to the south of Berlin. Organized into separate columns, repeated bombardments from artillery and the Red Air Force caused forest fires that led to the fragmentation of the breakout force. Although many of the retreating masses were either killed or captured, such was their desperation that around 25,000 soldiers and several thousand civilians reached the Twelfth Army outposts from 3 May onward.[7] The soldiers of Twelfth and Ninth Armies then fell back west to the Elbe and to surrender. Matthias Kleinheisterkamp, commander of the XI SS Panzer Corps, was one of those who failed to get to safety; captured by Soviet troops, he committed suicide.

GIVEN GERMANY'S HOPELESS position in early 1945, it was remarkable
how so many within the Waffen-SS continued to fight with undiminished resolve. The strength of Nazi propaganda was one element in maintaining such a level of military commitment, creating a commonly held
assumption that defeat would lead to the literal destruction of Germany
in a devastating apocalypse. The brutality of the war on the Eastern Front
encouraged such a view. The rank and file kept faith in what Goebbels
and Hitler told them, despite the mounting evidence to the contrary.
Soldiers still believed the official pronouncements of how Germany's new
"wonder weapons"—jet fighters, V1 and V2 rockets, and more—would
turn the tide of war in their favor. Erik Wallin of the Nordland Division
remained hopeful of such an outcome, even in March 1945: "Certainly,
on our side, we knew that important things were going on, that sensa-
tional weapons would soon be put into action, and, thanks to that, the
war would take on a completely new character. The new jet-propelled
fighter-planes, which were far superior to the best British and American
planes, were already in action and had caused heavy casualties among
their bombers. We knew that even better things were coming."[8] Wallin's
concern was that they might not be ready in time, and while this proved
to be the case, the new weapons would never have been sufficient to tip
the military balance in Germany's favor.

A further factor hovering behind all soldiers on the front line was the
harsh military discipline of the German armed forces, made harsher still
by the Nazi regime. During the war 15,000 German servicemen were put
to death for capital crimes,[9] and in 1945 roving patrols of military police,
Gestapo, and other SS units were authorized to hang any soldiers or civilians they believed to be lacking in resolve when encountering the invader.

Field Marshal Schörner earned a reputation for brutality toward wavering German troops. Günter Grass recalled his fear when escaping from
the Spremberg pocket: "Even though I had no direct contact with the
enemy, I was scared to death. The soldiers hanging from the trees along
the road were a constant warning of the risk run by every one of us who
could not prove that he belonged to a company or was on his way to
this or that unit with signed and sealed travel orders." Grass concluded,
"Schörner and his orders were more to be feared than the enemy."[10]

Arguably more powerful than such negative factors in maintaining a
fighting spirit was the intense comradeship that had developed within
the Waffen-SS, which also focused men's minds exclusively on the battle
before them. Hauptsturmführer Heinz Meier of Leibstandarte wrote of
the deep bonds that bound them together: "In the fighting arm we were
all as if sheltered in a family, which explains the preparedness, up until
the obviously recognizable final collapse, to risk our lives for it. What else
really remained in this comradeship? In officers' circles we never discussed
other possibilities, that we must just keep on fighting. Hardly anybody
considered how it would look at the end, let alone mentioned it openly.
It is certain that even in the last hopeless days there was no question of
laying down our weapons."[11]

The resolve to fight to the last was evident in the performance of those
Waffen-SS units assigned to the defense of Berlin. And as these soldiers
waged an impossible battle in the rubble of Germany's capital, Adolf
Hitler took shelter in the Führerbunker, a concrete construction dug
underneath the Chancellery. Hitler's physical and mental deterioration
was obvious to all who saw him in the final weeks of the Thousand-Year
Reich, but the power of his will was undiminished.

On 20 April the Red Army was sufficiently close to Berlin that its
long-range artillery could pound the city center. The date was also Hitler's
fifty-sixth birthday, and he welcomed a gathering of leading Nazis who
included Göring, Goebbels, Bormann, Speer, Ribbentrop, and Himmler.
During the conference that followed the birthday speeches, it was agreed
that command of German forces outside of Berlin should be delegated
to others. Admiral Dönitz would be responsible for northern Germany,
while Field Marshal Kesselring would have control to the south. Hitler
was undecided whether he should stay in Berlin or fly out to the southern
redoubt in Austria and join his SS panzer divisions. After the conference,
Himmler left for the sanatorium in Hohenlychen (to the north of Berlin),
where he once again conferred with Count Bernadotte to bring about a
negotiated peace.

On 21 April a confident but deluded Hitler set about preparing what
he believed would be the operation to destroy the Soviet armies now besieging Berlin. He issued orders for Ninth and Twelfth Armies to march

on Berlin once they had united. In the meantime, he ordered Steiner's Eleventh SS Panzer Army to immediately drive toward central Berlin. By this time Steiner's force had been reduced to little more than a headquarters, as division after division had been removed to fight elsewhere. Hitler seemed unaware of this development, and his sudden, manic enthusiasm for the assault was unbounded. He demanded that every available soldier, tank, or aircraft be subordinated to Steiner, making it clear that "any commanding officer who keeps men back will forfeit his life within five hours."[12]

On 22 April Hitler eagerly awaited details of Steiner's offensive, but no information was relayed to the bunker. At 3:00 p.m. the daily staff conference began, and it was only then that the news arrived: there had been no offensive at all, made worse by reports that Soviet tanks were now within the city boundary. Steiner had not followed Hitler's orders on the basis that the formations promised him had not arrived and that to attack with the untrained Luftwaffe infantry and Hitler Youth at his disposal would be totally irresponsible.

Hitler flew into a rage whose virulence had never been seen before. He lambasted the failures of the German armed forces, lamenting that he was the victim of treason of all kinds. The tirade lasted a full three hours, after which an exhausted Hitler quietly declared he had had enough; the Third Reich had let him down, and he would remain in the bunker to await his inevitable fate.[13] According to historian George Stein, the reason for Hitler's extraordinary outburst was not just the failure of the Wehrmacht— which had "failed" him many times before—but what he saw as betrayal by the Waffen-SS. Hitler's stenographer Gerhard Herrgesell explained that the Führer had lost "confidence in the Waffen-SS for the first time. He had always counted on the Waffen-SS as elite troops which would never fail him." Herrgesell concluded that in Hitler's eyes, his special guard had "lost heart" and that "no force however well trained and equipped could fight if it lost heart, and now his last reserve was gone."[14]

Hitler's suspicions of SS treachery were confirmed when he heard of Himmler's attempts to secure a negotiated peace with the Western Allies on 28 April. Bernadotte had informed Eisenhower of Himmler's proposals, and the U.S. general had passed on the information to the BBC for its regular European broadcasts. A furious Hitler dismissed Himmler from the SS and ordered his immediate arrest. Hitler then instructed Wilhelm Mohnke, commander of the SS troops defending the bunker complex, to interrogate Hermann Fegelein, the former SS cavalry general who had been appointed as Himmler's representative at Führer headquarters. A drunken Fegelein, who was already under arrest for attempting to flee his post, admitted to having some knowledge of Himmler's plans. He was taken out of the bunker and shot. Himmler, meanwhile, fled north to Dönitz's headquarters at Flensberg in northern Germany.

On 29 April the Red Army closed on the city center, and at 1:00 A.M. on the thirtieth the Führerbunker was informed that all attempts to reach Berlin and rescue Hitler had failed. On the afternoon of 30 April Adolf Hitler committed suicide with his long-term mistress and now wife, Eva Braun, their bodies doused with gasoline and burned in the Reich Chancellery garden. Goebbels and his family followed the Führer's lead the next day. According to the terms of Hitler's last will and testament, Dönitz was made head of what remained of the Nazi state.

While Hitler had been fulminating at the treachery of those around him, the rank and file of the Waffen-SS in Berlin were faithfully adhering to their motto: "My honor is loyalty." As well as the remnants of the Nordland Division, other Waffen-SS units in Berlin included those from the French Charlemagne Division, a depleted battalion of Latvians, soldiers from Himmler's escort unit, and Leibstandarte battalion based in Berlin. Fighting alongside the Waffen-SS were battered army units, men of the (overage) Volkssturm, and boys from the Hitler Youth.

For the assault on Berlin, the Red Army had massed a substantial portion of the 40,000 artillery pieces assigned to the 16 April offensive; the sheer weight of the bombardment was without parallel, most of the city reduced to rubble. In addition to the barrage of shells falling on them, the defenders repelled constant tank and infantry attacks, thrown into the battle without regard to loss of life.

While the Volkssturm faded away at this onslaught, the Waffen-SS veterans were impressed at the bravery and skill of the Hitler Youth boys. Testimony came from Hans-Göta Pehrsson, a Swedish volunteer in Nordland, on the fighting of 27 April: "What made the greatest

impression on me were the 12–14 year-olds, the Hitlerjugend boy volunteers who crept through house ruins looking to destroy Soviet armor with
their Panzerfausts. I still can't understand how certain commanders sat in
their bunkers and drank while they sent out these small children to fight
in Berlin."[15] Fellow Nordland soldier Erik Wallin also praised the boys'
"boundless contempt for death." But they, and all the other defenders,
were unable to match the power of the Red Army, as Wallin recalled
while holding an abandoned house:

> Then they put in the heavy artillery. It sang and thundered all around and
> the blast waves threw us, half conscious, to and fro between the walls. The
> defenders who were killed by collapsing walls, ceilings and iron girders
> numbered more than those who got a direct hit. It became unendurable
> to stay in this inferno. Whirling stone, scrap iron and bloody body parts
> made the air impossible to breathe, filled as it was with limestone dust
> and gunpowder gasses. All day we fought our way back in this way. Sur-
> rounded over and over again, we struggled on through narrow passages
> and back streets. We always got through but with steadily growing losses.[16]

As the Red Army advanced on the Reich Chancellery, just over 300
French troops from the Charlemagne Division joined with what was left
of Nordland's "Norge" and "Danmark" regiments, both at subbattalion
strength. While many German troops began to surrender or discard their
weapons and uniforms and slip into the civilian crowd, the foreign SS
units fought on.

After Hitler's death, negotiations with the Red Army were initiated
for the surrender of Berlin. On 2 May the German garrison commander,
General Weidling, accepted the Soviet demand for unconditional surrender and ordered all German troops in the city to lay down their arms.
During the night of 1–2 May a breakout attempt had been attempted.
Only one group managed to escape Berlin, and most of these were subsequently killed or captured by Soviet troops already encircling the city; the
remainder surrendered to the Red Army.

DURING THE FIRST week of May, German theater commanders, realizing the futility of further struggle and released from their oath to Hitler (if not his successor), began to capitulate. On 2 May German forces in Italy and the western parts of Austria surrendered to the British, although fighting continued against partisans and Soviet troops as German rearguard units held open escape routes for those fleeing through Hungary and northern Yugoslavia. The 13th, 14th, 16th, 24th, and 29th SS Divisions were able to surrender to the British, but 7th SS Volunteer Mountain Division Prinz Eugen was less fortunate, overrun by Tito's partisan army as it struggled northward toward safety.[17]

In northern and central Germany, Waffen-SS troops trekked westward to the Anglo-American stop line on the River Elbe. At some river crossings, the western Allies refused to accept the escaping Germans, but such was their desperation that most forced their way over the river or drowned in the attempt. Those unable to reach the Elbe were rounded up by the Red Army. On 4 May German forces in northwest Germany, Denmark, and the Netherlands surrendered to Montgomery. Two days later Dönitz authorized General Jodl to travel to Eisenhower's headquarters at Reims, and at 2:41 A.M. on 7 May he signed the document for the unconditional surrender of all German forces to the Allies. General Keitel signed a further surrender document in Berlin in the presence of Marshal Zhukov. All hostilities were to end at 11:01 P.M. on 8 May.

Dietrich's Sixth SS Panzer Army in southern Germany and Austria conducted a fighting retreat westward to surrender to the advancing Americans. The elite but much-reduced SS panzer divisions had defended Vienna between 6 and 13 April, but to avoid entrapment and further destruction to the city, Dietrich ordered them to continue the retreat.

On 30 April the U.S. and Soviet commanders in Austria decided that the demarcation line between their two armies would be the River Enns and that German units would surrender to the side they had most recently been fighting.[18] The SS divisions—still engaged in delaying actions against the Red Army—were desperate to avoid capture by the Soviets. They negotiated with the Americans for permission to cross the Enns until midnight on 8–9 May for capitulation to the U.S. Army.

Stadler's Hohenstaufen Division had the good fortune to be deployed opposite the U.S. 71st Infantry Division. The two formations had fought each other during the Battle of the Bulge, and the American division's commanding officer had briefly been captured by troops from Hohenstaufen. He remembered the good medical treatment he had received from his SS captors and consequently welcomed Stadler and his men. Similarly, the Wiking Division had an unimpeded transfer into captivity, driving through U.S. forward lines on 8 May.

Not all units reached the Enns before the deadline, and some found the U.S. troops holding the crossings less than cooperative. One soldier from Leibstandarte described how his unit—the 1st Panzergrenadier Regiment—arrived at the river twelve hours late and was refused permission to cross. The regiment's commander, Standartenführer Max Hansen, had to use the threat of physical force to pass over the bridge: "With the help of several combat-ready panzers in the column we crossed the Enns without a fight. During the evening, after the vehicles could go no further, we set them on fire. We continued marching to the west and into captivity."[19]

The Totenkopf Division suffered most, the entire division failing to reach the demarcation line in time. On 9 May Brigadeführer Becker, Totenkopf's commander, was summoned to a local Soviet headquarters to be given the details of the surrender terms. Realizing that the division was about to be taken over by the Red Army, he sent covert orders for the entire division to immediately drive west and break through the thinly held American forward screen. Once across the demarcation line, most SS troops joined other Germans in a large U.S.-organized encampment some 20,000–25,000 strong. According to German accounts, they were left without food for three days before being ordered to march to a new camp, which turned out to be behind Soviet lines.[20] Thus, despite their best efforts to the contrary, the men of Totenkopf were now in Soviet captivity.

In the final weeks of the war, Das Reich was divided into separate groups. Those troops sent to the Dresden area were captured by the Red Army, although the bulk of the division in Austria managed to successfully cross over to American captivity. Otto Weidinger's "Der Führer"

Regiment had been ordered to Prague to hold the city against an uprising by Czech insurgents. As Weidinger closed on the Czech capital, he changed his mission to help German civilians escape from the insurgents and soon-to-arrive Red Army. He successfully led his troops and the civilians to Pilsen (Plzen), then held by the Americans.[21]

THE WAR WAS over, and the Waffen-SS had paid a high price for its place at Hitler's vanguard. Although the Waffen-SS suffered heavy losses, so too did the German Army; in overall terms their casualty rates were broadly similar, with fatalities for both standing at a little more than 30 percent. Precise casualty figures are hard to ascertain, the SS having a poor record in keeping and publishing accurate statistics. In broad terms, the Waffen-SS reached a peak strength of just under 600,000 men in midsummer 1944,[22] although more than 900,000 men passed through its ranks. Of that number, 310,000 were killed or died of their wounds.[23]

For all survivors, unconditional surrender was a bitter pill to swallow. When still on the front line—no matter how hopeless the situation—their energies were focused on the fighting itself. Once it had stopped, they faced the stark realization that they were prisoners and not soldiers anymore, forced to consider a future over which they would have little or no control. The men of the Waffen-SS, for so long the victors, were now the vanquished. Totenkopf antiaircraft gunner Werner Volksdorf, captured by the Americans in Munich while training recruits in gunnery duties, spoke for many after the surrender: "It had not really sunk in yet that the war was over for us, and that we were now a defeated army, a defeated country, a country occupied by foreign forces. Over five years of fighting and the struggle in the cause we believed in. This was a demoralizing end after so much suffering and blood sacrifice, with the sad memory of comrades and friends whom we had buried in foreign soil. We just didn't know what had hit us."[24]

Chapter 31

AFTERMATH

WHEN HIMMLER HEARD that Dönitz had been made head of state, he tamely accepted Hitler's decision, although he put himself forward as a second in command to the new leader in the belief that he would have some negotiating sway with the Allies. Dönitz, however, rejected Himmler's offer. When Himmler persisted, Dönitz sent him a letter of dismissal on 6 May. Now that he had been formally removed from all positions of power, first by Hitler and then by Dönitz, Himmler was forced back on his own resources. He had four choices: to be killed fighting to the last (an order issued to all SS soldiers in such a position), suicide, surrender, or escape. Himmler—without much forethought—chose the last option. As part of a small group of SS men, he took the identity of a sergeant in the field-security police and marched southward, hoping to be lost within the vast streams of soldiers, civilians, and refugees crisscrossing Germany.

Himmler was stopped at a checkpoint on 21 May, and because of his security-police uniform he was detained for further questioning. While under interrogation he suddenly admitted he was Heinrich Himmler, and after this bombshell he was immediately rushed to the main British camp at Lunenburg. On 23 May, while undergoing a medical examination that included an oral inspection, he turned his head away from the examining doctor and bit on a hidden potassium cyanide pill. Although the British interrogators did their utmost to prevent the pill from taking effect, Himmler was pronounced dead within fifteen minutes.

Three days later the former Reichsführer-SS was buried by a British officer and three NCOs in an unmarked grave on Lunenburg Heath.[1] Himmler's unheroic demise at least minimized the possibility that any remaining followers might rally around his memory. In fact, almost all those who had previously been part of the SS were only too keen to distance themselves from their former chief.

While Himmler had departed the scene, the men of the Waffen-SS faced a new life as prisoners of the Allies. Those captured by the Red Army feared the worse, well aware that retribution for the excesses of Nazi Germany over the previous four years must follow. Some Red Army soldiers killed Waffen-SS prisoners without compunction; the SS blood-group tattoo on their left armpit made the veterans vulnerable to close inspection. Most, however, were marched away to camps within the Soviet Union.

During the middle part of the war on the Eastern Front—when victory or defeat seemed to hang in the balance—the Soviet authorities displayed no interest in the welfare of their German prisoners, the majority dying of disease, starvation, overwork, and the cold. Later in the war, conditions in the camps began to improve, especially when German prisoners—eventually amounting to nearly 3 million men—became a useful source of labor. In 1946 the Soviet Union began a phased release of German prisoners, initially to the newly created Soviet-controlled East Germany. By 1949 the majority of prisoners had been freed to both Germanies, although those considered war criminals—including many in the Waffen-SS—had to wait until 1956 for repatriation.

In Yugoslavia, now under Tito's communist administration, people who had supported the Germans experienced varying degrees of retribution. According to the divisional history of the Prinz Eugen Division,[2] its soldiers captured by Tito's partisans were badly treated, and throughout the country there was the inevitable settling of scores among different ethnic groups. Tito realized, however, that if he was to unite the country under his rule, he would have to tread carefully, especially as so many of his citizens had in some way supported the Axis cause. While those accused of specific war crimes against the Yugoslav people were subject to the full rigor of the courts, a general amnesty was extended to the mass of followers who included most ordinary soldiers from the Waffen-SS divisions raised within Yugoslavia. In Tito's view, these people had been merely "seduced" by the Axis and could be exonerated through their participation in a new communist Yugoslavia.[3]

The Axis troops who had surrendered to the British in Italy and Austria faced very different fates. The Cossacks raised by the German Army in the Soviet Union—which in some cases included their families—had been sent to Yugoslavia to destroy Tito's partisans and in February 1945 had been transferred to the SS, to become the XV SS Cossack Cavalry Corps. In line with an agreement reached between the Allies at the 1945 Yalta Conference, all foreign nationals were to be repatriated to their country of origin. Stalin was determined to punish those who had in any way been involved with the Germans, while the British and American governments were fearful that their former POWs under Soviet control might not be released. As a result, thousands of the Cossack fighters—along with their women and children—were forcibly repatriated by British troops, sometimes at gunpoint. Once in Soviet hands, the leaders were killed and the remainder sent to slave labor camps in Siberia.

The Ukrainian troops of the 14th Waffen Grenadier Division of the SS were more fortunate. Thanks to lobbying by the Vatican, the International Committee of the Red Cross, and the Polish II Army Corps (then in Italy), they were nationally reclassified and not returned to the Soviet Ukraine. Briefly kept in an internment camp in Italy, some 9,000 former SS soldiers were allowed to travel to Britain,[4] where some settled, although a greater number continued on to North America to join its well-established Ukrainian communities.

The Volksdeutsche in Eastern Europe and the Balkans suffered grievously at the hands of their new masters. Stalin had decided that all able-bodied Volksdeutsche were liable to perform labor service in the Soviet Union. The Banat region in Yugoslavia was swept of its ethnic Germans, Tito handing over as many as 100,000 people to Stalin.[5] Soviet-controlled Hungary and Romania also witnessed large-scale forced transfers of Volksdeutsche, often from communities that had been established since the Middle Ages. Other Volksdeutsche had, however, managed to follow the withdrawing German armies, to begin new lives in

West Germany. In communist Poland there was a vast forced exodus of both Reich Germans and Volksdeutsche to Germany.

Foreign volunteers recruited from western and northern Europe were now reduced to the status of traitorous collaborators in their home countries. Popular anger was chiefly directed at the men who had worked closely with the Nazi national administrations. Death sentences were passed on the most visible—such as Quisling from Norway and Laval in France—while the remainder received substantial prison sentences. The former Waffen-SS soldiers fell into the latter category, although most were released after a few years. Some men decided not to face the music and remained in Germany.[6]

The millions of Wehrmacht troops captured by the Western powers in Germany were held in hastily erected POW camps. Conditions were poor at the beginning—with inadequate shelter and limited food supplies—and former Waffen-SS soldiers complained bitterly of their treatment, which included widespread theft of watches and insignia by souvenir-hungry guards.[7] The conditions endured by the Waffen-SS were, however, no worse than those experienced by captive Americans in 1944 and the British in 1940.[8]

Late in 1945 the first German prisoners were allowed to leave the camps, with further releases continuing over the next eighteen months. Germans captured earlier in the war and imprisoned in Britain and the United States were held on to for longer, even though in direct contravention of the Geneva Conventions. For the other ranks, their value as labor for the Allies was too useful to give up easily, and for officers, especially the hard-liners in the Waffen-SS, U-boat arm, and paratroop formations, there was a worry that they might form a pro-Nazi resistance when back in Germany. But by the late 1940s most German prisoners, including Waffen-SS, had been released. As a result of the devastated condition of postwar Germany and the good treatment afforded them by the Western Allies, small numbers of ex-Waffen-SS soldiers joined others from the Wehrmacht to permanently settle in Britain and the United States.[9]

THE ALLIES WERE determined to hold the Nazi regime accountable for its actions during the war, and at the International Military Tribunal held at Nuremberg surviving Nazi leaders were put on trial. One of the judgments made at Nuremberg was the ruling that the SS—including the Waffen-SS—was a criminal organization. The ruling infuriated Waffen-SS veterans, who protested that they had been unfairly singled out by the tribunal. There was some truth in their argument, but only to the extent that the entire Nazi regime was essentially a criminal enterprise, and on that basis all of its institutions should also have been similarly condemned (although, of course, such a decision would have been quite impractical). Following on from the indictments of the leading Nazis were a series of trials of men accused of specific war crimes. These included former members of the Waffen-SS, their trials concentrating on massacres of British and American troops and of civilians in France, Belgium, and Italy.

One of the first trials to be completed was that of the Hitlerjugend's Kurt Meyer. In a Canadian military court he was found guilty of inciting his men to commit murder and of being the officer in charge of the Hitlerjugend soldiers who had killed Canadian prisoners in cold blood during the opening phase of the Normandy campaign. Meyer was sentenced to death on 28 December 1945, although, on appeal, the sentence was commuted to life imprisonment. In September 1954 he was released from prison. Bernhard Siebken and Dieter Schnabel, Hitlerjugend officers during the summer of 1944, fared less well. Found guilty of the shooting of Allied prisoners, they were hanged on 20 January 1949.

A larger and more complex trial involved Waffen-SS men accused of killing U.S. prisoners around Malmédy during the 1944 Ardennes offensive. Some seventy-three defendants, mainly from the Leibstandarte Division and I SS Panzer Corps, stood before a U.S. military court. Among them were Sepp Dietrich, Fritz Kraemer, Hermann Priess, and Jochen Peiper, the latter having led the Kampfgruppe directly involved in the massacre. The court found them guilty on 16 July 1946, with forty-three sentenced to death (including Peiper) and the remainder to imprisonment, with Dietrich given life, Priess twenty years, and Kraemer ten.

During the trial the defendants protested at prior ill treatment, which, they claimed, included mock trials, torture, and forced confessions.

Subsequent investigations by U.S. military authorities accepted that the pretrial investigations had not been conducted in a proper manner, and as a consequence all death penalties were commuted.[10] By the early 1950s Allied attitudes toward the Waffen-SS softened, especially as the Cold War began to dominate the international political sphere, with West Germany now an ally against the Soviet Union. The convicted men were steadily released from prison, with the last—Jochen Peiper—let go in December 1956.

The French government's attempt to bring to justice the perpetrators of the Oradour and Tulle Massacres from Das Reich Division were largely thwarted by the subsequent deaths of the main protagonists and the inability to extradite others living in Germany. Nonetheless, 2 military tribunals were held in Bordeaux in 1951 and 1953, and in the latter tribunal all but one of the twenty-one defendants present were found guilty of war crimes, the sentences ranging from death to varying terms of imprisonment.

Complicating matters at the trial was the Alsatian background of many of the subordinates involved in the killings, who, post-1945, were once again French citizens. They argued that they had been coerced into the division as *malgré-nous* (against our will), and following a wave of protest in Alsace they were released as part of a general amnesty in February 1953. The remaining convicted men were also subsequently set free. Heinz Lammerding, the Das Reich commander sentenced to death in absentia, lived openly in West Germany until his death in 1971, the French government unable to secure his extradition for lack of "incontestable evidence" that he had committed murder.

Of the massacres of British prisoners in 1940, Fritz Knöchlein of the Totenkopf Division was hanged in 1948 for his role in the Le Paradis shootings, while Leibstandarte's Wilhelm Mohnke—considered by the British to be the officer most responsible for the Wormhoudt killings—was not brought to trial because of insufficient evidence. Mohnke denied having any involvement in the killing of British prisoners, and after release from Soviet imprisonment in 1955 he settled in the Hamburg region, where he lived until his death in 2001, aged ninety.[11]

Although many Germans accused the Allies of administering "victor's justice"—with might triumphing over right—the Western Allies were, for the most part, scrupulous in their proceedings against the Waffen-SS, erring on the side of the defense when the evidence was uncertain. Such an approach was in marked contrast to the dealings of the Nazi legal system, an irony probably lost on the SS men in the dock. The inability to find evidence of a sufficient standard to guarantee a conviction was a consequence of many factors that included German witnesses' understandable reluctance to condemn old comrades, the loss or destruction of incriminating paperwork, and, from around 1950 onward, the influence of an ever-increasing passage of time clouding memories and reducing the desire to enact retribution. By the mid-1950s the prosecution of former Waffen-SS soldiers declined rapidly.

THE TRAUMA OF defeat left its mark on the soldiers of the Waffen-SS, made worse by the accusations leveled at them by some former comrades in arms in the Wehrmacht and from sections of the West German civilian population. In the years after the surrender the veterans kept their heads down, but a renewal of confidence was evident in the late 1940s, witnessing the emergence of local support groups. In 1951 this led to the official formation by Otto Kumm of HIAG: Hilfsgemeinschaft auf Gegenseitigkeit der Angehörigen der ehemaligen Waffen-SS (Mutual aid association of former Waffen-SS members).[12] The organization proved an immediate success: 376 branches were established, and leadership was provided by Waffen-SS luminaries that included Paul Hausser, Felix Steiner, and Herbert Gille. It soon saw itself as representing the interests of all Waffen-SS veterans.

By its stated aim, HIAG provided material assistance to former Waffen-SS soldiers. It also campaigned for the overturning of the criminality clause assigned to the Waffen-SS—not least to enable veterans to enjoy the same legal and pension rights as the Wehrmacht—and for the release of the remaining captives. These included Sepp Dietrich and Kurt Meyer, who, once out of prison, became leading figures in the organization. At its peak in the late 1950s, HIAG membership reached 20,000, and with the charismatic appeal of men like Meyer and Dietrich, it enjoyed wide publicity throughout West Germany, but as a lobbying group it failed to translate influence into governmental action in favor of the Waffen-SS.[13]

HIAG was always a controversial organization, not least because many in West Germany's new government feared that it might operate as rallying point for a possible Nazi revival. With this in mind, Hausser wrote to all the political parties in the West German parliament in December 1951, reassuring them that HIAG was "firmly committed to the new democratic system" and that its role was merely to encourage "comradeship" within its membership and look after its "legal, social, and economic rights."[14]

Shortly after its establishment, HIAG developed the idea of holding mass meetings—*Suchdiensttreffen*—nominally to exchange information about Waffen-SS soldiers lost in action but also to strengthen the cohesion of the organization and provide an opportunity for old soldiers to reminisce over the war. The first such meeting, held in 1952, was carefully stage-managed as leading ex-officers declared their loyalty to the West German government. Their good work was undone, however, by a surprise intervention from their guest speaker, former paratrooper general Hermann Ramcke. Deviating from the HIAG script, Ramcke set about lambasting the government and accusing the Western Allies of being the "real war criminals"—his outburst greeted with resounding applause by the veterans.

Wider public reservations about the true nature of HIAG seemed to be confirmed by reports from other meetings where veterans marched in torchlight processions, openly wore (banned) SS insignia, and sang their old wartime songs with undiminished enthusiasm. Hausser was sufficiently worried by the damage done to HIAG's image that he issued a warning not to use "words and images that can be falsely interpreted."[15]

During the 1960s membership of HIAG began to decline, while its political affiliations moved toward the Far Right. A journalist from the magazine *Stern* infiltrated a gathering of veterans from I SS Panzer Corps in 1985 and revealed that attitudes had not changed over the years, the SS veterans making rabid anti-Semitic remarks and sarcastically denying the existence of the Holocaust.[16] But no matter how odious their views, the veterans posed no political threat to Germany; they were merely a small rump of old, unrepentant Nazis speaking in their cups. Rejected by mainstream Germany and rent by internal divisions, HIAG was disbanded as a national organization in 1992, although local groups remained in existence.

While HIAG lobbyists experienced mixed fortunes in their attempt to improve the reputation of the Waffen-SS, they were more successful in their publishing program. After HIAG's formation in 1951, a newsletter-journal, organized by Otto Kumm, was issued to members and called *Der Ausweg* (The Way Out), soon followed by *Wiking-Ruf* (Viking Call), the latter published by Herbert Gille. Both were superseded in 1956 by a new magazine, *Der Freiwillige* (The Volunteer), a long-term venture that included news for SS veterans and positive articles on their military actions, while attacking those critical of Germany's role in the war. The magazines were useful in keeping the membership together and publicly waving the Waffen-SS flag, but of greater significance were the book-publishing ventures that reached a larger and more varied readership.

The first significant work was Paul Hausser's *Waffen-SS im Einsatz* (*Waffen-SS in Action*), published in 1953, which, as well as extolling the bravery and honor of the Waffen-SS, made the superficially appealing yet false argument that the Waffen-SS was a multinational force of idealists fighting for a common European destiny. Hausser and his publisher persuaded Heinz Guderian to write a glowing foreword to the book. This represented more than a straightforward endorsement by an eminent soldier; it was a public declaration that the Wehrmacht was extending a hand of friendship to the Waffen-SS, suggesting that the differences between the two were perhaps not so great after all.

The Cold War—with the looming threat of the Soviet Union and the creation of the North Atlantic Treaty Organization (NATO)—played perfectly into the HIAG narrative of the Waffen-SS as defenders of the West. Hausser's book was followed by others that developed the idea further, notably Felix Steiner's 1958 publication, *Die Freiwilligen der Waffen-SS: Idee und Opfergang* (*The Volunteers of the Waffen-SS: Idea and Sacrifice*). The notion of the Waffen-SS as a Pan-European proto-NATO encouraged foreign SS veterans to make their own contributions. Among them was Léon Degrelle, who issued several books from his hideaway in

Spain that praised the European contribution to the Waffen-SS, with appropriate emphasis given to the author's role in the struggle.

A few battlefield memoirs from leading SS officers followed, notably Kurt Meyer's pugnacious and self-serving account of his experiences with Leibstandarte and Hitlerjugend Divisions. But it was not until the end of the 1990s that SS war memoirs came into their own, as works by junior officers and other ranks met the demand by a new generation of readers eager to find out more from firsthand sources. They were supplemented by illustrated histories that showcased the vast treasury of photographs of the Waffen-SS. Commercial success brought their exploits to a wider audience, not only in Germany but, through translation, to North America and Western Europe as well.

The publication of divisional and unit histories provided the heavy-weight support in HIAG's "battle for history." They were serious ventures, which in some cases—notably the histories of the Leibstandarte and Das Reich Divisions—were vast, multivolume works. They made extensive use of combat reports within a detailed narrative of the unit's or formation's activities on the battlefield and, where available, included testimonies to SS valor from the Wehrmacht and opposing armies. They were typically silent on Waffen-SS shortcomings, whether in terms of combat performance or involvement in atrocities.

The traditional regimental history—from any nation—has rarely dwelled on its subject's negative aspects, but the refusal of these books to address the fundamental question of Waffen-SS involvement in Hitler's war of extermination undermined their veracity. In HIAG's eyes, however, such criticisms were quibbles by enemies attempting to divert attention away from their story of heroic self-sacrifice.

From the perspective of ordinary SS veterans, this positive narrative was eagerly sought after and no doubt beneficial to their psychological well-being post-1945. To lose the war in such a crushing manner and to be widely condemned as mass murderers was sufficiently bad, but the idea that their efforts and the deaths of their comrades had seemingly been for nothing would have been all but intolerable. Quite understandably, the veterans looked for some level of meaning to justify the suffering they had endured, a meaning provided by the idea of their participation in the battle to save Europe from communism.

The old cliché that "history is written by the victors" proved wrong in this instance. The books sponsored by HIAG and written by the veterans filled something of a niche void in post-1945 historiography: they were the first on the scene, and in the wider publishing sphere they outnumbered (and outgunned) the critical, more nuanced works of academic historians.[17] HIAG's victory was confirmed by a succession of popular histories from younger writers—without direct connection to the war—who readily adopted the SS viewpoint with little, if any, further historical scrutiny.[18] Their works became part of a new orthodoxy of the "honorable" Waffen-SS, although this viewpoint did not go unchallenged in other popular histories, which while admiring the prowess of the Waffen-SS in battle did not exonerate them from the charge sheet of war crimes.[19]

THE FALL OF the Berlin Wall in 1989 and the collapse of communism in Eastern Europe was seized upon by the old veterans and their supporters as further vindication of their part in Germany's war against the Soviet Union. Henri Fenet, an officer in the Charlemagne Division and survivor of the final defense in Berlin, reflected the mood of self-congratulation in a speech reproduced in *Der Freiwillige* in 1998: "After a half-century, history has justified our mission. We have paved the way to independence and self-sufficiency, and now the Europeans are walking down the road that we, then, paved."[20]

The differing attitudes of Eastern European countries toward Soviet communism and Nazi Germany also supported the Waffen-SS conception of recent history. These countries had suffered under both tyrannical regimes, and post-1989 there was a feeling in some of them—especially Hungary, Estonia, and Latvia—that Stalin was the more evil of the two devils. This chimed with a strongly held belief that any organization that even appeared to have fought for national sovereignty was to be applauded. The Eastern European units of the Waffen-SS were included in this category, ignoring the fact that Hitler and Himmler had rejected any notion of national self-determination and were using them for their own cynical ends.

Waffen-SS veterans groups from Germany and the rest of Western Europe were invited to Eastern Europe to take part in celebrations otherwise banned in their home countries. HIAG had always wanted to publicly honor its fallen comrades with the construction of fixed sites as a focus for these commemorations.[21] This had proved difficult to carry out in Western Europe, where even unofficial sites built on private land were regularly defaced or destroyed by protesters. Only in the extensive private grounds at Ulrichsberg in Austria—with tacit support from the Austrian government—were the veterans able to organize rallies with permanent memorials.

Hungary publicly acknowledged the Waffen-SS in its annual "Day of Honor" celebrations, first held in 1997, which commemorated the defense of Budapest in 1944–1945. In something of a festival atmosphere—complete with flying flags, martial music, and the laying of wreaths—veterans from the Waffen-SS marched alongside those of the Wehrmacht and the Hungarian Army, to the applause of an appreciative audience of right-wing and neo-Nazi groups.

Latvia and Estonia were also prominent in welcoming Waffen-SS veterans from across Europe, who in turn donated relief supplies and money to their hosts. Support for the Waffen-SS was somewhat more controversial in the Baltic States, however, with its large minority populations of Russian-speaking citizens opposing the erection of memorials glorifying SS troops as freedom fighters. Despite this, Narva in Estonia became a key site of commemoration, the former battleground where Waffen-SS units from the Baltic States, Germany, and Western Europe had fought together in the defense of the city in 1944.

During the war on the Eastern Front, the Wiking Division had established a cemetery and memorial at Uspenskaja in the eastern Ukraine. It was later bulldozed by the Red Army, but in 1993 a small group of former Wiking soldiers and their relatives established a wooden cross for their former comrades, which in subsequent years developed into a substantial memorial. This initiative was welcomed by Ukrainian nationalists, who were also determined to honor the contribution of their own people who fought for the Germans in World War II. The veterans of the Waffen-SS Ukrainian Division were lauded as heroes in the struggle against the

Soviet Union, with graveyards to the dead carefully tended by volunteers and the division's distinctive lion insignia publicly and reverentially displayed by young Ukrainians. Unsurprisingly, these celebrations irked many Russians and helped stoke the fires of ethnic antagonism between the two countries.

Support for the Waffen-SS within Eastern Europe has always been fiercely nationalistic, running counter to the Western European concept of a multinational Waffen-SS, but such differences seemed not to have upset the warmth of their mutual friendship.

A more pressing concern for the elderly veterans was to make sure their version of history continued into the future. As a defensive-minded self-help group, HIAG had steadfastly refused membership to those who had not served in the Waffen-SS. But as its members died off from natural causes and its political lobbying became less important, outside support to continue their legacy was looked upon more favorably.

When HIAG broke up as a national organization in the early 1990s, local old-comrades groups brought in younger members who subsequently took over the publication of *Der Freiwillige*. A looser successor to HIAG also came into being, the War Grave Memorial Foundation "When All Brothers Are Silent" (Kriegsgräberstiftung "Wenn alle Brüder schweigen"). As the twenty-first century progressed, the idea of "a passing on of the torch" to a new generation was promoted in Waffen-SS publications. These followers were a mixture of younger family members, various types of Waffen-SS admirers, and supporters of Far Right and Neo-Nazi groups.

The influx into Europe of migrants from Africa and the Middle East in the early twenty-first century also acted as an inducement for right-wing elements to reuse the SS fantasy that they were modern-day warriors defending Western Europe from external threat. At a commemoration in Estonia in 2005, a Swedish neo-Nazi described his meeting with a Belgian veteran: "I run into a gigantic old man from Léon Degrelle's division. I am so eager standing over here with this two-meter man. He asks me, for the sake of their honor, to free Sweden from the foreign occupiers and explains that we Aryans will die if nothing happens. His stone-hard gaze softens a little at the thought of the perishing of the white peoples."[22]

The fawning encounter, as described here, gave further support to the idea not only of the Waffen-SS as a chivalric order, but, more chillingly, that its work was not yet done and needed others to finish it.

HIAG AND ITS successors had achieved much in keeping alive the story of the Waffen-SS as a noble military caste, protecting it from the unpleasant truth of history and politics. But what of the Waffen-SS as it actually existed? The Waffen-SS was, of course, part of the overall SS and can be properly understood only in that context. And it was the SS that represented the future of Nazi Germany, rather than the other increasingly muddled and corrupt agencies of the Nazi Party.

In Himmler's view, the postwar role of the Waffen-SS was to provide military backing for an SS-controlled racially organized Pan-Germanic Europe. It would (probably) not replace the German Army but through its greater political flexibility would perform the difficult actions that the army might be reluctant to perform.[23] Himmler made himself the most powerful individual in the Nazi regime aside from Hitler, well placed to take over the helm when the opportunity arose.

The wartime transformation of the Waffen-SS from a small elite guard to a large multinational army was necessary to allow the SS to become masters of postwar Europe; no other Nazi organization would have such a wide and powerful reach. The mass expansion inevitably caused immense difficulties for the administration branches, exacerbated by Himmler's divide-and-rule policy, giving equal weight to Gottlob Berger's Main Office and Hans Jüttner's Leadership Main Office. Their overlapping areas of responsibility were a constant source of conflict between the two branches, which undermined efficiency. And the recruitment of men from across Europe was even more problematic for the German officers and NCOs who were to train and lead them into battle.

It was the case that as the war progressed, external differences between the German army and the Waffen-SS diminished; the hardship and shared experience of fighting against overwhelming numbers brought them together. This convergence gave some comfort to HIAG's assertion that the Waffen-SS were merely "soldiers like any other."[24] Himmler, however, was aware of this development from the outset and fought to maintain a distinction between the two, and had Germany won the war it would have reemerged.

In a military assessment of the Waffen-SS, the seven panzer divisions maintained a high level of battlefield efficiency to the end, a remarkable achievement given the progressive qualitative decline of their reinforcements from mid-1943 onward. The Leibstandarte and Das Reich Divisions were elite formations by any standard, owing much to the high caliber of their officers and NCOs and the long and imaginative training they received in the years leading up to war. They fought almost continuously from 1939 to 1945, and as well as suffering heavy casualties their core of excellence was constantly being chipped away by the dispatch of high-quality personnel to form other SS units. At their height, roughly between 1940 and 1943, they had few if any equals on the battlefield.

The Totenkopf and Wiking Divisions stood only a little way behind, redoubtable veterans of the Eastern Front who battled it out to the end. Hohenstaufen and Frundsberg only took part in the latter stages of the war but fought creditably on both Eastern and Western Fronts. The last SS panzer division—the Hitlerjugend—repeatedly distinguished itself in the defensive fighting in Normandy, even if it proved less adroit in offensive operations.

Himmler and his propagandists held high hopes for Germanic and Western European volunteers. Recruitment levels did not live up to expectations, however, and German training and supervision were initially poor. Although individual units fought well on occasion—such as the Danish Legion at Demyansk—it was only at the end of 1943 that the Waffen-SS deployed Germanic forces that had any sustained battlefield presence. The Nordland Division and the assault brigades from Belgium (Flanders and Wallonia) and the Netherlands made a solid, if small, contribution to the war on the Eastern Front, but, in the considered view of historian Kenneth Estes, "their numbers may not have justified the efforts made by the Germans to recruit them."[25]

The Baltic states of Latvia and Estonia provided both volunteers and conscripts to the Waffen-SS. Although indifferently equipped and armed, and without sufficient training, they fought with considerable resolve in the defense of their homelands. But, once again, their limited numbers and late deployment at the front were insufficient for them to have any bearing on the war.

Of the other Waffen-SS formations displaying varying degrees of military ability, 6th SS Mountain Division Nord overcame its initial poor showing in Finland to demonstrate a commendable fighting spirit in the retreat from Finland and in Operation Nordwind. The 7th SS Mountain Division Prinz Eugen had some success against its only conventional military opponent, the Red Army, although its overall military performance was weak. The Ukrainian 14th Panzergrenadier Division recovered from its disaster at Brody in 1944 to successfully engage in antipartisan operations in Slovakia and Slovenia. The Florian Geyer Cavalry Division also demonstrated an aptitude for antipartisan warfare before being thrown into the maelstrom of the defense of Budapest. The remaining divisions displayed little combat aptitude, although to Himmler their prime function was in the political rather than the military sphere.

The martial swagger, ruthless behavior, dashing uniforms, and awesome weapons and equipment of the best divisions have ensured continuing popular appeal. This attraction is understandable, but when divorced from a wider historical context, it makes the men of the Waffen-SS appear as ordinary soldiers, rather than active participants in one of the most evil tyrannies of history. The story of the Waffen-SS is not one to celebrate or commemorate, but it does at least demonstrate the dangers of a powerful military organization coming under the command of a man like Hitler, consumed by hatred and determined to act out his violent fantasies on the people of an entire continent.

APPENDIX A
Waffen-SS Divisions

1ST SS PANZER DIVISION LEIBSTANDARTE SS ADOLF HITLER

1. SS-Panzer-Division Leibstandarte SS Adolf Hitler

Originated as a 117-strong headquarters guard for Adolf Hitler on 17 March 1933, it progressively expanded into a regiment, reinforced brigade, and panzer division. Fought in all the major European campaigns, establishing a reputation as a ferocious, buccaneering combat formation. Surrendered to the U.S. Army in Austria in May 1945.

2ND SS PANZER DIVISION DAS REICH

2. SS-Panzer-Division Das Reich

Formed from the three SS-VT regiments "Deutschland," "Germania," and "Der Führer," it was one of the original Waffen-SS formations, achieving divisional status in 1939. A first-rate division that provided many officers and units to create new SS formations. Surrendered to the U.S. Army in Austria and Czechoslovakia in May 1945.

3RD SS PANZER DIVISION TOTENKOPF

3. SS-Panzer-Division Totenkopf

Drawing most of its troops from concentration-camp guards, Totenkopf was organized as a division in 1939 and fought in the 1940 campaign in the West. Thereafter it was exclusively deployed on the Eastern Front, acknowledged as a crack combat division. Surrendered to the U.S. Army in Austria in May 1945, before being turned over to the Red Army.

4TH SS POLIZEI PANZERGRENADIER DIVISION

4. SS-Polizei-Panzergrenadier-Division

Formed from police units under Himmler's control, it became a division in 1939, though not formally assigned to the Waffen-SS until 1942. After frontline service around Leningrad, it was deployed in antipartisan operations on the Eastern Front and in Greece. Sent to support the Oder front in early 1945, surviving remnants surrendered to the U.S. Army on the Elbe in May 1945.

5TH SS PANZER DIVISION WIKING

5. SS-Panzer-Division Wiking

Formed in late 1940, the division first saw combat in the Ukraine in June 1941 and fought with distinction on the Eastern Front for the rest of the war. Although intended to draw upon Aryan volunteers from northwestern Europe, it was mainly staffed by Reich Germans and Volksdeutsche. Surrendered to the U.S. Army in Austria in May 1945.

6TH SS MOUNTAIN DIVISION NORD

6. SS-Gebirgs–Division Nord

Formed from Totenkopfstandarten, Kampfgruppe Nord was sent to Finland in 1941. Withdrawn to reorganize after the defeat at Salla, it was upgraded as a mountain division in June 1942, reinforced by Reich and ethnic Germans. Transferred to Western Europe after the 1944 Soviet-Finnish armistice, it took part in Operation Nordwind. Destroyed by the U.S. Army in March–April 1945.

7TH SS VOLUNTEER MOUNTAIN DIVISION PRINZ EUGEN

7. SS-Freiwilligen-Gebirgs-Division Prinz Eugen

Formed from Volksdeutsche during the winter of 1941–1942, the mountain division was engaged in antipartisan operations in Yugoslavia for most of its existence, earning a reputation for brutality toward the civilian population. Briefly deployed against the Red Army in 1944, it was overwhelmed by Tito's partisans in Slovenia in May 1945.

8TH SS CAVALRY DIVISION FLORIAN GEYER

8. SS-Kavallerie-Division Florian Geyer

Based around the experienced SS Cavalry Brigade, the formation achieved divisional status in June 1942. Deployed on the Eastern Front as a specialist antipartisan force, increasing numbers of recruits were supplied by Volksdeutsche communities. Transferred to Hungary in October 1943, it took part in the defense of Budapest in 1944–1945, where it was destroyed.

9TH SS PANZER DIVISION HOHENSTAUFEN

9. SS-Panzer-Division Hohenstaufen

Organized in the spring of 1943 around a core of youthful recruits from the Reich labor service (RAD), the division first saw action in April 1944 on the Eastern Front. Transferred to the West in June, it was involved in heavy fighting in Normandy and later at Arnhem. Took part in the ill-fated offensives in the Ardennes and Hungary, before surrender to the U.S. Army in Austria.

10TH SS PANZER DIVISION FRUNDSBERG

10. SS-Panzer-Division Frundsberg

A sister division to Hohenstaufen, the RAD-recruited Frundsberg fought on the Eastern Front in April 1944 and then in Normandy and at Arnhem. It took part in the Nordwind Offensive before transfer to Pomerania in early 1945. Virtually destroyed in the final battles south of Berlin, remnants surrendered to the Red Army or the U.S. Army on the Czech-German border.

11TH SS VOLUNTEER PANZERGRENADIER DIVISION NORDLAND

11. SS-Freiwilligen-Panzergrenadier-Division Nordland

Based around Wiking's "Nordland" Regiment, the division was created in March 1943 and emphasized its Scandinavian background, although most of its recruits were Balkan Volksdeutsche. It was sent to the Leningrad front and took part in the long retreat through the Baltic States that included the defense of Narva. Remnants destroyed in Berlin, April–May 1945.

12TH SS PANZER DIVISION HITLERJUGEND

12. SS-Panzer-Division Hitlerjugend

Created in April 1943 using sixteen- and seventeen-year-olds from the Hitler Youth, the division's leadership cadre came from the experienced Leibstandarte Division. Hitlerjugend fought with great tenacity during the Normandy campaign and also took part in the Battle of the Bulge in the Ardennes and the final offensive in Hungary. It surrendered to the U.S. Army in Austria.

13TH WAFFEN MOUNTAIN DIVISION OF THE SS HANDSCHAR (CROATIAN NO. 1)

13. Waffen-Gebirgs-Division der SS Handschar (kroatische Nr. 1)

Raised from Bosnian Muslims living in Croatia, the division was formed in March 1943, and after training in France it saw action in Yugoslavia in February 1944. Of limited military value, it began to fall apart in September 1944, although a Kampfgruppe fought on until the end of the war, the remnants surrendering to the British in Austria.

14TH WAFFEN GRENADIER DIVISION OF THE SS (GALICIAN/UKRAINIAN NO. 1)

14. Waffen-Grenadier-Division der SS (galizien/ukrainische Nr. 1)

Formed in April 1943 from volunteers in the western Ukraine, the division was all but destroyed in the Brody encirclement battle in July 1944. Subsequently re-formed, it took part in antipartisan operations in Slovakia and Slovenia, before combat against the Red Army in March 1945. Renamed 1st Division of the Ukrainian National Army, it surrendered to the British in Austria in May 1945.

15TH WAFFEN GRENADIER DIVISION OF THE SS (LATVIAN NO. 1)

15. Waffen-Grenadier-Division der SS (lettische Nr. 1)

Formed in May 1943 from the Latvian Legion and other SS-sponsored police units, the division first saw combat against the Red Army in November 1943, the beginning of a long retreat through Latvia and East Prussia. A detached battalion fought in the final defense of Berlin, while the remainder fell back to surrender to the Allies on the Elbe and at Schwerin.

16TH SS PANZERGRENADIER DIVISION REICHSFÜHRER-SS

16. SS-Panzergrenadier-Division Reichsführer-SS

Formed in November 1943 from the assault brigade that had originally been Himmler's escort battalion, additional manpower was supplied from Volksdeutsche sources. It served in Italy, against the Allies and Italian partisans, and also in Hungary, before retreating into Austria and surrender to the British in May 1945.

17TH SS PANZERGRENADIER DIVISION GÖTZ VON BERLICHINGEN

17. SS-Panzergrenadier-Division Götz von Berlichingen

Established in France in October 1943 from replacement units and Volksdeutsche, it suffered heavy casualties fighting the Americans in Normandy. A reorganized division took part in Operation Nordwind in 1944–1945 before being forced back into Germany and eventual surrender to the U.S. Army in Bavaria in May 1945.

18TH SS VOLUNTEER PANZERGRENADIER DIVISION HORST WESSEL

18. SS-Freiwilligen-Panzergrenadier-Division Horst Wessel

Using the 1st SS Infantry Brigade as a leadership cadre on its creation in January 1944, its personnel were largely supplied by Volksdeutsche. Involved in antipartisan actions in Croatia and Slovakia and in the defense of Hungary from the Red Army in 1944–1945. Transferred to Silesia in February 1945, it suffered heavy casualties, the survivors surrendering to Czech and Soviet forces.

19TH WAFFEN GRENADIER DIVISION OF THE SS (LATVIAN NO. 2)

19. Waffen-Grenadier-Division der SS (lettische Nr. 2)

Formed from Latvian troops in the 2nd SS Infantry Brigade and the Latvian Legion, it achieved divisional status in January 1944. Suffering heavy casualties during the retreat into Latvia in 1944, it remained trapped in the Courland pocket for the remainder of the war, the survivors either surrendering to the Red Army or fleeing into Soviet-occupied Latvia.

20TH WAFFEN GRENADIER DIVISION OF THE SS (ESTONIAN NO. 1)

20. Waffen-Grenadier-Division der SS (estnische Nr.1)

Drawn from the Estonian Legion and Wiking's Estonian "Narwa" Battalion, the division was created in January 1944 and took part in the successful defense of Narva. Reconstituted in January 1945, it fought in the final battles in Silesia; a few survivors reached American lines, although most were captured by the Red Army or killed by Czech partisans.

21ST WAFFEN MOUNTAIN DIVISION OF THE SS SKANDERBEG (ALBANIAN NO. 1)

21. Waffen-Gebirgs-Division der SS Skanderbeg (albanische Nr. 1)

Formed in April 1944, predominantly from Muslim Albanians, with the intention of fighting Tito's partisans. Incapable of concerted military action, however, desertions rose swiftly, and even the inclusion of a batch of German sailors was unable to stop the rot. Disbanded in November 1944, some troops were reassigned to Prinz Eugen.

22ND SS VOLUNTEER CAVALRY DIVISION MARIA THERESIA

22. Freiwilligen-Kavallerie-Division Maria Theresia

With a nucleus of experienced troops provided by Florian Geyer, the division was formed in May 1944, the bulk of its manpower supplied by Hungarian Volksdeutsche, plus some ethnic Hungarians. It was sent to support the defense of Budapest and destroyed during the abortive breakout from the city in February 1945.

23RD WAFFEN MOUNTAIN DIVISION OF THE SS KAMA (CROATIAN NO. 2)

23. Waffen-Gebirgs-Division der SS Kama (kroatische Nr. 2)

Created in June 1944 with a training cadre from Handschar, this mixed Croatian, Volksdeutsche, and Muslim Bosnian force never achieved true divisional status. Elements fought against the Red Army in October, but the whole formation was dissolved at the end of the month, some troops involved in the creation of 31st SS Volunteer Grenadier Division.

23RD SS VOLUNTEER PANZERGRENADIER DIVISION NEDERLAND (NETHERLANDS NO. 1)

23. SS-Freiwilligen-Panzergrenadier-Division Nederland (niederlandische Nr. 1)

Taking its number from the disbanded Kama Division, the former Nederland Brigade was upgraded to divisional status in February 1945. Took part in the German offensive in Pomerania during February–March 1945 before being caught inside the Halbe pocket. Survivors from the breakout surrendered to the U.S. Army on the Elbe.

24TH WAFFEN MOUNTAIN DIVISION OF THE SS KARSTJÄGER

24. Waffen-Gebirgs-Division der SS Karstjäger

Originally a battalion and then a regiment formed for antipartisan operations in the jagged limestone Karst border areas of Slovenia, Croatia, and Italy, it was upgraded as a division. Lack of personnel, however, saw it downgraded as a brigade in January 1945, where it fought in defense of the region against Tito's partisans and the Red Army. Surrendered to the British in May 1945.

25TH WAFFEN GRENADIER DIVISION OF THE SS HUNYADI (HUNGARIAN NO. 1)

25. Waffen-Grenadier-Division der SS Hunyadi (ungarische Nr. 1)

Authorized in November 1944 from Hungarian Army conscripts and volunteers, it was sent to Neuhammer in Silesia for further training. While still undergoing instruction, it was involved in the final Soviet offensives of early 1945. Two battalions were caught in heavy fighting before rejoining the main division in a retreat to Bavaria and surrender to the U.S. Army in May 1945.

26TH WAFFEN GRENADIER DIVISION OF THE SS HUNGARIA (HUNGARIAN NO. 2)

26. Waffen-Grenadier-Division der SS Hungaria (ungarische Nr. 2)

A companion formation to Hunyadi, it was created in November 1944 and sent to Silesia and then Poland for training. The Soviet offensive forced it back into Silesia in February 1945; from there it began a retreat westward, surrendering to the U.S. Army in Austria in May 1945.

27TH SS VOLUNTEER GRENADIER DIVISION LANGEMARCK (FLEMISH NO. 1)

27. SS-Freiwilligen-Grenadier-Division Langemarck (flämische Nr. 1)

Based around the Flemish Langemarck Assault Brigade, which had seen extensive service on the Eastern Front, the formation was upgraded to divisional status in September 1944, although its numbers and equipment were never more than at brigade level. Assigned to Pomerania in February 1945, it also fought on the defensive Oder Line before surrender to the Allies on the Elbe.

28TH SS VOLUNTEER GRENADIER DIVISION WALLONIEN

28. SS-Freiwilligen-Grenadier-Division Wallonien

Tracing its origins to the army's Walloon Legion, it fought in the Caucasus before transfer to the Waffen-SS and subsequent upgrading to an assault brigade and involvement in the Korsun-Cherkassy encirclement battle. Converted into a division in September 1944, it fought in Pomerania and on the Oder in 1945, before surrender to Allied forces on the Elbe.

29TH WAFFEN GRENADIER DIVISION OF THE SS (RUSSIAN NO. 1)

29. Waffen-Grenadier-Division der SS (russische Nr. 1)

The notorious Kaminski Brigade was absorbed into the Waffen-SS in June 1944. Upgraded to divisional status in August 1944, it caused further controversy during the brutal suppression of the Warsaw Uprising. As a consequence, the division was dissolved, the remnants transferred to General Vlasov's Russian Liberation Army.

29TH WAFFEN GRENADIER DIVISION OF THE SS (ITALIAN NO. 1)

29. Waffen-Grenadier-Division der SS (italienische Nr. 1)

After Mussolini's fall from power, new Italian fascist units were raised, the Waffen-SS forming a brigade in September 1944 to take part in antipartisan operations. In early 1945 the brigade was upgraded to divisional status—taking its number from the former Russian division—although it was a division in name only. It surrendered to the British and Italian partisans in April 1945.

30TH WAFFEN GRENADIER DIVISION OF THE SS (RUSSIAN NO. 2)

30. Waffen-Grenadier-Division der SS (russische Nr. 2)

Drawing personnel from the pro-German Belorussian home guard and other police (Schuma) units, a brigade force was nominally upgraded as a division under Waffen-SS leadership in August 1944. Transferred to France for training, it fought against the Free French in November 1944. The formation was broken up early in 1945, prior to surrender to the U.S. Army in Bavaria.

31ST SS VOLUNTEER GRENADIER DIVISION

31. SS-Freiwilligen-Grenadier-Division

Raised in October 1944 from a last trawl of Volksdeutsche from the Batschka region between Hungary and Yugoslavia, it was sent to fight in Hungary and suffered heavy casualties. Withdrawn from the line to recuperate, it was thrown back into combat in January 1945 in Silesia and was overrun by the Red Army. (It is not to be confused with a unit raised from SS training schools in Bohemia, the so-called Böhmen-Mähren division.)

32ND SS VOLUNTEER GRENADIER DIVISION 30TH JANUARY

32. SS-Freiwilligen-Grenadier-Division 30 Januar

Formed in January 1945 from SS training-school personnel and miscellaneous ad hoc units, the formation was assigned divisional status in February and fought on the Oder Line. Much of the formation was destroyed in the Halbe pocket and in the defense of Berlin, with only a few survivors reaching the Elbe to surrender to the Western Allies.

33RD WAFFEN GRENADIER DIVISION OF THE SS CHARLEMAGNE (FRENCH NO. 1)

33. Waffen-Grenadier-Division der SS Charlemagne (französische Nr. 1)

The numerical designation had originally been assigned to a Hungarian cavalry formation but was transferred to the upgraded French SS brigade in February 1945. Combining former army and Waffen-SS units, the division fought in Pomerania before a retreat to the Western Allies and surrender. A volunteer battalion fought its way into Berlin; it was destroyed in the final battle.

34TH SS VOLUNTEER GRENADIER DIVISION LANDSTORM NEDERLAND

34. SS-Freiwilligen-Grenadier-Division Landstorm Nederland

A home-guard, paramilitary formation, drawn from old SS veterans and Dutch Nazi groups, this assembly of infantry units was given divisional status in February 1945. It remained in the Netherlands and was torn apart by the Allied attack from the Arnhem position in April 1945, most surrendering to the British.

35TH SS POLIZEI GRENADIER DIVISION

35. SS-und-Polizei-Grenadier-Division

Created from whatever police personnel could be found as the war drew to a close, the formation was based around an SS paramilitary police brigade formed in the summer of 1944. Designated as a division in February 1945, it fought on the Oder Line and was destroyed in the Halbe pocket in April 1945, a few survivors escaping to Allied lines on the Elbe.

36TH WAFFEN GRENADIER DIVISION OF THE SS

36. Waffen-Grenadier-Division der SS

A February 1945 redesignation of the Dirlewanger Assault Brigade, which had achieved notoriety on the Eastern Front and in the suppression of the Warsaw Uprising in August 1944. Some troops from the army, training schools, and Volkssturm reinforced the formation, although all were overwhelmed in the fighting along the Oder Line in March–April 1945.

37TH SS VOLUNTEER CAVALRY DIVISION LÜTZOW

37. SS-Freiwilligen-Kavallerie-Division Lützow

An ad hoc combination of replacements and reserves from 8th and 22nd SS Cavalry Divisions not involved in the Budapest disaster, reinforced by other Hungarian Volksdeutsche soldiers. By March 1945 a Kampfgruppe from the division was committed to combat and fought alongside the Leibstandarte Division during the retreat through Austria.

38TH SS PANZERGRENADIER DIVISION NIBELUNGEN

38. SS-Panzergrenadier-Division Nibelungen

Formed in March 1945 from SS cadets and staff at the Bad Tölz training academy, plus soldiers from several other Waffen-SS units with a substantial contribution from Hitler Youth and RAD members. Ordered into battle on 24 April, it conducted a spirited defense against the Americans in Bavaria until ordered to surrender on 8 May 1945.

APPENDIX B

Waffen-SS Knight's Cross Holders by Division

Division	Number of awards
1st SS Panzer Division Leibstandarte SS Adolf Hitler	52
2nd SS Panzer Division Das Reich	72
3rd SS Panzer Division Totenkopf	46
4th SS Polizei Panzergrenadier Division	19
5th SS Panzer Division Wiking	54
6th SS Mountain Division Nord	5
7th SS Volunteer Mountain Division Prinz Eugen	6
8th SS Cavalry Division Florian Geyer	23
9th SS Panzer Division Hohenstaufen	12
10th SS Panzer Division Frundsberg	13
11th SS Volunteer Panzergrenadier Division Nordland	27
12th SS Panzer Division Hitlerjugend	15
13th Waffen Mountain Division of the SS Handschar (Croatian No. 1)	4
14th Waffen Grenadier Division of the SS (Galician/ Ukrainian No. 1)	1
15th Waffen Grenadier Division of the SS (Latvian No. 1)	3
16th SS Panzergrenadier Division Reichsführer-SS	1
17th SS Panzergrenadier Division Götz von Berlichingen	4
18th SS Volunteer Panzergrenadier Division Horst Wessel	5
19th Waffen Grenadier Division of the SS (Latvian No. 2)	12
20th Waffen Grenadier Division of the SS (Estonian No. 1)	4

21st Waffen Mountain Division of the SS Skanderbeg (Albanian No. 1)	—
22nd SS Volunteer Cavalry Division Maria Theresia	5
23rd Waffen Mountain Division of the SS Kama (Croatian No. 2)	—
23rd SS Volunteer Panzergrenadier Division Nederland (Netherlands No. 1)	20
24th Waffen Mountain Division of the SS Karstjäger	—
25th Waffen Grenadier Division of the SS Hunyadi (Hungarian No. 1)	—
26th Waffen Grenadier Division of the SS Hungaria (Hungarian No. 2)	—
27th SS Volunteer Grenadier Division Langemarck (Flemish No. 1)	1
28th SS Volunteer Grenadier Division Wallonien	3
29th Waffen Grenadier Division of the SS (Russian No. 1)	—
29th Waffen Grenadier Division of the SS (Italian No. 1)	—
30th Waffen Grenadier Division of the SS (Russian No. 2)	—
31st SS Volunteer Grenadier Division	—
32nd SS Volunteer Grenadier Division 30th January	—
33rd Waffen Grenadier Division of the SS Charlemagne (French No. 1)	2
34th SS Volunteer Grenadier Division Landstorm Nederland	—
35th SS Polizei Grenadier Division	—
36th Waffen Grenadier Division of the SS	1
37th SS Volunteer Cavalry Division Lützow	—
38th SS Panzergrenadier Division Nibelungen	—
Total	410

A further 38 awards were presented to Waffen-SS soldiers outside these formations. The list includes awards made to men in SS brigades before divisional upgrading.

Source: Wegner, Waffen-SS, 312.

ACKNOWLEDGMENTS

A WORK OF this nature relies heavily on published and other documentary material and I would like to thank the following archives and libraries: the National Archives (UK); the National Archives and Records Administration (US); the Imperial War Museum; the British Library; and the London Library. My gratitude extends to the knowledgeable and highly efficient staffs of these institutions. Among a number of individuals who helped with the project I must single out Herbert Walter (ex-Leibstandarte/Hitlerjugend) who answered many questions during an extended interview in the now distant past. And, of course, I would like to acknowledge the various copyright holders who have kindly given me permission to use material in the book.

I would like to thank my agent Andrew Lownie and the staff at Da Capo and Perseus books, who include my editor Bob Pigeon, Amber Morris, and Annette Wenda. The maps were expertly drawn up by Ed Darack. Finally, a mention must be made to my immediate family, not least for great forbearance over an extended period.

NOTES

Works listed in the Bibliography are abbreviated in the Notes.

ABBREVIATIONS

IMT: International Military Tribunal (Nuremberg)
IWM: Imperial War Museum
NA: National Archives, United Kingdom
NARA: National Archives and Records Administration, United States

INTRODUCTION

1. For Himmler's postwar plans for Europe, see Wegner, *Waffen-SS*, 126–128, 332–336, 343–350; and Wegner, "My Honour Is Loyalty," 228–231.

2. Wegner, *Waffen-SS*, 355.

3. For a full account of this deception, see Smelser and Davies, *Myth of the Eastern Front*.

4. See, for example, Bartov, *Hitler's Army*; Neitzel and Welzer, *Soldaten*; and Wolfram Wette, *The Wehrmacht: History, Myth, Reality* (Harvard UP, 2006).

5. For further discussion of the Waffen-SS and its postwar "battle for history," see Chapter 31.

6. Pontolillo, *Murderous Elite*; Goldsworthy, *Valhalla's Warriors*.

CHAPTER 1. FOUNDATION STONES

1. See Longerich, *Heinrich Himmler*; Padfield, *Himmler Reichsführer-SS*; and Höhne, *Order of the Death's Head*, 29–50.

2. Longerich, *Heinrich Himmler*, 115.

3. Ibid., 743.

4. Messenger, *Hitler's Gladiator*, 19.

5. Höhne, *Order of the Death's Head*, 55.

6. Lumsden, *Himmler's Black Order*, 142–146.

7. NA, WO 205/1021, Dietrich/1.

8. Nikolaus Wachsmann, *KL: A History of the Nazi Concentration Camps* (London: Little, Brown, 2015), 54.

9. Hoess, *Commandant of Auschwitz*, 235, 236.

10. Krausnick and Broszat, *Anatomy of the SS State*, 178.

11. For the SS role in the Night of the Long Knives, see Höhne, *Order of the Death's Head*, 93–131.

12. Sydnor, *Soldiers of Destruction*, 17.

13. Stein, *Waffen SS*, 7.

CHAPTER 2. CREATING AN ELITE

1. Hausser, *Soldaten wie andere auch*, 45.

2. Wegner, *Waffen-SS*, 20.

3. See, for example, Bartmann, *Für Volk and Führer*, 10.

4. Wegner, *Waffen-SS*, 134.

5. Stein, *Waffen SS*, 13.

6. For details of Bad Tölz, see Hatheway, *In Perfect Formation*.

7. Williamson, *Loyalty Is My Honour*, 34.

8. Ibid., 35–36.

9. Ibid., 36.

10. Volkner, *Many Rivers I Crossed*, 12.

11. Höhne, *Order of the Death's Head*, 446.

12. Hausser, *Soldaten wie andere auch*.

13. Messenger, *Hitler's Gladiator*, 66.

14. Williamson, *Loyalty Is My Honour*, 46.

15. Ibid., 47.

16. Walther, interview with the author.

17. M. Williams, *SS Elite*, 241.

18. Weingartner, *Leibstandarte SS Adolf Hitler*, 17–18.

19. Lucas and Cooper, *Hitler's Elite*, 27.

20. Padfield, *Himmler Reichsführer-SS*, 388.

21. Höhne, *Order of the Death's Head*, 439.

22. Messenger, *Hitler's Gladiator*, 66.

CHAPTER 3. THE MARCH TO WAR

1. Hoess, *Commandant of Auschwitz*, 236, 238.

2. See Sydnor, *Soldiers of Destruction*, 28.

3. Ibid., 29n.

4. Blanford, *Hitler's Second Army*, 19.

5. Sydnor, *Soldiers of Destruction*, 26.

6. Wegner, *Waffen-SS*, Table 6.1, p. 95.

7. Hitler, Nuremberg Doc 467-PS, in Weale, *The SS*, 221.

8. Stein, *Waffen SS*, 16.

9. See Wegner, *Waffen-SS*, 128–129, 340–343; and Hale, *Hitler's Foreign Executioners*, 20, 198, 358.

10. Weidinger, *Das Reich*, 1:40.

11. Ibid., 41.

12. Höhne, *Order of the Death's Head*, 451.

13. Longerich, *Heinrich Himmler*, 249.

14. Rossino, *Hitler Strikes Poland*, 7.

CHAPTER 4. THE DESTRUCTION OF POLAND

1. Blanford, *Hitler's Second Army*, 46.

2. Weidinger, *Das Reich*, 1:122–124.

3. K. Meyer, *Grenadiers*, 2.

4. XIII Armeekorps report, NARA T314 (roll number 509), accessed from www.axishistory.com/axis-nations/119-germany-waffen-ss/germany-waffen -ss-divisions/1243-1-ss-panzer-division-leibstandarte-ss-adolf-hitler.

5. Weidinger, *Das Reich*, 1:129.

6. Ibid.

7. Ibid, 136.

8. Rossino, *Hitler Strikes Poland*, 105–107. The incident was thoroughly investigated by the German Army and (postwar) by Jewish institutions.

9. Weingartner, *Leibstandarte SS Adolf Hitler*, 34.

10. See Rossino, *Hitler Strikes Poland*, 154–166; and Messenger, *Hitler's Gladiator*, 74.

11. Rossino, *Hitler Strikes Poland*, 159–160 (detailed postwar investigations were unable to discover any provocation to provide justification for the atrocity).

12. Weingartner, *Leibstandarte SS Adolf Hitler*, 33.

13. Lehmann, *Die Leibstandarte*, 168.

14. K. Meyer, *Grenadiers*, 6.

15. Weidinger, *Das Reich*, 1:184–185.

16. Ibid., 217.

17. Sydnor, *Soldiers of Destruction*, 42.

18. Rossino, *Hitler Strikes Poland*, 109.

19. Lehmann, *Die Leibstandarte*, 209.

20. Weidinger, *Das Reich*, 1:240.

CHAPTER 5. DEPLOYMENT IN THE WEST

1. Weidinger, *Das Reich*, 1:277.

2. Goldsworthy, *Valhalla's Warriors*, 18.

3. Weingartner, *Leibstandarte SS Adolf Hitler*, 38.

4. Höhne, *Order of the Death's Head*, 453.

5. Ibid., 452.

6. Ibid.

7. Wegner, *Waffen-SS*, 304.

8. Ibid., 124–125.

9. Blanford, *Hitler's Second Army*, 52.

10. Stein, *Waffen SS*, 34n.

11. See Sydnor, *Soldiers of Destruction*, 48–52.

12. Ullrich, *Like a Cliff in the Ocean*, 14.

CHAPTER 6. INVADING THE NETHERLANDS

1. Weidinger, *Das Reich*, 2:19.

2. Lehmann, *Die Leibstandarte*, 1:229.

3. Hausser in Lucas, *Das Reich*, 38.

4. Weidinger, *Das Reich*, 2:44.

5. For a detailed narrative of the Grebbeberg battle, see A. M. A. Goossens, www.waroverholland.com; and Weidinger, *Das Reich*, 2:24–35.

6. Weidinger, *Comrades to the End*, 33.

7. Stein, *Waffen SS*, 65.

8. K. Meyer, *Grenadiers*, 15.

9. Weidinger, *Das Reich*, 2:67.

CHAPTER 7. THE ASSAULT ON FRANCE

1. Ullrich, *Like a Cliff in the Ocean*, 15.

2. Ibid., 18.

3. Leleu, "SS Division Totenkopf."

4. Ibid.

5. All figures (ibid.) drawn from local town registers.

6. Weidinger, *Das Reich*, 2:72.

7. Ibid., 79–83. See also Sydnor, *Soldiers of Destruction*, 98–101.

8. Reitlinger, *The SS*, 148. See also Sydnor, *Soldiers of Destruction*, 98–101.

9. Guderian, *Panzer Leader*, 117.

10. Sydnor, *Soldiers of Destruction*, 104–105.

11. For details of the massacre, see Cyril Jolly, *The Vengeance of Private Pooley* (London: Heinemann, 1956). For the problematic nature of battlefield surrender, see Adrian Gilbert, *POW: Allied Prisoners in Europe, 1939–1945* (London: John Murray, 2006).

12. Sydnor, *Soldiers of Destruction*, 108.

13. Weidinger, *Das Reich*, 2:96.

14. Stein, *Waffen SS*, 78.

15. Guderian, *Panzer Leader*, 118. See also Messenger, *Hitler's Gladiator*, 82–83.

16. Marcus Cunliffe, *History of the Royal Warwickshire Regiment, 1919–1950* (London: William Clowes, 1956), 59–60. See also Leslie Atkin, *Massacre on the Road to Dunkirk: Wormhout, 1940* (London: Kimber, 1977).

17. Sayer and Botting, *Hitler's Last General*.

CHAPTER 8. FRANCE DEFEATED

1. Weingartner, *Leibstandarte SS Adolf Hitler*, 43.

2. Ullrich, *Like a Cliff in the Ocean*, 31–32.

3. Ibid., 30.

4. Sydnor, *Soldiers of Destruction*, 112–113.

5. Ibid., 112.

6. K. Meyer, *Grenadiers*, 24.

7. Stein, *Waffen SS*, 88.

8. Weidinger, *Das Reich*, 2:165.

9. Ibid., 174.

10. Ullrich, *Like a Cliff in the Ocean*, 38.

11. Sydnor, *Soldiers of Destruction*, 117.

12. Ullrich, *Like a Cliff in the Ocean*, 39.

13. See Rafael Scheck, *Hitler's African Victims: The German Army Massacres of Black French Soldiers in 1940* (Cambridge: Cambridge University Press, 2010).

14. Neitzel and Welzer, *Soldaten*, 304.

15. Lehmann, *Die Leibstandarte*, 306.

16. Weidinger, *Das Reich*, 2:188.

17. Ibid., 201.

18. Yerger, *SS-Obersturmführer Otto Weidinger*, 52.

19. Wegner, *Waffen-SS*, 312.

20. Neitzel and Welzer, *Soldaten*, 283.

21. See Gordon Williamson, *Knight's Cross of the Iron Cross: A History* (Poole: Blanford, 1987).

22. Neitzel and Welzer, *Soldaten*, 283–284.

23. Leleu, "SS Division Totenkopf."

CHAPTER 9. TRANSITION AND EXPANSION

1. Blanford, *Hitler's Second Army*, 64.

2. Sydnor, *Soldiers of Destruction*, 127n.

3. Höhne, *Order of the Death's Head*, 467.

4. Weidinger, *Das Reich*, 2:218.

5. See Pieper, *Fegelein's Horsemen*, 2–46.

6. Ibid., 39.

7. Wegner, *Waffen-SS*, 342.

8. See Christensen et al., "Germanic Volunteers," 45.

9. Wegner, *Waffen-SS*, 341.

10. Longerich, *Heinrich Himmler*, 498–499.

11. Christensen et al., "Germanic Volunteers," 51.

12. Estes, *European Anabasis*, 31–35.

13. Ibid., 33.

14. Strassner, *European Volunteers*, 293.

15. Lumans, *Himmler's Auxiliaries*, 12. Hale, *Hitler's Foreign Executioners*, 54, suggests a higher figure of 13 million.

16. Höhne, *Order of the Death's Head*, 458.

17. Lumans, *Himmler's Auxiliaries*, 28.

18. Longerich, *Heinrich Himmler*, 502.

CHAPTER 10. BALKAN DIVERSION

1. Weidinger, *Das Reich*, 2:234.

2. Ibid., 236.

3. Ibid., 244.

4. Lehmann, *Die Leibstandarte*, 373–374.

5. Quassowski, *Twelve Years with Hitler*, 127.

6. Ibid.

7. *Canadian Military History* 11, no. 4 (2002): 3.

8. K. Meyer, *Grenadiers*, 51.

9. See Messenger, *Hitler's Gladiator*, 93–94; and Weingartner, *Leibstandarte SS Adolf Hitler*, 54–55.

10. Messenger, *Hitler's Gladiator*, 215.

11. Weingartner, *Leibstandarte SS Adolf Hitler*, 55.

12. K. Meyer, *Grenadiers*, 60.

13. Ibid., 62.

14. Messenger, *Hitler's Gladiator*, 94.

CHAPTER 11. OPERATION BARBAROSSA

1. Blanford, *Hitler's Second Army*, 74.

2. From John Erickson, *The Road to Stalingrad* (London: Weidenfeld & Nicolson, 1983), 98.

3. Dear and Foot, *Oxford Companion to the Second World War*, 434.

4. Erickson, *The Road to Stalingrad*, 98.

5. For these and ensuing figures, see Koehl, *Black Corps*, 200; and Stein, *Waffen SS*, 20.

6. Quassowski, *Twelve Years with Hitler*, 147.

7. The circumstantial evidence provided by Soviet defector Viktor Suvorov in *Icebreaker: Who Started the Second World War* (London: Hamish Hamilton, 1990) to support the idea of imminent Soviet invasion can be discounted.

8. IMT 31:84.

9. Goldsworthy, *Valhalla's Warriors*, 5.

10. Michael Jones, *The Retreat: Hitler's First Defeat* (London: John Murray, 2009), 23.

11. See, for example, Strassner, *European Volunteers*, 16; and Guderian, *Panzer Leader*, 152.

12. Förster, "Wehrmacht and the War of Extermination."

13. Neitzel and Welzer, *Soldaten*, 5.

14. Höhne, *Order of the Death's Head*, 469.

15. Tuff, in the Norwegian NRK TV documentary: Swww.nrk.no/doku mentar/--nordmenn-deltok-i-drap-pa-sivile-1.11262316. See also Richard Rhodes, *Masters of Death: The SS-Einsatzgruppen and the Invention of the Holocaust* (London: Vintage, 2003), 63–64.

16. Müller, *Unknown Eastern Front*, 128.

17. Estes, *European Anabasis*, 37.

18. Gutmann, "Debunking the Myth of the Volunteers," 585.

19. Smith, Poulsen, and Christensen, "Danish Volunteers in the Waffen SS," 92.

20. Estes, *European Anabasis*, 36–39.

21. Ibid., 44.

22. Blanford, *Hitler's Second Army*, 92.

23. Ibid.

24. Felix Steiner, *Die Freiwilligen der Waffen-SS: Idee und Opfergang* (Oldendorf: Pruess, 1973), 373.

25. See, for instance, Stein, *Waffen SS*, 139.

26. Hirschfeld, *Nazi Rule and Dutch Collaboration*, 287; Christensen et al., "Germanic Volunteers," 42.

27. Weidinger, *Comrades to the End*, 69.

CHAPTER 12. ADVANCE ON LENINGRAD: ARMY GROUP NORTH

1. Ullrich, *Like a Cliff in the Ocean*, 28.

2. Sydnor, *Soldiers of Destruction*, 163n.

3. Ullrich, *Like a Cliff in the Ocean*, 54.

4. Ibid., 73.

5. Ibid., 55.

6. Ibid., 90.

7. Ibid.

8. Manstein, *Lost Victories*, 113–114. See also Melvin, *Manstein: Hitler's Greatest General*, 215.

9. Sydnor, *Soldiers of Destruction*, 177.

10. Ibid., 187.

11. Ullrich, *Like a Cliff in the Ocean*, 99. Sydnor, *Soldiers of Destruction*, 186, has Eicke return on 21 September.

12. Sydnor, *Soldiers of Destruction*, 192.

13. Ullrich, *Like a Cliff in the Ocean*, 102.

14. Ibid., 119.

15. Blanford, *Hitler's Second Army*, 105–106.

16. Ullrich, *Like a Cliff in the Ocean*, 120.

17. Ziemke, *German Northern Theater of Operations*, 157–163; Stein, *Waffen SS*, 131.

CHAPTER 13. ACROSS THE UKRAINE: ARMY GROUP SOUTH

1. See Strassner, *European Volunteers*, 18. Strassner uses the term *Gefechtsgruppe* (fighting group) to describe the reinforced regimental unit; I have kept to the more usual, broadly synonymous *Kampfgruppe*.

2. Weingartner, *Leibstandarte SS Adolf Hitler*, 60.

3. Strassner, *European Volunteers*, 23.

4. www.http://yahadmap.org/#village/tarashcha-kyiv-ukraine.675.

5. Stahl, *Eyewitness to Hell*, 56–59 (previously published as *Dance of Death* by Erich Kern). Stahl/Kern is Reitlinger's source.

6. Reitlinger, *The SS*, 170–171. The normally reliable Stein, *Waffen SS*, 133, seems to confuse the supposed Kherson incident with the Taganrog

killings. For a balanced summary of the controversy, see Messenger, *Hitler's Gladiator*, 100–101.

7. Bartmann, *Für Volk and Führer*, 64; Maeger, *Lost Honour, Betrayed Loyalty*, 61; Christensen et al., "Germanic Volunteers," 66.

8. Robert Kershaw, *War Without Garlands* (Hersham: Ian Allen, 2008), 364–368; Messenger, *Hitler's Gladiator*, 102.

9. Strassner, *European Volunteers*, 32–33.

10. Ibid., 33.

11. Lucas and Cooper, *Hitler's Elite*, 101.

12. K. Meyer, *Grenadiers*, 123.

13. Strassner, *European Volunteers*, 41. Weingartner, *Leibstandarte SS Adolf Hitler*, 63, puts forward a higher figure of 100,000 prisoners.

14. Ibid., 42.

15. Ibid., 42–43.

16. Ibid., 47.

17. Lucas and Cooper, *Hitler's Elite*, 109.

18. Messenger, *Hitler's Gladiator*, 105.

CHAPTER 14. DRIVE ON MOSCOW: ARMY GROUP CENTER

1. Franz Halder, "War Journal" (prepared by the Office of Chief Counsel for War Crimes, Office of Military Government, United States), 3 July 1941, 6:196.

2. Eddie Bauer, *The History of World War II* (London: Orbis, 1979), 174.

3. Weidinger, *Das Reich*, 2:290.

4. Ibid., 308.

5. Lucas, *Das Reich*, 61.

6. Weidinger, *Das Reich*, 2:349.

7. Halder, "War Journal," 11 August 1941, 7:36.

8. Weidinger, *Comrades to the End*, 82.

9. Pieper, *Fegelein's Horsemen*, 88, 89, 120.

10. Lucas, *Das Reich*, 73.

11. Weidinger, *Comrades to the End*, 93.

12. Goldsworthy, *Valhalla's Warriors*, 64.

13. Weidinger, *Comrades to the End*, 95.

14. Lucas, *Das Reich*, 70.

CHAPTER 15. HOLDING THE LINE: EASTERN FRONT, 1941–1942

1. Dear and Foot, *Oxford Companion to the Second World War*, 113.

2. Halder, "War Journal," 17 March 1941, 6:27.

3. Messenger, *Hitler's Gladiator*, 105.

4. Trevor-Roper, *Hitler's Table Talk*, 168.

5. Richard Overy, *Interrogations: Inside the Mind of the Nazi Elite* (London: Penguin Books, 2002), 275.

6. Stein, *Waffen SS*, 135.

7. Strassner, *European Volunteers*, 20.

8. Ullrich, *Like a Cliff in the Ocean*, 148.

9. Weidinger, *Comrades to the End*, 108.

10. Weingartner, *Leibstandarte SS Adolf Hitler*, 70.

11. Sydnor, *Soldiers of Destruction*, 217.

12. Verton, *In the Fire of the Eastern Front*, 95.

13. *Military Improvisation During the Russian Campaign* (Washington, DC: U.S. Army, CMH), 51.

14. Verton, *In the Fire of the Eastern Front*, 79.

15. Ibid., 74–75.

16. Bartmann, *Für Volk and Fatherland*, 70.

17. Weidinger, *Comrades to the End*, 104–105.

18. Lucas, *Das Reich*, 78.

19. See ibid., 79; and Weidinger, *Comrades to the End*, 115.

20. Lucas, *Das Reich*, 80.

21. Pieper, *Fegelein's Horsemen*, 145.

22. Ibid., 144.

23. Ullrich, *Like a Cliff in the Ocean*, 144.

24. Sydnor, *Soldiers of Destruction*, 208–226.

25. Padfield, *Himmler Reichsführer-SS*, 369; Sydnor, *Soldiers of Destruction*, 239–230.

26. Ullrich, *Like a Cliff in the Ocean*, 172.

27. Smith, Poulsen, and Christensen, "Danish Volunteers in the Waffen SS," 80.

28. II Army Corps communiqué, in Ullrich, *Like a Cliff in the Ocean*, 172.

29. Estes, *European Anabasis*, 39.

30. Sydnor, *Soldiers of Destruction*, 244–245.

31. Ibid., 250.

32. Ullrich, *Like a Cliff in the Ocean*, 173.

CHAPTER 16. AT THE EDGE: THE EASTERN FRONT, 1942–1943

1. For the SS legions on the Eastern Front, see Estes, *European Anabasis*, 38–52; Böhler and Gerwarth, *Waffen-SS*, 51–60; and Müller, *Unknown Eastern Front*.

2. Estes, *European Anabasis*, 51.

3. Blanford, *Hitler's Second Army*, 112.

4. Ibid., 112–113.

5. Estes, *European Anabasis*, 42.

6. For the origins of Waffen-SS armored units, see Fey, *Armor Battles of the Waffen SS*; Tiemann, *Chronicle of the 7. Panzer-Kompanie*; Klapdor, *Viking Panzers*; and Agte, *Wittmann and the Waffen SS Tiger Commanders*, vol. 1.

7. Strassner, *European Volunteers*, 78, 70.

8. Ibid., 70.

9. Klapdor, *Viking Panzers*, 54.

10. Strassner, *European Volunteers*, 86.

11. Klapdor, *Viking Panzers*, 83.

12. For the Steiner-Ott dispute, see Strassner, *European Volunteers*, 87–94; and Klapdor, *Viking Panzers*, 78, 85–89, 96, 101.

13. Klapdor, *Viking Panzers*, 86–87.

14. Ibid., 96.

15. Ibid., 101.

16. Ibid., 141.

CHAPTER 17. KHARKOV COUNTERSTROKE

1. Stein, *Waffen SS*, 203.

2. Sydnor, *Soldiers of Destruction*, 258.

3. Kindler, *Obedient unto Death*, 23, 44.

4. For Tiger tanks in the Waffen-SS, see Agte, *Wittmann and the Waffen SS Tiger Commanders*, 1:1–26.

5. Sydnor, *Soldiers of Destruction*, 262–263.

6. Maeger, *Lost Honour, Betrayed Loyalty*, 81.

7. Lehmann, *The Leibstandarte*, 40 (this is a surprisingly high figure; Totenkopf managed with 120 trains for the same transit).

8. Ibid., 59.

9. Peiper has proved a magnet for biographers, among them Parker, *Hitler's Warrior*; Bouwmeester, *Beginning of the End*; Jens Westemeier, *Joachim Peiper: A Biography of Himmler's SS Commander* (Atglen, PA: Schiffer, 2007); Michael Reynolds, *The Devil's Adjutant: Jochen Peiper, Panzer Leader* (Staplehurst: Spellmount, 1995); and Patrick Agte, *Jochen Peiper: Commander Panzer Regiment Leibstandarte* (Winnipeg: Fedorowicz, 1999).

10. See, for example, remarks by Peiper's then battalion commander, Albert Frey, in Parker, *Hitler's Warrior*, 354n.

11. Lehmann, *The Leibstandarte*, 64.

12. Parker, *Hitler's Warrior*, 94. See also NA WO 208/4295.

13. Parker, *Hitler's Warrior*, 354. Peiper's unit was nicknamed the "Blowtorch Battalion."

14. Sydnor, *Soldiers of Destruction*, 267–268. Sydnor also suggests that this incident influenced Hitler to accept the Manstein plan (268).

15. Fey, *Armor Battles of the Waffen SS*, 14.

16. Weidinger, *Comrades to the End*, 130.

17. Meyer's actions were confirmed in two separate Waffen-SS accounts (as well as postwar Ukrainian testimonies). See Parker, *Hitler's Warrior*, 96.

18. Maeger, *Lost Honour, Betrayed Loyalty*, 130.

19. Weidinger, *Comrades to the End*, 138.

20. Manstein, *Lost Victories*, 435.

21. Weidinger, *Comrades to the End*, 145.

22. Parker, *Hitler's Warrior*, 95.

23. Agte, *Jochen Peiper*, 56.

24. Weingartner, *Leibstandarte SS Adolf Hitler*, 77.

25. Weidinger, *Comrades to the End*, 144 (individual divisional losses comprised Leibstandarte, 167 officers and 4,373 NCOs and enlisted men; Das Reich, 102 and 4,396; Totenkopf, 94 and 2,170; corps units, 2 and 215).

CHAPTER 18. KURSK: CLASH OF ARMOR

1. Messenger, *Hitler's Gladiator*, 117.

2. NA WO 205/1021, Wisch.

3. Gordon Williamson, *Knight's Cross, Oak-Leaves and Swords Recipients, 1941–45* (Oxford: Osprey, 2005), 30.

4. Weidinger, *Comrades to the End*, 177.

5. Dear and Foot, *Oxford Companion to the Second World War*, 660.

6. Volkner, *Many Rivers I Crossed*, 37–38.

7. Lucas and Cooper, *Hitler's Elite*, 213.

8. Lucas, *Das Reich*, 105.

9. Fey, *Armor Battles of the Waffen SS*, 20.

10. Agte, *Wittmann and the Waffen SS Tiger Commanders*, 103, 105.

11. Lucas, *Das Reich*, 108.

12. See Nipe, *Decision in the Ukraine*; and Glantz and House, *The Battle of Kursk*.

13. Kindler, *Obedient unto Death*, 85.

14. Nipe, *Decision in the Ukraine*, 49–50.

15. Ibid., 52; George M. Nipe Jr., "Battle of Kursk: Germany's Lost Victory in World War II," *World War II* (February 1998).

16. Stein, *Waffen SS*, 214.

17. Skorzeny, *Skorzeny's Special Missions*, 45–46.

CHAPTER 19. AN ARMY OF EUROPEANS

1. Estes, *European Anabasis*, 113.

2. Christensen et al., "Germanic Volunteers," 64.

3. Estes, *European Anabasis*, 119.

4. Ibid., 112n.

5. For the Walloon Brigade, see Bruyne and Rikmenspoel, *For Rex and for Belgium*.

6. For the Frankreich Brigade, see Forbes, *For Europe*.

7. For the British Free Corps, see Weale, *Renegades: Hitler's Englishmen*.

8. Kumm, *Prinz Eugen*, 17.

9. Wittmann, *Balkan Nightmare*, 71.

10. Casagrande et al., "Volksdeutsche," 232.

11. Figures from Stein, *Waffen SS*, 173.

12. Ibid., 172.

13. Blanford, *Hitler's Second Army*, 120.

14. Woltersdorf, *Gods of War*, 26–27.

15. Christensen et al., "Germanic Volunteers," 74.

16. Wittmann, *Balkan Nightmare*, 80.

17. Lepre, *Himmler's Bosnian Division*, 17—a detailed account of the Handschar Division. See also Bougarel et al., "Muslim SS Units," 252–283; and Hale, *Hitler's Foreign Executioners*, 262–292.

18. Lepre, *Himmler's Bosnian Division*, 42.

19. Bougarel, "Muslim SS Units," 256–257.

20. Lepre, *Himmler's Bosnian Division*, 52.

21. Hale, *Hitler's Foreign Executioners*, 300–302.

22. Melnyk, *To Battle*, 31.

23. Młynarczyk et al., "Eastern Europe," 200–201.

24. Heike, *Ukrainian Division "Galicia,"* 6.

25. For the involvement of the Baltic States within the Waffen-SS, see Müller, *Unknown Eastern Front*, 158–183; and Kott et al., "Baltic States," 120–164.

26. For Latvian SS formations, see www.latvianlegion.org; and Svencs, "Latvian Legion," 58–78.

27. For Estonian SS formations, see www.ecstileegion.com.

CHAPTER 20. DEFENDING THE UKRAINE

1. Fey, *Armor Battles of the Waffen SS*, 40.

2. Ibid., 43.

3. Mellenthin, *Panzer Battles*, 308.

4. Fey, *Armor Battles of the Waffen SS*, 52.

5. Agte, *Wittmann and the Waffen SS Tiger Commanders*, 177.

6. See Parker, *Hitler's Warrior*, 104–105.

7. Kindler, *Obedient unto Death*, 104.

8. Parker, *Hitler's Warrior*, 106.

9. Weidinger, *Comrades to the End*, 241.

10. Zetterling and Frankson, *Korsun Pocket*. See also Bruyne and Rikmenspoel, *For Rex and Belgium*, 119–125; and Strassner, *European Volunteers*, 135–153.

11. Kaisergruber, *We Will Not Go to Tuapse*, 204. For similar Soviet atrocities during the breakout, see also Erickson, *The Road to Stalingrad*, 178.

12. Zetterling and Frankson, *Korsun Pocket*, 277. Erickson, *The Road to Stalingrad*, 179, using only Soviet sources, suggests a figure of around 55,000 killed and wounded and 18,200 taken prisoner from an original force in the pocket of more than 75,000—surely too high in all respects.

13. See Degrelle's colorful memoir, *Eastern Front*.

14. Grass, *Peeling the Onion*, 110.

15. For II SS Panzer Corps, see Tieke, *In the Firestorm*; and Reynolds, *Sons of the Reich*.

16. Lehmann and Tiemann, *The Leibstandarte*, 75.

17. Weidinger, *Comrades to the End*, 241.

18. Estes, *European Anabasis*, 126.

19. Longerich, *Heinrich Himmler*, 341. See also Messenger, *Hitler's Gladiator*, 118.

20. Höhne, *Order of the Death's Head*, 480–481; Maeger, *Lost Honour, Betrayed Loyalty*, 127.

21. Wegner, *Waffen-SS*, 127.

22. Ibid., 215.

23. Ibid., 213.

24. Höhne, *Order of the Death's Head*, 480.

25. Wegner, *Waffen-SS*, 206–207.

CHAPTER 21. BATTLE IN THE NORTH

1. For details of III SS Panzer Corps' organization and operations, see Wilhelm Tieke, *The Tragedy of the Faithful* (Fedorowicz, 2001).

2. Poller, Månsson, and Westberg, *SS-Panzer-Aufklärungs–Abteilung 11 "Nordland,"* 56.

3. Williamson, *The Blood-Soaked Soil*, 136.

4. Estes, *European Anabasis*, 121.

5. Blosfelds, *Stormtrooper on the Eastern Front*, 133–134.

6. Voss, *Black Edelweiss*, 128.

7. For overviews of the Nord Division in Finland, see Rusiecki, *In Final Defense of the Reich*, 1–20; and Ziemke, *German Northern Theater of Operations*, 292–310.

8. Voss, *Black Edelweiss*, 147.

9. Ibid., 165–166.

CHAPTER 22. SHORING UP THE LINE

1. Melnyk, *To Battle*, 151. Melnyk provides a full account of the Ukrainian Division. See also Heike, *Ukrainian Division "Galicia."*

2. Melnyk, *To Battle*, 155.

3. Heike, *Ukrainian Division "Galicia,"* 46–47.

4. Ibid., 47.

5. Ibid., 48.

6. Ibid., 52.

7. Melnyk, *To Battle*, 181.

8. Strassner, *European Volunteers*, 156–160.

9. Klapdor, *Viking Panzers*, 277.

10. Strassner, *European Volunteers*, 167, 169.

11. Volkner, *Many Rivers I Crossed*, 140.

12. Klapdor, *Viking Panzers*, 349–352.

13. Ullrich, *Like a Cliff in the Ocean*, 243–244.

14. Strassner, *European Volunteers*, 178.

15. Ullrich, *Like a Cliff in the Ocean*, 249.

16. Volkner, *Many Rivers I Crossed*, 154.

CHAPTER 23. PARTISAN WARS: THE EASTERN FRONT

1. Hale, *Hitler's Foreign Executioners*, 160.

2. Matthew Cooper, *The Phantom War* (London: Macdonald & Jane's), 57.

3. Bartmann, *Für Volk and Führer*, 64; Maeger, *Lost Honour, Betrayed Loyalty*, 61; Christensen et al., "Germanic Volunteers from Northern Europe," 66.

4. Bartmann, *Für Volk and Führer*, 67.

5. Norman Davies, *Rising '44: The Battle for Warsaw* (London: Macmillan, 2003), 397.

6. Trevor-Roper, *Hitler's War Directives*, 144.

7. For a detailed examination of Bandenbekämpfung, see Blood, *Hitler's Bandit Hunters*.

8. Trevor-Roper, *Hitler's War Directives*, 197–202.

9. Blood, *Hitler's Bandit Hunters*, 122.

10. See Melson, *Kleinkrieg*.

11. Charles D. Melson, "German Counterinsurgency Revisited," *Journal of Military and Strategic Studies* 14, no. 1 (2011): 12.

12. Ibid., 17–24.

13. Bayer, *Kavallerie Divisionen der Waffen SS*, 12.

14. Dorondo, *Riders of the Apocalypse*, 191.

15. Ibid., 193, 198.

16. The "Stroop Report" (Jewish Virtual Library).

17. Ibid.

18. MacLean, *Cruel Hunters*, 177.

19. Dear and Foot, *Oxford Companion to the Second World War*, 1261.

20. Hale, *Hitler's Foreign Executioners*, 336.

21. Dear and Foot, *Oxford Companion to the Second World War*, 1262.

22. Judge, *Slovakia, 1944*, 18–19.

23. Heike, *Ukrainian Division "Galicia,"* 94.

CHAPTER 24. PARTISAN WARS: THE BALKANS

1. Kumm, *Prinz Eugen*, 19–20.

2. Wittmann, *Balkan Nightmare*, 146.

3. Melson, "German Counterinsurgency Revisited," 25–26; Kumm, *Prinz Eugen*, 30–40.

4. Kumm, *Prinz Eugen*, 40.

5. Casagrande et al., "Volksdeutsche," 246.

6. Christensen et al., "Germanic Volunteers," 66.

7. Melson, "German Counterinsurgency Revisited," 28.

8. Hale, *Hitler's Foreign Executioners*, 284.

9. Kumm, *Prinz Eugen*, 68.

10. Ibid., 70. See also Wittmann, *Balkan Nightmare*, 100.

11. Kumm, *Prinz Eugen*, 89.

12. Ibid., 107.

13. Lepre, *Himmler's Bosnian Division*, 150, 152.

14. For the action, see Melson, *Operation Knight's Move*; and Kumm, *Prinz Eugen*, 117–120, 142–149.

15. Melson, *Operation Knight's Move*, 49.

16. Kumm, *Prinz Eugen*, 144.

17. Bougarel et al., "Muslim SS Units," 266.

18. John Mulgan, *Report on Experience* (Barnsley: Frontline Books, 2010), 145.

19. Pontolillo, *Murderous Elite*, 68; Mark Mazower, *Inside Hitler's Greece: The Experience of Occupation, 1941–44* (London: Yale University Press, 2001), 180.

20. Mazower, *Inside Hitler's Greece*, 212–215; Pontolillo, *Murderous Elite*, 41.

21. Mulgan, *Report on Experience*, 161, 164.

22. Christian Jennings, *At War on the Gothic Line* (New York: St. Martin's Press, 2016), 204.

CHAPTER 25. BATTLE FOR THE BEACHHEAD

1. For the division's formation, see H. Meyer, *12th SS*, 1:1–30; K. Meyer, *Grenadiers*, 210–214; and Luther, *Blood and Honor*, 12–79.

2. Kraemer, "I SS Panzer Corps in the West in 1944," p. 3, IWM Department of Documents (Duxford).

3. Luther, *Blood and Honor*, 78.

4. Shulman, *Defeat in the West*, 124.

5. K. Meyer, *Grenadiers*, 223–224.

6. Ibid., 228.

7. For this complex subject, see Howard Margolian, *Conduct Unbecoming: The Story of the Murder of Canadian Prisoners of War in Normandy* (Toronto: University of Toronto Press, 1998); and Luther, *Blood and Honor*, 181–194. For useful summaries, see Beevor, *D-Day*, 180–181; and Reynolds, *Steel Inferno*, 92–96. The accounts by K. Meyer and H. Meyer both maintain a disingenuous silence on the matter.

8. According to postwar testimonies by Hitlerjugend soldiers, Kurt Meyer told his men to "take no prisoners," although at his subsequent trial he denied issuing such orders. See Sayer and Botting, *Hitler's Last General*, 154–155.

9. Neitzel and Welzer, *Soldaten*, 309.

10. K. Meyer, *Grenadiers*, 222.

11. Walther, interview with author, 1983.

12. C. P. Stacey, *Official History of the Canadian Army in the Second World War* (Ottawa, 1960), 3:137.

13. H. Meyer, *12th SS*, 1:186.

14. Fey, *Armor Battles of the Waffen SS*, 98.

15. H. Meyer, *12th SS*, 1:191.

16. Ibid., 197.

17. J. L. Cloudsley-Thompson, in Agte, *Wittmann and the Waffen SS Tiger Commanders*, 2:30.

18. Walther, ibid.

19. Messenger, *Hitler's Gladiator*, 128.

20. H. Meyer, *12th SS*, 1:241.

CHAPTER 26. UNEQUAL STRUGGLE

1. Shulman, *Defeat in the West*, 128.

2. Yerger, *Knights of Steel*, 55.

3. Weidinger, *Comrades to the End*, 268–269.

4. For a detailed narrative of Das Reich's advance to Normandy, see Hastings, *Das Reich*.

5. A series of apologias by Otto Weidinger for Das Reich's actions at Tulle and Oradour can be found in his *Das Reich*, 5:137–175; *Comrades to the End*, 272–301; and *Tulle and Oradour*. See also Michael Williams's comprehensive website on Oradour, www.oradour.info.

6. Pontolillo, *Murderous Elite*, 29–31, 224–225.

7. Quassowski, *Twelve Years with Hitler*, 183.

8. H. Meyer, *12th SS*, 1:373.

9. Chester Wilmot, *The Struggle for Europe* (London: William Collins, 1952), 377.

10. Shulman, *Defeat in the West*, 132.

11. Kraemer, "I SS Panzer Corps in the West in 1944," p. 54, IWM Department of Documents (Duxford).

12. 49th Division intelligence summary, 28 June 1944, in H. Meyer, *12th SS*, 1:422.

13. Lehmann and Tiemann, *The Leibstandarte*, 121. This is skirted over in H. Meyer, *12th SS*, 1:419.

14. Tieke, *In the Firestorm*, 89.

15. Reynolds, *Steel Inferno*, 138.

16. H. Meyer, *12th SS*, 1:433.

17. Beevor, *D-Day*, 269.

18. H. Meyer, *12th SS*, 1:504.

19. Lehmann and Tiemann, *The Leibstandarte*, 136.

20. K. Meyer, *Grenadiers*, 271.

21. Messenger, *Hitler's Gladiator*, 132.

22. Mitcham, *Retreat to the Reich*, 93.

23. English, *Surrender Invites Death*, 205.

CHAPTER 27. COLLAPSE AND RECOVERY

1. See Messenger, *Hitler's Gladiator*, 138; and Parker, *Hitler's Warrior*, 109.

2. Neitzel and Welzer, *Soldaten*, 301. See also Messenger, *Hitler's Gladiator*, 136; and Beevor, *D-Day*, 442.

3. Kraemer, "I SS Panzer Corps in the West in 1944," p. 76, IWM Department of Documents (Duxford).

4. NA WO 205/1021, Dietrich, p. 5.

5. Agte, *Wittmann and the Waffen SS Tiger Commanders*, 2:166–169; H. Meyer, *The 12th SS*, vol. 2, section 14 addendum. Some accounts claim that Wittmann's tank was destroyed by artillery fire, Typhoon rockets, or another tank unit, but are less than convincing.

6. H. Meyer, *12th SS*, 2:95.

7. Weidinger, *Comrades to the End*, 329, states a loss of twelve enemy tanks, surely excessive. See also Reynolds, *Steel Inferno*, 279; and Beevor, *D-Day*, 473.

8. These figures have been given more credence than they deserve. See, for example, Max Hastings, *Overlord: D-Day and the Battle for Normandy* (New York: Simon and Schuster, 1984), 313.

9. H. Meyer, *12th SS*, 2:117.

10. Lehmann and Tiemann, *The Leibstandarte*, 228.

11. Tieke, *In the Firestorm*, 200.

12. Figures from ibid., 222. In R. Kershaw, *It Never Snows in September*, 39, a combined corps figure of 6,000–7,000 soldiers is suggested, apparently based on Tieke's figures. Both Tieke and Kershaw provide detailed narratives of the Waffen-SS at Arnhem.

13. R. Kershaw, *It Never Snows in September*, 149.

14. Ibid., 206.

CHAPTER 28. FINAL GAMBLE IN THE WEST

1. Hirschfeld, *Nazi Rule and Dutch Collaboration*, 310.

2. See Estes, *European Anabasis*, 148–154.

3. For French involvement in the Waffen-SS, see Forbes, *For Europe*; and Carrard, *French Who Fought for Hitler*.

4. Mazière, *The Captive Dreamer*, 30.

5. Estes, *European Anabasis*, 150; Rikmenspoel, *Waffen-SS Encyclopedia*, 48.

6. Figures from Tieke, *In the Firestorm*, 312. Numerical strengths given for both sides in the battle vary considerably according to date of commitment and chosen geographical area.

7. Blanford, *Hitler's Second Army*, 175.

8. The Ardennes offensive of 1944 has been the subject of intense historical scrutiny. Recent studies include Peter Caddick-Adams, *Snow and Steel: Battle of the Bulge, 1944–45* (London: Arrow, 2015); and Beevor, *Ardennes, 1944*.

9. H. Meyer, *12th SS*, 2:255.

10. Blanford, *Hitler's Second Army*, 176.

11. Figures from Tiemann, *Chronicle of the 7. Panzer-Kompanie*, 125 (personnel); and Fey, *Armor Battles of the Waffen SS*, 186 (armored vehicles).

12. For the massacre, see James J. Weingartner, *Crossroads of Death: The Story of the Malmédy Massacre and Trial* (Berkeley: University of California Press, 1979); and Danny S. Parker, *Fatal Crossroads: The Untold Story of the Malmédy Massacre at the Battle of the Bulge* (Boston: Da Capo, 2013).

13. See Beevor, *Ardennes, 1944*, 162–164, 183–184, 212–213, 221.

14. Tieke, *In the Firestorm*, 315.

15. Fey, *Armor Battles of the Waffen SS*, 203.

16. Tieke, *In the Firestorm*, 330.

17. Ibid., 334.

18. Voss, *Black Edelweiss*, 189–190.

19. Rusiecki, *In Final Defense of the Reich*, 42.

20. Monroe-James, *Crossing the Zorn*, 141.

21. Tieke, *In the Firestorm*, 338–340.

22. See Messenger, *Hitler's Gladiator*, 161–162.

23. Ibid., 160.

CHAPTER 29. DISASTER IN HUNGARY

1. Lumans, *Hitler's Auxiliaries*, 226.

2. Wittmann, *Balkan Nightmare*, 171.

3. Figures from Krisztián Ungváry, *Battle for Budapest: 100 Days in World War II* (London: I. B. Tauris, 2011), 323.

4. Strassner, *European Volunteers*, 199.

5. Ibid., 202.

6. Ungváry, *Battle for Budapest*, 331.

7. Bayer, *Kavallerie Division der Waffen-SS*, 213.

8. Agte, *Wittmann and the Waffen SS Tiger Commanders*, 2:342.

9. Woltersdorf, *Gods of War*, 103–104.

10. Tieke, *In the Firestorm*, 365.

11. H. Meyer, *12th SS*, 2:412.

12. Tieke, *In the Firestorm*, 376.

13. Woltersdorf, *Gods of War*, 105, 106.

14. Ullrich, *Like a Cliff in the Ocean*, 263.

15. Tiemann, *The Leibstandarte*, 254.

16. Weingartner, *Leibstandarte Adolf Hitler*, 136.

17. Messenger, *Hitler's Gladiator*, 168.

18. Ibid., 169.

CHAPTER 30. THE WAFFEN-SS DESTROYED

1. For Himmler in 1945, see Longerich, *Heinrich Himmler*, 696–736.

2. Bartmann, *Für Volk and Führer*, 165.

3. Tieke, *In the Firestorm*, 344.

4. Grass, *Peeling the Onion*, 123–124.

5. Tieke, *In the Firestorm*, 400–410.

6. Figures from Antony Beevor, *Berlin: The Downfall, 1945* (London: Viking, 2002), 329.

7. Ibid., 337. Tieke, *In the Firestorm*, 433, though, suggests a higher figure of between 30,000 and 40,000.

8. Hillblad, *Twilight of the Gods*, 47.

9. Bartov, *Hitler's Army*, 6.

10. Grass, *Peeling the Onion*, 126.

11. Kindler, *Obedient unto Death*, 177.

12. Trevor-Roper, *Last Days of Hitler*, 117.

13. Hitler's outburst was famously captured in the film *Downfall* (2004).

14. Stein, *Waffen SS*, 242.

15. Poller, Månsson, and Westberg, *SS-Panzer-Aufklärungs—Abteilung 11 "Nordland,"* 225–256.

16. Hillblad, *Twilight of the Gods*, 83–84.

17. Kumm, *Prinz Eugen*, 266–267.

18. Tieke, *In the Firestorm*, 439.

19. Tiemann, *The Leibstandarte*, 352.

20. Ullrich, *Like a Cliff in the Ocean*, 271–273, 276–278.

21. Weidinger, *Comrades to the End*, 403–424.

22. Estes, *European Anabasis*, 183.

23. Rüdiger Overmans, *Deutsche militärische Verluste im Zweiten Weltkrieg* (Berlin: DeGruyter Oldenbourg, 2000), 257.

24. Volkner, *Many Rivers I Crossed*, 196.

CHAPTER 31. AFTERMATH

1. Longerich, *Heinrich Himmler*, 1–3.

2. Kumm, *Prinz Eugen*, 267–270.

3. See Steinacher et al., "Prosecution and Trajectories," 308.

4. Ibid., 342.

5. Lumans, *Himmler's Auxiliaries*, 260.

6. See, for example, Maeger, *Lost Honour, Betrayed Loyalty*, 244–245.

7. Weidinger, *Comrades to the End*, 426–445; Tieke, *In the Firestorm*, 445–456; Strassner, *European Volunteers*, 213.

8. Adrian Gilbert, *POW: Allied Prisoners in Europe, 1939–1945* (London: John Murray, 2006), 45–47, 153.

9. See, for example, Bartmann, *Für Volk and Führer*; and Volkner, *Many Rivers I Crossed*.

10. Parker, *Hitler's Warrior*, 187–188.

11. See Sayer and Botting, *Hitler's Last General*.

12. For HIAG, see Large, "Reckoning Without the Past"; and Mackenzie, "Waffen-SS in the Second World War."

13. Large, "Reckoning Without the Past," 82–83 (membership had fallen to 6,000 by 1963).

14. Ibid., 83.

15. Ibid., 91–92.

16. Parker, *Hitler's Warrior*, 389–390.

17. See, for example, Mackenzie, "Waffen-SS in the Second World War"; and Wegner, "My Honour Is Loyalty."

18. They include authors Richard Landwehr, Franz Kurowski, Mark Yerger, and Patrick Agte.

19. Among this category are works by Gordon Williamson, Tim Ripley, and Robin Lumsden.

20. Werther and Hurd, "Go East, Old Man," 334.

21. Ibid.; Hurd and Werther, "Waffen-SS Veterans." For Latvia, see Hale, *Hitler's Foreign Executioners*, 8–17.

22. Hurd and Werther, "Waffen-SS Veterans," 354.

23. Wegner, *Waffen-SS*, 126–128, 292, 332–336, 341, 343–350, 358.

24. Paul Hausser first popularized the phrase when giving evidence to the Nuremberg Tribunal.

25. Estes, *European Anabasis*, 183.

SELECT BIBLIOGRAPHY

BOOKS

Agte, Patrick. *Michael Wittmann and the Waffen SS Tiger Commanders and the Leibstandarte in WWII.* 2 vols. Mechanicsburg, PA: Stackpole Books, 2006.

Bartmann, Erwin. *Für Volk and Führer.* Solihull: Helion, 2013.

Bartov, Omer. *Hitler's Army: Soldiers, Nazis, and War in the Third Reich.* New York: Oxford University Press, 1991.

Bayer, Hanns. *Kavallerie Divisionen der Waffen-SS im Bild.* Osnabrück: Munin Verlag, 1982.

Bayer, Hans. *A Dog's Life.* Lanham, MD: University Press of America, 1993.

Beevor, Antony. *Ardennes, 1944: Hitler's Last Gamble.* London: Penguin Viking, 2015.

———. *D-Day: The Battle for Normandy.* London: Penguin Viking, 2009.

Blanford, Edmond L. *Hitler's Second Army: The Waffen SS.* Shrewsbury: Airlife, 1994.

Blood, Philip W. *Hitler's Bandit Hunters: The SS and the Nazi Occupation of Europe.* Washington, DC: Potomac Books, 2008.

Blosfelds, Mintauts. *Stormtrooper on the Eastern Front: Fighting with Hitler's Latvian SS.* Barnsley: Pen & Sword Military, 2008.

Böhler, Jochen, and Robert Gerwarth, eds. *The Waffen-SS: A European History.* Oxford: Oxford University Press, 2017.

Borowski, Tomasz. *Last Blood in Pomerania: Leon Degrelle and the Walloon Waffen SS Volunteers, February–May 1945.* Solihull: Helion, 2016.

Bouwmeester, Hans. *Beginning of the End: The Leadership of SS Obersturmbannführer Jochen Peiper.* N.p.: CreateSpace, 2004.

465

Brett-Smith, Richard. *Hitler's Generals*. London: Osprey, 1976.

Bruyne, Eddy de, and Marc Rikmenspoel. *For Rex and for Belgium*. Solihull: Helion, 2004.

Burdick, Charles, and Hans-Adolf Jacobsen, eds. *The Halder Diaries*. London: Greenhill Books, 1988.

Carrard, Philippe. *The French Who Fought for Hitler: Memories from the Outcasts*. New York: Cambridge University Press, 2010.

Combs, William L. *The Voice of the SS: A History of the SS Journal "Das Schwarze Korps."* New York: Peter Lang, 1986.

Dear, I. C. B., and M. R. D. Foot. *The Oxford Companion to the Second World War*. Oxford: Oxford University Press, 1995.

Degrelle, Leon. *The Eastern Front: Memoirs of a Waffen SS Volunteer, 1941–1945*. Newport Beach, CA: Institute for Historical Review, 2014.

Dorondo, David R. *Riders of the Apocalypse: German Cavalry and Modern Warfare, 1870–1945*. Annapolis, MD: Naval Institute Press, 2012.

English, John A. *Surrender Invites Death: Fighting the Waffen SS in Normandy*. Mechanicsburg, PA: Stackpole Books, 2011.

Estes, Kenneth W. *A European Anabasis: Western European Volunteers in the German Army and SS, 1940–45*. Solihull: Helion, 2015.

Fey, Will. *Armor Battles of the Waffen-SS, 1943–45*. Mechanicsburg, PA: Stackpole Books, 2003.

Flaherty, Thomas H., ed. *The SS*. Alexandria, VA: Time-Life Books, 1989.

Fleming, David. *Weapons of the Waffen SS*. St. Paul, MN: MBI, 2003.

Forbes, Robert. *For Europe: The French Volunteers of the Waffen-SS*. Solihull: Helion, 2006.

Forczyk, Robert. *Tank Warfare on the Eastern Front, 1941–1942: Schwerpunkt*. Barnsley: Pen & Sword Military, 2013.

Gersdorff, Rudolf-Christoph Freiherr von, et al. *Fighting the Breakout: The German Army in Normandy from COBRA to the Falaise Gap*. London: Greenhill Books, 2004.

Gilbert, Adrian. *Germany's Lightning War: From the Invasion of Poland to El Alamein*. Newton Abbot: David & Charles, 2000.

Glantz, David M. *Operation Barbarossa: Hitler's Invasion of Russia*. Stroud: History Press, 2011.

Glantz, David M., and Jonathan M. House. *The Battle of Kursk*. Lawrence: University Press of Kansas, 1999.

Goldsworthy, Terry. *Valhalla's Warriors: A History of the Waffen-SS on the Eastern Front, 1941–1945*. Indianapolis: Dog Ear, 2007.

Grass, Günter. *Peeling the Onion*. London: Harvill Secker, 2007.

Greger, Albin. *Memoirs of a German Soldier*. N.p.: CreateSpace, 2015.

Guderian, Heinz. *Panzer Leader*. London: Penguin, 2000.

Hale, Christopher. *Hitler's Foreign Executioners: Europe's Dirty Secret*. Stroud: History Press, 2011.

Hastings, Max. *Das Reich: Resistance and the March of the 2nd SS Panzer Division Through France, June 1944*. London: Pan Books, 1983.

Hatheway, Jay. *In Perfect Formation: SS Ideology and the SS-Junkerschule-Tölz*. Atglen, PA: Schiffer Military History, 1999.

Hausser, Paul. *Soldaten wie andere auch: Der Weg der Waffen-SS*. Osnabruck: Munin Verlag, 1966.

Heike, Wolf-Dietrich. *The Ukrainian Division "Galicia," 1943–45: A Memoir*. Toronto: Shevchenko Scientific Society, 1998.

Hillblad, Thorolf, ed. [Eric Wallin]. *Twilight of the Gods: A Swedish Volunteer in the 11th SS Panzergrenadier Division "Nordland" on the Eastern Front*. Mechanicsburg, PA: Stackpole Books, 2009.

Hirschfeld, Gerhard. *Nazi Rule and Dutch Collaboration: The Netherlands Under German Occupation, 1940–1945*. Oxford: Berg, 1988.

Hoess, Rudolf. *Commandant of Auschwitz*. London: Weidenfeld & Nicolson, 1959.

Höhne, Heinz. *The Order of the Death's Head: The Story of Hitler's SS*. London: Penguin Books, 2000.

Judge, Sean M. *Slovakia, 1944: The Forgotten Uprising*. Maxwell, AL: Air University Press, 2008.

Kaisergruber, Fernand. *We Will Not Go to Tuapse: From the Donets to the Oder with the Légion Wallonie and 5th SS Volunteer Assault Brigade "Wallonien," 1942–45*. Solihull: Helion, 2016.

Kershaw, Ian. *Hitler*. London: Penguin, 2009.

Kershaw, Robert. *It Never Snows in September*. Addlestone: Ian Allen, 2004.

Kersten, Felix. *The Kersten Memoirs, 1940–1945*. London: Hutchinson, 1956.

Kindler, Werner. *Obedient unto Death: A Panzer Grenadier of the Leibstandarte-SS Adolf Hitler Reports*. London: Frontline, 2014.

Klapdor, Ewald. *Viking Panzers: The German 5th SS Tank Regiment in the East in World War II*. Mechanicsburg, PA: Stackpole Books, 2011.

Koehl, Robert. *The Black Corps: The Structure and Power Struggles of the Nazi SS*. Madison: University of Wisconsin Press, 1983.

Krausnick, Helmut, and Martin Broszat. *Anatomy of the SS State*. London: Paladin, 1970.

Kumm, Otto. *Prinz Eugen: The History of the 7th SS Mountain Division "Prinz Eugen."* Winnipeg: J. J. Fedorowicz, 1990.

Kuusela, Kari, and Olli Wikberg. *Wiking in Suomalaiset / Finnish Volunteers of SS-Division Wiking*. Helsinki: Wiking-Divisiona Oy, 1996.

Lehmann, Rudolf. *Die Leibstandarte*. Vol. 1. Osnabrück: Munin Verlag, 1977.

———. *The Leibstandarte*. Vol. 3. Winnipeg: J. J. Fedorowicz, 1990.

Lehmann, Rudolf, and Ralf Tiemann. *The Leibstandarte*. Vol. 4, pt. 1. Winnipeg: J. J. Fedorowicz, 1993.

Lepre, George. *Himmler's Bosnian Division: The Waffen-SS Handschar Division, 1943–45*. Atglen, PA: Schiffer Military History, 1997.

Longerich, Peter. *Heinrich Himmler*. Oxford: Oxford University Press, 2012.

Lucas, James. *Das Reich: The Military Role of the 2nd SS Division*. London: Cassell, 1991.

Lucas, James, and Matthew Cooper. *Hitler's Elite: Leibstandarte SS, 1933–1945*. London: Grafton Books, 1990.

Lumans, Valdis O. *Himmler's Auxiliaries: The Volksdeutsche Mittelstelle and the German National Minorities of Europe, 1933–1945*. Chapel Hill: University of North Carolina Press, 1993.

Lumsden, Robin. *Himmler's Black Order: A History of the SS, 1923–45*. Stroud: Sutton, 1997.

Luther, Craig W. H. *Blood and Honor: The History of the 12th SS Panzer Division "Hitler Youth."* San José, CA: R. James Bender, 1987.

MacLean, French L. *The Camp Men: The SS Officers Who Ran the Nazi Concentration Camps*. Atglen, PA: Schiffer Military History, 1999.

———. *The Cruel Hunters: SS-Sonderkommando Dirlewanger*. Atglen, PA: Schiffer Military History, 1998.

Maeger, Herbert. *Lost Honour, Betrayed Loyalty: The Memoir of a Waffen-SS Soldier on the Eastern Front*. Barnsley: Frontline Books, 2015.

Manstein, Erich von. *Lost Victories*. London: Arms and Armour Press, 1982.

Mazière, Christian de la. *The Captive Dreamer*. New York: Saturday Review Press/Dutton, 1974.

Mellenthin, F. W. *Panzer Battles: A Study of the Employment of Armour in the Second World War*. London: Futura, 1977.

Melnyk, Michael James. *To Battle: The Formation and History of the 14th Galician Waffen-SS Division*. Solihull: Helion, 2002.

Melson, Charles D. *Kleinkrieg: The German Experience of Guerrilla Warfare, from Clausewitz to Hitler*. Oxford: Casemate, 2006.

———. *Operation Knight's Move: German Airborne Raid Against Tito, 25 May 1944*. Quantico, VA: Marine Corps University Press, 2012.

Melvin, Mungo. *Manstein: Hitler's Greatest General*. London: Weidenfeld, 2010.

Messenger, Charles. *Hitler's Gladiator: The Life and Military Career of Sepp Dietrich*. London: Brassey's, 2001.

Meyer, Hubert. *The 12th SS: The History of the Hitler Youth Panzer Division*. 2 vols. Mechanicsburg, PA: Stackpole Books, 2005.

Meyer, Kurt. *Grenadiers: The Story of Waffen SS General Kurt "Panzer" Meyer*. Mechanicsburg, PA: Stackpole Books, 2005.

Mezmalis, Andrejs M. *The Latvian Legion: Information, Facts, Truth*. Riga: privately published, 2008.

Mitcham, Samuel W. *Retreat to the Reich: The German Defeat in France, 1944*. Mechanicsburg, PA: Stackpole Books, 2007.

Monroe-Jones, Edward. *Crossing the Zorn: The January 1945 Battle of Herrlisheim as Told by the American and German Soldiers Who Fought It*. Jefferson, NC: McFarland, 2010.

Müller, Rolf-Dieter. *The Unknown Eastern Front: The Wehrmacht and Hitler's Foreign Soldiers*. London: I. B. Tauris, 2014.

Neitzel, Sönke, and Harald Welzer. *Soldaten: On Fighting, Killing and Dying*. London: Simon & Schuster, 2012.

Nipe, George M., Jr. *Decision in the Ukraine: German Panzer Operations on the Eastern Front, Summer 1943*. Mechanicsburg, PA: Stackpole Books, 2012.

———. *Last Victory in Russia: The SS-Panzerkorps and Manstein's Kharkov Counteroffensive, February–March 1943*. Atglen, PA: Schiffer Military History, 2000.

Noakes, J., and G. Pridham, eds. *Nazism, 1919–1945*. Vol. 3, *Foreign Policy, War and Racial Extermination*. Exeter: University of Exeter Press, 2001.

Padfield, Peter. *Himmler Reichsführer-SS*. London: Cassell, 2001.

Parker, Danny S. *Hitler's Warrior: The Life and Wars of SS Colonel Jochen Peiper*. Boston: Da Capo, 2014.

Pieper, Henning. *Fegelein's Horsemen and Genocidal Warfare: The SS Cavalry Brigade in the Soviet Union*. Basingstoke: Palgrave Macmillan, 2015.

Pierik, Perry. *From Leningrad to Berlin: Dutch Volunteers in the Service of the German Waffen-SS, 1941–1945*. Soesterberg: Aspekt, 2001.

Poller, Herbert, Martin Månsson, and Lennart Westberg. *The SS-Panzer-Aufklärungs—Abteilung 11 "Nordland" and the Swedish SS-Platoon in the Baltic States, Pomerania and Berlin, 1943–1945*. Stockholm: Leandoer & Ekholm, 2010.

Pontolillo, James. *Murderous Elite: The Waffen-SS and Its Record of Atrocities*. Stockholm: Leandoer & Ekholm, 2009.

Quassowski, Hans, ed. *Twelve Years with Hitler: A History of 1. Kompanie SS Adolf Hitler, 1933–1945*. Atglen, PA: Schiffer Military History, 1999.

Reitlinger, Gerald. *The SS: Alibi of a Nation, 1922–1945*. London: William Heinemann, 1956.

Reynolds, Michael. *Sons of the Reich: The History of II SS Panzer Corps*. Staplehurst: Spellmount, 2002.

———. *Steel Inferno: I SS Panzer Corps in Normandy*. Staplehurst: Spellmount, 1997.

Rikmenspoel, Marc J. *Waffen-SS Encyclopedia*. Bedford, PA: Aberjona Press, 2004.

Rossino, Alexander B. *Hitler Strikes Poland: Blitzkrieg, Ideology and Atrocity*. Lawrence: University Press of Kansas, 2003.

Rusiecki, Stephen M. *In Final Defense of the Reich: The Destruction of the 6th SS Mountain Division "Nord."* Newbury: Casemate, 2010.

Ryan, Cornelius. *A Bridge Too Far*. London: Hamish Hamilton, 1974.

Sayer, Ian, and Douglas Botting. *Hitler's Last General: The Case Against Wilhelm Mohnke*. London: Bantam Press, 1989.

Shulman, Milton. *Defeat in the West*. London: Secker & Warburg, 1949.

Skorzeny, Otto. *Skorzeny's Special Missions: The Memoirs of Hitler's Most Daring Commando*. Barnsley: Frontline Books, 2011.

Smelser, Ronald, and Edward J. Davies. *The Myth of the Eastern Front: The Nazi-Soviet War in American Popular Culture*. New York: Cambridge University Press, 2008.

Stahl, Erich. *Eyewitness to Hell: With the Waffen-SS on the Eastern Front in World War 2*. Bellingham, WA: Ryton, 2009.

Stein, George H. *The Waffen SS: Hitler's Elite Guard at War*. Ithaca, NY: Cornell University Press, 1984.

Strassner, Peter. *European Volunteers: 5th SS Panzer Division Wiking*. Winnipeg: J. J. Fedorowicz, 1988.

Sydnor, Charles W. *Soldiers of Destruction: The SS Death's Head Division, 1933–1945.* Princeton, NJ: Princeton University Press, 1990.

Theile, Karl H. *Beyond "Monsters and Clowns"—the Combat SS: De-mythologizing Five Decades of German Elite Formations*. Lanham, MD: University Press of America, 1997.

Tieke, Wilhelm. *In the Firestorm of the Last Years of the War: II. Panzerkorps with the 9. and 10. SS Divisions "Hohenstaufen" and "Frundsberg."* Winnipeg: J. J. Fedorowicz, 1999.

Tiemann, Ralf. *Chronicle of the 7. Panzer-Kompanie 1. SS-Panzer Division "Leibstandarte."* Atglen, PA: Schiffer Military History, 1998.

———. *The Leibstandarte*. Vol. 4, pt. 2. Winnipeg: J. J. Fedorowicz, 1998.

Trevor-Roper, H. R., ed. *Hitler's Table Talk, 1941–1944*. London: Pan, 1966.

———, ed. *Hitler's War Directives, 1939–1945*. London: Phoenix Press, 2000.

———. *The Last Days of Hitler*. New York: Macmillan, 1947.

Ullrich, Karl. *Like a Cliff in the Ocean: The History of 3. Panzer-Division "Totenkopf."* Winnipeg: J. J. Fedorowicz, 2002.

Verton, Hendrik C. *In the Fire of the Eastern Front: The Experiences of a Dutch Waffen-SS Volunteer, 1941–45*. Mechanicsburg, PA: Stackpole Books, 2010.

Volkner, Werner. *Many Rivers I Crossed*. St. Austell: W. Volkner, 2004.

Voss, Johann. *Black Edelweiss: A Memoir of Combat and Conscience by a Soldier in the Waffen-SS*. Bedford, PA: Aberjona Press, 2002.

Walther, Herbert. *Die Waffen-SS: Eine Bilddokumentation*. Echzell: L. B. Ahnert-Verlag.

Weale, Adrian. *Renegades: Hitler's Englishmen*. London: Pimlico, 2002.

———. *The SS: A New History*. London: Little, Brown, 2010.

Wegner, Bernd. *The Waffen-SS: Organization, Ideology and Function*. Oxford: Basil Blackwell, 1990.

Weidinger, Otto. *Comrades to the End: The 4th Panzer-Grenadier Regiment "Der Führer," 1938–1945*. Atglen, PA: Schiffer Military History, 1998.

———. *Das Reich*. Vols. 1–2. Winnipeg: J. J. Fedorowicz, 1990–1995.

———. *Division das Reich*. Vols. 3–5. Osnabrück: Munin Verlag, 1977–1986.

———. *Tulle and Oradour: A Franco-German Tragedy.* N.p.: privately published, 1985.

Weingartner, James J. *Leibstandarte SS Adolf Hitler, 1933–1945: A Military History.* Nashville: Battery Press, n.d.

Williams, David G. *SS Leibstandarte, Ace of the Waffen SS: Werner Herman Gustav Pötschke.* N.p.: Lulu, 2015.

Williams, Max. *SS Elite: Senior Leaders of Hitler's Praetorian Guard.* Vol. 1. Oxford: Fonthill Media, 2015.

Williamson, Gordon. *The Blood-Soaked Soil.* London: Brown Books, 1995.

———. *Loyalty Is My Honour.* London: BCA/Brown Packaging, 1995.

Wittmann, Anna M., ed. [Fred Umbrich]. *Balkan Nightmare: A Transylvanian Saxon in World War II.* New York: Columbia University Press, 2000.

Woltersdorf, Hans Werner. *Gods of War: A Memoir of a German Soldier.* Novato, CA: Presidio, 1990.

Yerger, Mark C. *Knights of Steel: The Structure, Development and Personalities of 2. SS-Panzer-Division "Das Reich."* Vol. 2. Hershey, PA: Michael J. Horetsky, n.d.

———. *SS-Obersturmführer Otto Weidinger: Knight's Cross with Oakleaves and Swords, SS Panzer-Grenadier Regiment 4 "Der Führer."* Atglen, PA: Schiffer Military History, 2000.

Zetterling, Niklas, and Anders Frankson. *The Korsun Pocket: The Encirclement and Breakout of a German Army in the East, 1944.* Havertown, PA: Casemate, 2011.

Ziemke, Earl F. *The German Northern Theater of Operations, 1940–1945.* Washington, DC: Department of the Army, 1959.

ARTICLES, SEPARATE CHAPTERS, THESES, AND DISSERTATIONS

Antoniou, Georgios, et al. "Western and Southern Europe: The Cases of Spain, France, Italy, and Greece." In *The Waffen-SS: A European History*, edited by Böhler and Gerwarth.

Binkowski, Rafael, and Klaus Wiegrefe. "The Brown Bluff: How Waffen SS Veterans Exploited Postwar Politics." *Der Spiegel*, no. 42 (2011).

Böhler, Jochen, and Robert Gerwarth. "Non-Germans in the Waffen-SS: An Introduction." In *The Waffen-SS: A European History*, edited by Böhler and Gerwarth.

Bougarel, Xavier, et al. "Muslim SS Units in the Balkans and the Soviet Union." In *The Waffen-SS: A European History*, edited by Böhler and Gerwarth.

Casagrande, Thomas, et al. "The Volksdeutsche: A Case Study from South-Eastern Europe." In *The Waffen-SS: A European History*, edited by Böhler and Gerwarth.

Christensen, Claus Bungård, et al. "Germanic Volunteers from Northern Europe." In *The Waffen-SS: A European History*, edited by Böhler and Gerwarth.

Förster, Jürgen. "Barbarossa Revisited: Strategy and Ideology in the East." *Jewish Social Studies* 50, nos. 1–2 (1988–1992): 21–36.

————. "The Wehrmacht and the War of Extermination Against the Soviet Union." *Yad Vashem Studies* 14 (1981).

Gelwick, Robert A. "Personnel Policies and Procedures of the Waffen-SS." PhD diss., University of Nebraska, 1971.

Gutmann, Martin. "Debunking the Myth of the Volunteers: Transnational Volunteers in the Nazi Waffen-SS Officer Corps During the Second World War." *Contemporary European History* 22, no. 4 (2013): 585–608.

Hurd, Madeleine, and Steffen Werther. "Waffen-SS Veterans and Their Sites of Memory Today." In *The Waffen-SS: A European History*, edited by Böhler and Gerwarth.

Kott, Mathew, et al. "The Baltic States: Auxiliaries and Waffen-SS Soldiers from Estonia, Latvia and Lithuania." In *The Waffen-SS: A European History*, edited by Böhler and Gerwarth.

Large, David Clay. "Reckoning Without the Past: The HIAG of the Waffen-SS and the Politics of Rehabilitation in the Bonn Republic, 1950–1961." *Journal of Modern History* 59, no. 1 (1987): 79–113.

Leleu, Jean-Luc. "From the Nazi Party's Shock Troops to the 'European' Mass Army: The Waffen-SS Volunteers." In *War Volunteering in Modern Times: From the French Revolution to the Second World War*, edited by Christine G. Krüger and Sonja Levsen. Basingstoke: Palgrave Macmillan, 2011.

————. "The SS Division-Totenkopf—Facing the Civilian Population in Northern France in May 1940." *Revue du Nord* (*Northern Journal*) 4, no. 342 (2001): 821–840. www.cairn.info/revue-du-nord-2001-4-page-821.htm.

Mackenzie, S. P. "The Waffen-SS in the Second World War, 1939–45 Europe's Übermenschen?" In *Revolutionary Armies in the Modern Era: A Revisionist Approach*, edited by S. P. Mackenzie. London: Routledge, 1997.

Melson, Charles D. "German Counterinsurgency Revisited." *Journal of Military and Strategic Studies* 14, no. 1 (2011): 1–33.

Młynarczyk, Jacek Andrzej, et al. "Eastern Europe: Belarussian Auxiliaries, Ukrainian Waffen-SS Soldiers and the Special Case of the Polish 'Blue Police.'" In *The Waffen-SS: A European History*, edited by Böhler and Gerwarth .

Nipe, George M., Jr. "Battle of Kursk: Germany's Lost Victory in World War II." *World War II* (February 1998).

Rempel, Gerhard. "Gottlob Berger and Waffen-SS Recruitment, 1939–1945." *Militärgeschichtliche Zeitschrift* 27, no. 1 (1980).

Reynolds, Michael. "Hitler's Last Offensive: Operation Spring Awakening." *Warfare History Network* (October 2016).

Smith, Peter Scharff, Niels Bo Poulsen, and Claus Bundgård Christensen. "The Danish Volunteers in the Waffen SS and German Warfare at the Eastern Front." *Contemporary European History* 8, no. 1 (1999): 73–96.

Steinacher, Gerald, et al. "Prosecution and Trajectories After 1945." In *The Waffen-SS: A European History*, edited by Böhler and Gerwarth.

Svencs, Edmunds. "The Latvian Legion (1943–45) and Its Role in Latvia's History." Master's thesis, U.S. Army Command and General Staff College, 2013.

Sydnor, Charles W. "The History of the SS Totenkopfdivision and the Postwar Mythology of the Waffen SS." *Central European History* 6, no. 4 (1973): 339–362.

Thomas, M. J. "The Waffen SS 1933–45: 'Soldiers, Just Like the Others'?" *Military History Journal* (South African Military History Society) 12, no. 5 (2003).

Trașcă, Ottmar. "Andreas Schmidt and the German Ethnic Group in Romania (1940–1944)." *Euxeinos* 19–20 (2015): 16–19.

Wegner, Bernd. "My Honour Is Loyalty." In *The German Military in the Age of Total War*, edited by Wilhelm Deist. Leamington Spa: Berg, 1985.

Werther, Steffen, and Madeleine Hurd. "Go East, Old Man: The Ritual Spaces of SS Veterans' Memory Work." *Culture Unbound* 6 (2014): 327–359.

INDEX